# Studying Educational and Social Policy

## Theoretical Concepts and Research Methods

# Sociocultural, Political, and Historical Studies in Education
## Joel Spring, Editor

# Studying Educational and Social Policy

## Theoretical Concepts and Research Methods

### Ronald H. Heck
*University of Hawai'i at Mānoa*

Routledge
Taylor & Francis Group
New York   London

Routledge is an imprint of the
Taylor & Francis Group, an informa business

Lawrence Erlbaum Associates, Inc., Publishers
10 Industrial Avenue
Mahwah, New Jersey 07430

Cover design by Kathryn Houghtaling Lacey

**Library of Congress Cataloging-in-Publication Data**

Heck, Ronald H.
Studying educational and social policy: theoretical concepts
and research methods/ Ronald H. Heck.
     p. cm.
     Includes bibliographical references and index.
ISBN 0-8058-4460-0 (cloth. : alk. paper)
ISBN 0-8058-4461-9 (pbk. : alk. paper)
1. Policy sciences.   I. Title.

H97.H43 2004
320.6—dc22                       2003049528
                                          CIP

Books published by Lawrence Erlbaum Associates are printed
on acid-free paper, and their bindings are chosen for strength
and durability.

Printed in the United States of America
10  9  8  7  6  5  4  3  2

# Contents

# Foreword

Ronald Heck's *Studying Educational and Social Policy: Theoretical Concepts and Research Methods* is a valuable introductory textbook covering a wide range of methods for analyzing federal, state, and local school policies. Future school administrators must be prepared to cope with a steadily increasing number of educational directives coming from the desks of federal and state executives and legislators. Educational administrators at every level of government are affected by continually changing directions of educational politics. I welcome Heck's book into my series because of my firm conviction that future educational leaders must be prepared to analyze, evaluate, and understand the impact of federal, state, and local educational policies.

—*Joel Spring*
*Series Editor*

# Preface

The purpose of this book is to introduce beginning researchers to the study of policymaking, how it has been examined from a scholarly perspective, and the salient issues to consider in conceptualizing and conducting policy research. The emphasis is on "introduce," as the various policy fields within the public sector (e.g., education, energy, health, labor) are much too diverse to include in one text on theoretical concepts and research methods. The book is not directed so much at the substance of policymaking—other volumes do an excellent job of covering information about how the policy system works (e.g., Fowler, 2000; Guthrie & Reed, 1991; Van Horn, Baumer, & Gormley, 1992)—as it is toward understanding the interplay between how policy is made and implemented and the various conceptual approaches and methods researchers can use to frame and conduct policy studies. The worth of the research in answering important policy questions is assessed by a variety of different audiences including policymakers, the public, practitioners, and the research community itself (Anfara, Brown, & Mangione, 2002).

The consideration of social problems and how they are studied is important in policy fields such as education, where there is currently a heightened demand for more research, but research that policymakers perceive is of a higher quality and greater utility than has been the case in the past (Feuer, Towne, & Shavelson, 2002) . In education, policymakers continue to direct attention toward upgrading the quality of educational outcomes by mandating greater accountability (e.g., setting standards, requiring assessments of student progress) and by increasing parents' educational options, while also lessening educators' control over school decision making and entry into the teaching and administrative professions. To date, many of the corresponding policy changes resulting from these demands (e.g., curricular standards and performance benchmarks, use of technology to enhance instructional capacity, site-based management, school vouchers, open enrollment, privatization, alternative preparation and certification) have proven to be mixed or ineffective. Policy interventions have been criticized as not consistent with research and, consequently, uninformed and ineffective (Finn, 2002; Witte, 1998). As Feuer and colleagues concluded, whether exaggerated or not, there is a common perception among policymakers that other social policy fields (e.g., health) do a better job of integrating research findings into practice, and education needs to catch up.

Demands for increased productivity and accountability, coupled with a renewed recognition of the potential of research to provide information about the impact of policy changes, suggest that policy researchers have a new opportunity to produce studies that policymakers perceive as important. In education, however, this opportunity comes at a price—as recent federal legislation in education (e.g., No Child Left Behind Act of 2001) details requirements for obtaining federal research grants that prescribe acceptable research methods (i.e., experimental trials) and promote a rigid definition of research quality (Feuer, Towne, & Shavelson, 2002). One key issue in this is whether policymakers or researchers will decide what aspects of educational policy will be studied and how. Another issue is that the educational research community itself has been quite divided over the nature of research and standards for its design and conduct. A third issue is whether policymakers will continue to look to universities to provide policy research or whether they will look elsewhere in the future.

Criticism of the quality and utility of research in the public sector suggests the need to consider its theoretical underpinnings, design, and conduct. How researchers account for and disclose their approach to all aspects of the research process is essential if readers are to evaluate their results substantively and methodologically (Anfara et al., 2002; Sabatier, 1999). Framing the policy study is the key to providing results that are compelling and useful for readers—that is, our analyses should advance the field's thinking about the problem and should also serve as exemplars of its evolving scholarship. Advancing knowledge and scholarship are the essence of good research, policy or otherwise.

Increasingly, both the theoretical concepts and the analytic tools are becoming available that allow a more rigorous and thorough investigation of policy problems. The assumption of this book is that a critique of the substantive, theoretical, and methodological issues involved in studying policy can help researchers develop and conduct policy studies that are more informative in guiding policy development and more effective in assessing the impact of policy reforms. More specifically, the intents are to help those interested in studying policy understand (a) the environmental context and policymaking system, (b) the essentials of policy scholarship, including various frameworks and methods researchers use to study policy problems and policies empirically, and (c) the assumptions and considerations involved in conceptualizing and conducting policy research.

The book provides an overview of several basic conceptual and methodological tools used to study policy processes and outcomes. They are not the only concepts and methods that can be used to examine policy. They are, however, approaches that have been used successfully in conducting policy research. Most of the substantive discussion concerns educational policy issues and example studies, because that is the policy field with which I am most familiar. I have found, however, that many of the issues involved in the study of social policy are similar across various fields. Policy researchers have a variety of different home disciplines including political science, economics, sociology, history, public administration, psychology, and anthropology. Disciplinary affiliations influence to some degree what social problems are of interest to researchers, how they define the problems, and what methods they use to investigate them. Readers are encouraged to examine the studies described in each chapter more closely on their own and to find other published studies illustrating the theoretical lenses and methodological approaches from their own particular policy fields or topics of interest. Other generic types of examples and exercises are provided throughout the book to help readers think about conceptual and methodological issues salient to conducting their own policy research.

Much of the material in the text comes from introductory and seminar courses that I teach in educational policy and research methods. The book is designed to be used in a semester course focusing on theoretical concepts and methods of studying policy. In this seminar, I generally spend 6 weeks developing a number of substantive concepts about the policy system (e.g., how the federalist system encourages and blunts policy activity; how policy is formulated, implemented, and evaluated; how policymakers' belief systems and institutional arrangements structure their interactions, how organizations resist policy changes) and the theoretical perspectives used to study it (e.g., rational, structural, cultural, critical, and poststructural); another 5 or 6 weeks highlighting research methods (e.g., design, data collection, analysis) for investigating policy problems; and the remaining 4 weeks focusing on how students can begin to translate their interests in particular policy problems and dilemmas into feasible research studies. In addition to their substantive courses in educational policy and administration, students taking the policy seminar typically have had a research design course, introductory courses in qualitative and quantitative methods, and perhaps advanced course work in one of these areas. Students' reactions to the course material—their comments and questions about "how things work," and our discussions about formulating their own research studies in educational policy and subsequently conducting them have also shaped the subject matter that is presented in the following chapters.

In Part I, I present an overview of substantive issues related to the study of policy. This section addresses how the environmental context, institutions, and actors shape policies and, consequently, their study. Chapter 1 provides an overview of what policy is and some of the challenges of its study. Chapter 2 explores how the nature of the American federalist system has helped to shape policy in education over time. Chapter 3 develops the "policy stages" approach that has traditionally been most often used in studying policymaking processes.

Several alternative conceptual approaches are presented in Part II that provide different perspectives on the study of policy problems. These lenses originate in rational, political, cultural, and critical perspectives for researching social problems. Chapter 4 develops the concept of political culture and its use in understanding policy activity at both the national and state levels. Chapter 5 presents two political perspectives—the punctuated-equilibrium framework and the advocacy coalition framework—and applies them to the study of policy processes over time. Chapter 6 introduces several economic (production functions, cost/benefit, cost effectiveness) and organizational lenses (rational organizational theory, institutional rational choice, and institutional theory) for examining policy. Chapter 7 provides an introduction to other promising critical lenses and more personal perspectives that depart from established ways of studying policy.

Part III focuses on research methods for studying policy. Chapter 8 provides an introduction to methodology, focusing primarily on research designs. Calls for upgrading the quality and usefulness of policy research are directed at how research is designed relative to the types of questions one is interested in answering and how useful the research is in helping policymakers and educators solve policy problems. Several types of designs are introduced including experimental, quasi-experimental, nonexperimental, case, and historical.

Chapter 9 provides an overview of qualitative methods with a focus on their use in case study and historical research. Chapter 10 provides an introduction of quantitative modeling for conducting policy research with an emphasis on multilevel analyses. The chapter begins with a brief review of multiple regression and then introduces multilevel regression and multilevel structural equation modeling as techniques for analyzing policy-related data. A series of examples is also presented to illustrate how to set up and conduct basic multilevel analyses. Data and software set-ups are also included in the appendix for those students who would like to practice with some of the analyses. In Chapter 11, the use of longitudinal methods to study policy processes is presented. Another set of examples is provided, along with data and software set-ups in the appendix.

Finally, in Part IV, the diversity of approaches used by policy scholars is compared in Chapter 12 with respect to their strengths and weaknesses in studying the policymaking process, and some thoughts are presented on a number of issues for further consideration in conducting policy research. It is hoped that a discussion of theories and methods of conducting policy research will give prospective researchers an appreciation for the relationship between policy problems, empirical methods, and practice, and will also contribute to their skills in conceptualizing and conducting policy research that answers important policy questions.

## ACKNOWLEDGMENTS

I would like to thank a number of people for their help at various stages of the writing process. I am indebted to Linda Johnsrud, Doug Mitchell, Vicki Rosser, Alan Shoho, Naomi Silverman, Scott Thomas, and Lawrence Erlbaum Associates series editors George Marcoulides and Joel Spring for numerous discussions, helpful insights, and comments on earlier versions of the manuscript. Thank you also to Linda and Bengt Muthén of *Mplus* for helpful advice regarding multilevel and longitudinal analyses. Finally, I am grateful to Sara Scudder of Lawrence Erlbaum Associates for her outstanding work in preparing the manuscript for publication.

# Introduction

Few policy fields have been as volatile as education over the past several decades. Since the early 1980s, many nations, including the United States,
have experienced significant changes in how people think about education
and what is demanded of schools. These developments are related to the
world's political and economic events and to larger changes in how we think
about government and services, organizations and management, and industry and technology (Boyd, 1992). Legislation (e.g., Individuals With Disabilities Education Act, No Child Left Behind Act), policy directives (e.g.,
the Brown Decision), and the release of reports (e.g., *A Nation At Risk*) generate considerable debate among policymakers, practitioners, the public,
special interest groups, and researchers over the definition of policy problems; the nature of responsibility; the structuring, funding, and effectiveness of interventions; and the role of research in contributing knowledge
that leads to the alleviation of social and educational problems.

Embedded in these debates are value preferences of American society at
given points in time, political and professional agendas about what views
will dominate, who will be served, what policies and programs should be developed and implemented to achieve particular societal goals, and what levels of funding should be provided now and over time. In the American
federalist system, policy change occurs as a result of collective action. How
people organize and make choices about where to pursue ideological agendas are key to understanding the movement of policy issues through the system. Policy actors' beliefs and values as well as institutional arrangements
within the federalist system play an important part in supporting or isolat-
ing the advancement of policy activity.

As Schattschneider (1960) concluded, the scope of political conflict in
American government has gradually widened since the founding of the
country, as industrialization, urbanization, nationalization, and globalization have altered the meanings of both local and national government. The

development of American political institutions (courts, executive branch, Congress) reflects their widening involvement in national politics. Although the federal role in education could traditionally be described as an "interested bystander" (because education is a state function), during the 1950s and early 1960s, federal policymakers became more active in education in order to address a number of social problems facing the nation (e.g., segregated schooling, Civil Rights, poverty). One example of federal activity was the Elementary and Secondary Education Act (ESEA) of 1965, which allocated federal money to schools where students experienced differential educational opportunity resulting from poverty.

The increased federal role in allocating funds to schools through federal projects brought with it the necessity for schools to evaluate the results of their efforts to increase educational opportunity. Where equity had been an important social value during the 1950s and 1960s, accountability emerged during the 1970s as a dominant and influential value, often directed at the actions of government (e.g., spending, energy policy, environmental policy). The demand for information relevant to policy problems and the effectiveness of government spending and interventions created an initial impetus for policy research in fields such as education. The Coleman Report (1966) created an intellectual stir by suggesting that students' backgrounds played a more powerful role in the quality of their academic achievement than school-based resource variables. The popular (and incorrect) conclusion drawn from the study was that schools make no difference. Fallout from the report has been credited for the beginnings of the "effective schools" movement in the late 1970s, which sought to dispute Coleman's research by identifying school variables that were related to student learning (Bidwell & Kasarda, 1980; Teddlie & Reynolds, 2000). A few years after Coleman's research, the Rand study on *Federal Policy Supporting Educational Change* (Berman & McLaughlin, 1975, 1977, 1978) reported on the implementation of nearly 300 federal education projects to change educational practices. The report concluded that the implementation of federal projects was largely mixed due to a number of local school factors that mediated their implementation. This report alerted attention to the dynamics of local organizational and political factors that can affect the implementation of policies to improve schools developed at other levels of the political system.

*A Nation At Risk*, released by the Reagan Administration in 1983 made the case that the nation was at risk of economic mediocrity, ironically because of years of federal overinvolvement in education. *A Nation At Risk* was not really a research report, but rather, a document outlining a policy agenda that used some description and much more prescription. While it did not signal an end of federal involvement in education (i.e., Reagan was not entirely successful in blunting the efforts of legislators to continue their support of ESEA), it was effective in advancing the Reagan Administration's objective of returning primary oversight of education and accountability for educational results to the states. It focused states' educational reform efforts on student outcomes and school improvement. A considerable number of its recommendations were implemented by states over the next decade or so.

As these early reports on federal educational policy efforts demonstrate, the use of information generated from policy research has been widely recognized as central to debates about educational problems and their proposed solutions. In the past few years, unprecedented federal legislation in education has called for an increase in the scientific rigor of research as the key to improved policy and practice (Feuer, Towne, & Shavelson, 2002). For example, the federal government has appropriated increased funding for schools to adopt "proven, comprehensive reform models," called comprehensive school reform (CSR) models (U.S. Department of Education, 1999). Congress appropriated $150 million per year in 1998, which increased to $310 million annually in 2001 and provided funding to over 2,600 mostly high-poverty schools (Slavin, 2002; Southwest Educational Research Laboratory, 2002). In this legislation, *proven* was defined in terms of experimental trials with treatment–control comparisons on standards-based measures (Slavin, 2002). Whereas the emphasis is supposed to be on programs with "proven effectiveness" based on rigorous research, there is considerable discretion at the state and local levels about which programs to adopt, and funding is still being given to programs with little evidence of effectiveness (Herman, 1999).

Similarly, the Bush Administration's reauthorization of ESEA as the No Child Left Behind Act of 2001 defined scientifically based research as having "rigorous, systematic and objective procedures" (U.S. Congress, 2001) to obtain valid knowledge that is generated through the use of experimental designs, preferably with random assignment of subjects (Feuer et al., 2002; Slavin, 2002). This type of design is intended to serve as the basis for Title I programs, as well as for various reading programs for early grades. Moreover, as Slavin noted, the Office of Educational Research and Improvement (OERI) will likely be reorganized to focus resources on randomized and rigorous "matched" educational research on programs and policies that are used in educating large numbers of pre-K through 12th-grade students. In fact, the OERI strategic plan for 2002–2007 is to have 75% of all OERI-funded research that addresses program or policy effects use random-assignment experimental designs by 2004 (U.S. Department of Education, 2002).

As a practical matter, the type of large-scale experimental designs now favored within federal policy circles can be very difficult and costly to implement in educational settings. As a result, educational research has produced few rigorous evaluative studies of programs and practices that could serve as a solid base for improving policy and practice (Slavin, 2002). It is uncertain yet what will be the outcome of these recent demands for "evidence-based" policy developments in Washington. For example, No Child Left Behind has produced considerable debates among policymakers, practitioners, and researchers over the definition of "adequate yearly progress" and its validity in categorizing schools as low performing (e.g., Linn, Baker, & Betebenner, 2002; Linn & Haug, 2002). It is too early to tell what its impacts will be on educational funding and changed practices, however. While the promise is potentially far-reaching (Slavin, 2002), it is not certain yet the extent to which states and districts may be left to pick up funding shortfalls. Some states have even contemplated pulling out of federal programs due to uncertainties regarding the funding of many federal mandates.

## POLICY RESEARCH AS A SCHOLARLY FIELD

These recent debates over the quality of research to inform policy and practice, as well as prescriptions for what should constitute scientific research methods, focus attention on what policymakers are currently demanding of policy research and the status (real and perceived) of educational policy as a scholarly field. Educational problems in particular have drawn the attention of numerous researchers in diverse social science disciplines (e.g., anthropology, sociology, economics, political science, psychology). This is because of a long tradition among policymakers of viewing education as a primary means to solve the nation's social problems. Education is perceived as being related to many problems of importance in other fields (e.g., poverty, unemployment, international economic competitiveness, health, crime, political behavior).

Despite the growing professional literature on educational policy that has accumulated over its first two and a half decades, early reviews of its impact have concluded that this work produced little agreement on the goals or methods of policy research, few classic studies that defined the area's central thrust and overall theoretical perspectives for studying policy activity, and no standard textbooks (Boyd, 1988; Marshall, Mitchell, & Wirt, 1989; Mitchell, 1984). A decade or so later, Fowler (2000) completed one of the first policy texts in education aimed at acquainting practitioners with the theoretical and substantive aspects of educational policy. She also found that there were no suitable textbooks available in the educational field that provided basic information about the policymaking process. Fowler suggested that most students in her policy courses did not have a suitable background in political science to understand the changing political and social landscape surrounding policymaking in education.

Other scholars have suggested that previous research on educational policy has too often focused on specific issues and narrow time frames and, therefore, has been of little use in guiding policy development and change beyond limited settings (Mawhinney, 1993; McDonnell & Elmore, 1987; Ouston, 1999). As Boyd (1988) concluded, policy research may illuminate or obscure—even distort—what it views. At its best, policy research may make an independent, and influential, contribution to the beliefs and choices of policymakers. At its worst, it may be used as a device to support a preconceived value preference and legitimate a particular policy choice (Boyd, 1988; Jenkins-Smith, 1990).

Criticisms of policy reforms and policy research suggest there is often a disconnect among the worlds of policymakers, practitioners, and researchers (Birnbaum, 2000). In part, this is because they work within different worlds, each with its own values and traditions, and they speak somewhat different languages (Birnbaum, 2000; Marshall et al., 1989). Policymakers live in political arenas where turnover is high and, therefore, the pressure is greater for quick results from their legislative efforts if they wish to stay in office (Firestone, 1989). By the time research can produce empirical results that respond to interests and results of policymakers' efforts, the nature of the policy problem may have changed (Birnbaum, 2000).

Critics of policy research argue that it is of little use to policymakers, does not attend to the questions they want answered, is poorly conceived and conducted, and is seldom disseminated in ways that educators can put the results to use (Birnbaum, 2000; Feuer et al., 2002). Educational leaders believe that policymakers do not understand the complexity of running educational organizations. Researchers suggest that policymakers do not adequately fund research efforts and also lament the potential effects of federal government's current narrow definition of scientific research and its likely effects on shaping the field of policy research (e.g., Feuer et al., 2002; Slavin, 2002). This seems to represent a "cycle of blame" where no one accepts responsibility, and in many ways, signals a need to reassess the possibilities and prospects for policy research.

Such criticisms and controversies about policy research and its potential to inform policymaking are based on several assumptions that are important to consider. First is the implied assumption that it is necessary for policymakers and researchers to agree on the nature of policy problems and the type of research they would find most useful (Birnbaum, 2000). It is certainly the case that policy research can provide useful information for policymakers to use in decision making. It is also a fact, however, that the preferences of policymakers (i.e., their values and preferred actions) can change over time as political pressures are brought to bear in shaping policy agendas. Researchers could never respond to the myriad of policy problems that policymakers at the federal, state, and local levels are considering at any particular moment in time. Moreover, it is often not feasible to predict what those will be in any particular legislative session. Over time, therefore, policy scholars are likely to attend to a set of problems defined in the professional literature (e.g., tracking, grouping practices, opportunity to learn, gaps in student achievement, resource equity, dropouts) that are at least somewhat different from those more immediate problems attended to by policymakers.

Second is the assumption that research in the field of education is of generally poor quality in comparison to other applied fields such as medicine and, because of this shortcoming, requires guidance from the federal level to strengthen its design and methodology. As Feuer and colleagues noted (2002), the lack of confidence in the quality of educational research is a perception generally shared among federal policymakers, educational practitioners, engineers, business leaders, social scientists and, to some extent, educational researchers themselves. Critics argue that educational studies have weak or absent theory, poor research designs, inadequate sampling, weak methods of analysis, cannot be replicated, and lack policy relevance. At the present moment, federal policymakers seem to favor funding research that produces evidence of effects based on experimental trials among established school reform programs. Whereas this is certainly a carrot for some policy researchers interested in pursuing this more narrowly focused research program, it is only a small subset of the broader scope of educational policy problems that are worthy of researchers' attention.

A third assumption is that policymakers would act on the basis of relevant studies if they existed. Although policymakers often call for evidence they can use in decision making, in actuality, however, their actions result from a complex number of factors including their own value preferences; perceptions of others' value preferences; societal values (e.g., equality, liberty); their accumulation of power, resources, and knowledge; and their assessment of the evolving policy environment (Fowler, 2000). Most important, their decision making takes place in a political arena (e.g., a policy subsystem), as opposed to in an academic arena. Although universities, think tanks, foundations, and other agencies may contribute to idea development and discussion, it would be unrealistic to expect policymakers to act on the basis of the results of separate studies. It is unlikely that policymakers would act on the basis of a single study, even if one were to exist that answered a particular policy problem directly.

In contrast, because policymakers are currently interested in programs and policies that are shown to improve schools, it is reasonable to think that when evidence begins to accumulate on the worthiness of particular programs and approaches to improve student outcomes, they will support and fund disciplined policy inquiry. Weiss (1991), for example, noted that policymakers' thinking and actions are influenced by the cumulative policy research on a particular topic. As Weiss suggested, policymakers assimilate generalizations, concepts, and perspectives from research that shape their actions. This accumulated knowledge "creeps" into the policy environment (Lindblom & Cohen, 1979). Some recent examples of this type of accumulated knowledge include lengthening of the school year, adopting educational standards, providing differential financing to students with greater need, and reducing class size.

## STUDYING POLICY

Because of the complexity of the policy process in addressing social problems—one that involves a changing environment; numerous actors, arenas, and institutional factors; and often uneven results—its study requires one to simplify the situation in order to understand it (Sabatier, 1999). The limitations of previous research have revealed several salient points for studying policy. One point concerns the quality of research produced and its potential usefulness in resolving policy problems. Research has the capacity to be very persuasive in policy discourses. Studies are used, and misused, to provide support for particular policy positions. Debates often focus on the conduct of the study and the credibility of its findings. It is therefore incumbent on researchers to both read and conduct policy studies with a critical awareness of how blind spots or other biases may be embedded in the conceptual frameworks, research designs, and processes of data collection that are used (Wagner, 1993). Choices about conceptual underpinnings and research methods will impact what is illuminated—or what is obscured. Critiques of conceptual lenses and methodological approaches that are used in conducting policy research are therefore important in examining how our assumptions structure that which we observe. Thoughtful discussion of theories and methods and self-correction are ways that a field progresses (Popper, 1959).

A second point is that longer time frames are needed to study policy change appropriately (Sabatier, 1999; Tyack, 1991). Policy activity is affected by larger social, economic, and cultural determinants that influence the purposes of education and at least partially structure policymakers' actions (Benham & Heck, 1998; Plank, Scotch, & Gamble, 1996; Tyack, 1991). Policies take time to develop, to become implemented, and to have their effects identified. Because of the complexity of interrelationships and the length of time it takes for policy activity to unfold, it may take a decade or more to study a policy cycle.

A third point is that policy activity resides primarily within policy subsystems, as opposed to single governmental institutions (Congress, the courts) consisting of multiple individuals and groups whose values and beliefs are central to the processes (Marshall et al., 1986). As such, policy is socially constructed by its participants. Within the political context, it is often managed by those with greater access and familiarity with the policy system. The policy that results, therefore, often focuses on problems and solutions identified by those in positions of power (Marshall, 1997).

A final point is that because policy often represents the views of those who can gain access to policy subsystems, it is essential to understand why some groups and values have been so much—or so little—represented in society and schooling at different times in our nation's history (Tyack, 2002). A goal of policy research should be to illuminate relationships among power, culture, and language that underlie policies that marginalize people primarily on the basis of race, gender, and social class (Bensimon & Marshall, 1997; Tillman, 2002). Policies may be read, interpreted, and negotiated into practice quite differently among a number of different groups. As a constructed activity, policy discourses and actions may both shape and be shaped by the norms, values, and daily operations of the school and its staff, students, and parents (Blackmore, Kenway, Willis, & Rennie, 1993). Because of criticisms about previous policy research, researchers have recently given more attention to using alternative theoretical lenses and methods of analysis in developing programs of policy research (McDonnell & Elmore, 1987; Marshall, 1997; Martin & Sugarman, 1993; Mawhinney, 1993; Sabatier, 1999).

Flexibility in examining a policy problem from alternative perspectives, as opposed to holding to traditional conceptualizations and methods that have dominated past research and practice, opens up new possibilities for understanding problems in expansive ways that move us toward viable policy solutions. A number of new perspectives hold much promise for examining policy problems in education and in other fields, but they have yet to be adequately developed in empirical work. One of the tests of the usefulness of a conceptual framework or theory is its ability to further our understanding of important policy problems. Thus, while particular approaches may describe certain realities of policy life, they should also result in serious, cumulative empirical work (Sabatier, 1999; Willower & Forsyth, 1999).

## DEVELOPING A POSSIBLE STUDY

The intent of this book is to help beginning researchers understand how conceptual models and methods contribute to the study of policy problems. Several elements have to be brought together including a knowledge of policy environments and processes (i.e., the context of the research), the definition and development of the policy problem, the goals of the research, the objects of study, the method of investigation, and communication with potential users of the study's results (e.g., policymakers, educators, researchers, the public). There are also potential constraints to consider including time, costs, and the data one needs versus what can actually be obtained.

Finding a policy problem to research is a highly individual endeavor. I have observed that for some students, it is easy. Others struggle with where to "find" one. Potential research problems can be found in a variety of places— from personal interest and experience, the workplace, academic journals, grant opportunities from governmental and private funding agencies, as well as in the unfolding news stories that are covered in professional newspapers (e.g., *Education Weekly, Chronicle of Higher Education*). These latter two newspapers can be an important source on politics and policy in education. Problems may be ideas we have carried with us over the years. In other cases, the "light just goes on," and one may get an idea for a research study out of something that was covered in the media, or a problem that presents itself for the first time during the course of a conversation with a mentor.

It can take some time to define the problem and then to figure out what one wishes to find out about it. Usually it is a process that unfolds gradually. I have gone back to my course notes from graduate school and found the scribbles where my dissertation topic began to emerge in the margins. I began by "floating" two competing short proposal ideas (identifying what I wanted to study and how) to different professors and receiving their feedback. These were initial efforts to frame the problem in a couple of pages. Underneath the topic that I settled on, however, was also a personal conviction about the detrimental effects on students from ways that school personnel assign them to classes and structure their subsequent learning experiences. My interest in student assignment and student grouping developed from my experiences as an elementary school student (where we sat at three tables grouped by ability) and later as a elementary school teacher observing how students were assigned to classes and moved through the school year to year. These assignment decisions had a profound impact on students' educational experiences.

The art of crafting a quality policy study is to take a problem of personal concern and commitment and frame it in such a way that its results will be important to policymakers, practitioners, and researchers—no matter what is found; that is, the importance is more in the framing than in the results themselves. If the study is framed correctly, it should be important—whether the results are "significant" or not. After students settle on a topic of interest, therefore, they should spend a good amount of time working on the conceptualization of the research problem. Gaining access to the literature on a particular problem and determining what others have done is a good place to begin. I often have students begin their literature searches by examining what research has been done on the topic within the past 5 years. In education, the *Current Index to Journals in Education* (CIJE) and annual meeting programs for the American Educational Research Association (AERA) conferences are good places to start. They should not, however, be viewed as exclusive sources of extant research on a particular topic. If the topic is not listed, it may be an indication that it is either a new and emerging area, or an area that has been exhausted and is not drawing much current attention.

One of the important tasks of a literature review is to identify the key conceptual frameworks, theories, models, and methods within a field and examine their interrelationships. A reviewer may have to deal with conflicting findings and the limitations of individual studies in conceptualizing progress in the field. A literature review is not simply a chronological summary of all the studies that have been done previously. Rather, it is a conceptualization of the various theories, methods, patterns of findings, conclusions, and limitations of empirical previous work. It is therefore a challenge to evaluate and integrate the work that has been done on a particular topic, paying particular attention to the theories, concepts, and methods that are used to advance knowledge in the field, with one's own interests, experiences, and perspectives.

This preliminary process helps the researcher begin to shape potential research questions. The types of questions one asks will influence the type of data that are collected. I encourage students to play with the phrasing of the questions to see where each would lead. Suppose a student is interested in studying education in high schools. This topic would lend itself to a myriad of research questions. A question like "What is the impact of school improvement efforts in math on student outcomes?" would suggest a quantitative type of investigation. In contrast, a question like "How do high school students value their educational experiences?" may suggest a qualitative type of investigation. "What sorts of issues influence high school teachers to become involved in, or resist, school improvement?" would suggest a third focus and data collection. Although the questions asked should drive the data collection, the reality is that most researchers generally think of themselves as doing either quantitative or qualitative type of work. These preliminary decisions about topic, data needed, and methods of investigation will begin to structure the data collection part of the study.

It is often useful to cap off this preliminary process of thinking about what to study and how with a short two-page paper. One should identify the background of the problem, what the research intents are, and how the problem will be studied. This is part of the problem formulation stage. The idea is to be able to state relatively succinctly what one wishes to study and how. If the research proposal may eventually become a dissertation, one might entertain several preliminary research ideas that could be presented to different faculty members in order to receive some feedback. In the previous example about high school education, one might think about each of the three questions and share the ideas with different faculty members to receive their perspectives on whether it is a project that would be feasible and has merit. A faculty member who studies school effects might be knowledgeable and interested in a study on how school improvement processes may affect student outcomes. A faculty member interested in the social construction of meaning (e.g., constructivism, feminism) might provide insight on the second question. A faculty member who does research on school reform might provide feedback on the third question concerning teacher resistance to change.

It is often at this stage that a student begins to identify a dissertation chair. Ideally, at this point in the process there is a suitable match made between the area of research the student is proposing and a faculty member's interest and expertise. Then it is important to think about other faculty members who could contribute to the research process through their interests, expertise, and methodological perspectives.

Once some of the preliminary work has been completed, students can put together more complete research proposals. At this point, researchers usually talk in terms of conceptualizing (or framing) the research study. Theories, frameworks, and models are conceptual tools that help researchers investigate relationships that underlie phenomena empirically. They can be a valuable aid in helping researchers distinguish between what to include (e.g., setting, variables, interview data, analyses) and what can be safely ignored (Sabatier & Jenkins-Smith, 1993). Other research perspectives may imply the more limited use of conceptual models at the early stages of problem formulation. The choice of conceptual framework and methodological approach underpinning a proposed study, therefore, is an essential part of the research design in helping to recognize previous work, mold the problem statement, develop the research questions, and add necessary structure to the collection and organization of the data (Miles & Huberman, 1984; Yin, 1994).

Sabatier and Jenkins-Smith (1993) argued that conceptual and methodological underpinnings should be explicit rather than implicit in research studies. Whereas the scientific foundations of studies are often hidden from the author and readers, making them explicit encourages the linking of theoretical propositions to research questions, methods of conducting the study, empirical findings, and the logic of conclusions. This requires the researcher to label the relevant propositions that are derived from the theory and (or) the methodological approach being employed. These activities are fundamental to the conduct of rigorous research on educational policy, because relative to one's research purposes, some conceptual groundings and methods provide greater insights about policy problems and their solutions than do others. In the following chapters, conceptual tools and methods that can be used in formulating policy studies are addressed in more detail.

## EXERCISES

1. Identify a policy issue that is currently being discussed. Describe some differing views on the issue. What values and assumptions about education underlie these contrasting views? Are there disconnects among policymakers, researchers, educators, and the public that you can identify? What might be some of the reasons for these differences among various groups?

2. Take some time to consider one or two possible policy problems that you might be interested in studying further. Write a short (two-page) preliminary overview of one of the policy problems you have been thinking about. Identify the background and importance of the problem, what you might want to find out about it, how you might study it, and what data you would need (and can get) to study it. In subsequent chapters, you will be able to think about other conceptual and methodological aspects of the problem.

# *1*

# *AN OVERVIEW OF THE POLICY PROCESS*

Policies are developed and implemented to advance particular political viewpoints or to address problems perceived as pressing. An understanding of the dynamics of the policymaking process is important in studying why some policies are effective, whereas others fall short of their intended goals, or produce unintended, negative results. Process connotes temporal conditions that affect how events, strategies, actions, and decisions unfold. Uncovering the reasons why some policies succeed whereas others fail and understanding the political dynamics that accompany policy activity form the basis for conducting policy research.

The policy process has been described as dynamic and disorderly, with time spans that often last over a decade to several decades. The process focuses on disputes involving deeply held values, different perceptions about the causes of problems and the probable impact of solutions to problems, contrasting amounts of resources, often considerable political stakes in the outcomes of the debates. Policy issues, which are by definition disagreements about how given problems should be approached and solved, are the basic precursors to future policy activity. They are typically found within a subset of policy domains, within which numerous special interest groups, governmental agencies, legislatures, and other individuals are involved in various aspects of the process over a period of time.

Over time, an issue may become politically defined and placed on the policy agenda within the policy domain. For this reason, some have suggested that the policy subsystem is the appropriate unit of analysis, as opposed to a specific program, governmental branch, or agency. Once an issue is receiving serious attention, it may be expressed in written form and eventually adopted by an appropriate legislative branch or agency (U.S. Department of Education, state departments of education, local school districts). From this more formal phase, the policy must then be implemented by those in the field charged with educating students (state and local administrators, teachers). Policy implementation carries its own set of dynamics that often form the basis for policy study. Other efforts may also be directed at determining whether the policy is reaching its intended targets and whether it is successfully achieving its goals. This process can lead to further modifications of the policy (e.g., changes in language, levels of resources allocated to support the policy, termination). Because of the complicated life each policy has, it can be challenging to evaluate its development, implementation, and impact. Moreover, it can be difficult to reach conclusions about policy regularities based on the idiosyncratic nature of individual policies. Although individual policies have been perhaps most studied, the complexity of policy processes suggests a number of different focal points for analysis.

The first section of this book develops an overview of the policy process in the United States and its study. Chapter 1 presents an introduction to the field of educational policy and its study. Chapter 2 provides an overview of the federalist system and how it impacts educational policy processes. Chapter 3 examines in more detail how educational policy develops and is implemented.

# An Introduction to Policymaking and Its Study

Tinkering with the education system in the United States has always drawn the interest of policymakers and educational reformers as a means of improving society's social and economic ills (Tyack, 1991). For over a century and a half, Americans have translated their cultural hopes and anxieties into demands for public school reform. In their historical examination of American education, Tyack and Cuban (1995) concluded that people in the United States supported public education because they believed that progress was the rule and that better schooling guaranteed a better society. From the early beginnings of the nation, communities recognized that education played a powerful role in the socialization of children. School committees ensured that the curriculum content taught in the schools functioned to shape the minds of students (Finkelstein, 1978). As Tyack and Cuban (1995) suggested, it was generally easier to coerce the young by teaching reading skills, moral principles, and citizenship than it was to shape the minds of adults. A good example of this was the Americanization movement in the schools during the early 20th century. Schools were used as a means to socialize the children of immigrants to American norms and language.

Schools therefore were primary vehicles for implementing social policies. As political scientist Thomas Dye (1972) commented about the role of schooling in American society:

> Perhaps the most widely recommended "solution" to the problems that confront American society is more and better schooling. If there ever was a time when schools were only expected to combat ignorance and illiteracy that time is far behind us. Today schools are expected to do many things: resolve racial conflict and build an integrated society; inspire patriotism and good citizenship; provide values, aspirations, and a sense of identity to disadvantaged

children; offer various forms of recreational and mass entertainment (football games, bands, choruses, majorettes, and the like); reduce conflict in society by teaching children to get along well with others and to adjust to group living; reduce the highway accident toll by teaching students to be good drivers; fight disease and ill health through physical education, health training, and even medical treatment; eliminate unemployment and poverty by teaching job skills and malnutrition and hunger through school lunch and milk programs; produce scientists and other technicians to continue American's progress in science and technology; fight drug abuse and educate children about sex; and act as custodians for teenagers who have no interest in education but whom we do not permit either to roam the streets unsupervised. In other words, nearly all of the nation's problems are reflected in demands placed on the nation's schools. And, of course, these demands are frequently conflicting. (p. 131)

Policy changes often result from shifting demographic, social, economic, and political trends (Iannaccone, 1977; Ward, 1993; Wirt & Kirst, 1989). Because these trends affect political interests, participation in the system, and ultimately can change the distribution of political power among various groups, they affect expectations in policy fields such as education. These forces bring pressures on schools to make educational changes. Proposals to makes changes in education reveal much about how problems are diagnosed and solutions are proposed. Once a problem is identified, policy debate typically ensues, which can lead to various policy actions—a new course or curriculum, a different school structure, a stronger set of academic standards, a new way of teaching, higher standards for the preparation of professionals—that are intended to bring about the desired end.

Despite policymakers' intentions to solve social problems through policy actions, the historical record suggests that changes in institutional practices often lagged behind (or were unaffected by) the political rhetoric demanding educational reform (Tyack & Cuban, 1995). As Tyack and Cuban argued, there is a complex relationship between periods of "policy talk," or the way reformers and politicians talk about changes, and the actual institutional changes that result. Policymakers are not always able to control the outcomes of change (McLaughlin, 1990). This is because institutional practices can be resistant to the mandates and directives of external policymakers because implementation is shaped by the local context and, therefore, represents a "constructed" activity among stakeholders.

Although policy talk about change can be blunted by the norms, practices, and values within those institutions, over time, institutions do change (Tyack, 1991). In the past, some innovations were easily incorporated into the educational system without much political rhetoric or debate. Tyack and Cuban (1995) indicated that these types of little changes occurred regularly and were typically structural "add ons" (e.g., kindergarten, junior high school) that disturbed established norms of educational practice little. In a few instances, the institutional changes resulting from policy actions were more visible, dramatic, and widespread, such as fundamental restructuring of local school governance that took place at the turn of the 20th century (Plank, Scotch, & Gamble, 1996). In contrast, however, some issues needed to be constantly renegotiated (Tyack, 1991). Recurring policy debates about "the failure of public schools" were sometimes triggered by single events (e.g., the launch of Sputnik in 1957, the publication of *A Nation At Risk in* 1983).

Tyack (1991) concluded that eras of social, political, or economic turmoil, which often create much talk about educational change, do not necessarily lead to subsequent institutional changes in educational practice. He noted, for example, that the Depression and subsequently the New Deal during the 1930s had very little impact on educational activities in the schools. Similarly, World War II did not seem to disrupt the daily lives of children in school. Even the social turmoil of the Vietnam War, while certainly causing unrest on college campuses, did not substantially affect daily public school instructional routines.

Public schools in the 21st century are expected to do more than schools in past eras. Charter schools, special education litigation, technological innovation, federal legislation such as the No Child Left Behind Act (U.S. Congress, 2001), vouchers to support private (religious) schools, open enrollment, standards-based curriculum, race-linked enrollment policies, certification requirements for educational professionals, violence on campus, and the minority–white achievement gap are all concerns that have garnered considerable attention within the education landscape over the past decade. These new demands and expectations for education are very different from those in the nation's beginning or a century ago. Understanding patterns of educational change in the past, however, can inform our thinking about current pressures and trends.

## WHAT IS POLICYMAKING?

Changing political, social, and economic forces such as the increasing cultural diversity of the United States and the recurring theme of reforming the country's schools over the past century are appropriate places to begin a discussion about policymaking in education. Policymaking has been described in a number of different ways (e.g., Boyd, 1988; Cibulka, 1995; Easton, 1965; Firestone, 1989; Fowler, 2000; Lindblom, 1968; Mann, 1975; Marshall, 1997; Sabatier, 1999; Scribner & Englert, 1977). The various descriptions reflect differences in views about the nature of society and its problems, the proper role of government in pursuing policy goals and resolving conflicts, and who should be involved in crafting policy solutions.

Some definitions focus on policymakers' formal efforts (e.g., legislation, policy directives and regulations, court decisions) to resolve complex, consequential problems of a public nature through making a series of decisions according to some set of values (e.g., Fowler, 2000; Mann, 1975; Sabatier, 1999). Sabatier, for example, described the process of policymaking as including the manner in which problems get conceptualized and brought to various governmental branches and agencies for solution. Policy actors define policy problems, interpret values and proper courses of action, and the effectiveness of solutions in different manners depending on how much of their welfare is determined by the problem.

This view of politics and policymaking has been referred to as rationalist (Scribner, Aleman, & Maxcy, 2003), suggesting that those in power have the legitimacy to decide what means and policy ends to pursue. The focus is on the intentional actions of governmental actors and special interests operating within the political system in pursuit of goals that fulfill their self interests (Levinson & Sutton, 2001; Scribner et al., 2003). The rational view of political activity is rooted in economic theory; that is, from a range of choice options, individuals decide on the alternative that maximizes benefits and minimizes costs. From this perspective, policymakers' intentional pursuit of their own interests underlies all collective political activity that moves policy through a sequence of rational decision-making steps (or stages) from agenda setting, to formulation, enactment, and implementation. Rational choice theory is the most recent of several political theories examining how individuals organize to pursue collective policy action that grew out of the rationalist tradition (Scribner et al., 2003).

Especially within a democracy, however, this power is not absolute. Policymakers' choices are also bound by the social structures and economic conditions in which they operate (Elster, 1986). This has been referred to as *bounded rationality* (Simon, 1945). The complexity of problems of consequence and the public nature of policy issues imply the potential for controversy over what values will predominate in selecting a course of action. As some have noted (e.g., Coplin & O'Leary, 1981; Fowler, 2000), until various groups disagree about how government should approach a problem, it does not become a policy issue. As Shipman (1969) succinctly put it, "policy is the value content of administrative process" (p. 122). Not only is a value scheme embedded in using policy to resolve problems, but the choice itself announces the values of policymakers and the system (Mann, 1975). Hence, policy concerns the formal and informal mechanisms, visible and unseen, by which individuals, or groups of individuals, influence decision-making processes as well as resulting outcomes (Stout, Tallerico, & Scribner, 1995).

Where some rational perspectives focus on the intentional behavior of individuals, systems theory focuses on the rational behavior of the system itself in responding to policy demands (Easton, 1965). Easton's systems framework, which was a dominant way to examine policymaking in the 1970s and 1980s, suggested that within the political system, rational decisions are made about how individuals would be allocated valued, but limited, resources. Easton referred to policy actions as the "authoritative allocation of values" and, ultimately, the determinants of who benefits and who loses. From a systems perspective, policy may be defined as the process through which a political system responds to demands to handle a public problem—which includes government's expressed intentions and enactments as well as its patterns of activity and inactivity (Cibulka, 1995; Fowler, 2000). The link between the political system and other subsystems in the environment is key to the policymaking process because the other subsystems create stresses in the form of input demands. The political system then converts these demands into policy decisions or outputs, which feed back the allocated values to the society's environment where the process began (Wirt & Kirst, 1982). Efficiency becomes one measure of success in pursuing policy goals.

Other definitions of policymaking focus greater attention on identifying the formal structures of government (e.g., federal, state) and their respective arenas (e.g., legislatures, courts) in which policy activities take place. These definitions of policymaking pay particular attention to the specific arrangements in government and school systems and how their configurations affect policymaking processes and outcomes. For example, Iannaccone and Cistone (1974) suggested that educational governance within a federalist system consists of a "loosely coupled" family of governments in which "each sphere of authority and responsibility tends to obscure the operational realities of educational policymaking" (p. 17). Over time, the particular structural arrangements within federalism create distinctive patterns of rules and behavior that influence the educational policy process. Governmental institutions formulate alternatives, select solutions, and the solutions get implemented, evaluated, and revised. Similarly, the loosely coupled nature of schools represent micropolitical arenas where politics and the social system of teachers, administrators, and students interact (Iannaccone, 1975). Ball (1987) suggested, therefore, that schools were better understood as arenas of struggle. Structural definitions of policy provide an explanation why it is often difficult to implement policies crafted at various levels of government within schools.

Newer definitions center on policymaking as a socially constructed activity. These views emphasize the social settings in which policy actors compete, negotiate, or compromise and cooperate over time in integrating diverse interests to create coalitions in support of policy actions. As opposed to the focus on the intents of policymakers to maximize benefits and minimize costs in pursuing policy goals, the emphasis is on identifying their belief systems, perceptions, interpretations, and actions within multiple arenas. Firestone (1989), for example, described educational policy as a "chain of decisions stretching from the statehouse to the classroom" (p. 23) that represent the by-product of multiple agendas, available resources, political influence, and social relationships. In a similar manner, Marshall, Mitchell, and Wirt (1989) used a cultural paradigm to describe how cultural values underlie the process through which policies are made. They emphasized that policymakers play a key role in transforming cultural values into policy actions. Cultural values shape institutions and their traditions, and these values are imbedded in the policies that result. Marshall and colleagues described policy as "a set of values expressed in words, issued with authority, and reinforced with power (often money or penalties) in order to induce a shift toward those values" (p. 6). Thus, policymaking is dynamic, value laden, and focuses on both formal and informal activities over time.

A cultural approach to describing political activity, therefore, differs from rational and structural approaches in its attention to values, meanings, rules of behavior, power and influence, and the social and historical contexts that surround policy activity. The cultural approach focuses on ascertaining these intersubjective meanings and investigating the political dynamics of social interaction (Scribner et al., 2003). As Marshall and colleagues (1989) noted, social institutions represent the "cultural stage set built by the prior and present understandings of culture held by policy actors" (p. 5). Marshall (1997) took the cultural approach one step further, describing policy as "authoritative agreements among powerful people about how things should be" (p. ix).

By focusing almost exclusively on governmental action, conventional definitions of policy give privilege to those policy actors in formal roles (e.g., legislators, judges, agency bureaucrats). Understanding how policy has been socially constructed in past eras, and to what purposes, is key in modifying or transforming how policy works to maintain, or to transform, the social order. Critical and feminist perspectives on policy emphasize "going against the grain" of conventional definitions, models, and methods of examining policies. Going against the grain suggests researchers should focus on the cultural values embedded in policies; the deconstruction of policy documents into various readings, interpretations, and actions; the analysis of policy intention and effects for groups of people often silenced in conventional studies (e.g., women, nondominant minorities, Native Americans, urban poor); the impact of institutional structures that reinforce policy domination, oppression, and racism; and analyses of policies, programs, and political stances that focus on neglected needs in schooling (López, 2003; Marshall, 1997).

## THE STUDY OF POLICY

Policy problems by nature are public, consequential, complex, dominated by uncertainty, and affected by disagreement about the goals to be pursued (Mann, 1975). The nature of policy problems has implications on policymaking as an activity, as well as on its empirical study. From a diversity of ways to describe policymaking, Sabatier (1999) derived several important conclusions about the policy process. First, policymaking is diverse in scope, dynamic and often disorderly in process, and embedded in the cultural, political, and historical contexts of the United States. It involves an extremely complex set of interacting elements over time including hundreds of policy actors from interest groups, governmental agencies, legislatures, researchers, and journalists. Second, the process usually spans a decade or more as a minimum for most policy cycles (often reaching a much longer time frame). It is therefore best understood through examining events and social relations as they unfold over time. Third, most policy conflicts involve deeply held values and interests, large amounts of money, and sometimes, authoritative coercion.

## Evaluation, Policy Analysis, and Policy Research

As diverse as the definitions of policymaking are, it has also been studied from a variety of different perspectives and disciplines. In one of the first texts on conducting policy research, Majchrzak (1984) drew several distinctions between evaluation, policy research, and policy analysis. Evaluation research, which was a force from the middle 1960s, is directed more at judging the effectiveness and utility of existing programs. The focus is on providing information about the effects of programs (e.g., their benefits vs. costs, their impact on students) and whether they have reached their goals. In this context, evaluation research has been relatively limited to funded programs that the government had sponsored. There is some recent evidence, however, that this particular type of research will become influential once again in funded efforts to establish which types of school reform packages produce increased outcomes for large numbers of students (Slavin, 2002).

Policy analysis has been described as the analysis of alternative policy choices to arrive at the optimal decision in light of given goals, constraints, and environmental conditions (Nagel, 1984). Although this may have been a more limited initial technical focus, the field of policy analysis has expanded in many directions over the past few decades to include examining not only decision choices, but also many other associated aspects of the policy process including social, economic, political and cultural processes that underlie policy activity, developmental and implementation strategies, costs versus benefits associated with particular policy choices, the intended and unintended effects of policies, as well as the politics surrounding policy research and its utilization. In the past, policy analysis has probably drawn the most attention from researchers interested in educational policy.

Coplin and O'Leary (1981) further categorized policy analysis studies into four different types. *Monitoring* policy analysis consists of collecting ongoing data about a particular policy domain. In education, this could include attendance data, achievement data, data about the teaching force, graduation rates to name a few. By far, this is the preferred way in which school personnel collect data. They monitor certain types of processes to see if there are any changes in the trends. *Prescription* policy analysis may identify a policy problem, or a set of issues, and provide various kinds of decision options for policymakers to consider. Typically, they do not entail direct empirical data, but may consist of relevant research others have conducted that leads to a particular type of recommendation for action. *Evaluation-related* policy analysis examines the effects of a program to see how well the program has met its objectives, how well it was implemented, and whether it has produced any impacts. Often the intent is to decide whether to continue, modify, or terminate the program. Finally, *forecast* policy analysis addresses the future needs for teachers, administrators, or particular types of services in schools. These are usually based on an analysis of trends.

Whereas the objective of policy analysis may be to improve the quality of policy actions in alleviating social problems, in the past, analysts have thought of the process as more rational than it actually is in practice. As White (1983) argued:

> Policy analysis … is turbulent and open-ended rather than neat and easy. Decisive studies are very much the exception rather than the rule. Problems throw at analysts more variables for consideration and interests for accommodation than single studies can encompass. The task of policy analysis is not to produce that decisive recommendation, but, instead, to contribute toward consensual understanding of actualities, possibilities, and desirabilities. (p. 11)

In the political arena, policymakers often have a number of competing forces (e.g., time, resources, lack of relevant data when needed) that interact with the "rationality" of their decision choices. One of the benefits of policy analysis is that it offers a variety of frameworks that can be used to think about policy problems (Fowler, 2000). In recent years, in the United States, there has been a great effort to improve government's response to social problems through the analysis of its various activities (e.g., grants, educational innovations, mandates).

At the same time, however, policy analysis has been criticized as destructive to the practices of American politics (Jenkins-Smith, 1990). For one, it has been largely dominated by economic concerns (Boyd, 1988). Pressures for efficiency and productivity influenced by tight economic budgets have characterized many governments in recent decades. Often, policy analysis has heightened political tensions and even created new political issues (Warwick & Pettigrew, 1983). Instead of bringing scientific objectivity to the policy process, sometimes it brings subtle forms of bias (Callahan & Jennings, 1983). As policy has been increasingly seen as more dynamic and messy, policy analysis has been criticized as not living up to its early promise of improving government's policies and programs by providing objective and scientific analysis (Boyd, 1988).

In education, policy analysis (which is aimed at the analysis and evaluation of particular policies) and the politics of education (which focuses largely on political dynamics associated with educational policy activity) form subsets of the larger field of educational policy research. The goal of policy research is to conduct research on, or provide an analysis of, fundamental social problems to provide policymakers with technical information and pragmatic, action-oriented recommendations for alternative ways of alleviating the problem. Broadly speaking, policy research includes those efforts to produce knowledge about fundamental social problems that have implications for policymakers, educators, and others seeking to utilize the research in future policy activity to alleviate those problems. As Coleman (1972) argued, policy research originates in action and is fed back into action, whereas theory-based research originates in the disciplines and is fed back into disciplines. This focus largely separates policy research from other types of research endeavors (e.g., resolving problems of interest to other researchers in a discipline, testing theories about social processes, identifying and describing a new set of relationships that exist in a particular discipline). For example, in other research endeavors, researchers may have little concern about whether their results are actually utilized by policymakers or practitioners in resolving social problems that may be related to their research. They tend to focus their writing on how their results contribute to the advancement of disciplinary knowledge.

## Goals of Policy Research

Given the complicated nature of policy problems and policy actions, we can begin to identify several purposes or goals of policy-related research. As suggested, traditionally, the most basic goal is to identify choices, or courses of action, that lead to optimal decisions to resolve identified problems. This goal has formed the basis of much past research (i.e., policy analysis) that has been done in the field. Yet, for a variety of reasons, this type of policy research has received a mixed reception from policymakers.

A second goal is examine the processes through which purposes and values in the public sector are translated into policy actions. The study of policies and their associated politics must seek to understand the complexity of human interaction through examining the roots of these actions. Policy debates over the severity of problems, their causes, and the probable impact of proposed solutions play an important role in the outcomes of policymaking processes. These debates concern opposing political perspectives, values and interests, amounts of resources, and political coercion. Within particular institutional arrangements, various policy rules, norms, and strategies affect individuals' decision choices in the process of developing collective action. Different theoretical perspectives attend to policy coalition belief systems, to institutional arrangements that affect policymakers' strategies, and to social and cultural beliefs that may shape policymakers' interactions and actions. Because of their controversial nature, policy issues take time to be turned into legislation, implemented, and their effects realized. As this process can take several years, longitudinal approaches to its study are preferred to examine the intended and unintended effects and changes that result from policy activity.

A third goal is to identify the outcomes and impacts resulting from policy actions. All theories of policy activity must account for policy change

(Schlager, 1999). Some theories attend to the types of events, strategies, and factors that precede policy change. Other perspectives attend more to the results of policy activity on individuals and on the future activity of policymakers and the external environment. Intended effects refer to the extent to which policies reach their intended goals and targets. In contrast, unintended effects are not related to the goals of the policy but, rather, appear as by-products of the policy's implementation.

In education, intended (and unintended) effects often occur considerably after policy debates and may penetrate the existing institutional structures of schools in an uneven fashion (Tyack, 1991). The junior high (as a structural concept to bridge the K–8 and 9–12 school experience), the middle school, merit pay for teachers, and computers in classrooms all represent examples of educational innovations that were uneven in their ability to change existing educational structures and practices. Studies of innovations in education often require the examination of broad trends over time to determine how and the extent to which these trends impact the structure of the educational system. Uncovering the reasons for differing impacts of policy innovations represents a challenge for policy researchers. Most policy theories have been unsuccessful in identifying the conditions that lead to desired impacts versus those that lead to failure.

In recent years, policy researchers have also directed attention at how policy activity produces differential effects on particular groups (e.g., Anderson, 1990; Benham & Heck, 1998; Marshall, 1993, 1997). These studies help identify policy activity that has persisted over time, and focus attention on the outcomes of the policy process for particular targeted groups.

A fourth goal is to produce evidence that helps to resolve policy debates over different courses of action. Although policy research is often viewed as a means of solving problems or providing technical information for policy decision making, it is important to recognize the importance of analysis in reconceptualizing policy problems or in illuminating our understanding of complex policy questions (Boyd, 1988). For example, research on schools was initiated in response to the often-cited conclusion of the Coleman et al. Report (1966) that schools don't make a difference. This focus on school effects has produced over three decades of research that has significantly increased our understanding of how various school structures, policies, and processes affect student learning (Teddlie & Reynolds, 2000). The shift in thinking from students and their families as responsible for student outcomes to schools' responsibility in the educational process was momentous in thinking about systematic efforts to improve education (Boyd, 1992).

It is clear that policy research has produced scientific evidence about many different aspects of the policy process and the impacts of policies. Yet, it is also obvious that it has fallen short of some of its early promise of producing a science of policy. Disenchantment with the results of policy research over its first few decades have come from several sources—policymakers, practitioners, and scholars themselves. In education, federal policymakers are focused on school accountability and innovation. To assess the success of educational interventions, policymakers have directed attention at prescribing the nature of educational research that counts as scientific evidence (Feuer et al., 2002). Practitioners lament the irrelevance of university research to the training and practice of educators. Scholars have criticized the impact of the Theory Movement in educational administration that attempted to create a science of administration by incorporating social science theory and method (Culbertson, 1988). Conceptual and methodological wars have created separate camps of policy researchers with varied interests and beliefs about the scholarly purposes of the field. Some advocate that policy research has not gone far enough in identifying oppressive structures and working to replace them.

Over time, therefore, the increasingly diverse goals of policy research have favored the development of an eclectic set of conceptual lenses and methods that draw from disciplines such as anthropology, economics, political science, decision sciences, and sociology. The introduction of diverse theoretical frameworks, methods, and norms of inquiry used to understand educational policy activity has moved the field considerably from its political science roots. This has enriched the knowledge base of educational policy (Johnson, 2003). On the other hand, as Johnson suggested, because the field's focus and scope have broadened, its multidisciplinary nature also complicates attempts to bring needed theoretical clarity and a more integrated intellectual identity. Because numerous fields focus on different parts of the policy system, seemingly contradictory conclusions may be reached, which adds to the debate over the specific topic being studied, as well as the value of research in aiding policy activity (Feuer et al., 2002).

## EDUCATIONAL POLICY RESEARCH AS SCHOLARLY ACTIVITY

Willower and Forsyth (1999) indicated that the "history of a field of study is a recital of its landmark events, including the problems emphasized, the lines of inquiry pursued, and the issues contested" (p. 1). Similarly, as Robert Lynd noted, "the controlling factor in any science is the way it views and states its problems" (as quoted in Katznelson, 1976, p. 216). Understanding the historical context surrounding important policy debates and actions provides clues to what were considered to be the important policy problems of an era, the solutions that were favored, the data that were collected to provide evidence about solutions, and the ways in which the evidence was used to legitimate particular policy solutions.

The collection of data to provide information about schooling is relatively old in the United States. A key original purpose of the U.S. Office of Education, founded in 1867, was to collect data about schools and diffuse worthy innovations (Tyack, 1991). However, its staff was never fully able to get states to submit data, generally because the data had to be collected from local officials. The result was that educational data from the 1800s were generally unreliable and focused on such basic educational inputs as student enrollment, attendance, administrator and teacher numbers, and rudimentary fiscal information. For these reasons, it can be very difficult to assess policy trends and changes in schools during the early years of public education.

Of course, the collection of data is not neutral. Data collection represents political decisions about what types of information are useful in determining how the schools are doing. The presence of data can therefore provide clues about the values of policymakers in particular eras and what the important policy problems were. To illustrate this idea, much of the early statistical information was concerned with how the schools were expanding to serve greater numbers of students—as this was one dominant policy issue at the turn of the 20th century (Tyack, 1991). Policymakers were interested in getting children in school and keeping them out of the factories. The data available from this era generally focused on enrollment trends and responses of the system to deal with greater numbers of students (e.g., numbers of teachers and administrators, budgets, information about school board size). In contrast, it is difficult to find data on achievement before the "accountability era" in schooling (i.e., the 1970s and 1980s). Student performance and school effectiveness were not identified as important policy issues until then.

The formal study of educational practices began about the turn of the 20th century in an effort to create a "science of education" (Lagemann, 1997). During this period, the reliability and validity of the data collected improved substantially (Tyack, 1991). By the 1930s, subfields had emerged that centered on different subjects within the school curriculum. The one constant over the past 100 years has been the criticism of educational research. The most important criticism has been that it has failed to yield dramatic improvements in practice.

Although debates over education's goals, its study and practice, and its uneven impact have pitted groups against each other in our nation's history, the systematic study of educational policymaking is relatively new. Its roots are primarily found in studies of politics and governmental actions. During the 1930s and 1940s, statistics gathered by economists were often analyzed and published with recommendations (Nelson, 1991). These were generally not linked to government actions, however. The actual study and analysis of governmental policy, described as techniques and criteria with which to evaluate policy options and select among them (e.g., Boyd, 1988; Nagel, 1984), has been promoted since the 1950s. Lasswell (1951) was among the first to suggest a type of "policy science" (see also Lasswell & Kaplan, 1950) in terms of how this new approach could be used in studying government. His view was to improve government by improving the quality of information used, paying particular attention to various stages that a particular policy went through during its "policy life." This type of scientific analysis of governmental activity was seen as a means to provide information to use in promoting greater efficiency and equity in allocating re-sources. Concerned with the nature, causes, and effects of alternative policies (Nagel, 1980), policy analysis aimed to help policymakers under-take more effective action to solve or reduce significant policy problems. The dominant model used to organize the analysis of policy activity today is still heavily embedded in Lasswell's original organizing scheme to examine different stages in the policymaking process.

## The Politics of Education and Educational Policy

Only since the mid-1960s has research related to educational politics and policy been identified and discussed as an approach for understanding the dynamics of educational decision making. Much of the early research fo-cused on the "politics of education," or ways in which the "political struc-tures, actors, and processes of educational politics have become so fundamentally reorganized" (Wirt & Kirst, 1982, p. v). Early studies were conducted primarily by political scientists interested in the educational sec-tor (Johnson, 2003). In one of the seminal articles, Eliot (1959) outlined a research agenda for the emerging field. He called for the systematic study of ideologies, institutions, interests, decision-making processes, and voting patterns surrounding educational issues, noting that "if all the significant political factors are revealed, the people can more rationally and effectively control the governmental process" (p. 1036). Eliot's focus was on structural, behavioral, and voting aspects of educational issues at the district, state, and federal levels (Johnson, 2003). Iannaccone (1977) broadened the concern to consider how educational politics were related to various types of changes in educational governance; that is, changes in the service function of government (i.e., what is provided), the political function of government (i.e., how conflicts are managed), and the ideological assumptions and or-ganizational structures that manage political conflict (i.e., how governmen-tal systems are changed).

Although there was a proliferation of studies on educational politics in the 1960s and 1970s, there were few attempts to integrate them into a cohe-sive whole, or to provide a more comprehensive framework (Scribner & Englert, 1977; Wirt & Kirst, 1982). Much of the work was directed at under-standing sources of conflict in education and how these sources determined various changes in education (e.g., local board of education politics, super-intendent turnover, dynamics of educational decision making). By the mid-1970s, Scribner and Englert (1977) had identified four core concepts that structured much of the scholarly work done in the field. These concepts included government, conflict, power, and policy. Although researchers have since focused on an expanded range of topics, using a variety of con-ceptual lenses that extend from sociology to economics, these four concepts continue to be central to understanding policy processes in education (López, 2003). It was not clear, however, exactly where the developing interest in politics in education should be situated within the larger educational subfields. For example, Iannaccone (1975) described the field as specialized interest within educational administration in which scholars applied political science methods and knowledge to write about educational problems and constituencies.

While work was being done in understanding the politics of education during the 1960s and 1970s, research was also beginning to accumulate on the impact of planned programs designed to produce educational change. The primary source of this was an increased federal role in promoting educational reform projects. Against a backdrop of social unrest, by the mid-1960s as Congress implemented Johnson's "Great Society" ideals, social policy was very much a part of the federal government's domestic agenda. Evaluation, as a growing force in governmental accountability, was tied to money allocated to a number of equity programs. Beginning with the Elementary and Secondary Education Act (ESEA) in 1965, Congress insisted on documenting that federal funds intended for impoverished children under Title I of ESEA were actually helping to improve schooling for these children.

As a result, evaluation studies became a feature of federally funded education (and many noneducation) policies and their resultant programs (Lagemann, 1997). As part of ESEA, regional educational laboratories were also established to serve as brokers in improving the links between research and school practice (Kearney, 1967). These types of efforts focused interest on educational policy made at the federal level and its resulting implementation. The study receiving the most attention during this initial period was the Rand study of *Federal Policies Supporting Educational Change* (FPSEC). The first part consisted of surveys of 293 projects and intensive visits to 29 sites (Berman & McLaughlin, 1975). The second part looked at the institutionalization of change in 100 of the original 293 sites (Berman & McLaughlin, 1977). The study identified a number of factors that affected the successful (or unsuccessful) implementation of change. Most important, it suggested that features of the local context (e.g., implementation strategies, administrative support, quality of training, teacher perceptions) had greater impacts on the levels of implementation, as opposed to features under control of federal or state policy agencies (Firestone & Corbett, 1988).

The Rand study on the implementation of federal policies provided initial information about the nature of policymaking efforts at federal and state levels (e.g., mandates, grants, dissemination of knowledge-based products) and the challenges of penetrating established school practices to reach intended policy goals—a concern that has remained a consistent focus of policy research from the 1970s to the present. Through coupling governmental policy and evaluation, the resultant growth of policy research in the past three decades has been tremendous. In 1984, Mitchell made one of the first efforts to summarize the literature on educational policy. He described the voluminous, but uneven, writing and research on educational policy in the previous 20-year period (amounting to some 28,000 pieces on educational policy between 1975 and 1981 in the Educational Resources Information Center alone).

Over time, the politics of the education field moved away from its parent discipline in political science, becoming more multidisciplinary, and from a behavioral-oriented to a policy-oriented field (Johnson, 2003). Cibulka (1995) concluded that during the 1980s and 1990s, educational policy studies largely replaced studies of educational politics that were more popular in the 1960s and 1970s, although the politics of education as a field remains viable today (see, for example, Johnson, 2003; Scribner et al., 2003).

This shift in research focus was likely related to a number of forces including growing concerns with governmental accountability, a decline in the equity agenda of the 1960s and 1970s, rising conservatism, and pragmatic educational reforms that would produce stronger educational outcomes (as reflected in the publication of *A Nation At Risk* in 1983). The growing interest in educational policy led to the creation of several policy research journals in education (e.g., *Educational Evaluation and Policy Analysis, Educational Policy, Journal of Education Policy, School Effectiveness and School Improvement*) that have the intent of providing a forum for bridging the gap among practitioners, policymakers, and researchers on issues of educational importance.

By the mid-1990s, educational policy and politics also became one of the standing divisions within the American Educational Research Association. One concern that has arisen is the need to clarify what the relationship of educational politics as a field is to the larger field of educational policy. Educational politics and policymaking are inextricably linked and at times, difficult to distinguish because policy is at the center of political action (Johnson, 2003). As Johnson suggested, although they often overlap in studying educational processes, they can and should be separated for conceptual purposes. Each also has its own particular scholarly history.

The distinction between the two likely rests on the intellectual purposes and questions of interest to a researcher. For example, policy research questions often focus more on resolving identified problems (e.g., How do we improve educational practices in the schools?), whereas political questions focus more on assessing the political dynamics and milieu (e.g., What political forces, groups, and individuals dominate the identification, enactment, and implementation of educational improvement strategies in schools?) that may underlie particular policy situations (Johnson, 2003). Obviously, decision makers are concerned with more pragmatic questions such as, "How can we improve educational outcomes?" or "What is the most effective improvement strategy to implement?" Although these are important concerns, the political focus allows the researcher to also look at how politics influences the development, enactment, and implementation process for a given policy.

A second concern is the future direction of educational policy scholarship. Previous reviews of educational policy have pointed to the uneven results of scholarly endeavors to move forward in contributing to the improvement of practice (e.g., Boyd, 1988, 1992; Mitchell, 1984). Critiques of dominant perspectives point to their limited scope and assumptions (rationality, stable environments, and organizational structures) and failure to produce results that policymakers and practitioners can use in solving policy problems. Critical approaches to social analysis entail a critique of social and political inequities and an advancement toward desired ones. Yet, they, in turn, have been criticized for failing to address issues related to changing oppressive structures. Alternative frameworks have been better able to describe oppressive structures and inequities than they have to formulate and pursue policy changes.

In some ways, the field may be at a type of intellectual crossroads. At the end of the day, it will be challenging to reconcile differences about the field's proper directions, its scientific assumptions, and its conceptual and analytic methods among scholars, at the same time as policymakers are dictating the scope of educational reform and the nature of scientific research. This represents an challenge for moving future policy scholarship forward.

## HOW INFLUENTIAL IS POLICY RESEARCH?

Although the purposes and methods of policy scholarship have become more diverse over time, assessments of the impact of accumulated scholarly work have been skeptical about its utilization to resolve educational problems in a satisfactory manner. It is often difficult to separate the politics, values, and historical traditions from the technical activity of conducting an unbiased scientific inquiry and the politics surrounding its use. Differences in explanations about the adequacy or failure of reforms to actually change educational practices suggests competing conceptual models influence our explanations of events (Boyd, 1992). Researchers themselves often frame policy problems quite differently, employ varied methods of investigating problems, and reach very different suggested solutions to policy problems such that, short of any real agreement, we cannot expect policymakers to choose between them (Birnbaum, 2000; Donmoyer, 1996). Because of these shortcomings, assessments on the role of analysis in understanding policy problems have oscillated between belief and doubt (Boyd, 1988; Jenkins-Smith, 1990). Wirt and Kirst (1982) noted that despite the growing amount of work on educational policy and politics through the 1970s, it was characterized by a "grab bag of partial theories and contrasting methods" with "no over arching general theory that generates hypotheses" (p. 27).

Coleman (1972) commented on the political nature of policy research; that is, it tended to produce findings that added to the power of certain groups while diminishing the powers of others—a feature not found in basic research. Because of the high stakes surrounding policy actions, policy disputes often involve misrepresentation, selective presentation of information, coercion and the discredit of opponents in the name of gaining an advantage (Moe, 1990; Sabatier, 1999). This political context results in both the use and misuse of policy research. Research is often selectively presented to further a political agenda. The phrase "based on research" is very influential in many policymaker and practitioner circles. We can wonder about whose research is represented as well; because policymakers do not have the expertise or time to evaluate the quality of research studies, peers, subordinates, and political ideology can exercise a great deal of control over what gets on the political agenda. The potential is always there to affect future policy, funding, and alter educational programs.

As Feurer and colleagues (2002) noted, the unprecedented federal legislation (e.g., No Child Left Behind Act) today praises scientific evidence as a key driver for educational policy and practice. In contrast, however, recent federal actions (e.g., legislation and embedded references to what constitutes acceptable research evidence) have also tended to narrow the view of what is counted as "scientific evidence." Recently, the federal government approached the National Research Council (NRC) of the National Academies (of Science, Engineering, and the Institute of Medicine) for advice about educational research (Feuer et al., 2002). NRC authored a report that articulated the nature of scientific research in education and offered a framework for the future of federal educational research (NRC, 2002). The committee acknowledged that educational research was of uneven quality. The report argued for a careful linking of research questions to particular types of methods that could be employed to address each, noting that the choice of method should be governed by the particular purposes and circumstances of the research (Feuer et al., 2002). It also suggested that a diversity of perspectives is likely to emerge in education (given its history, the role of values and democratic ideals in defining schooling, and the diversity of roles, curriculum, and governance across settings), and that this actually lends vitality.

Perhaps one of the benefits of the NRC report is that it will contribute to a debate among policy researchers about the nature of the research endeavor and its potential to contribute scientific evidence to policy discussions. This would be welcome, because the growth of standards-based reform has created a new arena for educational research and policymaking. Since the mid-1980s, demands have focused on improving the quality of educational outcomes. In response, there has been a greater emphasis on using reform packages that are based on research over the past decade in the search for improved educational outcomes.

There has also been debate over the relationship of accountability standards for educators (preparation, certification, continuing licensing), recent educator shortages, and alternative routes to certification. Because of growing shortages of teachers and administrators across the nation, there has been increasing policymaker support for reducing (or removing) such credentialing requirements as well as for opening up alternative routes to becoming a teacher or administrator. For example, a number of states have enacted legislation to increase alternative routes for individuals to become teachers. A few states have also acted to reduce or remove initial administrative certification requirements (e.g., Hawai'i, Michigan).

Research has been used as a political ping-pong ball in some of these recent policy debates. The underlying policy issue centers on the relationship of teacher education and certification to student learning. On one side of the teacher certification debate are those who conclude that teacher quality is an important influence in student learning, and those most affected by not having access to quality teachers are disadvantaged children in central cities who are substantially abandoned by the funding and hiring protections that should operate to provide a foundation for their education (Darling-Hammond, 2002). On the other side are those who believe that certification represents some type of professional roadblock controlled by State Departments of Education and Colleges of Education that creates an entry barrier keeping many qualified individuals out of classrooms. Addressing the politics of the debate, Darling-Hammond (2002) noted that the U.S. Secretary of Education cited the report from the Abell Foundation[1] purporting that there is "no credible research that supports the use of teacher certification as a regulatory barrier to teaching" (Walsh, 2001, p. 5) as the sole source for concluding that teacher education does not influence teacher effectiveness. As Darling-Hammond argued:

> In this report, the Secretary argued that teacher certification systems are "broken," imposing "burdensome requirements" for education course work that make up "the bulk of current teacher certification regimes" (p. 8). The report argues that certification should be redefined to emphasize higher standards for verbal ability and content knowledge and to de-emphasize requirements for education course work, making attendance at schools of education and student teaching optional and eliminating "other bureaucratic hurdles" (p. 19). The report suggests that its recommendations are based on "solid research." However, only one reference among the report's 44 footnotes is to a peer-reviewed journal article (which is misquoted in the report); most are to newspaper articles or to documents published by advocacy organizations, some of these known for their vigorous opposition to teacher education. For the recommendation that education preparation be eliminated or made optional, the Secretary's report relies exclusively on the Abell Foundation's paper. Though written as a local rejoinder to Maryland's efforts to strengthen teacher preparation and certification, it appears to have become a foundation for federal policy. (p. 2)

That the political debate hinges significantly on the citations and interpretations of a sustained program of research into the relationship be-

---

[1]"Teacher Certification Reconsidered: Stumbling for Quality" is published through the Abell Foundation website (www.abellfoundation.org). The version of the report that was published on this website in October, 2001 is the basis for Darling-Hammond's article. According to Darling-Hammond, the report has since been amended.

tween teacher certification and student learning is evidence of the manner in which research can be intentionally selected (or ignored) and represented in ways that support a particular policy choice. Much of Darling-Hammond's (2002) discussion was directed at taking apart the report's arguments, patterns of citing, and misrepresentations of empirical findings, and its criticism of the methodological approaches (e.g., sample size and design, measures for assessing performance, level of data aggregation) used in previous studies that have examined this teacher quality and student achievement. As Darling-Hammond further suggested, a recent review that analyzed 57 studies that met specific research criteria and that were published after 1980 in peer-reviewed journals, concluded that the available evidence demonstrates a relationship between teacher education and teacher effectiveness (Wilson, Floden, & Ferrini-Mundy, 2001). The review shows that empirical relationships between teacher qualifications and student achievement have been found across studies using different units of analysis and different measures of preparation, and in studies that employ controls for students' socioeconomic status and prior academic performance.

The illustration aptly demonstrates the potential importance of systematic research to weigh in on political discussions and provide evidence that can lead to eventual solutions. Systematic research that can be used to resolve important problems is one indicator of a field's progress. It requires the sustained commitment of groups of researchers to study particular problems and solutions in a variety of settings, under varied conditions, and using diverse methods of analysis. This specific focus of policy research (i.e., using policy research to help resolve debates over potential courses of action) is one concrete way that researchers can aid policymakers in answering questions about whether policies attain the goals for which they were intended or, perhaps, in identifying how certain policy solutions may have negative effects on particular groups. The challenge for educational policy researchers is to bring diverse communities together to integrate theories and empirical findings across domains, cultures, and methods (Feuer et al., 2002).

The particular mix of politics, values, and traditions, and perceptions about research in education creates numerous debates over the priority of policy problems, optimal solutions, funding sources, the role of research itself, as well as the roles of researchers, politicians, funding agencies, and educational practitioners in the policymaking process (Lagemann, 1997). As suggested in the introduction, policy researchers have been criticized in the past for their lack of clarity and understanding of the policy issues being addressed, the limitations of their analytic techniques, and their interpretations of findings. As a result, after initial enthusiasm for research on educational programs sponsored by Congress in the 1960s, federal support for educational research dropped consistently throughout much of the 1970s and 1980s (National Academy of Sciences, 1996). Recent evidence from Washington, however, suggests that federal perspectives and priorities for educational research are again shifting (Slavin, 2002). It is also the case that where scientific evidence can be presented to policymakers for use in decision making, because of the complex set of factors that influence policy decisions, they may well choose to ignore it. Thus, within the research community, the complaint is often heard that policymakers ignore the results of research, whereas policymakers contend that there is not much produced within the research community that is of value in decision making (Birnbaum, 2000; Lagemann, 1997; Lindblom & Cohen, 1979).

These arguments speak to the ambiguity of purposes and the challenges of methods and communication in increasing the utilization of policy research. Lest the reader despair about even attempting to do policy research, although the direct influence of policy studies on making particular policy decisions has been modest, the indirect influence on policymaking has been more significant, due to the role policy research has had in sharpening and reformulating policy issues and sometimes leading to new strategies for approaching social problems (Boyd, 1988). Although policymakers may not routinely act based on the results of a particular research study, studies of their behavior suggest that they do assimilate information, concepts, generalizations, and perspectives from a variety of sources including research that shape their understandings (Lindblom & Cohen, 1979; Weiss, 1982, 1991).

## CONCEPTUAL FRAMEWORKS, THEORIES, AND MODELS

Policy research and policy analysis attempt to bring understandings to complex problems and processes. Conceptual models help bound our inquiries into these complex problems and processes. They direct our attention to critical features—contextual conditions, institutional arrangements, cultural norms and belief systems—that influence policy activity and change (Schlager, 1999). Easton (1953) suggested that it is one thing to collect the facts, but they may not explain or lead to the understanding of the actual event. What must be done, then, is to order the facts around a conceptual framework or theory that may explain, analyze, and predict the "confusion of reality" (Marshall et al., 1989, p. 4). With respect to dealing with issues such as time lags between policy debates and implementation, the uneven penetration of policies on institutional changes, the differential impact of policies on various groups, and the tendency of some values to dominate while others have been silenced, previous policy theory has been severely lacking.

Broadly speaking, educational policy and politics have been studied from diverse conceptual lenses derived from rational, structural, and cultural research perspectives (Lichbach, 1997; Scribner et al., 2003). Past theories in these fields have emphasized structure, goals, inputs, outputs, and roles (Marshall et al., 1989) or stages in the policy development, enactment, and implementation process. *Rational* explanations focus on the intentional activity of policymakers in pursuit of clearly defined organizational goals. Rational explanations can be traced to economic theories and the bureaucratic model of organizations. They have also been widely used in political science in explaining individuals' intended actions. The rational model focuses on events within a limited time frame (i.e., viewing the policy system as more static), and policy activity as consisting of a number of steps or stages where demands are turned into policy outputs. Easton's (1965) "systems analysis" framework was one defining theoretical heuristic in the field. It provided one way of organizing analysis about how the political system influences policy development, implementation, and outcomes. The framework focused on the interplay among stresses in the environment that generate inputs of demand on the political system. The system then converts these inputs into rational decisions or outputs representing favored values, which in turn feed back the allocated values into the environment so that the process can begin again (Wirt & Kirst, 1982).

At the same time, however, this paradigm's hold on the field has represented a handicap in examining policy from other perspectives. Numerous criticisms have been raised over the past decade about the limitations of rational approaches to understanding how policy activity unfolds and how resulting institutional change occurs over time. Rational models tended to focus on equilibrium, stability, and incrementalism as opposed to systemic change (Johnson, 2003). Whereas attention is drawn to policy as an iterative process that results in a type of policy cycle (i.e., agenda setting, formulation, enactment, and implementation) surrounding the specific life of a particular policy, less attention is directed toward policy impact, because the impact often takes a longer time frame to unfold. It also tends to exclude concerns with issues outside the model including structured exclusion and marginalization (Johnson, 2003).

In contrast to the rational perspective, *structuralism* suggests that human behavior is externally conditioned by society's institutions, as opposed to emanating from the internal goals of actors (Scribner et al., 2003). Scott (1995) argued that the early studies on institutions examined the formal structures of government or broader social structure, while paying little attention to organizations as institutional forms. These classic studies focused on the relative effectiveness of various types of organizational arrangements (Scribner et al., 2003). For example, Weick (1976) described schools as "loosely coupled," as opposed to the "tight coupling" posited in traditional bureaucratic theory (Scribner et al., 2003). Within schools, this structural arrangement was said to result in different domains of authority for teachers and administrators.

In the structural approach, the nature of schools themselves (e.g., their size, grade-level configurations, their internal organization, such as student grouping and tracking) is found to produce particular types of outcomes. Structural examinations of educational policy within schools might focus on the effects of particular types of arrangements (e.g., lowering school or class size, creating particular types of student grouping) on outcomes. Newer views on structuralism (e.g., institutional theory) also examine how organizations both shape and are shaped by the economic, political, and cultural milieu (Scribner et al., 2003). This view rejects the notion that organizations are rational and goal oriented. They do not merely represent arenas for individual actions. Instead, institutional behavior is viewed as the enactment of broad cultural prescriptions (Ogawa & Bossert, 1995).

*Cultural* approaches to policy focus on the historical or temporal context and how this contributes to policy patterns that develop over time. Cultural approaches often examine value conflicts, tensions, the dynamics of negotiation and coalition building among actors, and the various environmental and institutional conditions that lead to social and political changes. This can also include conflict theories that focus on the emergence and persistence of conflict within social or cultural systems.

More recently, the cultural perspective has deepened and expanded (e.g., critical theory, critical constructivism, feminism) to examine how systemic features structure, disguise, suppress, and silence conflict for marginal groups (Johnson, 2003; Marshall, 1997). For example, the radical feminist perspective has been used to examine how policy results differentially affect groups by gender, class, or race (e.g., Blackmore et al., 1993). Although the studies are wide ranging in orientation and focus, currently, there are fewer theoretical and methodological guidelines to offer in developing and conducting studies that apply newer approaches (Johnson, 2003).

The challenge for policy theorists is to develop more comprehensive conceptual frameworks that explain how policy environments and policy actors working within specific arenas impact the policy process, both in its processes and in its results (Marshall et al., 1989). New ways of looking at policy problems need to be bridged with methodological approaches that can be used studying the problems in ways that provide new insights. Unfortunately, there is often little guidance available to researchers on what lenses and methods are most appropriate for various policy problems. It would be a mistake to think that any single scheme would capture the breath and depth of work on educational policy (e.g., see Boyd, 1988; Mitchell, 1984). As in other fields, there are conceptual and methodological debates about what ways should dominate in examining problems.

Scientific fields tend to advance through a complex combination of professional criticism and self-correction (Popper, 1959). New conceptualizations can illuminate some aspects of policymaking that are ignored in other frameworks (Johnson, 2003). As Johnson argued, the nature of inquiry is such that each theory should be "examined for what it includes and excludes, what it frames in and out, the questions/phenomena it highlights and the questions/phenomena it ignores, the assumptions it makes, and its inherent limitations.... The acceptance or rejection of any framework ... should not come at the cost of sacrificing theoretical and methodological rigor" (p. 50).

Policy frameworks "may be understood as mechanisms for comprehending empirical situations with simplification" (Shapiro & McPherson, 1987, p. 61). Different conceptual approaches to the study of policy provide alternative ways through which to view the phenomenon. Each approach tends to emphasize different features and to provide somewhat different explanations of events. Policy experts draw some useful distinctions between the terms *framework, theory,* and *model* in conducting policy research. A conceptual framework identifies a set of variables and the relationships among them that are believed to account for a set of phenomena (Sabatier, 1999). The complexity can vary from a simple set of variables to something similar to a paradigm. It does not need to identify causal directions among all relationships, but will likely include some hypotheses. A theory contains more abstract, logically interrelated sets of propositions. It may apply numerical values to some of the variables and specify how relationships may vary depending on the values of critical variables (Sabatier, 1999). A useful theory, therefore, implies that a number of propositions may be stated that can then be subjected to empirical tests across a number of settings. Importantly, numerous theories could be consistent with the same conceptual framework. In contrast, a model is a representation of a particular situation, more narrow in scope and more precise in its assumptions (Sabatier, 1999; Shapiro & McPherson, 1987).

Frameworks, theories, and models are therefore conceptualized as operating along a continuum involving increasing logical interconnectedness and specificity, but decreasing scope (Sabatier, 1999). Analyses conducted at each level of logical interconnectedness provide different degrees of specificity with respect to a particular policy problem (Ostrom, 1999). Conceptual frameworks provide the most general list of variables that should be used to analyze all types of institutional arrangements. For example, a multilevel conceptual framework for explaining student achievement would include student (e.g., socioeconomic status, previous achievement, gender, ethnicity), classroom (e.g., teaching effectiveness, curriculum coverage, student time on task), and school (e.g., context, opportunity to learn, expectations, curricular standards, school leadership) variables.

Theories allow the researcher to specify which parts of a conceptual framework are most relevant to certain types of questions (Ostrom, 1999). It is usually the case that several theories are compatible with a single conceptual framework. For example, a number of different theories (e.g., psychological theories, sociological theories) about students' behavior might be compatible with a conceptual framework identifying factors that lead to their decisions to leave school before graduating.

Finally, models makes more precise assumptions about a limited set of variables (Ostrom, 1999). Experiments, mathematical models (e.g., structural equation modeling), and simulations are various means for exploring a set of proposed relationships among a defined set of variables. It is important to note that multiple models may also be compatible with a particular theory. Using structural equation modeling, for example, the analyst might test competing models and determine which one fits the data best.

## CHALLENGES IN STUDYING POLICYMAKING

Given the complexity of the policy process, researchers who study it must find ways of simplifying it in order to understand it (Sabatier, 1999). An ideological focus on how policy problems are viewed and solutions conceptualized is key because erosion in consensus about accepted ideas and the appropriateness of previous policy solutions is often an impetus for creating change within the educational system (Iannaccone, 1977). Because of the inherent complexity of ideas, events, and structures that envelop the educational policy process—a theme to which we return often in examining educational policy—its scholarly study has presented a number of challenges and raised a number of questions for future research.

### To What Extent Do Policies Penetrate the System?

Despite the political rhetoric directed at changing public education, it is difficult to determine under what conditions policies will actually penetrate the educational system and produce institutional change. Conceptualizing how external factors and institutional arrangements affect the strategies, interactions, and actions among policy coalitions represents an ongoing challenge for policy theorists. As Tyack and Cuban (1995) concluded, historically, educational policy reforms in the United States tinkered at the edges of the educational process. Actual reforms rarely matched reformers' aspirations. Successful reforms were generally structural add-ons (as opposed to radical changes), noncontroversial, required by law and easily monitored, and those that produced community constituencies that wanted to see them continue were more likely to become institutionalized. Historically, public schools implemented new practices at different rates (Tyack & Cuban, 1995). There was often a considerable lag between policy debate, advocacy, and implementation. Some schools adopted new ideas to solve specific problems, whereas others followed along to look innovative as a way of maintaining policymaker support (Plank et al., 1996). At other times, however, major changes took place in relative silence (Tyack & Cuban, 1995). As Tyack and Hansot (1990) suggested, the adoption of coeducation during the first half of the 19th century was one such change. Only afterward did it become a more debated topic. Research on these types of educational reforms suggests that it often takes several decades to identify and track policy cycles and to assess their impact in producing institutional changes.

One explanation about the uneven ability of policies to penetrate the schools has to do with the structure of policy subsystems within government (e.g., whether the policy originates at the federal level or the state level), the dynamics of implementation processes, and specific features of schools to blunt external changes. As McLaughlin (1990) argued, policies are typically formulated at higher levels of government; however, the nature, amount, and pace of change at the individual school level is a product of local conditions that are largely out of the control of federal or state policymakers. Teacher practices in classrooms are layers away from policy debates conducted within government. Features of local school context and the specific implementation process (i.e., how people read, interpret, and respond to policies) largely determine the actual influence of change-oriented policies on educational practices. The pace of change, therefore, may be different within policy subsystems versus the organizations that they seek to change. Politicians need results to satisfy constituents, often seeking reelection in 2-, 4-, or 6-year intervals. The time it takes for changes to be implemented at the site level, however, is often much longer—for example, 4 to 7 years (Louis & Miles, 1990). As Swanson and Stevenson (2002) concluded, individual layers and actors attempting to influence educational policy further decouple the federal and local poles of the policy system, resulting in what Pressman and Wildavsky (1984) termed the "complexity of joint action" that makes the attainment of a policy's intended objectives more difficult.

Other concerns about policy impact focus less on its ability to influence institutional changes but, rather, on how policies affected groups of students differentially. As Tyack (2002) concluded, one of the themes about American education historically concerns the tendency for some groups and values to dominate whereas other groups and values have been little represented in the schools. While some groups received benefits, others were marginalized. Such disparate outcomes challenge researchers to consider that events, policies, and their meanings are multidimensional and must be examined as social fabric woven together to produce a greater whole (Everhart, 1988). In more recent years, groups that were marginalized have sought access and influence in education. They have also expanded views about how researchers examine the impact of policy.

Newer views of policy implementation and impact (e.g., critical theorist, feminist) focus more on how policies are read and understood by those who implement (or are affected by) policies within the specific school setting. These perspectives provide a more personal view of the policy process. For example, Blackmore and colleagues (1993) demonstrated that reform policies created at different levels of government to influence how girls experience schooling are often read, interpreted, and acted on in diverse ways within schools. Often, these subtle differences are missed in conventional policy analyses that are aimed at assessing the level of implementation across a number of settings. Therefore, research is also needed that examines how policy is received, interpreted, and used within school settings. Such fine-grained analyses can help illuminate how policies operate at the level of institutional practice.

## How Does Research Reinforce and Shape Our Thinking?

Thus far, we have discussed some of the challenges in moving the field forward in terms of its conceptual and theoretical underpinnings. Another challenge that emerges from the study of educational policy is that our assumptions and views of the policy system and our subsequent research efforts are often mutually reinforcing. As Popkewitz (1981) reminded us, researchers who investigate social phenomena are not just technicians trained to gather facts. Rather, they are members of a culture and thus reflect "certain hopes, beliefs, and commitments to that which is, has been, and is seen as possible" (Everhart, 1988, p. 712). As Boyd (1988) noted, "How we think about our problems determines both *what we see* and *what we fail to see*" (p. 505).

In the past, a narrow set of views has tended to dominate the investigation of policy processes (e.g., economic models, structural–functionalism, rational views of organizations). In more recent years, however, numerous critiques of dominant ways of doing research have provided more varied perspectives on conducting policy research. These new lenses include phenomenology, constructivism, critical theory, feminist theory, postmodernism, and poststructuralism. Most reviews of the scholarship within the field have emphasized the need for greater flexibility in thinking about policy. Less commentary has addressed the research tools that are needed to create sound scientific knowledge (Johnson, 2003). Sound analytic tools and methods are the means by which conceptual progress is made in a field. Moving the field forward involves skillfully grounding concepts and theories in the empirical world. Theoretical development in a field thus takes time and commitment on the part of scholars to disciplined inquiry.

There are, however, a number of factors that work against efforts to move toward more disciplined inquiry (Johnson, 2003). The press and demands of the policy world often mean that theoretical, conceptual, and methodological concerns of scholars are rendered less important. The pressing nature of policy problems brings an impatience with more abstract theoretical concerns in the field (Johnson, 2003). As Johnson noted, the discussion of theory often fails to provide quick answers to complex problems. Policy problems and solutions are often identified and acted on by those who dominate (special interests, politicians, agency directors). Therefore, what gets funded for data collection and research is often the result of what dominant groups prefer.

The intermixing of politics and funding in the process of defining problems and solutions can have a powerful effect on what issues get recognized and who receives support in making claims about the effects of policies. Moreover, data often are not available until the policy activity has been made legitimate by a dominant group (Tyack, 1991). Because of this, the focus is more on the policy problems, debates, and solutions developed by those with power—obscuring the needs, values, and aspirations of those who are on the margins of the policymaking processes (and therefore policy analyses) because they do not have sufficient power to provide input into policy discourses.

Researchers therefore must consider the importance of examining how their assumptions about how the policy system works and what they subsequently see empirically can be related. This process should entail examining the assumptions of particular lenses or frameworks for studying policy and how these can structure the analysis and interpretation of policy events. Theoretical work in applied fields such as educational policy will continue to be an uphill endeavor pursued by a minority of scholars (Johnson, 2003). Policy scholars should, however, continue to attend to work aimed at increasing the theoretical underpinnings of explanations of the policy world.

To illustrate how this process works in a bit more detail, one prevailing view of the failure of educational policy efforts was attributed to the disconnected, loosely coupled relationship between government and educational system. This view received affirmation from early empirical evaluations of the federal role in establishing reform initiatives beginning with the Elementary and Secondary Education Act of 1965. Federal programs to provide money to improve the educational opportunity and academic progress of disadvantaged youth were found to be largely unsuccessful (Berman & McLaughlin, 1978). The explanation was that several layers of educational organizations (state, district, school) and government appeared to intervene between federal funding and the students who were to receive the aid.

A similar failure was observed in other federal efforts to equalize educational opportunity—most notably with the Brown decision—where schools were ordered desegregated with "all deliberate speed." The mode of deliberate transportation was the school bus. From the late 1960s until well into the 1990s, districts tried busing and various structural arrangements (e.g., magnet schools) to achieve racial balance in the schools. Almost 50 years after this historic decision, however, large urban districts have been released from their federal court orders. Recent reports suggest that schools are becoming more racially and economically segregated once again (Jacobson, 2002).

In contrast to these documented failures, it is clear that at other times, policies that begin at the federal level have a profound impact on daily classroom practices. An example is the impact of the Individuals With Disabilities Educational Act (IDEA), which virtually structures day-to-day activities in schools and classrooms all over the nation. The loosely coupled nature of the federalist system does not explain this success. In these situations, successful implementation is often explained by alternative theories focusing on coalitions among groups that work successfully within appropriate policy subsystems to achieve desired goals. Policy theories have been less successful in explaining the ability of some policies to penetrate the system whereas others fail. This has led some to concede that policy is best studied in hindsight.

These types of conflicting empirical results bring into question a number of issues for those interested advancing educational policy research. Some of these include the importance of considering the relevance of the particular theoretical model used to examine specific cases, the usefulness of particular types of policy levers (e.g., funding ones vs. regulatory ones) in various circumstances, the effectiveness of particular branches of government (e.g., courts vs. legislatures) and other actors and groups in pursuing various policy goals, and the consideration of the needs and involvement of particular targets of policies (e.g., urban poor, women, culturally assimilated groups) who are often left out of policymaking processes and policy analyses (Marshall, 1997). They represent considerable opportunities for researchers in deciding how to conceptualize policy problems, design empirical studies and collect relevant data, and interpret that data in competent ways that answer important policy questions.

## What Methods Are Used?

A third set of challenges involves the various types of data collection and research methods that can be used to investigate policy problems. The complexity of policymaking processes within the structure of the American political system makes the study of educational policy difficult. Policies begin in various subsystems sponsored by different levels of government This makes their particular implementation paths quite diverse. The targets of intended policies also reside in hierarchies—states, districts, schools, and classrooms. As a consequence, examining the implementation and impact of policies across different levels of the educational system has proven to be challenging from a research standpoint. Analyses range from quantitative studies of policy implementation across a large number of settings (states, districts, or schools) to up-close case study examinations of a particular policy in a particular setting.

There can be considerable data challenges in studying certain policy problems. Unfortunately, there is little similar data that is collected routinely across all 50 states. States use a variety of different assessment procedures that may bear little resemblance—that is, each state typically develops its own assessments. What similar data are available across states may be reported in very different ways. For example, the reporting of dropout statistics across the states provides one case where varied meanings about dropping out and reporting procedures make it difficult compare state dropout figures or to examine trends reliably (Viadero, 2001). In other cases, types of data that might help policymakers understand the progress of educational reforms have not been collected. Although national statistics have been collected for over a hundred years, they are limited in scope. As Tyack (1991) reminded us, one important sign that reform has become legitimate is the collection of relevant data. This temporal relationship can be an important limitation in trying to identify changing values and practices over time. For example, the push for routine collection of instructional practice data only began in the late 1980s (Mayer, 1999).

As a result of this complexity, the scope of the scholarly field has become considerably larger over time from the original, limited goal of policy analysis in providing information that would lead to improved governmental decision making. As suggested, this broadened scope has resulted in a diversity of theories and methods from a number of different disciplines. This conceptual and methodological diversity also has made it more difficult to integrate the knowledge into a distinct set of concepts and methods. In this newer state of the field, the definitions of what constitutes a policy study, policy research, policy analysis, or a "politics of education" study have become more blurred. In this book, policy research and policy study are used as the most general terms to describe research that is focused on policy problems and issues, and whose findings are structured in a way that have implications or recommendations for actions that can alleviate or resolve those problems. Policy analysis is more focused on understanding policy processes and effects as they relate to particular policies. Politics of education studies are concerned more specifically with the political dynamics and environmental milieu underlying policy situations.

The methodological approaches used to examine policy problems and activities have also broadened considerably. There is no denying the bias toward narrow methods of inquiry in educational policy that has characterized the field since its beginnings. In the past, relatively limited analytical means were used to examine policy problems, actions, and solutions. Investigations were generally limited to case studies of single policies, conducted from narrow conceptual views. The goal was to help policymakers find more efficient (e.g., cost effective) ways of pursuing goals (Ball, 1990). This analytic approach was well suited to a rational view of political and organizational processes where decision makers pursued clear goals. Case studies are not easily generalized to other policy situations, however.

In more recent years, criticism of past research lenses for constructing knowledge about policy processes and outcomes has expanded the conceptual and methodological approaches used to investigate policy (Banks, 1998; Bensimon & Marshall, 1997; González, 2001; Ladson-Billings, 2000; Parker & Lynn, 2002). For example, there are beginnings of national and international databases regarding educational inputs, processes, and progress. This makes the quantitative study of academic achievement, access to resources, and the efficacy of educational practices more practical across multiple states or national policy domains (Raudenbush, Fotiu, & Cheong, 1998). Interpretive, phenomenological, and constructivist methodological approaches use methods of analysis (e.g., narrative, ethnography, discourse analysis) that can uncover how meaning is constructed among individuals participating in policy processes. The critical (or emancipatory) orientation entails a critique of existing social relationships that are influenced by educational policy and advancement toward those that are desired (Keith, 1996). Postmodern and poststructural approaches focus on deconstructing the scientific knowledge base gained from traditional theories and raise questions about how researchers and the construction of text influence social scientific inquiry (Lather, 1992).

Some of these newer perspectives look more closely at policy on the microlevel—that is, where policies actually encounter their intended targets—at the school and classroom level. Analysts operating within these lines of inquiry evidence a concern for "blind spots" that result from societal and cultural inequities in power and social relations (Wagner, 1993). They often provide analyses "that go against the grain" (Marshall, 1997), or that give voice to those who are not often at the center of policy analyses (Dunbar, 2001; Henry, 1998). These analyses focus on those who often fall "between the cracks" in macroanalyses of educational policy. They emphasize those who struggle to gain access to the policy system, they use alternative types of analytic frames (e.g., institutional theory, critical theory, feminist theory, critical race theory, postmodernism, poststructuralism) and methods, and the results are contextualized—that is, they do not assume that policies affect individuals without regard to gender, social class, and ethnicity. Hence, they place these latter issues at the center of their theories and analyses, instead of at the fringe. There has also been a growing indigenous voice in educational policy scholarship over the past decade (e.g., Benham, 1993; Kahumoku, 2000; Lomawaima, 2000 Rains, Archibald, & Deyle, 2000).

**Whose Voices Are Heard?**

Because the study of educational policy has often concerned the definition of problems and policy choices of those in power, other perspectives are often silenced, declared irrelevant, postponed, or ignored (Marshall, 1997). Traditional perspectives on educational policy tend to emphasize formalized structures (e.g., government) and roles that comprise the policy system. The dominant perspective on policy analysis in the past found its roots in utilitarian theory derived from economics; that is, the goal of public policy is to emphasize legislation that pursues a set of benefits for the greatest number of individuals. This prescriptive role is embodied in the notion of economic efficiency that underlies the allocation of resources in a democracy. In societies with limited resources, where individuals compete for resources including education as primary means to satisfy wants, Jenkins-Smith (1990) noted that improvement of individuals' standard of living can occur either without reduction (and perhaps improvement) in the standard of living of others, or with a concomitant decrease in the standard of living of others.

For groups who have been outside the dominant perspective, however (e.g., Native Americans, African Americans, immigrants), policy action was often based on an underlying goal of assimilation (Banks, 1988)—that is, replacing one set of cultural values with a new set of Euro-American values including, for example, individual rights and individual productivity to replace collectivism and ownership of private property instead of shared ownership. Although most would view this culturally neutral or reflective of the values of the norms of many in the country (i.e., expanding the whole to include the various different groups), this type of policy activity has had a devastating effect on these groups in terms of satisfying their needs and wants.

From this largely mythological mainstream view, the history of the United States has been one of continuous progress toward democratic ideals, with education playing a key role in assimilating ethnically diverse immigrants into U.S. values and institutions by giving them the tools to compete economically. Alternative interpretations of historical trends point to powerful institutionalized structures that are developed to reinforce dominant views and ensure a comparative advantage over less-powerful groups in economic, social, and political spheres. Bell (1992) noted that racism is a permanent structure in the United States, and schools as organizations often mirrored this through creating oppressive structures. Because various groups have been marginalized over time, mainstream policy has neglected the educational needs of many Americans.

Although the United States has become more culturally diverse in recent years, the experiences of these Americans are conspicuously absent from the literature on educational reform. Cultural diversity has become a popular phrase in educational circles; however, exactly what the term means with respect to understanding the nation's past educational practices and establishing new goals for the education of the nation's various cultural groups has been openly debated (Adams, 1988; Banks, 1993; Benham & Heck, 1998; González, 2001; Marshall, 1993; Stanfield, 1994). In fact, different viewpoints regarding ethnicity, culture, and social class have arisen since the decline of the liberal consensus favoring equity that largely shaped federal policy in the mid-1960s.

Alternative research lenses allow us to see our educational history and policy processes in more diverse and expansive ways. They help uncover instances of oppression, domination, or marginalization, and help to create policies that meet the lived realities, needs, and aspirations of those who have been silenced by past policies and practices (Marshall, 1997). These views have implications for the redefinition of policy problems and solutions. They also suggest the development of more culturally sensitive research (Dillard, 2000; Gordon, 1997; Sleeter, 2000; Tillman, 2002).

## SUMMARY

From its initial home in political science, interest in the field of educational policy has rapidly expanded since the late 1970s. With this interest has come a broadened scope and greater conceptual and methodological diversity. Although the field has become accepted as one of the long-standing intellectual subfields within education (e.g., administration, curriculum studies, measurement and research methodology, postsecondary education) over the past decade, a number of challenges remain. The complexity of policy processes themselves and the diversity of current research approaches to their studies make it more difficult to integrate a singular set of findings about particular policy problems.

As Scribner and colleagues (2003) concluded, the field has never been characterized by a single paradigm. In contrast, they noted that it has advanced through the dynamic interplay among paradigms and research traditions, critiquing and complementing one another, as each competes to define the study of policy problems. In many ways, the diversity of perspective calls into question some of the assumptions about a cumulative type of policy knowledge base and method. It also creates challenges for policy researchers to structure pathways for their research results and recommendations to actually be read and incorporated into the proper political arenas for future political action to improve the educational system. The study of policy problems and their solutions, and the role of policy research in contributing to dialogue among policymakers, will likely continue to benefit from a critical discussion of problems, concepts, and methods.

## EXERCISES

1. The rhetoric about how to solve social problems through intervening in schools has been much more consistent over time than the actual impact of educational policy reforms on changing fundamental school practices. What may be some of the reasons for this?

2. Identify some of the contrasting features of rational, structural, and cultural explanations of policy activity. How might these represent blind spots in examining policy issues and solutions?

3. From your perspective, which of the several challenges in studying policy problems mentioned in the chapter represents the most formidable obstacle for conducting policy research? Why? Support your argument with a particular policy example.

# Chapter 2

# Federalism and Policymaking

Policies in the public sector are shaped by the political philosophy associated with governments and the surrounding social and cultural contexts of the settings in which those governments exist. The process and products of policymaking in the United States are therefore influenced by its federalist form of democratic government and the guiding principles, traditions, and cultural values of American society. Federalism is a type of government in which a constitution distributes powers between a central government and subdivisional governments. The key is that both levels of government receive their powers from the Constitution. Both have substantial powers and responsibilities, including the ability to collect taxes and pass laws regulating the conduct of individuals. State and local governments are also policy institutions within the federalist system. They implement federal domestic programs, which typically leave many aspects to the discretion of state and local policymakers (Van Horn et al., 1992). They also create policy of their own.

The nature of our governance system—emphasizing shared control and authority over education among federal, state, and local governments as well as the public and private sectors (Weiss & Gruber, 1987)—in part structures policymakers' interactions and actions in pursuing their efforts to address social problems. Federalism is a particular type of institutional arrangement that sets a general context that affects political decision making. Institutions not only establish a general framework, but are also critical in defining the strategies individuals and groups use in search of ways to accomplish their policy goals. Over time, choices made within policy subsystems that are loosely coupled among the local, state, and federal levels form distinctive patterns of rules and behavior that influence the policy process in diverse policy fields including education (Benham & Heck, 1998; Fowler, 2000; Marshall et al., 1989). Moreover, the results of policy activity—policy documents (e.g., statutes, rules, procedures) and speech—can have a wide range of reception, interpretation, and impact on their intended targets. Policies are often experienced in ways that differ widely from the intents of policymakers.

Relations among the various agencies and arms of government, policy subsystems, special interests, and individual policy actors have evolved over the almost 400 years since the settlement of the English colonies. Federalism itself does not constitute a conceptual framework or theory for understanding educational policy processes. It is, however, a significant institutional arrangement that plays a role in policy change. Within any particular policy domain such as education, there are typically dozens of different programs involving multiple levels of government that are operating within any particular state or local area. Because these programs deal with interrelated issues and involve many of the same policy actors, policy scholars tend to focus on policy subsystems, as opposed to specific levels of government or governmental programs (Sabatier, 1999). That said, however, examining how the federalist system is structured and how the various relationships among the various governmental units, and their related agencies and actors, have evolved over time can provide one useful window to understanding how governmental action to address policy problems proceeds. At the center of this activity are debates among actors over the severity of problems, their causes, and the probable impact of alternative policy solutions (Sabatier, 1999). As Sabatier reminded us, it is important to understand the role these debates play in the overall policy process.

The political traditions of republican democracy in the United States require universal public education (Alexander & Alexander, 2001). The public educational system in the United States is large and diverse in authority. The 50 states have unique historical and social contexts that add to the diversity of educational philosophy, goals, and practices. Because legally binding authority over public education resides with the states, historically each has been relatively free to chart its own course in meeting its citizens' educational needs. One recurrent theme in studying educational policy in the United States is the potential for tension between state autonomy in pursuing educational goals and federal interest and oversight. The over 14,500 separate school districts (ranging from 1,040 in Texas to 1 in Hawai'i and the District of Columbia) also contribute to the complexity of the governance system (National Center for Educational Statistics, 2003). The decentralized nature of the educational governance system creates a structural complexity of administrative units, legislatures, and courts that influences policymaking. Differences in the politics within these various arenas result in different policies and outcomes (Van Horn et al., 1992). Moreover, the political strategies and politics can vary according to the particular policy issue being debated.

## THE STRUCTURE OF FEDERALISM

Federalism is both the fundamental character of American government and the source of its flexibility (Grodzins, 1966). With its structural distinctions and separations of powers, federalism is basic to the American system of educational governance and efforts to reform public education—both externally in the system's separation from the general government and internally in its national, state, and local units (Iannaccone, 1977). Because educational governance is shared by various branches and agencies of government, their separate authority and responsibility impacts the process and outcomes of educational policymaking. Even with broad societal changes over time and periods of considerable internal political turbulence (e.g., Civil War, the Depression), the stability of our nation's federalist system itself, with inherent checks and balances and corresponding multiple points of access, has for the most part ensured that its institutions, including schools, remained relatively stable and reflected the dominant social, economic, and political interests of the times (Iannaccone, 1977; Van Horn et al., 1992). Policy challengers must overcome a number of places where their preferred policies may be stalled or stopped (Schlager, 1999). The pace of political change has typically been very slow (e.g., with relatively few amendments to the Constitution). As Van Horn and colleagues concluded, the nation's political institutions were designed to inhibit change.

Because public education is a governmental function in the United States, a number of structural, legal, and historical issues should be considered in determining how educational policy activity takes place. Federalism creates several layers of government, and a number of different policy arenas. One primary source of influence in educational policymaking is formal government institutions such as legislatures, chief executives, and the courts. Educational policymaking is also created through several other sources of influence (Van Horn et al., 1992). These include governmental administrators (e.g., federal and state administrative agencies who make rules with the input of special interest groups, legislatures, and chief executives), the business sector (e.g., their decisions that impact policy in education), and the public (e.g., grassroots involvement in initiatives, political activism, voting, and media).

The fundamental principles of legal control governing the conduct of the federal government and the 50 states are described in the Constitution. Except for its inherent power over foreign affairs, the Constitution delegates powers to the federal government. Within the scope of its operation, the federal government is supreme. Its powers, however, are specifically limited by the Tenth Amendment that states, "The powers not delegated to the United States by the Constitution, nor prohibited by it to the States, are reserved to the States respectively or to the people."

The Constitution gives Congress the authority to make laws, tax and appropriate funds, and regulate interstate and foreign commerce; the President as chief executive (and a growing administrative bureaucracy) has the responsibility to administer them, and the Supreme Court the authority to interpret them (Van Horn et al., 1992). In addition to express powers, the Constitution delegates to Congress implied powers, which may be inferred from the express powers. The source of this implied power is the "necessary and proper" clause (Article 1, Section 8, Clause 18). Essentially, this gives the right "to make all Laws which shall be necessary and proper for carrying into Execution the fore-going Powers, and all other Powers vested …" in the government. In this con-stitutional arrangement, legislators are the principal lawmakers in the system.

## Constitutional Authority For Education

The constitutions at both levels of government are basic to the federalist sys-tem because they specify the powers each holds and also serve as restraints to protect people from unwarranted denial of their basic constitutional rights and freedoms (Alexander & Alexander, 2001).The power to operate public education originates in the states' constitutions with delegation to the legislature to provide for such systems. All state constitutions make pro-visions for free public education. Public schools are governed by statutes ex-ecuted by state legislatures. The provisions range from very specific educational provisions to broad mandates that the legislature of the state provide funds in support of public schools. This variation in how state con-stitutions establish the goals of education within each state can even be seen in the statutes that grant each state's support for public education. Some ex-amples of the statutes for public education include:

> Wisdom, and knowledge, as well as virtue, diffused generally among the body of the people, being necessary for the preservation of their rights and liber-ties; and as these depend on spreading the opportunities and advantages. (Massachusetts)

> The legislature shall provide for the maintenance and support of a system of free common schools, wherein all the children of this state may be educated. (New York)

> Religion, morality and knowledge being necessary to good government and the happiness of mankind, schools and the means of education shall be for-ever encouraged. (Michigan)

> The General Assembly, at its First Session after the adoption of this Constitu-tion, shall by Law establish throughout the State a thorough and efficient Sys-tem of Free Public Schools; and shall provide by taxation, or otherwise, for their maintenance. (Maryland)

Boards of education (BOE) receive their powers from the state legisla-ture and must act within the powers granted in governing the schools. Within the powers granted, local boards pass rules and regulations (poli-cies). In 1931, there were 127,000 local school districts and corresponding boards of education. Over the past 80 years, however, this number has de-creased dramatically, as the trend has been to consolidate these smaller ed-ucational systems into larger systems, with greater state control being exercised in important educational domains (e.g., finance, curriculum).

The combination of constitutions, statutes, and case law from judges forms the legal foundation on which public schools are based. This diversity across the 50 states also results in considerable variation in other policy areas regarding education including, for example, goals for education, attendance, funding, professional standards, the types and scope of student assessment, and the curriculum. States, in turn, delegate much authority to operating the public schools to the local school districts. Thus, policy results from a variety of governors, legislators, state officials, state courts, state and local school boards, and superintendents. Moreover, to maintain principles of diversity, choice (or liberty), and self-determination, there exists a parallel system of private education that operates relatively free from government intervention and oversight.

## Descriptions of Federalism

Political scientists differ over the exact definitions and descriptions of federalism and its various forms over the years. The term *dual federalism* has been used to describe the historical separation of powers between the federal government and the various state governments. Under this view, each level of government is dominant within its own sphere. The Supreme Court serves as the referee between the national government and the states regarding which should be in charge of a particular activity. During the first 100 years of the nation, this interpretation was often used. The underlying rationale for this interpretation is that Jefferson and the other framers of the Constitution believed that government at all levels should be relatively limited in its scope. The Articles of Confederation, which tended to be too weak, was discarded in the attempt to create a separation of powers between the states and central government. Whereas Jackson favored a strong federal government, Jefferson tended to emphasize states' rights.

Whereas the original concept of dual federalism attempted to delegate to the national government certain necessary and limited functions, over time, substantial power has shifted to the federal government. Both social and economic reasons led to this. There have been few crises over principles of government during our nation's political past once the Constitution was written and adopted in 1788. One of those times was the Civil War, although it would be incorrect to think of this war as merely a test of power between the federal government and the loose confederation of state governments (which gave limited power to the centralized government) in the South that formed the Confederacy. These conflicting arrangements did form a test case, however, in the vertical power of governmental units in our federalist system. The Civil War firmly established the scope and power of the national government to resolve both social and economic issues.

Grodzins (1960, 1966) contended that dual federalism never implied a genuine separation between governments. The local, state, and federal levels are not separate layers of government. Instead, he used the metaphor of a marble cake, suggesting that the various layers interact with and influence the other levels. In fact, he suggested federalism as a plan for sharing functions of government and not for separating them (Campbell, Cunningham, Nystrand, & Usdan, 1990). Federal education programs during the 1960s were to be "marbled"—that is, formulated and financed at the federal level, but administered and operated at the state and local levels (Jung, 1988). Policymakers interpreted this as meaning that it was possible to implement reform through infusing large amounts of federal money (Peterson & Wong, 1985).

Yet, considered together, federalism today results in well over 80,000 governmental units in the United States. This decentralized arrangement has been referred to as "competitive federalism" (Dye, 1990), which suggests that they all compete with one another to put together packages of services and taxes—such that Dye suggested that we have some choice over which state and city we want to use for our services. Other descriptions include cooperative federalism, which suggests that the various levels work together to provide services and permissive federalism, such that while there is a sharing of power and authority between the states and the national government, the states' share rests on the permission and permissiveness of the national government (Reagan & Sanzone, 1981).

As these various descriptions emphasize, federalism fosters participation in a variety of arenas by different actors, yet it also encourages a variety of conflicts—over state versus local control or legislative versus executive dominated governance. As Cohen (1982) concluded, the system tends to operate not so much as a hierarchy, but as a broad flat plain, whereon multiple interests exercise influence over various aspects of decision-making processes, including policymaking in education. This decentralized arrangement of separate institutions and overlapping jurisdictions creates relatively open access to the system. Control is spread among the systems' myriad and competing parties. Much of the time, policy activity occurs within policy subsystems that allow for incremental adjustments. Once collective action is mobilized, however, there is the potential for other governmental actors to get involved in a new policy area (True, Jones, & Baumgartner, 1999). At this point, the policy momentum has the potential to expand. Yet, because each arm of the system (e.g., courts, legislature) or level may respond somewhat independently to public demands, researchers have noted that the momentum often dissipates, creating considerable difficulties in bringing about change in this decentralized type of political system (e.g., Cuban, 1990; Marcoulides & Heck, 1990; McLaughlin, 1990; Tyack & Cuban, 1995). This is because reform efforts begun at higher levels of the governmental policy channels must weave their way through a variety of political arenas to reach their intended targets at the local level. On other occasions, when policy subsystem processing breaks down, policy problems may be addressed by the senior political institutions (i.e., Congress, Executive Branch, or the Supreme Court).Within these institutions, major policy change can occur (Schlager, 1999).

## HOW FEDERALISM AFFECTS EDUCATIONAL POLICYMAKING

The legislative process of lawmaking in the United States has been described as decentralized and fragmented. As opposed to being accountable to a particular party or governing body (as in a unitary governance system), legislators are broadly accountable to their constituents at identified intervals of 2, 4, or 6 years (Van Horn et al., 1992). There is a socialization process that takes place as well—senior senators have one goal; to get reelected. Freshmen senators must not only pursue this goal, but they must learn the rules of the game as it is played in Washington (Lewellen, 1992). In reality, therefore, they have much latitude to support their own particular policy views.

The process through which a proposed bill must travel to become law is difficult, as it must pass through a committee system (existing across both Houses) where power is concentrated. For senior senators, committee chairs may be the primary means of exercising power. For new senators, serving on less desirable (i.e., powerless) committees provides an illusion of power for constituents back home. The committee phase has been referred to as a graveyard, because the overwhelming majority of bills die in committee. If a bill manages its way out of committee, it must be approved by the general legislature. This makes legislation extremely difficult without considerable consultation, coalition building, or compromise. The legislative process thus has its own concentrations of power, socialization processes, and rules of engagement.

The historical context has also shaped the manner in which educational policy is developed. Although responsibility for education was not expressly mentioned in the Constitution, the federal government has always been a type of partner with the states in creating educational policy (e.g., setting aside tracts of land for public schooling). In the early years of the nation, the role was very limited, although there was much debate among the Constitution's framers about the relationship of education and governmental control in maintaining peace and stability in the new country. The authority to run schools was largely delegated to the local level. By the mid- to late-19th century, states began to assume a greater role in conducting educational business (e.g., consolidating schools into larger entities, mandating public school attendance, changing the governance structure, attempting to equalize the financing of schools).

Since World War II, the federal role in educational policymaking has expanded in a number of ways (Atkin & House, 1981). Increasing globalization was one notable trend leading to greater federal involvement in education. The Cold War with the Soviet Union and the subsequent "space race" led to important federal legislation to enhance the curriculum and the professional preparation of educators. One such example was the National Defense Education Act in 1958. Financial support included an array of categorical programs for educationally disadvantaged students (e.g., by language, special needs, poverty status). Many of these new programs provided opportunities for regulatory services along with funds to implement them (e.g., those regulations followed grant-in-aid programs referring back to protecting civil rights). In 1965, the Elementary and Secondary Education Act (ESEA), which was part of Johnson's "Great Society" proposals, provided funds for students in need. There were also several demonstration and innovation types of curricular projects aimed at elementary and secondary schools. The federal courts, including the Supreme Court, have also had considerable influence on the nation's educational policy historically; the entry points have often been class action suits associated with the First (e.g., religion, free speech), Fifth (e.g., due process), and Fourteenth Amendments (e.g., equal protection, due process). Further legislative efforts have included the Civil Rights Acts of 1964 (which opened issues concerning the lack of equal educational opportunity), and Title IX of the Educational Amendments of 1972 (PL 94-142 on special education in 1975).

This apparent tension between independence and control is a key structural feature of the American political system. Each branch and level of government has an amount of authority that makes it independent to a large degree. Although there is little argument today over which level of government has the constitutional authority to deal with the nation's key issues, there is still concern over how much freedom the states should enjoy from federal intervention. The states have all powers not granted to the national government, subject to the limitation of the Constitution. For many issues, state governments are almost completely free from federal control (e.g. banking, insurance). Powers not given exclusively to the national government may be concurrently exercised by states as long as they do not conflict with national law (e.g., interfere or complicate). For example, states can levy a tax on gasoline concurrently with the federal tax. States are prohibited from certain activities that would conflict with the federal government's role (e.g., making treaties with foreign governments, entering into agreements with other states that would increase their political power, coining money, engaging in war). In other areas (e.g., education, social programs), the federal government can extend its support by offering incentives (e.g., grants) or by imposing sanctions (e.g., regarding discriminatory practices).

Because the delegation of authority is qualified by other provisions, their powers are also shared (Van Horn et al., 1992). States must cooperate with each other—for example, give full faith and credit to each other's public acts, records, and judicial proceedings; extend to other states' citizens the privileges and immunities of their own citizens (e.g., protection of the laws, rights to work and reside); and return people fleeing from justice. Within the federalist system, cities are not considered to be sovereign entities; that is, only two levels of government are recognized by the Constitution. Yet, local governments (who receive delegated powers from the states) are granted considerable control over everyday life (e.g., neighborhood quality of life, zoning regulations, building ordinances).

Because the governance system is decentralized, various groups (i.e., special interests, lobbyists, political parties, media) or individuals outside of government also have access to the decision-making process (Van Horn et al., 1992). Interest groups can work with legislators and various administrators in the executive branch to develop policies within particular policy subsystems. Most often, these interests organize around particular types of policy issues. One Gallup poll in 1987 described this as almost 16,000 national voluntary membership organizations and over 200,000 state and local community groups. Of course, much of this lobbying rests on the use of money. At times, the public also participates in the policymaking process, either by directly placing issues on the ballot and voting through referenda or by focusing public opinion such that policymakers are persuaded to yield. The media also play an important role in shaping policymakers' views and in influencing elections.

Moreover, there are differences in regions, states, and communities that reflect the individualism that Americans value. Marshall and colleagues (1989) explored how differences in policymaking agendas and decisions were related to cultural and historical traditions and values. They found great variation in principle and practice at the state level. Similarly, the tremendous variation in local politics across American cities was explored in Banfield's (1965) *Big City Politics* and later in Savitch and Thomas's (1991) volume *Big City Politics in Transition*.

Policymaking is thus distributed among a variety of different governmental units and actors, contributing to a decentralized, and often fragmented, system. The various governmental layers in the system also present difficulties in policy implementation. A program policy passed may have to make its way through a number of regional federal administrators, state, perhaps county, and local officials. In the education arena, school districts are also involved. One explanation is that the structure of educational organizations buffers them from change efforts. For several decades, theorists have referred to the educational system as loosely coupled (Weick, 1976). The concept originated with the study of educational decision making (e.g., Cohen, March, & Olsen, 1972), suggesting that the technical aspects of schooling such as teaching and learning were only marginally related to the activities of administrators at other levels of the system. In this conceptualization, the work of teachers in the classroom was largely buffered from policy activity, including change, at other levels of the system.

In some situations, this structural arrangement may be beneficial, in that it protects the core technology of schooling from the whims of policymakers. Yet, in other situations, this loose coupling within educational organizations and the senior governments that govern education can be a barrier for states and school systems attempting to implement systematic change (Firestone & Corbett, 1988). From this perspective, the loosely coupled and hierarchical nature of the policy and educational systems ensures participation in a variety of policymaking arenas by different actors, yet it encourages a variety of conflicts over the structure of institutional arrangements (e.g., state vs. local control, legislative- vs. executive-dominated governance) and the substance of policy activity (e.g., interactions, mobilization of collective choice, decision making) that takes place within the various arenas and corresponding targeted educational structures (i.e., state departments of education, districts, schools, classrooms).

Thus, a variety of structural, procedural, and conceptual constraints (e.g., past practice, institutional arrangements and rules, political culture) may await a policy that has been developed. Whereas basic constitutional structures, rules, and cultural values may remain as relatively stable influences on policy actions, other contextual parameters may be more dynamic. Socioeconomic conditions change in the external environment. Van Horn and colleagues (1992) reminded us that the institutions themselves do change over time and are, themselves, subject to public opinion. The political leanings of the various governmental units may change as well. The courts may use their latitude to interpret cases at the state level somewhat differently than at the federal level (Gormley, 1988). This suggests that the political institutions themselves change. Moreover, because the institutional setting and policy domain may affect the outcomes of policy disputes, it is not uncommon for those involved to try to shift the dispute from one arena to another, to prevent such a shift from occurring, or to displace one dispute with another (Schattschneider, 1960). Policy activity can therefore be seen to result from shifting dynamics in the environment and from institutional arrangements that are coupled with individuals' beliefs and values, perceptions of evolving policy situations, and strategies that will be beneficial for achieving policy goals.

## THE HISTORICAL CONTEXT OF FEDERALISM AND EDUCATION

One of the most direct ways to examine this evolving relationship of government to educational policy is through the results of policy activity. The most direct way governmental intentions are announced is through the laws that are enacted. It is in this manner that societal values, principles of government, and intentions are expressed. In this section, we examine briefly some of the ways in which government's role in educational policy has evolved.

### Education in the Colonies

In the early years, the American colonies had to alter the accepted pattern of the class-oriented English system of education. In this type of system, the rich received education whereas lower class children received little or no education, or became apprentices to learn a manual trade. Education in the colonies was not seen as a governmental function. Lower education in those times was largely private and restricted to a religious focus (Callahan, 1960). Education was a matter for parents and the church. Higher education was also private in the 18th century. Early in the country's history, schools were identified as important policy instruments in formulating an American society. The first step was to establish the legal basis for education in the colonies. Cremin (1970) noted that most of the colonies made provisions for schooling during the latter part of the 17th century.

Massachusetts set up the first rudimentary educational system. It is first mentioned in a 1642 General Court law establishing public schooling (Callahan, 1960). In 1647, General Court also passed the Old Deluder Satan Act, which directed every town to set up a school or pay money to a larger town to support education. The act required towns with at least 50 families to appoint a teacher and towns with more than 100 families to establish a secondary school. It also provided for schools' monetary support. Pulliam (1987) noted that the first tax on property for local schools was in Dedham, Massachusetts in 1648. By 1693, New Hampshire also required the support of elementary schools. Hence, local control of education was established early on, with each town functioning as a school district.

## Framing the Constitution

It was not really until the middle of the 18th century, during the Enlightenment, that public education became more accepted as essential to the welfare of the state. A republican democracy implied a responsibility of government to ensure the participation of citizens in government. As Montesquieu wrote in his 1748 treatise *The Spirit of Laws,* in a democracy everything "depends on establishing this love in a republic, and to inspire it ought to be the principal business of education.... It is in a republican government that the whole power of education is required" (p.130). In 1758, Rousseau argued that the responsibilities of citizenship were dependent on education and that public education "is one of the fundamental rules of popular or legitimate government" (p. 149).

During the 1760s and 1770s in the colonies, the idea that there should be a free system of public education received support. The federal government's involvement begins virtually with the beginnings of the nation (even before the Constitution was adopted). In the Ordinance of 1785, Congress declared that section 16 of every township in the Northwest Territory should be reserved for the maintenance of public schools. In one section of The Ordinance of 1787, it was suggested that religion, morality, and knowledge are necessary for good government and for the happiness of people; therefore, means of education should be encouraged. As part of the Northwest Ordinance of 1787, tracts of land in the newly opened territory were set aside for public schools.

Although there was a general recognition of the importance of education, spearheaded by the Constitution' framers such as Thomas Jefferson, one of the first to propose a free public school system, the view needed until the mid-1800s to become legally binding within state constitutions. As an early advocate of universal education, Thomas Jefferson argued that peace and stability in the new nation were best preserved by giving people access to education instead of giving government more authority to control their actions. As Spring (1986) summarized this beginning period of education and government: "What distinguishes education in pre-Revolutionary and post-Revolutionary America is the concept of service to the broader needs of government and society. After the Revolution, many Americans began to believe that a public system of education was needed to build nationalism" (p. 28).

Besides the traditions of local control from the English Colonies, another reason for the decentralized nature of America's government was the mind set of the Constitution's framers. Certainly, the writers of the Constitution struggled with the balancing of individual rights versus collective will. Undergirding these debates were different feelings about the relative merits of elite or pluralistic government (Kramnick, 1987). These fundamentally different conceptions of governance have significant influence on the selection and function of governmental institutions (March & Olsen, 1989). As Scribner and colleagues (2003) noted, elite governance is integrative, the pursuit of a common good by a single public; in contrast, pluralistic governance is aggregative—the pursuit of many interests by numerous individuals and groups.

Because the framers of the Constitution were concerned about the potential for a dominant form of centralized government (as in a monarchical or unitary type of government), they did not want to grant too much power to a national government. Federalism was thought to keep tyranny in check. If one party lost control at the national level, it would still be likely to have influence within the states. This would tend to keep a singular thinking majority in check (see Madison, *The Federalist*, No. 10). Freedom to choose among alternatives and self-determination were held in high regard; thus, people should be free from governmental interference whenever possible. Hence, we have the system of checks and balances present in our government to ensure that any one part of the government does not become too powerful. It is important to emphasize, however, that the Constitution itself did little in terms of ensuring individuals' rights. Those rights were addressed in the first 10 amendments. It is these 10 amendments (and the 14th Amendment) that have had the most influence on education in this country.

Thus, the first major changes in American schooling involved providing a public education, getting students into school, and changing the purposes of education from supporting the goals of parents and the church to supporting the goals of the state. Recognizing, however, it was difficult to control schools from the state level, local lay boards were created, with the argument being that they would function in place of parents and the church. Throughout most of the 19th century, local boards were the main source of control in the public schools.

Interestingly enough, state support for higher education in the United States paralleled the K-12 sector. In colonial times, colleges were primarily to enhance preparation for religious and civic responsibilities among the social elite (Spring, 1986). After the Revolutionary War many leaders, including Thomas Jefferson, began to view colleges as a source of republican leadership (Spring, 1986). Over time, a more secular view of education emerged, as leaders realized the need for freedom of thought, as opposed to indoctrination, and saw the power of education to provide intellectual tools and scientific knowledge that could create a better society (Spring, 1986). Early in the 19th Century, colleges were established at an increasing rate in response to public demand and rivalries among religious groups. As Spring noted, concerns soon grew over the appropriate curriculum and the mixing of public and private financial support and governing control. The test case for mixing public and private institutional support came in 1819, when the State of New Hampshire tried to establish control over Dartmouth College (Heller, 2002). Whereas the New Hampshire Superior Court ruled that Dartmouth was a public entity and subject to state control, the Supreme Court decided that Dartmouth as a private entity had been granted a state charter to operate. This charter was a contract protected by the Constitution against future alteration or interference by the state (Spring, 1986).

## Establishment and Bureaucratization of Public Education (1800s–1900s)

By the beginning of the 19th century, there was more interest in public education. Horace Mann's common school in Massachusetts provided one of the first experiments of free public education. Mann conceived of education as a natural right (i.e., a property right under the Constitution). Madison had earlier conceived of property as those things to which a person might attach value. Madison argued, an individual has an "equal property in the free use of his facilities," and his facilities encompass knowledge and learning (as cited in Meyers, 1973, p. 186). Under this view, public schools became a means for ensuring the transfer of knowledge between generations.

As the cities grew, and as they became wealthier than the rural areas, it created problems in financing education within each state. Gradually, policymakers moved to establish statewide educational systems. By 1820, 21 of the 23 states in existence had constitutional or statutory provisions regarding public education (Thurston & Roe, 1957). At the same time as the legal basis was being established, laws providing tax supports for public education were also being enacted. As Ellwood Cubberley (1929) noted, the battle for the establishment of tax supported schools was bitter, but after about 1850, it was won in every Northern state. Using Massachusetts as an early example, up until the 1820s, schools were under the direction of the town meeting and a town selectmen. The schools' management was in the hands of typical citizens. In 1826 and 1827, however, the Massachusetts General Court (legislature) established the town school committee (school board) as a separate governmental body. Over time, this action was followed in other states as well (Campbell et al., 1990). These actions shifted the control of schools to state government. Along with this, teaching administrators began to take over many duties needed to run schools. For example, Cincinnati had a principal-teacher in each school by 1838 (Pierce, 1934).

Higher education was also affected by federal and state desires to increase access to public education (Spring, 1986). Over the first half of the 1800s, federal land grants established a federal interest in, and furthered the wide development of, colleges and universities. During the 1850s, several state legislatures (e.g., Michigan, Illinois) made requests to Congress for funds to establish colleges that pursued more specific and practical curricular ends such as agriculture and industry, in addition to the traditional higher education curriculum (Campbell et al., 1990). Such requests culminated in the Morrill Act in 1862. This legislation established land grant colleges and universities that emphasized agriculture, mechanic arts, sciences, and liberal arts for the industrial class (Rudolph, 1990; Spring 1986). By the mid-1800s, the important sources for funding public higher education included state general fund tax revenues, revenues from land grants, and the tuition charged to students (Heller, 2002).

As schools and universities took on more of an economic role, policymakers recognized the need to have children in school. Funding of higher education from the states and the Morrill Act led to large increases in enrollments in universities during the latter part of the 19th century. Similarly, the common school was locally run and financed and was open to all children free of cost. The argument was advanced that only if education reached all children would the return on the investment made in taxes for public schools be realized (Glenn, 1988). Beginning in Massachusetts in 1852 (nearly 200 years after it began the first public system), states in turn enacted compulsory education laws, making education a responsibility of the state (Campbell et al., 1990). In Massachusetts, the first general attendance law required children between the ages of 8 and 14 to attend schools for 12 weeks per year (Van Geel, 1987). With that, came governmental responsibility for financing free public education. Such issues as compulsory education and its financing, however, were not universally accepted. The issues were in fact hotly debated (Tyack, 1976).

The actual test case on compulsory attendance can be found much later in the Supreme Court decision *Pierce vs. Society of Sisters* (268 U.S. 510, 45 S.Ct. 571, 69 L.Ed. 1070) in 1925. This decision, which concerned Oregon's children's requirement to attend a public school, determined that although children should attend some school, and that these schools could be regulated, inspected, supervised, and examined by the state, they could not be forced to attend a public school only. The decision affirmed that government should not unreasonably interfere with the liberty of parents to direct the upbringing and education of children under their control—that is, the fundamental theory of liberty excludes the general power of the state to standardize its children by forcing them to accept instruction from public school teachers only. The decision made (i.e., that children must attend some school) established a compromise between the parents' individual rights and freedom regarding schooling options and the state's right to educate its citizens. Multiple views were to be encouraged, even if the majority chose to send their children to attend public schools.

The second major stage involved the bureaucratization of the schools, which was brought on by changing social, economic, and demographic trends. By the close of the 19th century the American frontier had been conquered (see Turner, 1894) and the nation was shifting from an economy based on agriculture to one based on industry. These changes produced shifts in the nation's settlement patterns. As Tyack and Cuban (1995) argued, "Increasing urbanization and consolidation of rural districts produced a concentration of population required for larger and more differentiated high schools" (p. 48). The educational structural change resulting from these tensions was the high school. Child labor laws and compulsory attendance resulted in greater numbers of teenaged students enrolled in high schools. In a country that was rapidly changing from agriculture to industry, high schools grew rapidly and became more differentiated in terms of their curricular offerings. In 1895, John Dewey suggested the high school's intent was to provide a link between the lower grades and college as well as to serve as a final educational stage for those who would move directly into the workforce (Dewey, 1972). In 1900, only 1 out of 10 children ages 14 to 17 was enrolled in high school; by 1940, 7 in 10 were enrolled; and by 1980, 9 out of 10 students were enrolled in high school (Tyack & Cuban, 1995). Correspondingly, graduation rates also rose. In 1900, only 8% of those enrolled were graduated from high school; by 1920, 17% were graduated; by 1940, 51%; by 1960, 69%; and by 1980, 71% were graduated (NCES, 1993).

The key change characterizing this period was the reform of educational governance that took place within the nation's cities at the turn of the 20th century. Progressive school reformers wanted to rid city schools of political corruption that had evolved at the local level. Local control resulted in a decentralized, ward-based system (i.e., where board members were elected by their own wards to advance special interests) that accentuated opportunities for local political favors. Elected board members often responded to their own neighborhood needs and ignored the needs of the school district as a whole. Reformers countered this system with at-large elections and ended up with smaller boards that they contended were more professionally driven. Financial and professional leaders did not like the decentralized ward system because it empowered recent immigrants who were members of the lower and lower middle classes (Hays, 1963). With the growth of cities near the turn of the 20th century, the political solution was to turn over management of the schools to superintendents and other professional administrators, as opposed to lay members of large and diverse boards of education.

## Providing Alternatives to the Public Education Bureaucracy

The third major stage seems to be dealing with the problems of the bureaucratic nature of American schools over the past several decades—segregation, unequal resources and opportunity, and the fact that as America grew more diverse, large numbers of people were marginalized by the policy process. Much of this chapter focuses on how federalism influenced the development of policy and, more specifically, how the role of particular governmental branches has changed over time. The federal government itself (with its various actors) must be seen as an important actor in policy-making processes. Its participation has waxed and waned within dominant liberal and conservative political eras. It is not clearly spelled out, however, how the institutional arrangements between federal government and the various states interact during times when the political system is in relative flux over educational concerns. Further refinement of the impact of shifting institutional arrangements (e.g., the roles and structures) may help sort out the dynamics between these types of processes and various policy actions and outcomes (Schlager, 1999). States obviously play an important role in inhibiting or promoting major policy change. This is a fruitful area for research.

Conceptual lenses must account for the dynamics of policy change. Theories that attend to policy change focus on similar types of events and factors that set the stage (Schlager, 1999). These types of major changes are preceded by series of events and activities that may unfold over several decades. Appearance on the government's agenda is the outcome of these longer processes of change as belief systems coalesce, but this alone does not guarantee major change (Schlager, 1999). Merelman (2002) argued that the federal government has taken on two massive social experiments in the 20th century. One was the additional support system for the disadvantaged and the elderly—sometimes referred to as the welfare state. It provided entitlements to health care for the elderly, Social Security, unemployment compensation, a minimum wage, and other types of monetary support for those in need. Americans argue about the scale and shape of the programs, but not about their existence. Powerful constituent groups guard the continued existence of these programs.

The other social program was the social and racial integration of America's schools. The key legislation here was the Brown Decision in 1954 and other decisions on issues related to segregated schooling. The Brown Decision affirmed that separate but equal doctrine (*Plessy vs. Ferguson*, 1819) as applied to education did not hold. Separate schools were neither equal nor constitutional. This began the long, complicated federal attempt to desegregate the nation's schools and thereby improve educational opportunities for groups of students marginalized by the nation's past educational policies and practices. During the years of Johnson's "Great Society," federal policymakers diligently tried to improve schooling opportunities for minority and poor students through such policy actions as adjusting resource allocations (e.g., to create racial balance and financial equity), eliminating formal tracking practices, and busing students to achieve racial balance within schools. Their primary focus was on utilizing various policy inputs to increase educational equity. Critiques of these efforts suggested they were mixed at best (Berman & McLaughlin, 1978) and a failure at worst (Merelman, 2002; Murphy, 1971; Sarason, 1990).

By contrast with the welfare state, however, this latter experiment has failed. Racially integrated schools are not a foundation of American educational policy—nor do constituent groups protect their existence. As some have suggested, there were more African American students in schools with student minority populations greater than 50% in the 1990s than there were in the early 1970s before busing programs began. Other integration programs have similarly not stopped this trend (e.g., magnet schools), nor have some court decisions (Milliken vs. Bradley in 1974) that effectively let suburban districts out of metro busing plans to desegregate inner city schools. By the 1990s, most of the districts under mandatory desegregation were released from their court orders. These failures suggest that at least part of the national policy agenda has not been realized.

These were both examples of attempted major changes in the policy core aspects of governmental programs (Sabatier & Jenkins-Smith, 1999). Theories are unclear at present, however, as to how to predict successes and failures of major policy efforts. It is clear, however, that the perceived failure of educational reforms over the past few decades to deal with prominent issues such as school segregation, achievement gaps between minority and dominant students, dropouts, and the general quality of American students in comparison to other students internationally, has increased the support for efforts to provide educational alternatives. A sample of these include policies to reduce bureaucratic restrictions and promote alternative types of school structures (e.g., open enrollment, charter schools, privatization), hold schools accountable for learning results (e.g., through standards-based instruction), promote packaged, whole-school reforms in curriculum and instruction (e.g., *Success for All*), and encourage innovation in teaching practices from within the school.

During these more open periods of policymaking, governmental roles may be more multiple because beliefs are varied and conflicting. Some of these newer reforms suggest a considerable extension of the regulatory role for the federal government. Whereas previous federal activity in the 1960s and 1970s attempted to improve student achievement indirectly through the imposition of federal funding formulas or regulatory requirements, standards-based reform is based on a prescribed, concrete model of practice that specifies new high standards for curricula and instructional techniques in classrooms. Swanson and Stevenson (2002) provided preliminary evidence indicating considerable policy implementation of this national policy movement across the individual states in a relatively short period of time. The scope and implementation of standards-based reform suggests a means for integrating policy activity at distant levels of the educational system with activities in the classroom—a capacity generally lacking in earlier reform efforts. It was punctuated by several key federal policy activities including President George H. W. Bush's national conference with governors regarding education in 1989 and President Clinton's initiation of *Goals 2000*. Importantly, prior to *Goals 2000*, in its over 200-year history, the United States had never outlined any explicit policy regarding educational content goals (Marshall, Fuhrman, & O'Day, 1994). Recent federal attempts to extend regulatory aspects to increase accountability are most focused on one new mandate. The 2001 No Child Left Behind reorganization of ESEA represents a considerable expansion of the federal involvement in education in a number of key ways (e.g., mandating who to test, how often, defining adequately yearly progress, requiring alignment of testing to curriculum standards, describing school failure, outlining student movement to other schools, raising teaching standards, and determining who can be hired).

On the other hand, school choice, charter schools, and voucher programs have also found considerable support in various coalitions of policymakers at various levels of government. These are examples of educational reforms that bring value conflicts over the purposes of education into public display. As Godwin and Kemerer (2002) concluded, school choice philosophically tends to conflict with traditions of local control over schooling. For parents, controlling their children's education is an important liberty right. Choice brings a number of issues regarding the goals of education—for example, should all the schools be culturally diverse, or should diversity be encouraged across school types—that is, should a school be set up to serve only a single sex, or to promote a particular type of ethnically based curriculum? This brings to the forefront the issue of how much regulation to place on these schools, for example, in terms of staffing, curriculum, and accountability. The seminal 1925 Supreme Court ruling *Pierce vs. Society of Sisters* decision upheld the notion that parents have the right to educate their children in private schools.

Charter schools also tend to blur the lines between public and private education. They seek to reform public education by introducing elements of private schooling including choice, autonomy, and flexibility (Miron & Nelson, 2002). The blending of these elements in Cleveland (where the Supreme Court examined the issue of whether public funds can be used for private religious school attendance) creates controversy, such as the constitutionality of voucher systems and the question of separation of church and state. As Miron and Nelson argued, charter schools have brought a new definition of "public" in public education—one that emphasizes outcomes for the public "good," rather than public control and ownership. Charter school reform hits at the core of public education, for example, are the schools controlled by citizens and their elected representatives (a control-based definition of public schools), or are they to be controlled by private (e.g., private, for-profit organizations) or religious elements, but yet perform agreed-upon public functions (public defined educational outcomes, but privately controlled means to those ends). The design of these types of reform programs require policymakers to make trade-offs among value positions such as equality, liberty (or choice), and diversity.

## SUMMARY

As these examples detail, the political process that yields educational policy is obviously complex and rooted in the structure of federalism and the historical traditions of education in the United States. Policy is developed by a relatively diverse set of institutions, groups, and individuals. These policymakers have diverse expectations of government and widely different concerns. Policy is also shaped by the nature of the policy environment and the historical time. Trends in political and economic conditions can provide links between the changing policy environment and resulting ideological shifts in policy activity. These trends provide one important source of influence on the policymaking process. Demographic trends in the United States during the 1800s (e.g., immigration, urbanization) had important consequences for the growth of large public school systems in the nation's cities. Concerns with segregated schooling led to a number of policy remedies aimed at increasing educational equity beginning in the 1950s. World economic developments brought tight budgets and pressure for greater efficiency and productivity that translated into demands for increases in educational quality and accountability during the 1980s. During the 1990s, these demands translated into increasing educational options through privatization, choice, vouchers, and tax credits.

Although in the typical community, these types of policy disputes are played out in the local arena among boards of educations, superintendents, and parents, it is important to consider that educational policy processes often begin through the force of higher levels of government. As Wirt and Kirst (1989) suggested, this is because local authorities often frustrate the efforts of those who would attempt to change the schools (e.g., structure, services delivered, curriculum, finances). Those locked out of the local policy process may appeal to higher levels of the government within the federalist system. They may achieve favorable policy in the form of state or federal statutes, administrative rulings, or court decisions. Some examples include bilingual education, programs for disadvantaged and impoverished students, special education services. Other types of programs, curricula, financing, and testing programs have also been mandated. As many of these new programs are funded separately by federal or state categorical programs, over time, this has tended to erode the local control of schools.

## EXERCISES

1. Describe several ways that the institutional arrangements present in federalism impact on various aspects of policymaking processes. In what ways does federalism contribute to the expansion or isolation of policy debates?

2. If you think of the federalist system as multilevel (federal, state, local) and consisting of multiple branches (executive, legislative, judicial), what are some of the structural tensions that are implied? How have these structural tensions influenced several previous policy efforts (e.g., No Child Left Behind Act of 2001, *Brown vs. Board of Education* in 1954, Education for All Handicapped Children Act of 1975).

# Chapter 3

# Studying Policy Development, Implementation, and Impact

Policymaking is relatively complicated, so policy researchers have looked for ways to simplify it in order to study it in more detail. Because of this complexity (i.e., multiple issues and actors in numerous political arenas seeking to influence the formulation, implementation, and outcomes of policy actions), no one research approach is likely to yield a complete picture. In contrast, a number of different conceptual models and methods are used in investigating policy. Over the past several decades, one popular way of looking at the policymaking process has been to break it up into a number of different regular events or stages.

One focus concerns the political dynamics surrounding the development and movement of ideas (e.g., policy issues) from policy subsystems to formal government decision-making arenas. In formal arenas (e.g., legislatures, courts, governmental agencies), ideas may be sponsored, negotiated, supported, and eventually, the results of the political process may produce outcomes such as initial policy adoption, policy change, or policy termination. This part of the process entails the definition of policy issues (i.e., ways policy problems should be approached), agenda setting (reaching the attention of formal decision makers), and the specific strategies that coalitions of individuals use to influence policy formulation. Researchers may gain understandings of regularities of policy activity by applying theory that explains the dynamics of policy interactions (e.g., conflicts, participants, strategies for attaining goals, mobilization of support, formal legislation) within various policy arenas that lead to policy decisions. Other theories of policy development are more suited to explaining long-term policy trends by following the movement and management of ideas (and the controversy that may surround them) in and out of governmental policy agendas. For example, for an idea like educational vouchers, this ideological movement may take several decades (i.e., vouchers have appeared periodically in the federal agenda since the mid-1960s).

A second research focus on the policy process is the implementation of policy decisions. Implementation concerns the process of putting formally adopted policies into practice. In education, this job falls on numerous government agencies (e.g., U.S. Department of Education, state departments of education), groups (e.g., school boards), and individuals (e.g., professional employees). In the 1970s, researchers began to discover the difficulties of implementing policy directed at producing educational change (Berman & McLaughlin, 1975). Researchers pursuing this focus have produced sustained results over time identifying a number of environmental conditions, policy-related variables, and supports and barriers that enhance or hinder the implementation of policies (Firestone & Corbett, 1988). One of the consistent challenges of this research has been to develop theory about why policy implementation is rarely uniform across local school sites.

A third concern is with assessing the impact of policies. This is sometimes referred to as policy evaluation. Examples of this research can include how policies are understood and incorporated into practice (e.g., a policy to reduce gender bias in the schools), the extent to which policies reach their intended goals (e.g., raises the achievement of targeted students or reduces the achievement gap), or the benefits versus costs relative to other policy options. Although the formation and implementation of policies has garnered much of the attention of researchers, the third concern is currently a major focus of federal policymakers, as they seek to structure the nature of policy research in education (e.g., demanding the use of experimental trials for funded research to determine the effectiveness of policy program interventions).

This chapter describes some of the factors that affect policy decision making and examines the policy development process itself more closely—that is, how various policy problems become policy issues (i.e., intended for governmental action), how policy issues are negotiated within policy subsystems, and how some policy issues become formalized (e.g., mandates, directives). To deal with some basic concepts in the policy-making process, first, a general framework is presented to organize some of the key variables that influence policy development. Then some of the routine events in the process are described. These events have emerged from empirical work using the policy stages typology developed over the past several decades. This tool has been useful in describing a chronological sequence of regular policy events. Of course, when we examine a particular policy against what are described as "routine events," we find that this linear chronology seldom holds. Whereas there is a tendency for textbooks to describe policy development as routine and sequenced, in reality, the process is much less predictable.

## A FRAMEWORK FOR STUDYING POLICY PROCESSES

Researchers have employed a number of conceptual models to examine policy processes. In the past, theory drawn from economics and political science has had a dominant role in the analysis of educational policy—for example, in areas such as determining how environmental demands are translated into governmental policy intentions and actions; describing how the process of developing particular policies unfolds (i.e., forming, adopting, implementing, evaluating); explaining how various actors are involved in competition, negotiation, and compromise at different parts of the agenda setting, development, and implementation process; examining the particular types of policies produced, and evaluating how policies are received within districts and schools. In fact, the traditional policy analysis paradigm itself represented this blending politics and economics. The purpose of policy analysis was to consider the associated benefits and costs of various policy choices in order to assist policymakers in choosing the optimal (i.e., efficient, utilitarian) decision in light of given goals, constraints, and environmental conditions. The paradigm generally assumed that a relatively stable environmental conditions and rational behavior led to efficient policy decisions that maximized net benefits for individuals. Hence, it was more useful in explaining policy behavior under conditions where the system was in relative stability and policymaking was incremental in nature.

Schattschneider's (1960) seminal work on the role of conflict in American politics suggested that conflict was much more at the center of politics than theorists had realized, and that one of the possible outcomes of political conflict was that the audience could be drawn into the debate. At this point, it would become much more difficult for policymakers to manage the conflict and predict the outcomes. Schattschneider proposed that longer periods of stability within the political system, which described incremental policymaking, were occasionally interrupted by shorter periods of intense conflict, where values changed, and once mobilized, led to new ideas and major policy changes being incorporated into the system. The result over time was that the policy system tended toward institutionally reinforced stability (e.g., through characteristics of federalism such as decentralization and checks and balances), interrupted by bursts of change (True et al., 1999). It took considerable time, however, for policy theorists to shift from a focus on rational decision-making behavior to a focus on conflict and policy change at the center of their explanatory frameworks.

While conceptual maps can be useful representations of reality, they are not the phenomenon itself. They are based on assumptions made about important relational aspects of the phenomenon under study. Conceptual frameworks identify major types of concepts and propositions that affect policy activity and the scope of inquiry. These help describe how different variables may be interrelated and provide a common language that can be used to compare antecedent conditions, actions, and outcomes across a number of different situations. This can help analysts identify questions that need to be addressed when they first conduct an analysis (Ostrom, 1999).

Importantly, because of the assumptions they make, alternative frameworks will likely lead to very different understandings of the phenomenon under study. Frameworks help organize inquiry, but they do not provide explanations for actions and outcomes (Schlager, 1999). They set the stage for theory development through empirical research. Theories and models can be used to examine more specific aspects of a framework by positing relationships among a limited number of key variables and by making predictions about outcomes. Several different theories are usually compatible with a particular type of research framework. Theories are like the staging of action within the play (or framework). The researcher, as director, makes decisions about which actors are relatively more important in the scene, and which ones should remain in the background.

As we might expect, there is often a relationship between the conceptual models used in research and the researchers' home disciplines. Most conceptual models used to study policy have been associated with the researchers' home disciplines. Because the study of policies began as a specialized interest within political science, political frameworks have been widely applied. These are likely to focus on the politics of decision making—identifying the conflicts, particular courses of action to pursue, who among various political actors holds the power, and who wins and who loses (Easton, 1965; Wirt & Kirst, 1982).

**Easton's Systems Framework**

One of the most prominent conceptual lenses used to organize policy research in the 1970s and 1980s was David Easton's (1965) systems framework. In their influential educational politics and policy text, *Schools in Conflict,* Wirt and Kirst (1982, 1989), applied the systems framework extensively to explain how political demands were converted into educational policies at the federal, state, and local levels. This framework represented an attempt to apply scientific theory about how systems are organized and operate to explain human behavior. It focused attention on some of the determinants of policy activity (i.e., primarily environmental conditions and political variables). The framework generally helped describe how environmental demands and stresses (e.g., economic, political conditions) become policy inputs that are converted within the political system into policy outputs that are fed back into the environment (see Fig. 3.1). It tends to focus on the formulation (i.e., inputs and the political system) and the adoption of policies (outputs).

Systems theory provided one explanation of why the policy system persisted over time (as organisms do), because it was perceived as open, self-regulating, and able to adapt through time to changing environ-

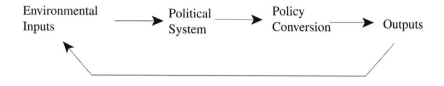

FIG. 3.1.  Systems analysis framework for studying educational policy.

mental conditions. It said much less about the causal processes and conditions under which the system was open (or closed) or self-regulating,
and what types of environmental stresses led to minor adjustments, or
even systemic revolutions.

In retrospect, although the systems framework was a useful organizing
device for examining how levels of government operated in general ways to
formulate and enact policies, as an empirical tool to examine educational
policy activity, it was lacking in several major ways. First, it was not sufficiently developed (e.g., concepts, interrelationships, causal connections) to
generate sustained empirical work in educational policy. Second, the unit
of analysis was the policy system at the macro level (i.e., focusing primarily
on the state level because there is only one federal unit and 50 state units).
By aggregating data to the state level, it was not well suited for examining
individual variability within states (including policymakers' preferences).
Third, it described more routine, incremental relationships when the policy system was in relative stability. The more interesting research question is
what happens to systemic relations (e.g., institutional responses to stress)
when the system itself is in flux (Heck, 1991; Iannaccone, 1977); yet it is
hard to find opportunities in education where systemic relations are breaking down and the system itself is changing. Reform in Chicago during the
mid- to late-1980s is one example (Wong & Rollow, 1990). Fourth, the
framework was not of much use in examining the developmental process of
particular policies, because it proposed no causal relations about how environmental demands were actually converted to policies (i.e., it contained a
huge "black box" about the actual policy process). For example, being a systems perspective (often focusing on the state as the unit of analysis), it could
not focus on explanations related to the interactions and actions of policy
actors (e.g., their beliefs, goals, strategies, perceptions of institutional arrangements) within policy subsystems. Fifth, it did not address policy implementation (which also seemed to hinge on characteristics of individual
locations as opposed to systemic processes). Other variants of systems theory (chaos theory, nonlinear dynamics, complexity theory) have also generated little interest among policy researchers since the early 1990s.

## Political Dynamics of Policy Development

Several alternative political lenses focused on the political dynamics of individual and group (e.g., legislators, pressure groups, special interests, media) involvement in the conflicts leading up to policy decisions. Rather than attending to policy at the macro level, they directed more attention on the various institutional arrangements within federalism (hierarchical governments, separation of powers, checks and balances) and how the role of each governmental unit may contribute to the policy process. Some of the early attempts to capture policy activity within and across governmental units included the policy stages typology, elite theory (which was concerned with the goals and preferences of governing elites), group theory (which focused on how groups manage conflict and competing interests), and incrementalism (i.e., which examined the tendency for policymakers to continue past practices). Of these latter approaches, the policy stages typology has formed the basis for organizing the policy development process.

Although these other models had success in organizing policy research, they also have received ample criticism. The policy stages model identified various important steps in development, but it offered no explanation about how the steps were related, or conditions that influenced movement from one stage to another. Elite theory tended to focus too much on formal roles and governmental arenas within the political structure (e.g., viewing policy development as a more closed activity conducted within formal arenas such as senates, courts, or executive offices). It did not do well, for example, in explaining how multiple and conflicting beliefs sometimes widen policy conflicts and create nonlinear outcomes. Incrementalism described more routine policy processes under stable environmental conditions and relative agreement over policy problems and solutions, but it did not account for times (e.g., Municipal Reform) when the system itself was under attack and institutional arrangements themselves might change (Iannaccone, 1977).

More recently, concepts and theories borrowed from other disciplines (e.g., institutional theory, culture, feminism, game theory) have enriched the study of policies. They have broadened the scope of policy inquiry to include how cultural and social factors and a variety of personal variables (e.g., belief systems of policymakers, perceptions of the challenges of particular policy situations, strategies, and the availability and use of information) also affect policy activity. To incorporate these types of factors into the analysis, they have also shifted researchers' attention away from aggregate data on systems and formal arenas of government toward disaggregated data on individuals within policy subsystems and policy coalitions.

The policy framework in Fig. 3.2 and described briefly represents a summation of several conceptual frameworks and lenses that have been used to study policymaking over the past 2 to 3 decades. The figure suggests that policy activity within a policy subsystem (comprised of individuals from various organizations and interests who regularly seek to

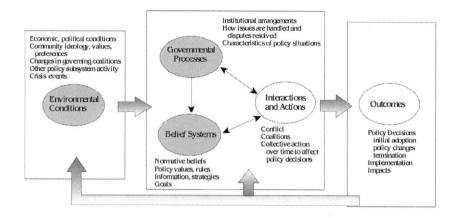

FIG. 3.2.　One possible conceptual framework for studying policy activity. *Note.* Shaded ovals are multilevel.

influence policy in that domain) results from (1) the interplay of changing environmental conditions with community and cultural values; (2) the changing political dynamics and influence between governmental units and competing policy coalitions; (3) and individuals' belief systems (e.g, normative beliefs, policy values, goals, strategies) and patterns of interaction that have shaped their previous policy efforts. In turn, as a result of these policy interactions and collective actions, various policy outcomes are realized. Formal decisions may be made to adopt a policy initially, or to change or terminate a policy. Because the focus is on policy development, implementation is treated as an outcome in this framework. This can include questions like, what agencies were involved or to what extent was the policy implemented? Research specifically on implementation has identified a number of variables that impact on implementation processes. Another common outcome studied is policy impact on targeted individuals and groups, the wider external system, as well as on policy-making individuals and groups themselves.

Some of the conceptual lenses following in this chapter and in chapters 4 through 7 address various aspects of the framework in more detail. Readers will notice that in an evolutionary sense, it still looks like a systems theory model, with some attention to multilevel characteristics of policy systems and more emphasis on the workings within the policy conversion process (i.e., focusing on activity within policy subsystems). Shaded circles represent variables that can have multilevel effects (i.e., effects on the same level as the unit of analysis and levels above) on the lowest levels of analysis (i.e., the policy subsystem, policy outcomes). Most often, researchers are interested in policy results conducted at the individual (or disaggregated) level of analysis. For example, their interest is on the beliefs and actions of individuals within a policy subsystem or outcomes related to individual policies. Occasionally, the interest is in an aggregate level, such as state-level policy outcomes. Arrows with double heads represent reciprocal processes, which suggests the two constructs affect each other over time. This more traditional policy framework forms a basis for comparing alternative perspectives on policy research in chapter 7.

## Environmental Conditions

Environmental variables are a first important source of influence on policy activity. This is the case, even if policymakers do not entirely perceive these factors. Changes at the federal level, shrinking state budgets, increasing poverty numbers, increasing gaps between rich and poor, less support for tax increases can all signal problems for financing education. During these times, education may be competing with various other social service agencies. Demographic shifts including increasing diversity may place new demands on schools for curricula that reflect diversity, for bilingual programs, and for the accommodation of a broader range of religious practices (Fowler, 2000). Changes in ideology, as represented by different political parties that dominate, may also bring changes in educational policymaking. Liberals and conservatives may pursue different educational agendas and structure widely different solutions to school problems. Moreover, various policymaking activities in other parts of government may also impact on other policy subsystems in intended and unintended ways.

Forces outside of the government can also include what are often referred to as random events. These are events that occur that result in some type of policy activity. They are typically not predictable, but may crystalize debate that has been ongoing about a particular policy problem and potential solutions. For example, the launch of Sputnik in 1957 by the Soviet Union during the Cold War led to the passage of National Defense Education Act in 1958 and the Elementary and Secondary Education Act in 1965. The event crystalized considerable debate that had been ongoing about the quality of the curriculum. Both mandates aimed to upgrade the quality of the nation's elementary and secondary curriculum and schools. Similarly, in the 1980s, the publication of *A Nation At Risk* focused attention on the perceived failure of the American educational system due to the federal government's involvement in pursuing educational equity. It signaled a shift in the relative influence of governmental units (i.e., decreasing the federal and increasing the state role) and correspondingly led to a wave of state reforms aimed at upgrading quality through increasing standards and lengthening the school year.

Some of the environmental parameters may be more stable over time (e.g., fundamental social and cultural values). Other parameters may be more unstable (e.g., economic conditions and political conditions, policy decisions in other subsystems, changes in governing coalitions, crisis events).

Environmental influences are important to consider in studying policy problems because they form the context in which policy activity is conducted. They are multilevel in that they can affect education policy formulation and implementation on the federal, state, and local levels. As Sabatier and Jenkins-Smith (1999) argued, these sets of contextual factors affect interactions and policy actions within a policy subsystem (i.e., a number of competing coalitions consisting of individuals with various affiliations that share particular beliefs and engage in a degree of coordinated activity).

## Belief Systems

Within a policy subsystem, individuals' belief systems (e.g., normative beliefs, core policy values, institutional rules), their perceptions of the policy situation, their policy goals, and strategies influence the nature of policy interactions and actions over time. These variables represent the inner life, or assumptive worlds, of policy actors (Marshall et al., 1989). Belief systems include the various views and meanings actors as individuals hold (e.g., about individual freedom, the role of government, about their commitments to particular value priorities, their perceptions about particular policy problems). These various beliefs and perceptions help influence what is important to them (e.g., what issues they support, what stances they take, and what commitments they make). As Sachen and Medina (1990) noted, policymakers are socialized into a distinctive policy culture that creates sets of expectation about appropriate ways of behaving, rituals, and the feasibility of various policy options.

Ideologies and values are translated into collective policy actions through conflicts surrounding what values to pursue, what policy alternatives to support, and where to pursue government action. Within a policy subsystem, there are likely multiple conflicting belief systems about the nature of policy problems, the ends to pursue, and the strategies to achieve goals. Policy actors seek information about policy issues and devise strategies with others holding similar beliefs (through forming policy coalitions) to translate policy goals into concrete collective actions. The duration of interactions to achieve policy ends can be considerable (lasting a decade or more) and can involve multiple governmental arenas. Over time, they also learn from their policy interactions. Importantly, Marshall and colleagues (1989) demonstrated that there is a collective component to policymakers' cognitive processes. Their actions also result from their own personal views, beliefs, and values (therefore, belief systems is a multilevel construct in the figure).

## Governmental Processes

Third, a broader definition of policymaking suggests that policy activity occurs both within governmental structures and also in the larger society (Baumgartner & Jones, 1993; Firestone, 1989). Institutional arrangements are therefore an important influence on the nature of policy arenas (because they suggest how relatively open access to policymaking processes will be). The nature of the federalist system itself (with multiple levels, a decentralized structure, and divided responsibilities) favors the development of coalitions among governmental actors, special interests, and others who may work collectively over time to bring government attention to resolving a particular policy problem. Federalism creates multiple points of entry into the policymaking system. Once support for particular issues becomes mobilized, it creates many opportunities for governmental actors to get involved (Schlager, 1999).

It is not enough just to study formal governmental structures (e.g., legislature, executive, judicial branches), however, and how they respond to policy problems (e.g., where issues develop, how policy decisions are made). Formal governmental policy decisions are the end result of more complex policy actions that take place within policy subsystems. The perceptions of coalitions about characteristics of evolving policy situations and the likelihood of obtaining governmental response can influence the strategies coalitions use to achieve policy goals. This can include which governmental policymakers have power, or are insiders, in making policy decisions. Recent studies using this type of framework have determined that the ability to change levels of political action is an important strategy in pursuing policy goals (Ostrom, 1999). This suggests the importance of conceptualizing this set of variables as multilevel. Moreover, various groups and individuals may also play differing roles in the policy formulation and implementation process. This makes participation in policy cycles a very fluid process.

## THE POLICY STAGES APPROACH

The policy frameworks in Figs. 3.1 and 3.2 represent ways that research into the determinants of policy activity has been organized over the past several decades. The competing alternative conceptual lens that is still widely used to examine policy activity is the policy stages typology. Instead of being directed at determinants of policy activity, it focuses on the identification of an ordered sequence of stages, or steps (e.g., agenda setting, policy formulation, implementation, evaluation), in the life of a particular policy. The policy stages model has been the "textbook approach" that numerous policy analysts employ to simplify the policymaking process. It was the dominant approach included in numerous texts for examining policy activity during the 1970s and 1980s, although, as suggested, a number of other approaches were also used. It stems from Lasswell (1951), who viewed the decision-making process about a policy as consisting of several identifiable steps that came to be closely associated with the science of policy analysis. These steps in analyzing a policy included identifying the process through which it is initiated, examined, selected, and carried out, and continued or eliminated (deLeon, 1999; Lasswell, 1956).

The specific steps are somewhat arbitrarily defined points by various authors (e.g., Brewer, 1974; Fowler, 2000) such as initiation (i.e., defining policy issues, developing an agenda), choosing among alternatives (policy formulation and adoption), implementation (i.e., how the policy is put into practice), and evaluation (e.g., analysis of impact, policy effects, and effectiveness). Over time, research using this approach has focused on describing the life of particular policies as they move through several developmental phases to enactment and implementation. Individual studies have generally examined particular stages separately (e.g., development and enactment, implementation, evaluation), often without reference to research in other stages (Sabatier, 1999). The collection of empirical studies has been useful in focusing attention on the debates and values underlying choices made especially during the policy's period of formulation. This can reveal that the timing of a political action is as important as the power resources that support it. It has also led to numerous studies on how policies are implemented, what types of barriers preclude policy implementation, and how to evaluate the success of policy implementation.

It is useful to highlight several of the criticisms that have been raised about the stages approach as a research tool (e.g., Sabatier & Jenkins-Smith, 1993; Schon & Rein, 1994) before actually discussing the various stages that have drawn researchers' attention. First, the approach tends to force one to view the process as rational and linear, consisting of a number of steps through which a value position (or approach to resolving a particular problem) becomes legislated and implemented. Critics, therefore, have noted that heuristics like the stages approach are often misleading because they introduce artificial symbols and divisions that make the policymaking process look more ordered and rational than it really is. For example, research from this perspective often focuses on discrete aspects of the process (i.e., one stage such as policy formulation or implementation) as opposed to the entire process (deLeon, 1999). Research within each stage tended to develop in its own manner without regard to research on other stages (Sabatier & Jenkins-Smith, 1993). Moreover, because attention is focused on formal "steps" through which a policy passes, it often ignores the role of more "grassroots" efforts (e.g., among coalitions in policy subsystems) that may take place on the fringes of the more visible legislative part of the process. This often makes each part seem larger than the process itself, as each has its own literature and set of concepts.

Second, the policy stages heuristic tends to reduce the life of a policy to a single set of discrete stages. More recently, however, researchers have found that there are often multiple interacting cycles involving many policy proposals and statutes and involving multiple layers of government that best describe the process (Sabatier, 1999). The reduction of these complex cycles to a single sequence of steps results in a considerable reduction in reality and also makes the process seem more linear than it actually is.

Third, critics note that the policy stages approach falls short of being a theory, because it neglects the role of ideology—in particular, ideas involving the relatively technical aspects of policy debates in policy evolution (Sabatier, 1993). Sabatier and Jenkins-Smith (1993) noted that the stages model is not really causal, because it does not identify a set of causal variables that govern the process within and across the stages. It does not imply that each policy moves through the same set of policy stages, or that one stage must be completed before another begins. Proponents have not derived a set of theoretical propositions that explain the types of factors that "cause" a problem to become a policy, that cause a policy to be implemented more thoroughly in one situation versus another, or to have an uneven impact on changing educational practice. The approach has been primarily used to describe past events as opposed to predict future ones. While useful for that purpose, it does little to advance explanations about when and why certain types of policy activities occur.

## STAGES IN THE POLICY DEVELOPMENT PROCESS

***Problems, Issues, and Agenda Setting.*** Studying the policy process really begins with the identification of policy problems. These are social problems that are often solved through educational means. Often, these problems are larger than educational in nature. Examples might be poverty, inflation, economic competitiveness, racial segregation, and teen alcohol and drug use. Some of the problems may be more related to the education system specifically—students dropping out, minority student access to higher education, and admission policies at universities.

Policy problems share a number of characteristics (Majchrzak, 1984; Mann, 1975). They are public in nature—that is, they are visible and involve governmental solutions that have consequences for the public. They may involve the allocation of resources (Easton, 1965), for example, adding resources to particular groups, or taking away resources from other groups. Policy problems also tend to be complex, as they are embedded in economic, political, social, and moral components. They are often hard to describe with certainty or to form a simple solution.

The identification of policy issues is at the center of policy analysis. In contrast to problems, policy issues are more controversial in nature, because they involve an interpretation of the problem, a set of values, and an expected role that government should play in resolving the problem (Fowler, 2000). An issue only exists if groups disagree about how a problem should be approached. Issues, therefore, drive the policy process because they represent attempts to create support for particular types of action to resolve a problem. Policy issues develop as a result of political interactions among those inside and outside of government. Often, the main players are agencies in the executive branch, members of congressional committees, and special interest groups (Guthrie & Reed, 1991). They may also arise from a variety of other sources as well including media articles, policy think tanks, or academic research. Sometimes, a catalyst, or outside event, occurs that may move things along. It may receive a wide variety of attention and crystalize debate that has been ongoing. These events often have the ability to get the wider public involved in mobilizing support for a particular action.

The analyst may strive to understand the various issues surrounding a problem, as this will tend to dictate the types of recommendations about resolving the problem that would be seen as acceptable and feasible. By identifying various related policy issues, the multidimensional nature of the problem often becomes apparent, as well as how the problem has been approached in the past. Many reform policies represent the concrete examples of different ways of solving a similar problem. For example, open enrollment, vouchers, and charter schools represent ways to increase choice in schooling as a way of promoting accountability and improved outcomes. Groups may disagree over the extent to which each represents a desirable way to resolve the problem. For many years, choice was not as controversial an issue in schooling, because districts made decisions about where children went to school (e.g., neighborhood school, bused to a school of the district's choice). More recently, as parents perceived they had been locked out of the decision-making process, increasing parental choice became a policy issue. Parents demanded to send their children to schools they perceived as good.

Policy issues embody underlying sets of values. They are an interpretation of the problem and imply a role that government should play in resolving the problem (Fowler, 2000). Policy issues are decided within policy subsystems. Within a policy subsystem, a number of groups seek to define problems or to get issues on the move (e.g., foundations, think tanks, corporations, educational associations). Over time, the interactions around a particular policy problem or set of problems and their related issues take place within a policy subsystem. Within the subsystem, problems get turned into issues that are described as intended government actions or inactions (Fowler, 2000). Individuals seeking similar policy ends form coalitions that over time act in a collective manner to realize their policy goals. It is important to realize that these various groups often have their own political leanings and agenda. These can determine what types of ideas, or policy issues, develop support (e.g., through funding) and how the solutions to various issues are framed.

In order for an issue to become formal policy, however, it must reach a governmental policy agenda. This is often the key stage of the process, because having control over the agenda determines what issues make it to become more public. Large numbers of issues are typically vying for attention on a governmental policy agenda at any point in time. Only a limited number, however, will receive governmental attention. Whereas it is difficult for issues to get on the policy agenda of government, it is relatively easy for them to fall out (Fowler, 2000). This is known as the issue–attention cycle (Baumgartner & Jones, 1993). Some issues get inadequate attention, or they may be displaced by more important issues (Schattschneider, 1960). Because the capacity of government to address issues is limited, there will be competition over the various issues and approaches taken to resolve policy problems.

Developing a policy agenda involves determining what issues are important enough to continue to be under discussion. This may include a broad set of issues that are under discussion outside of government. These may include issues that professionals are thinking about (e.g., education associations, policy centers, researchers), those that the media is interested in (e.g., publishing test scores, or other incidents that are believed to attract attention), and those that are in the public arena (e.g., opinion polls). Although there may be some overlap among these, it is also the case that the issues may be relatively separate for different groups. For example, educational issues are more likely to be defined among professional education groups—perhaps less frequently in the media, and only occasionally in the public arena (e.g., violence in the schools)

Research suggests that access to these various policy subsystems is highly competitive (Fowler, 2000). Time and other resources are limited. Therefore, coalitions supporting particular policy issues have to identify what the most favorable arenas are likely to be for a particular policy. There is likely competition among coalitions within a policy subsystem over what types of actions to sponsor and how to mobilize to develop broad-based legislative support for the intended action. This is because individual legislators may hold quite different conceptualizations of the problem—that is, in the previous case, the solution might be seen in terms of an economic problem (i.e., can we afford to give money needed for vouchers or provide support programs, is this a proper role of government, can we afford the strain on the economy over time to support those who drop out?) or perhaps a social problem (what will be the impact on society of additional individuals who are on the fringe or will this lead to an increase in crime among 18–24-year-olds?).

Looking at the legislative history of various policy issues that have been applied previously can be revealing about how government has attempted to handle the problem. It is therefore helpful to understand the formal part of the process. Importantly, however, the pattern of political influence is different depending on the issue. While it is important to understand the movement of ideas within the political context (Iannaccone, 1977), it is also the institutional arrangements (suggesting roles for various policy actors) and skill of various players in the policy system that move policy issues along. Not all actors are equally positioned in policy decision making; those who have more power have more influence on the process (Cobb & Elder, 1972). In their study of state policymaking activity, Marshall and colleagues (1989) provided one way to organize groups of policy actors who exert varying influence in policy actions (e.g., agenda setting, collective action, formal decisions) within given policy situations.

- *Insiders*—participate consistently in setting the agenda and in moving policy proposals forward. Policy insiders can include the governor, legislative committees, or even an individual legislator. Major political leaders such as the president and governors, and also prominent legislators, may play a key role in agenda setting. They have access to the media and public through their speeches.

- *Near circle*—those who sit in groups that can persuade insiders. The near circle could include various business or special interests, education agencies of the executive branch, the state legislature. They may provide information about issues to key policymakers and mobilize pressure to draw attention through lobbying. An example might be the Business Roundtable. This group was influential in moving site-based management along in the late 1980s and early 1990s. They tended to focus on a limited set of educational issues of importance to them.

- *Far circle*—these members are less critical to decisions that are made, but they can often influence policy implementation from their organizational positions. These actors might include members of professional interest groups such as teachers' unions or state educational superintendents.

- *Sometimes players*—can occasionally influence based on a particular issue.

- *Forgotten players*—these are groups on the margins. Although they may have some indirect influence at particular times, they generally do not influence agenda setting. Behavior that falls into such occasions could include student protests, demonstrations, or violence. There is a long history of these tactics in the United States that do influence policy.

In one study of 20 educational issues in Minnesota that emerged over a 20-year period and eventually became state law, Mazzoni (1993) showed that usually policy proposals were developed by coalitions of actors. In terms of cumulative involvement, legislators were involved about 50% of the time, governors about 35%, interest groups about 35% of the time (with greater involvement by noneducation groups), and the state department of education about 20%. This was consistent with Marshall and colleagues (1989) finding that policy is most often made by those in the near circle and by policy insiders.

***Formulating and Enacting Policy Choices.***    The formulation of policy choices is also relatively complex. This is, however, the part of the policymaking process that is more visible to the public. This phase has also drawn considerable attention from researchers (e.g., Wong & Rollow, 1990) because it is where the mobilization of efforts to support a particular policy issue are realized through the enactment of formal policies in government. This is the stage at which the intent of the policy issue is expressed in writing, often taking the form of a statute, court decision, or an administrative rule (Fowler, 2000).

The legislature is probably the most open branch in the sense that much of what goes on there is public. At both the federal and state level, legislatures are focal points for both insiders (legislative committee members, governmental administrators) and outsiders (business interests and other lobbyists, citizen activists, journalists). No major policy activity can take place without legislative consent, as money is often required. Of course, not every statute is passed with financial support. Passing statutes has been described as conservative, in that it is difficult for a bill to negotiate the variety of barriers that are there to prevent its passage. This is the case from passing amendments to the Constitution (requiring ultimately three fourths of the states to vote in favor of ratification) to typical bill that must first get out of committee, then move typically through two houses of Congress, and be signed by the executive.

At the federal level, Congress takes on a broad set of policy issues including economic affairs, defense and foreign policy, environmental protection, education, and health (Van Horn et al., 1992). Both houses of Congress are largely dominated by committee activity. For example, in 1990, the House had 22 major legislative committees and 138 subcommittees, whereas the Senate had 16 committees and 86 subcommittees (Ripley, 1988). The committee process disperses power for individual representatives to influence policy (Van Horn et al., 1992). The committees system, therefore, is largely responsible for shaping policy.

Proposed bills need sponsorship and they need to be sent to the appropriate committee for revision. As Fowler (2000) suggested, the bill's life may be decided by the leadership of the legislature (e.g., either a committee or an individual) and if these leaders wish, they can send a bill to a standing committee where it is either likely to find support or to be killed. For example, in 1996, Oleszek noted that in the 102nd Congress, 10,238 bills were introduced, 1,405 made it out of committee (14%), 677 bills (7%) passed both houses, and only 590 (6%) eventually became law. This suggests that the committee system has a tremendous effect on channeling the direction (supporting, changing, eliminating) of proposed policies.

If a proposed piece of legislation makes it out of standing committee, it goes to "rules" committee (or an individual), where the regulation of the flow of legislation to the floor for debate takes place (Oleszek, 1996). At this point, the bill's priority in reference to other bills is determined, as well as the length of its debate and the extent to which it can be amended. Obviously, its priority can have a major influence, if it is late or if time is short. Finally, bills must be approved in both houses of the legislature. Even if corresponding bills are introduced simultaneously, there is little likelihood that they will be the same after moving through each legislative hall separately. If differences are not worked out informally, then the bill must go to the "conference" committee where the disagreements are worked out (Fowler, 2000). As Oleszek (1996) summarized this, during the 103rd Congress, 13% of the bills went to Conference Committee. Here, the bill may also die due to power and politics. After going through this committee, the bill must go back to both houses for a majority vote and then go on to the chief executive for approval.

If the bill goes through all those previous steps successfully, there is still the chance that it will not be funded. So the funding part becomes another set of hurdles. This means it has to go through the government's budget for the next fiscal period. Of course, a policy that is not funded would likely be of little use. Controlling the money is therefore a key part to understanding the life of a policy. There is considerable variation across states on how these funding practices work (Rubin, 1990). Importantly, state governments cannot have deficit budgets—they must balance. Moreover, at the state level, most governors have legal power to use a line-item veto to eliminate spending approved at the legislature.

Since the latter half of the 20th century, the courts also have had substantial increase in interest and corresponding impact on educational policy. As Van Geel (1988) noted, Brown decision in 1954 was the beginning of a dramatic increase in involvement of the courts in schools. The issues have been varied including further clarifying the relationship between private and public schooling, expanding the rights of teachers, expanding the rights of students, expanding services to students, examining religious versus secular issues, the appropriateness of the curriculum and its materials, the placing of students, equalizing finances, and testing. As Van Geel concluded, however, although the judiciary's activities since 1954 have been extensive, there is need to exercise caution in assuming that the level of activity has actually caused changes in the behavior of school personnel, because there is little existing research. A judicial decision, however, may place the issue on the political agenda of the community (Elmore & McLaughlin, 1982).

Administrative agencies are also an important source for policy enactment. Agencies often must fill in the details for policies passed by the legislature. As Fowler (2000) suggested, these may have been unrecognized by legislators or they may have left the details to be filled in later. They may also expand on key terms in a law or in how the laws fit together in a specific policy area. Agencies may also write rules that define their own procedures. Although agencies have broad discretion in writing regulations, these rules must also be reviewed by outside sources and they can be challenged in court. The process aids in the implementation of policies, as if rules were too specific from the legislatures bills might never get passed because of the politics. Also, people in the agencies tend to be closer to the conduct of schools than are legislators, so they are more familiar with practices. In addition, the rules can be amended more easily than the laws, so personnel can revisit the regulations.

*Policy Implementation.* The dynamics surrounding policy implementation are important because implementation often implies a change
in behavior on the part of professionals within education. This could range
from the implementation of an important court decision (such as the Brown
decision) or a state policy. Policy implementation is the stage that has been
most studied in recent times; hence, it is also one of the areas that we know
the most about (Fowler, 2000). Implementation research grew out of a
number of practical concerns having to do with whether policy changes
were effective. Policymakers wanted to determine whether allocated funds
were producing desired changes. So along with federal money came the
mandate to evaluate new programs.

In the 1970s, the implementation of federal policy to create change was
extensively studied (Berman & McLaughlin, 1978). The results indicated
that the implementation phase is where many policy-related changes break
down. One reason was the difficulty in implementing policies across several
layers of government. Another reason was that policies were often not cus-
tomized to the local set of circumstances (e.g., Sarason, 1971). These findings shifted the perspective during the 1980s and 1990s to how policies
were implemented in the local setting. From this standpoint, implementation was less about following a rational process, and more about culture and
values. Much of this knowledge on implementation has been studied in relation to school improvement (e.g., see Louis, Toole, & Hargreaves, 1999).

*The Evaluation of Policy Outputs and Outcomes.* Research concerned with this stage often focuses on whether the policy has produced the
intended output and whether there are also other outcomes and shortcomings that may be notable. Research has shown that educational practices are
often resistant to the mandates and directives of external policymakers
(e.g., Firestone & Corbett, 1988; Louis et al., 1999). This is particularly evident when attempting to implement policies that support schools' academic improvement. There has been no clear blueprint that has resulted
from various efforts that describe how the key parts of the system interrelate
and that should be used to foster academic improvement (Ouston, 1999).
As McLaughlin (1990) concluded, it is difficult for reform policies to change
educational practices, especially across levels of government, because the
nature, amount, and pace of change at the individual school level is a product of local factors that are largely out of the control of higher level
policymakers. Policies may set directions and provide a framework for
change, but they do not determine the outcomes directly. Rather, features
of the local site context and the specific implementation process largely determine the eventual influence of reforms on student achievement (Berman
& McLaughlin, 1978; Teddlie & Reynolds, 2000). Policy mandates have
been found to work best when the goals to be met and the measure of their
attainment are clear, as well there is a balance of public and professional
support, and the target sites can reasonably achieve the mandated ends

(Firestone & Corbett, 1988). Public support is a key, as is the feasibility of the proposed change.

Although previous research often focused on the effects of policy outcomes as a discrete stage, it is possible to examine both the manner and degree of policy implementation and its effects. The combination of both implementation and impact phases of the policy process has been less studied (Heck, Brandon, & Wang, 2001). For example, at the site level, variables of the implementation process (e.g., how committed individuals are, how much support exists, what funding is available and how it is spent, how extensively a policy is implemented) affect the level of a policy's effects. To do so would require a longitudinal approach, perhaps collecting data at several places during the implementation and effect stages. To give a full accounting of a policy to reform student achievement in schools may involve utilizing a combination of methods and data taken from its implementation and afterward (e.g., student test scores, budget reports, attendance, interviews, ethnographic study of individual schools). It is often necessary, therefore, to delimit exactly what goals of a particular policy are being evaluated and for what purposes.

**Flexibility of the Policy Stages Approach**

Despite the criticism, however, the description of the various stages serves a number of purposes for studying policy activity. First, as deLeon (1999) argued, initially, the policy stages approach is one way to identify and describe the issues that drive the policy process. This allows one to identify what issues are competing and what values and contextual conditions may underlie the competition over issues. Second, the approach provides a convenient way of viewing and categorizing actors and actions so that analysts can unravel the set of political moves made. This may focus attention on how policy coalitions develop and interact over the pursuit of particular solutions. Third, it provides a means of tracking the modifications that are made over time in the process of policy development. Fourth, it focuses attention on the dynamics of implementation and how this part of the process affects whether or not policy changes are incorporated into practice. Fifth, it also suggests attention to describing the outcomes and impacts of the policy process. And finally, the stages approach has also been fairly adaptable to other substantive theories and to different epistemological approaches (e.g., constructivist, postpositivist, critical theorist).

The more pressing question is whether this approach can be useful in moving policy studies toward a set of policy-oriented theories (deLeon, 1999). The linkages between the stages remain elusive, but we have gained a more thorough picture of what makes up (and what does not make up) the various parts of the policy process due to research on its various parts. This has led to greater understanding about how policy issues develop, how agendas are formulated, how alternatives are considered, how actors work to move policies forward, the conditions that favor (or inhibit) implementation, and some of the ways that policies can be judged as effective or not. The challenge for researchers is to move beyond simple description and single case studies of policies toward an understanding of the policy process across a number of cases. Single case studies can give too much weight to idiosyncratic aspects of a policy problem. Future research using this perspective should help researchers seek more powerful explanations that hold across a number of varied cases by using the comparative method (see chap. 9).

## AN EXAMPLE STUDY: WONG AND ROLLOW (1990)

There are numerous research examples of the use of the stages typology in describing the development or implementation of educational policies. Wong and Rollow (1990) provided one excellent example of the purposes of this type of research. Wong and Rollow used a descriptive case study to identify and organize the dynamics leading to educational governance reform in Chicago during the 1980s. They described the political, social, and economic events that led to the issue formation and agenda setting, the mobilization of support, and the legislative phases of a policy to reform the governance of Chicago's public schools.

The focus of the Chicago school reform proposal was to raise student achievement by creating a system of school-based decision making that moved the Chicago public schools from a bureaucratically controlled system to a decentralized one—that is, the reform was primarily concerned with governance and power. The policy's intent was to change the relative decision-making power for the policy system's key actors (e.g., parents, teachers, principals, subdistrict and field superintendents, board of education, superintendent, central administration, and the Chicago Teachers Union) in order to provide a system that was more responsive to parental concerns. The Chicago School Reform legislation was signed into law in July, 1988. It culminated several years of citywide effort to mobilize support for the reform and to craft a legislative package at the state level that could be passed by the legislature and endorsed by the governor.

In analyzing the politics of the reform bill, Wong and Rollow (1990) emphasized two key phases of the policy development process (i.e., issue determination and mobilization, and enactment). The authors used the stages typology as an organizing scheme to examine the politics that led to the adoption of the reform and to specify the extent to which key organized policy interests had an impact on policy decisions at each stage leading to enactment of the final reform bill. Their choice of lens to structure the analysis focused the analysis on the issues, key players, events, and documents produced in each phase.

***Issues and Agenda Setting.***   The issues and agenda-setting phase centered on the grassroots involvement among parent, community and business interests, and professional educators (Wong & Rollow, 1990). The local mobilization of the policy issue depends on a number of factors including gaining access to the policy decision-making process. First, community interests (parents, mayor, business interests) become more active in reforming the local community. Second, they concluded that mobilization was more likely to occur in a policy domain that has seen more reform, such as public education. They determined that the policy subsystem handling education permits the existence of more demands from clients, including those that have had limited access to the policy process. Third, collective action was facilitated by the formation of broad-based coalitions that represented sources of local influence (e.g., business, local political leadership).

An educational summit meeting generated a set of written agreements. These agreements (dominated by local groups) were designed to bring about decentralization of the public school system. Some of the key proposals to create local parent and community school councils to increase parental control and access to school decision making, to adopt an effective schools approach (favoring a technical understanding of school problems and effective approaches to their improvement), to reduce administrative inefficiency (as the system was perceived to be administrative heavy), to limit the influence of administrators and teachers, and to gain more direct assistance to individual schools from central administration (Wong & Rollow, 1990). Many of these ideas were embodied within the document's call for creating a more decentralized governance structure. In contrast, however, the locally produced agreements had little to say about the reform of the top part of the school system and on external oversight. In the absence of clear agreement, these issues generated more conflict among key actors at the legislative phase.

***Enacting Policy Choices.*** In contrast to grassroots involvement of local interests, the formal legislative (enactment) stage was dominated by partisan influences and institutional constraints. Politicians and organized lobbying groups became more dominant. Wong and Rollow (1990) characterized this phase as one of conflict and compromise to achieve the legislative package. The analysis suggested that mobilized community-based policy preferences can either be endorsed or modified by key institutional actors in the state legislative process. As they noted, state political leaders were more willing to support issues that involved a clear consensus among diverse local interests. In contrast, where there was a lack of clear local consensus, it was likely that more intense politics at the state level would occur. This enactment phase took two legislative sessions.

Wong and Rollow (1990) noted that the committee system in the legislature played a critical role in filtering competing demands on school reform—that is, diverse proposals were introduced and channeled through the legislative process—in particular the Education Committee, which drafted the initial reform legislation (SB 1839) under the direction of its chair and other key Democrat members. Here, key legislators were able to introduce their own views, language, and preferences for reform—that is, they set the agenda for decision making (Wong & Rollow, 1990). Although the first bill passed the senate and the house, because there was significant Republican disagreement (i.e., wanting to reduce the power of district central administration, wanting more parent opportunity for school choice, allowing principals more discretion, and breaking the power of the teachers' union power), the bill was vetoed by the Republican governor. Specifically, the governor wanted to increase his oversight influence and he wanted to increase principals' ability to hire teachers without regard for seniority.

This disagreement from key players led to a compromise bill (SB 1840). It was very similar to the previous bill, except for oversight of the school system from the top. More specifically, the appointments were to be divided between the mayor of Chicago and the governor. The oversight committee's responsibilities were broadened from financial oversight of the district to responsibilities for the entire set of reform activities of the Board of Education.

Wong and Rollow's (1990) descriptive study provided a systematic analysis of the reform policy's development. They focused on two distinct phases; mobilization, which crated a broad-based reform coalition within the city of Chicago; and formal legislative activities, which shifted the influence to key legislators, party leaders, and organized interest groups. They used the stages lens to suggest that both phases produced reform documents that were similar to the original grassroots intent of the reform, resulting in a new governance system that would be more accountable to parents and the oversight authority that functioned above the school board. Thus, there was consistency across the phases of the process, demonstrating how coalitions develop within a policy subsystem that operates over time. As they concluded, the reform produced a broad-based coalition that survived the political process resulting in greater influence of parents and community in control over crucial school resources.

## SUMMARY

The policy stages typology has been a useful means of identifying key parts of policy processes that provide a focus for structuring analyses. It has led to a number of excellent descriptive studies such as Wong and Rollow's (1990) study. As a theoretical framework to understand policy, however, it is lacking in several ways. Most importantly, the next challenge for researchers using this approach is first to find similarities and differences in the dynamics of events across a number of these types of studies. Second, they can posit causal relations that will lead to the development of stronger theory that explains how these types of reforms develop, as well as how policies move from one stage to another.

## EXERCISES

1. Identify a policy issue. Use the policy framework (Fig. 3.2) presented in the chapter to identify some of the environmental factors, governmental factors, and policymakers' beliefs that influence activity regarding the issue.

2. Assume the role of aide to a state legislator who sends you the following memorandum. Keep in mind that legislators are busy people who respond more warmly to compact, well organized, and direct pieces of paper than to typical scholarly works. "I have just learned that at the next session of the Legislature several proponents of _____(select a policy issue) will initiate a major push for legislation. What I need from you are (1) a review of the background of the proposed legislation (if any exists)—who are the protagonists, what does the record show as to previous legislative intent; (2) a thorough but compact review of the arguments pro and con about the issue; and (3) a statement of optional political positions for me to consider, with rationale for each, including the one you recommend as the preferred position for me to take and why."

3. Select a current policy issue. Compose a short newspaper editorial (300 words or less) taking a particular stance on the issue.

# II

# CONCEPTUAL
# FRAMEWORKS
# AND THEORIES

In the second section of the book, a several conceptual lenses that have been used in studying policy are presented. As suggested in chapter 3, until recently, the most influential ways of studying policy were to examine it at a macro level (i.e., how the political system converts environmental demands to outputs) or as a series of stages (as discussed in the last chapter). As suggested, both approaches have drawn ample criticism. Most importantly, the systems approach examines the behavior of the policy system as [a] therefore, it is not very clear on how value preferences, institutional [ ] ments, and various groups of policy actors contribute to the convers[ion] [of en]vironmental demands and supports into actions and decisions. T[he] stages approach really does not constitute a theory, because it neve[r ] a set of causal variables that influence the process within and [ ] stages. Although it has led to a considerable amount of descripti[ve] [ ] within each of the various stages (e.g., policy development, policy [imple]men[ ] tation), it has not really moved researchers' thinking forward pa[st ] fication of behavior within each stage. Moreover, it does not capture the full range of the policy process over time—instead, generally focusing on one visible, legislative cycle, as opposed to multiple interacting cycles over time.

Previous critiques of the accumulated scholarly work on policy in education (e.g., Boyd, 1988, 1992; Johnson, 2003; Mitchell, 1984) have found the field to be somewhat muddled. Although it has not perhaps lived up to its early promise of creating a "science" of educational policy, certainly we now know considerably more about particular aspects of the policy process. For example, we know more about the nature of the policy process as an unfolding of actions and events (e.g., agenda setting, policy formulation) that lead up to policy decisions. Policy implementation has also received a tremendous amount of attention from researchers. Moreover, accountability has brought a particular interest in policy outcomes from policymakers.

It is also the case, however, that there is some lack of direction. For example, there seems to be no real agreement among educators, policymakers, and researchers on what the pressing policy problems are facing education, the appropriate methods to study them, and who should conduct the research. As chapter 3 notes, the policy process itself seems to be arbitrarily divided into the dynamics of policy activity before formal decisions, the implementation of those policies that make it through the development process, and the assessment of policy impact. In many cases, there are few empirical building blocks for answering important questions. In the past, researchers have generally worked in relative isolation, defining and investigating research problems in their own manner. The format of professional journals often adds to this by publishing articles across a broad range of topics. It may be years, if ever, before someone decides to extend an article and publish it in the same journal. A glance at some of the articles in one journal during the past few years includes achievement gaps due to ethnicity and class, professional development and teacher instruction, charter schools, high school graduation exams, performance-based assessments, whole-school reform, and class size. All of this may suggest the need to prioritize particular types of policy concerns and work on those problems and possible interventions from an empirical standpoint.

Another need is to get new researchers thinking about the conceptual tools they use in their craft. It is often dissatisfaction with traditional paradigms (e.g., they don't answer the questions of interest any longer) that leads researchers to articulate and develop new ones. The frameworks, theories, and models presented in chapters 4 to 7 meet the criteria for a scientific theory reasonably well. These criteria include having a set of concepts and propositions that are broad in scope (so they cover a number of different instances), identify a set of causal variables, and give rise to some testable propositions (Sabatier, 1999). Conceptual lenses should also include sets of factors that policy researchers have found to be previously important, for example, changes in the socioeconomic environment; the impact of institutional arrangements in federalism; conflicting values, interests, and strategies; and temporal considerations.

# Political Culture
# and Policymaking

Understanding the relationship among culture, politics, and decision making is a relatively new area of policy research. As chapter 3 suggests, Schattschneider (1960) noted that conflict is at the center of political life in a democracy. The political system is the means of mediating value conflicts. The political system consists of the institutions, formal structures, constitutional arrangements, and laws that govern the conduct of education. In contrast, the culture is the socially constructed set of assumptions surrounding the political system and influencing its daily operation and outcomes. It is a system of subjective, but socially shared, symbols and meaning including language, myths, rituals, politics, social standing, and economics. Wildavsky (1987) asserted that culture may be conceived of as a theoretical lens from whose "few initial premises many consequences applicable to a wide variety of circumstances may be deduced" (p. 6).

The concept of culture has both an ideological component and a sociological one (White, 1959). The ideological component is comprised of ideological beliefs and values, whereas the sociological component includes customs, institutions, rules, and patterns of behavior. Culture, therefore, is an ideological orientation toward the world that provides a structured set of rules that govern social behavior. A cultural focus on policymaking examines the ideological system and values that underlie it. As Iannaccone (1988) noted, ideas operate as a driving force in American politics, especially in domestic affairs including education. Ideological beliefs help define policy problems and their accepted solutions. A case in point is Americans' prolonged belief in education to resolve the nation's social ills (Tyack, 1991).

## A CULTURAL PERSPECTIVE ON POLICY

The purpose of this chapter is to introduce the cultural lens as a means of examining national and state policymaking activities. A cultural perspective tends to focus our attention on the movement of ideas; that is, how ideas develop, gain support, and become influential over time. Swartz, Turner, and Tuden (1966) suggested the study of politics "is the study of the processes involved in determining and implementing public goals and in the differential achievement and use of power by members of the group concerned with these goals" (p. 7). Ideas form a guide to governmental actions (Fowler, 2000). Isaak (1987) defined ideology as "a fairly coherent set of values and beliefs about the way the social, economic, and political systems should be organized and operated and recommendations about how these values and beliefs should be put into effect" (p. 133). As Iannaccone (1988) argued, ideology provides an analysis of the current situation, a vision of the ideal society, and a plan for bringing society closer to the ideal.

Because fundamental ideological conflicts often recur (Cuban, 1990; Iannaccone, 1977), the closer study of these conflicts and their determinants can help reveal whether patterns exist. To do so requires identifying the dominant cultural ideology (e.g., beliefs, assumptions, traditions, language, and other customs) and values, and understanding how they are translated into policy. As Garms, Guthrie, and Pierce (1978) suggested, "The outcomes of public policy can be predicted to some extent by careful examination of the cultural system in which they are made" (p. 12). Educational policies are explicit expressions of underlying cultural values.

Most commonly, studies using culture as a lens tend to be process oriented and constructivist in nature—that is, they focus on how actors create shared meanings about their roles and their participation in policymaking. This has been referred to as the social construction of policy problems, belief systems, and other frames of reference (Sabatier, 1999). Focusing on process is important in studying policymaking in an historical, or temporal, context. It shifts our emphasis from static systems to the dynamics of change. It focuses our interest on shifting contextual settings (e.g., political, economic, social factors) that influence how groups interact with formal institutions. It also draws our attention to the activities of individuals and groups who are exercising power over time to influence policy action.

As a lens through which to view policy activity, culture works in a number of ways. First, because education is a state function, patterns of activity develop over time that reflect state policymaking preferences (e.g., Benham & Heck, 1994; Garms, Guthrie, & Pierce, 1978; Marshall et al., 1989). State governments have their own unique political traditions. Cultural values may be more directly or indirectly embedded in policies. As Marshall and colleagues suggested, "The ongoing activity of the policy actors is to transform cultural values into policy—to allocate values" (p. 5). These expressions, which become educational policy, guide the behavior and actions of educators. We can track policymaking activities over time to determine what regularities exist.

Second, culture is also relevant to discussions of policy at the national and international levels. American political institutions are part of a larger national culture and socioeconomic system. One way this national cultural orientation is manifested is seen in the historical debate over the influence of the federal government and national cultural norms and values in managing education (Marshall et al., 1989). State governments must react to national influences that are imposed externally. These external forces have been felt across the states in the 1800s in terms of common schools, compulsory education, consolidation of local ward governance systems, and in the 1900s as "Americanization," desegregation, bilingual education, special education, accountability, site-based governance, standards setting, and performance-based assessment, to name a few national trends.

## National Political Culture

Political culture has been defined as the collective beliefs and values of policymakers and citizens about how political institutions and policy processes work, about the role of each institution in the policy process, and the proper rules of the game (Lipsitz, 1986). It is exercised in such institutions as political campaigns, elections, legislatures, courts, and school board meetings. Its products include speeches, laws, court decisions, and policy directives. The concept of political culture provides a set of cognitive and affective indicators that mediate between the environment and structural variables and policy outcomes (Marshall et al., 1989).

Merelman (1984) concluded that there is no single culture or unifying myth that binds American people. Instead, there are a number of ideological principles and values that have shaped American political thinking over time. These principles are heavily embedded in policies. At one time, Puritanism provided an ideological framework that bound together New England society. The formation of a national ideology and the corresponding formal role of education in transmitting cultural principles to the young really began, however, with the establishment of the new government after the United States revolted from Great Britain. The shaping of democracy by the forefathers of the Constitution was an important part of the national political culture of Americans. The founding Americans held several ideological principles to be fundamental to the workings of government (Fowler, 2000).

- individualism—the right of people to pursue their own self-interests and own well-being.
- economic self-interest—the individual's right to act in her or his self-interest in acquiring economic resources without government interference (represented by support for the free-market economic system).

- liberty and personal freedom—the right to pursue self-improvement without government interference. Liberty was an important value underlying the addition of the Bill of Rights. Liberty assumed a structure of institutions and rules that defined rights and duties (Rawls, 1971) which balanced personal freedom.
- equality—the equal right of all citizens to participate in society and the political process. Ensuring due process (as represented in the 5th Amendment) and equal protection under the law to individuals and groups (formalized in the 14th Amendment) regarding issues such as gender equity, civil rights, and appropriate educational opportunity) has been a value often pursued in the courts.
- fraternity, or brotherhood. Developing a sense of community was essential to Jefferson's view of democracy. For example, one way this played out in educational policymaking during the Municipal Reform of the 1890s to 1920s was the creation of a melting pot ideology (or common American identity) for immigrants through education.
- order as a general social principle underlies American society and many educational policies to assure Americans safe schools.

It is useful to examine some of the debates about ideological principles a bit more closely, as the debates represent value positions that recur in the development of policies. Several of these ideological principles were at the core of debates over the proper role of central government versus the rights of individuals (e.g., individualism, economic self-interest, liberty, fraternity, order). In a sense, the Constitution represents a blending of diverse value positions about these ideological principles. At the time the Constitution was being written, Thomas Jefferson and others questioned whether peace and stability in society were best preserved by giving the government greater control over people's lives, or by giving individuals more responsibility and freedom by providing education. The debate was not really about education so much as it was about how people should participate politically in the new country. The new leaders were worried about possible rebellions from various factions creating political chaos (e.g., Shay's rebellion between debtor farmers and city creditors, struggles between abolitionists and slave holders) before the country had a chance to get firmly established.

Jefferson concluded that an educated populace was essential to developing the sense of community that was at the core of a republican democracy. He reasoned that an educated populace would see and act on the common good by placing the welfare of society above the individuals' own self-interests. As he argued, "Educate and inform the whole mass of people. Enable them to see that it is in their interest to preserve peace and order, and they will preserve them.... They are the only sure reliance for the preservation of our liberty" (as cited in Kemmis, 1990, p. 11). Jefferson believed that agriculture was the foundation of a participatory type of democracy. He saw the new nation's expanding territory as ensuring the republican goals of building civic participation in small communities. As long as the frontier was expanding, it encouraged the belief that the future of the nation was in agriculture. Jefferson's view of civic virtue and the need to encourage enlightened participation were partly behind his suggestion that tracts of land should be set aside for schools as the nation expanded westward. This would ensure community-based involvement and smaller governmental units.

Whereas the republican form of democracy placed high value on the engagement of citizens in public life, the Federalist view proposed an elaborate system of governmental checks and balances to minimize instability in society by limiting citizens' voices. As Sullivan (1982) noted, the Federalist position urged abandoning the language of civic virtue. Federalists favored balancing diverse interests by protecting the working of a commercially competitive economy (i.e., by ensuring that the invisible hands of the economy could operate). In this view, individuals could freely pursue their own self-interests with government serving as an umpire of sorts. Under the free market ideal, free exchange leads to efficiency. The Federalist position focused on ensuring fair competition; that is, free and open entry. The free market ideal suggested that government should work to protect certain economic, social, and political norms and rules of conduct against the freely exercised self-interests of individuals. These concepts stemmed from Adam Smith's (1775) *Wealth of Nations*. As Kemmis (1990) concluded, Madison (one of the primary architects of the Federalist view) applied the invisible economic hand, which suggested that the highest good would result from the actions of individuals who were pursuing their self-interest (as opposed to rising above their own self-interest to act for the common good), to the politics of the nation. Ensuring free exchange and balancing political interests provided a justification for laissez-faire capitalism and representative democracy.

The other key to ensuring domestic tranquillity was the vast landscape in the new country. Federalists believed the vastness of the frontier would keep people from developing too much common unity, thereby preventing rebellion (Kemmis, 1990). Madison reasoned that an expanding territory would tend to balance a variety of interests, so that one view could not dominate. In the context of a geographically expanding country rapidly coming under the philosophical view of Manifest Destiny, Madison argued for a dispersed, disconnected citizenry that was kept in check by government.

Eventually, the Constitution institutionalized an elaborate system of checks and balances that strengthened the power of centralized government versus states and individuals—so much so that the Bill of Rights had to be added before the Constitution was rarified. Yet, the debate over how much the federal government should be involved in overseeing the states in various areas (including education) has been debated ever since. In Jefferson's view, the strongest threat to self-government was the potential for shifting away from an agriculturally based society to one based on industry, because people would not meet face to face to solve community problems. Over the next century, however, the procedural democracy won out over participatory democracy, as the United States became an industrial power.

Like Jefferson, Frederick Turner in the late 1800s saw "the existence of an area of free land" as foundational to the nature of American politics. He noted, "The peculiarity of American institutions is the fact that they have been compelled to adapt themselves to the changes of an expanding people—to the changes involved in crossing a continent, in winning a wilderness ..." (as quoted in Kemmis, 1990, p. 26). In 1893, Turner delivered a paper to the American Historical Association in Chicago. He referred to a recent census:

> Up to and including 1880 the country had a frontier of settlement, but at present the unsettled area has been so broken into by isolated bodies of settlement that there can hardly be said to be a frontier line. In the discussion of its extent, its westward movement, etc., it can not, therefore, any longer have a place in the census reports. (as cited in Kemmis, 1990, p. 26)

Turner (1894) went on to suggest: "This brief official statement marks the closing of a great historic movement.... The existence of an area of free land, its continuous recession, and the advance of American settlement westward, explain American development" (p. 1).

The closing of the American frontier in the 1890s coincided with the election of 1896 that pitted the "Populist" agriculturalists (who stressed methods of cooperation in economics and politics) against the consolidated commercial and manufacturing interests that elected McKinley. As Goodwyn (1978) concluded, "A critical cultural battle had been lost by those who cherished the democratic ethos.... The demonstrated effectiveness of the new political methods of mass advertising meant, in effect, that the cultural values of the corporate state were politically unassailable in twentieth-century America" (p. 278).

Importantly, as America changed from an agricultural to an industrial nation, the public sector of government grew to check inequities in the private sector. For example, in 1887, Congress passed the Interstate Commerce Act (which among other things established that the national economy was supreme and therefore states had to subordinate their own economic activities to the national economy), which created a vast new regulatory bureaucracy. This precisely signaled a shift in ideology where governmental bureaucracy became more sovereign, in that it could limit the free choices of individuals. The regulatory role of government was not to choose one preferred way but, rather, to offer a framework of rights—that is, to provide a means for laying out rules and regulations that would help balance individual interests and uphold rights. Many other types of regulations arose in response to checking business interests, for example, protecting the environment from the timber industry, checking air pollution, and resolving water rights issues in the West, to name a few.

## State Political Culture

Although national political culture provides one lens to understand some broad consistencies in the American political system over time, state policy systems have proven more difficult to analyze. As Sachen and Medina (1990) argued, "Policymakers are socialized into a distinctive state policy culture that creates sets of expectations as to appropriate behaviors, rituals, and feasibility of different policy options" (p. 391). Policymakers pursue fundamental political values that can be defined in ways that permit us to view their presence and effect (Wirt & Kirst, 1989). The concept of state political culture implies that some of the underlying variation in state policymaking is due to differing value structures that can be identified in the characteristic actions and behavior of each state. Each state's political culture may be somewhat unique because of local history, but states with certain traditions are likely to pursue certain types of political values.

Political scientists tried to identify alternative cultural ideologies and values that led to policy differences across the United States. For example, Key (1949) noted how the South's cultural emphasis on race had produced distinctive policies and politics. Dye (1966) examined the extent to which political and economic factors affected state policies. Patterson (1968) identified regional differences in attitudes on political polls. Fairbanks (1977) found that religion was related to state policy activity. Marshall and colleagues (1989) applied the concept of political culture to educational policymaking. They identified great variation in scope and intensity of educational policymaking activities across six states (examined in more detail later in the chapter).

## Elazar's Typology of State Political Cultures

Elazar (1970, 1984) developed a typology of three distinctive state political cultures that were useful in explaining differences in states' political behavior. His orientation focused on perceptions the public and policymakers have about what politics is and what is expected from government, the types of people that get involved in government and politics, and the actual way that government is practiced in light of their perceptions. As Elazar (1984) suggested, state political culture is "the set of perceptions of what politics is and what can be expected from government, held by both the general public and the politicians" (p. 12). Researchers have applied this typology on a few occasions with positive results to explain differences in educational policymaking across states. Some states fit more easily into one dominant cultural type than others, however.

In *traditional* political cultures, government's main function is perceived to be maintaining stability and the established order (i.e., traditional patterns). Leadership is provided by a governing elite, with partisanship subordinated to personal ties. Membership in the governing elite tends to come through social and family ties. Resistence to change and elitism discourages widespread political participation in elections (Elazar, 1984). Traditional political cultures are dominant in the South and in regions of the country where Southerners originally settled (Fowler, 2000).

In *moralistic* political cultures, government is viewed as a means for achieving an idealized "good" community or commonwealth through positive action. Moralist culture focuses on public-centered activity (i.e., active role of government, widespread public participation) to attain public good and to advance public interest (Elazar, 1984). For example, governmental bureaucracy (e.g., regulations, civil service) is viewed as a positive agent of the people by ensuring the fair implementation of policies (Fowler, 2000). Moralistic political culture is originally modeled on the New England colonies.

In *individualistic* cultures, government is viewed as a marketplace that responds to diverse public demands. As opposed to a service function of government, states with individualistic cultures rely primarily on the political party as the vehicle for satisfying individual needs. The party machine, based on a complex system of obligations and loyalty is typical of this culture. This view favors economic development and implies that government should not intervene in the private sector such as business, family, and the church.

### Applying the Political Cultural Lens to Examine Differences in State Policymaking

For the state political culture lens to be useful, we should be able to derive a set of propositions about the relationship of political culture to policy activity. A first proposition is that differences in political culture should explain variation in subsequent policy behavior across the states. Tests of Elazar's typology yielded differences in a wide array of state behavior including party competition (Hanson, 1980), legislators' attitudes toward social and economic welfare issues (Welch & Peters, 1980), and the extent of state control of local schools (Wirt, 1980).

More recently, Marshall and colleagues (1989) applied this approach to study how political culture affects state educational policy activity. They proposed that states with different political cultures should produce different educational policy activity. They used Elazar's typology to select the states in their sample and then set out to determine if they could operationalize and measure political cultures in the six states they chose (two of each of the three cultural types). Their preliminary analyses supported the existence of Elazar's three archetypal political cultures; that is, policymakers in each state tended to provide higher responses on items comprising their state's proposed cultural type than on items comprising the other two cultural types. They also determined that those designations fit with historical accounts. As Marshall et al. (1989) concluded,

History has had consequences for the kinds of political systems that evolve in our states. Religious and ethnic strains have generated differences that can be separated by only a state border ... For our purposes these historically rooted differences which led to Elazar's (1984) classification also match (with some looseness) contemporary elites' perceptions of their constituents' attitudes about objects in the political world. Both measures and our constraining tests suggest that there do exist varying state political cultures ... (p. 119)

Importantly, however, Marshall and colleagues (1989) argued that state political culture appears to be more salient to educational policymaking during times when nationwide policy reforms are not being felt. They noted (p. 129) that the explanatory power of state political culture "is limited when all states are swept by specific policy reforms—such as finance—that arise out of currents that are national (Boyd & Kerchner, 1988) and indeed international (Wirt & Harman, 1986)." It may be the case, however, that even within a particular dominant national era (e.g., accountability), states may still pursue different policy paths. For example, some states might pursue school choice as a means to improve educational accountability (i.e., arguing that choice improves accountability by creating competition among schools). In contrast, other states might pursue efficiency (e.g., allocating resources more carefully) or quality (e.g., implementing standards, aligning curriculum and assessment instruments) policy levers.

Lee (1997) also applied Elazar's political culture typology to a state-by-state study of policy enactment activity during the mid-1980s and early 1990s. The 50 states make a useful database that allows some quantitative modeling in attempting to identify possible determinants of state policymaking. Lee reasoned that state implementation of policies was contingent on several factors. First, characteristics of the policy would likely affect policy enactment. For example, policies that are more expensive, complex, and redistributive are less likely to be enacted (Firestone, 1990). Second, the political culture of the state would affect the level of implementation of the policies. Third, if a pattern of activity were found to exist within each state, then policy adoption at one point in time (i.e., 1984) should also affect subsequent adoption at another time (i.e., 1991).

Lee found some support for these hypotheses. First, as proposed, policy cost, complexity, and innovation factors affected the level of state implementation. Low-cost, easy-to-implement, and conventional polices were more likely to be adopted by states. Second, state political culture was also found to affect policy implementation; however, the conclusion had to be qualified. Lee determined that traditionalistic states were able to implement regulatory policies that were common in the early 1980s more frequently. There was no specific implementation pattern found for moralistic and individualistic states. Finally, between 1984 and 1991, Lee found that state activism in education reform changed; that is, the types of policies implemented shifted from input-oriented regulations to content-driven (i.e., curriculum) reforms. In this new environment, some of the moralistic and individualistic states seemed to advance further than did traditionalist states in terms of policy implementation. At the same time, Lee also found that as the decade progressed, reform activity became more widespread throughout the nation. During these periods, there may be less patterned state policy activity.

## Describing Core Policy Values

A second proposition derived from the political cultural lens is that different political cultures should pursue different core ideological values. In turn, the pursuit of alternative core policy values should lead to different policy outcomes. Kaufman (1956) described three social values that were present in the policies developed at the state level (technical competence, democratic legitimacy, and organizational efficiency). These value preferences were referred to by Marshall and colleagues (1986, 1989) as quality, equity, and efficiency. Garms and colleagues (1978) identified a fourth value preference that was basic to the American political culture—liberty (or choice). Each has its roots in basic political ideology that helped shape the nation.

*Choice* is perhaps the most basic American public value. Liberty is one of the underlying principles of democracy and individual rights. The Constitution suggests that Americans' rights to self-determination, choice of religion, and freedom of choice must be preserved, and government must not intrude on citizens' basic freedoms. Policies to promote school choice is one obvious manifestation of this policy value. Ensuring the rights of citizens to choose to send their children to private or religious schools is another. Site-based management is third example of choice as a policy value position. As Rollow and Bryk (1993) argued, site-based management in Chicago in the late 1980s represented a type of democratic localism, in that it was a new form of institutional arrangement to apply to a wide range of human services. It replaced the traditional bureaucratic control of schools with local school politics directed at promoting greater engagement of school professionals with their local communities.

*Quality* as a policy value suggests that government actions should enhance citizens' quality of life. This value position is at the core of American way of life, in that providing free, public education is perceived as a basic responsibility of government. Many of the school reforms since the mid-1980s directly address this value position—that is, upgrading education is viewed as a means of increasing people's quality of life and as a means of strengthening the economy (e.g., access to better paying jobs, addressing the need for more technical training required in an age of information). Examples of educational policies expressing quality are to develop standards by which resources are to be allocated, increase training for teachers, set higher academic standards, or align the curriculum with assessment procedures.

*Efficiency* provides for either economic control or accountability. Efficiency policies ensure that standards are met. Efficiency also applies to the government's role in creating and maintaining order; for example, mandating that superiors have authority to develop and implement policies or to regulate potential inequities. Examples include maximizing gains to optimize program performance while minimizing costs, making programs more cost effective, improving the use of tax dollars, implementing a year-round school schedule to reduce overcrowding.

*Equity* focuses on ensuring equal opportunity. Another principle underlying American democracy was that the role of government should ensure citizens' equal rights. To do so often requires government to guard against inequities that develop in society. An example is ensuring equal opportunity. Policymakers have often used education to further this policy value. Hence, the government's role has been to create laws and programs that redress inequities. It is often a remedy approach—equalizing the playing field (opportunity) as opposed to the outcomes. Examples of equity policies include allocating resources that provide for the education of children with special needs, redressing identified wrongs (e.g., discrimination) equalizing educational resources, or ensuring broader participation in decision making (Marshall et al., 1989).

### Marshall, Mitchell, and Wirt's Study

After differentiating states according to their political cultures, Marshall and her colleagues (1989) wanted to determine the extent to which the core policy values (i.e., efficiency, equity, quality, choice) would be apparent within seven educational policy domains that they identified (e.g., finance, personnel, program, governance, curriculum) and whether any specific patterns existed. To examine whether the core values were present in educational policies, they content analyzed the educational codes that were in place in each state at the time they conducted the study. They reasoned that written educational codes would reflect these basic core values because they represent the allocation of resources to preferred ends.

Marshall et al. (1989) first developed working definitions of each value position. They then matched these definitions against the actual wording of the educational codes in two of the six states in their sample (i.e., two states with different political cultures). For example, an item in a statute that required teachers to hold a certificate of qualification granted by the state would reflect the value position of quality. A statute requiring a state testing program for students would also reflect quality. Ensuring due process rights of employees would be an example of an equity policy.

Next, the researchers wanted to determine whether these value positions would be treated differently by alternative political cultures; that is, would some value positions be favored over others? They proposed that different configurations of these values would mark differences in state culture, although they reasoned that quality would tend to dominate across all the states because of the national impact of works such as *A Nation At Risk* (1983) that focused attention on the lack of quality in public education. And finally, they wanted to determine whether or not the values had a type of historical sequence.

First, Marshall et al. (1989) found that the educational codes indeed reflected the four identified value positions. Second, they found that different value positions dominated in different states. In the two example states, they found that efficiency policies dominated, whereas quality and equity were about equal. Choice policies were the least favored. There were some variations across the two states as well—enough for them to conclude that the configuration of the codes across the two states was different. The two states also differed in the core values pursued across the seven educational policy domains. For example, one state favored an equity approach to finance, whereas the other favored a more efficiency-laden approach. In contrast, the second state used a more equity-based approach to personnel than did the first state. This finding suggested the values were distributed unevenly across the two states. More specifically, as opposed to a blanket approach to all the educational policy domains, these states used the core values differently across the identified policy domains.

Across the six states, and the full range of programs within each of the seven policy domains, Marshall and her colleagues found substantial correlation between core values and policy activity. For example, there were sharp distinctions in how the states dealt with school finance issues. Some states favored equalization of resources and an overall increase in state funding for education, whereas others favored reducing restrictions on local budgets and improving the use of existing tax dollars. More specifically, West Virginians favored an equity and quality perspective, whereas Arizonans favored a choice and efficiency approach. Marshall et al. (1989) concluded that some value positions tend to conflict (e.g., quality and equity, equity and choice), whereas others may reinforce (e.g., quality and efficiency, equity and efficiency). These inherent tensions in the value positions themselves created disputes over policymakers' efforts to resolve educational problems.

With respect to the extent that political culture might account for these findings, the researchers' results had to be qualified. First, there was a strong national influence on policy values that cut across all six states. They confirmed that at the time of the study (early 1980s), quality was the dominant concern of state policy leaders. Second, this attention to quality was linked to the levels of attention given to each of the seven policy domains they had identified. So, for example, where states ranked quality as the most strongly embraced value position, there was also a strong tendency to rank school finance as the most prominent policy mechanism. Hence, certain state value positions were related to certain policy mechanisms.

Third, they found considerable variation across the states in terms of the other core value positions (i.e., equity, efficiency, and choice). This suggested to the researchers that state political culture might also help explain policy activity, but only when nationwide policy reform was not present in that area (p. 125). Yet, state culture did explain certain kinds of educational priorities. For example, traditional political culture emphasizes elite dominance and a distrust of school professionals. There was evidence supportive of the hypothesis that legislatures in traditionalist states gave more attention to policies that would override educators' professional judgments (e.g., student testing and program definition).

Fourth, Marshall and colleagues (1989) concluded that although there was evidence of a state political culture in some policy areas, there was also considerable variation in policymakers' personal beliefs within each state. These differences among policymakers within each state were often played out in policy subsystems among those with differing influence in policy decision-making processes. They noted a lack of real state "cultural vision" except in the necessity to use power to implement their policy values—that is, policymakers did not pursue an integrated agenda of singular core values at points in time. Hence, they identified a series of subcultures (e.g., insiders, near circle, far circle, sometimes players) based on their relative influence in the policy process. They noted that it was the structure of the subcultures, vying for a impact in the process, that largely determined what core values were pursued within each state and in what policy domains they were pursued.

Finally, the presence of national policy values on top of state preferences suggested to the researchers that there may be a policy sequence in the pursuit of these core values in policymaking. Quality is often the first value sought in any new era of education policy, when the political will arises to improve an educational service for the public. On a national level, we see this played out over a 150-year period. For example, Horace Mann strove for free public education as a means of uplifting citizens economically. To implement the universal mass education policy, however, required policies rooted in efficiency to use resources effectively. Toward this goal came the public financing of education and compulsory attendance laws. The logical end, therefore, was the Municipal Reform, which put power in the hands of business elites (i.e., within small, efficient local boards of education) with superintendents overseeing school operations as scientific educational managers. Efficiency then seemed to dominate through the 1920s and 1930s (i.e., dealing with educating the children of immigrants and bringing them into the American way of life).

Equity goals then arise when a gap develops between desired standards and actual conditions for specific groups. This creates calls for additional funding to bring that group up to standard. Equity, beginning with the Brown Decision in 1954, seemed to dominate the policy agenda during the 1960s and 1970s. Quality also was at the root of reports about how America's schools were slipping in the 1980s and early 1990s.

Marshall and her colleagues (1989) suggested that choice is often present in various ways throughout the policy sequence—in terms of guaranteeing rights to choose school settings. When they measured these values across six states in the 1980s, choice was a distant last in value preference. It is likely, however, that over the past decade, choice has become a more viable value preference for reforming schools (i.e., choice schools/open enrollment, charter schools, voucher programs). Lately, much has been centered on increasing parents' choice in education.

As they concluded, differing state histories of resources and group demands create different experiences, so differences in educational policy are to be expected. These differences are evident in how education is financed across the 50 states, as well as in the amount of local control that exists. Because of the nature of democracy, differences in value preferences are negotiated at the local, state, and national levels. The various policymaking arenas are designed to accommodate such diversity and conflict. Marshall et al. (1989) suggested that the cultural frame does not offer a single, encompassing explanation of policymaking. Rather, it provides possibilities for understanding how historical traditions, cultural values, individuals' preferences, and the structure of policy elites themselves may lead to different types of meaning. It opens up the examination of the relations among the various aspects of the policymaking phenomenon—as opposed to the nature of the phenomenon itself (Marshall et al., 1989).

## Benham and Heck's Case Study in Hawai'i

Maenette Benham and I (1994) applied Marshall and colleagues' (1989) work on political culture to a single-state, longitudinal case study. As opposed to studying political culture in multiple states at a single point in time, we wanted to study policymaking processes longitudinally within the context of one state to determine what core values were pursed, who the major players were in policy decision making, and whether there would be policy regularities that would emerge across time. The fundamental relationship between education and the political and social order suggested using a longitudinal orientation for understanding how broader changes in cultural values and political ideology may impact the schools.

From the early days of the common schools, communities recognized that education played a powerful role in the socialization of children. The public and private schools have always been potentially important instruments of political and social indoctrination in their replication of broader social class structures. In this first study, we focused on identifying who the influential policy groups were and what core values (choice, efficiency, equity, quality) they pursued over time across the seven policy domains Marshall et al. (1989) identified. We selected three periods of political change covering approximately 150 years of public school history in Hawai'i. We reasoned that during turbulent periods, the chances that educational change would be manifested were greater. These periods included the arrival of the missionaries in the 1830s, the overthrow of the Hawaiian monarchy (and subsequent occupation by the United States) beginning in 1893, and the period of social change after World War II (culminating in statehood in 1959). Importantly, each turbulent period produced a new set of educational laws that could be analyzed across the seven policy domains to determine the policy preferences that were embedded in the statutes.

With its historical traditions in agriculture (e.g., sugar cane, pineapple), plantation social organization, and consistently low ranking among the states in political participation, Hawai'i has elements of a traditional political culture. With its one-party politics (i.e., there had not been a Republican governor since Hawai'i became a state in 1959 until this past election) and preference for obligation, Hawai'i also has elements of individualistic political culture (Elazar, 1984, p. 136). Hawai'i represents an interesting case study in educational politics because of its unique history as an independent nation (overthrown illegally by the United States) and its historical traditions in public schooling that are among the oldest in the western United States. Public schools date from 1831. The notion of common schools came with the missionaries in the 1830s at the same time common schools were taking hold in New England. Conflicts over educational purposes between private "select" schools (for the children of the ruling elite) and public "common" schools (for Native Hawaiians and children of immigrants) date from the initial arrival of the missionaries. Thus, similar educational traditions exist between Hawai'i and New England states—the background of religious education (as various religious groups fought to dominate policy in Hawai'i) and considerable influence of private schools—and between Hawai'i and other regions—how to integrate large numbers of immigrants who arrived during the 19th century and early 20th century, cultural and language diversity, formally segregated schooling.

We constructed three historical cases by content analyzing a variety of data sources including archival data, documents, historical texts, and actual statutes for the core policy values embedded in them. We then compared the three case studies to determine whether policy regularities existed across time (see chaps. 8 and 9 for details on this type of design and analysis). Each state's political culture may be somewhat unique due to local history, but we thought that a state with a strong tradition of centralized control (and roots in traditional and individualist political culture) would be likely to exert a more forceful role over time and, hence, pursue certain types of political values. More specifically, it would likely pursue efficiency, which is at the root of policy elites' thinking about the usefulness of governmental bureaucracy.

We reached a number of conclusions about policy regularities. First, over time, Hawai'i's policy making could be described as rule by elite (i.e., policy insiders such as the governor, key cabinet members, and legislators) with limited participation of others. Second, the core value of efficiency dominated most policy domains across time, with considerable attention also given to quality. Third, over time, the policy domains of finance and governance drew the most attention. This is consistent with meritocratic cultures that pursue combinations of quality and efficiency (Marshall et al., 1989). As one of the first school public school laws of 1842 suggested, "It is not proper that all teachers should be paid alike. A very wise teacher who is exceedingly laborious in his business, and has many pupils, should be paid a high price, while he who is less wise and less laborious in his business should be paid a lower price" (cited in Benham & Heck, 1994, p. 434). This reasoning is similar to the current notion of providing monetary incentives for teachers as a policy lever to increase accountability (efficiency) and improve school quality.

Finally, the policy process was mostly closed—tending to be privatized by the controlling elite (i.e., Hawai'i still ranks about last among the 50 states in terms of grassroots political participation). Efficiency supported Hawai'i's growing economic concerns over competing with Western nations and institutionalized a clearly defined social hierarchy that was present in the early debates over the common and select schools. Quality and efficiency are reinforcing policy values because one seeks a standard to be applied across the board, whereas the other (rooted in rationality of the bureaucracy) seeks the most efficient and effective means of realizing the desired quality end (Marshall et al., 1989). Therefore, the discussion often concerns the most efficient or effective means to reach the end, but there is little disagreement over either the efficiency goal itself or the quality end. This historical tradition explains the current reluctance of Hawai'i to give up the centralized control of its one school district, although debate often centers around other structures that might be more efficient and effective. For example, whether to create seven local school boards, or 15 local district complexes was recently debated during a legislative session, but ultimately both bills died in favor of maintaining the current one district that everyone agrees is not producing a quality education for students.

Policymaking over time can be seen as providing a system of controls (fiscal, regulatory, ideological) designed to shape and limit schools' behavior in ways that reflect culturally based values (Benham & Heck, 1994). Differences in states' control reflect these underlying differences in values. Hawai'i's school policies "have resulted from partisan political activity pursuing efficiency that consequently focuses on the policy domains of finance (efficient allocation) and governance (efficient control). The rhetoric that emerged during each of the periods resulted in educational policies that were symbolic expressions of these values and preferences" (p. 444).

In a second study (1998), we added one more socially turbulent period (i.e., the influence of Native Hawaiian efforts toward gaining sovereignty since the 1970s) and focused more specifically on the impact of these policies over time on Native Hawaiians. We wondered why, despite very different local political history, there were similarities between the educational history of Hawai'i and other parts of the United States. We also wanted to examine the interplay between national cultural ideologies and state political culture in determining educational policy over time.

There has been considerable agreement among scholars, especially since the 1970s, about what some of these national cultural ideologies were (e.g., Adams, 1988; Banks, 1988; Tamura, 1994). Adams (1988) concluded that at least three broad cultural values defined educational policy toward Native Americans (and immigrants) during the 1800s and early 1900s. These formed a mutually reinforcing system with public education as a primary vehicle used to assimilate other cultures into the American culture. The first of these was religious ideology based on teaching students to read the Bible and elevating them spiritually through teaching about individual salvation and morality.

The second was the acceptance of a type of cultural or social evolution from savage to civilization. As Jefferson suggested, a journey beginning in the Rocky Mountains to the eastern seacoast would "in fact [be] equivalent to a survey, in time, of the progress of man from the infancy of creation to the present day" (as cited in Pearce, 1965, p. 155). Policymakers at the time believed that native cultures would either die out because of their cultural inferiority or would be assimilated into White culture (Adams, 1988). They concluded that schools could be used to bridge the inherent inferiority of native cultures in one generation—as opposed to what might take many generations biologically.

The third ideological belief was Manifest Destiny, which provided a rationale for taking lands and assimilating native cultures as the United States expanded westward across the continent and the Pacific Ocean. It was in the name of raising the natives spiritually and helping them evolve upward from savages to civilized participants in a democracy that justified taking and controlling their lands (Adams, 1988). Policymakers in Jefferson's time reasoned that native cultures had too much land for their specific needs as civilized farmers (Adams, 1988). They reasoned that roaming over the lands to hunt was not as desirable as owning the land, as when one farms a particular tract of land. On the other hand, the forefathers had plenty of civilization but were in need of land (Adams, 1988).

In this study, we used institutional theory to examine the interplay between these three larger cultural ideologies and local educational policy in Hawai'i over time. Because we were interested in how the state educational political activity responded to these broad cultural values, we traced the existence of the three broad cultural ideologies in Hawai'i's schools over a 150-year period. Once again, we content analyzed documents, archival records, and laws. We constructed four separate case studies from these data. Then we compared the case studies to determine whether there were policy regularities present across time.

We reached several additional conclusions in this study. First, we traced the three cultural ideologies outlined by Adams (1988) as they spread from the continental United States across the Pacific to the Hawaiian Islands (i.e., religious education, centralization and control of education by business elites, assimilation of Native Hawaiians and immigrant children). These larger cultural ideologies were present despite local political and social conditions that were unique in Hawai'i. For example, we noted that the centralization of schooling at the turn of the 20th century (the Municipal Reform) was also present in Hawai'i. The missionaries' beliefs and unfolding federal policy toward native cultures and other colonized people were central to institutionalizing a social hierarchy in the state's schools. This culminated in the creation of private schools, "English Standard" public schools (i.e., where students had to speak English at an accepted level to be admitted), and regular public schools (i.e., for the children of plantation workers) by the early 1900s. Moreover, instruction in Hawaiian, which had been encouraged during the early to mid-1800s as a way of acculturating students to the Bible, was officially outlawed in 1896.

Second, we found that over time, shifting amalgamations of elite groups defined and refined traditional Euro-American values (e.g., Protestant work ethic, individual ownership of land, assimilation to a melting pot) that influenced cultural boundaries and corresponding social and educational priorities. Missionaries set out to translate the Bible in native languages. Public schools sought to replace Hawaiian traditions, beliefs, and behaviors, with one Christian god, Calvinistic ethics, and Puritan behavior.

Third, institutional structures were created within education (i.e., social hierarchy of schooling) that allowed the implementation of these widely endorsed values. For example, the missionaries managed to move education out of the hands of Native monarchical rule and into the domain of the growing economic authority. The pursuit of efficiency as a policy goal ensured that schools were tightly regulated with respect to finance and held accountable to a prescribed school curriculum. Similarly, policies to track Native Hawaiian children and other immigrant children into remedial programs in separate schools began soon after contact with the American missionaries. This social differentiation remained within the public schools until the last vestiges of school segregation were removed with the 1960 graduation at the final English Standard school.

Fourth, the debates over Native Hawaiian issues (e.g., education, political sovereignty, health and welfare) can be placed within a larger set of conflicts and relationships among the federal government and its policies toward Native Americans, the states, and individual Native American groups over such issues as illegally acquired lands, beliefs about governance, sovereignty and self-determination, economic and human resources, and cultural status (Benham & Heck, 1998). The relationship of Native Hawaiians to the federal government similarly evolved over a period of years, driven by changes in federal policy toward native groups. From an initial position of independent sovereigns, the relationship evolved to a trustee and ward relationship. The primary intent was the dispossession of their lands after which the effort was made to acculturate them into the dominant culture through education. With respect to both the federal and state government, Native Hawaiians have had difficulty gaining greater self-determination. What makes these evolving relationships so fascinating is that they are at the core of democratic ideals long held as uniquely American. They help define how people will participate in and benefit from society.

## SUMMARY

The existence of policy ideals over time further suggests a more universal question that policy analysts may ask: "What is the relationship between political culture and educational policy?" Choices about analytic lenses definitely influence how one views the policymaking process. This is important because policy is an applied, practical activity. It is not only essential to present theoretical discourse that outlines the conceptual lenses and methodological processes through which to evaluate politics and educational policymaking processes, but the outcome and impact of the policy cannot be missed. A cultural perspective appears to be another useful means of understanding the policymaking process. The process of defining this relationship through frames provided by strong theory to analyze policy trends will temporally enable analysts to understand more clearly the supports or barriers to current policy actions. The concept of state political culture represents an evolving set of norms about the rules of the educational policy process. The concept can be used to understand how policy problems and dilemmas are resolved.

Policy values exist across a number of policy domains (e.g., program, finance, organization and governance, personnel, curriculum, facilities). Whether it is characterized as privatized and limited or socialized and participatory, political culture appears to impose rules and restrictions on what reforms will be proposed and implemented. As Marshall and colleagues (1989) noted, preferences for particular value positions lead to different types of behavior. For example, equity-oriented states endorse equalization funding. States preferring quality might embrace a finance approach focused on directing state revenues to particular school functions (Marshall et al., 1989). In personnel, an efficiency-oriented state would favor accountability, an equity-oriented one might favor professional development, a quality-oriented one might pass laws on training and certification, and a choice-oriented one might broaden job options through redefinition of roles and responsibilities. They also produce tensions, for example, choice versus equity. Choice favors individualism, whereas equity favors ensuring equal opportunity for individuals and groups.

Thus, the choices that policymakers have exercised over time affect how the game is played in today's educational arenas. Conflicts between these values produce policy dilemmas—for example, pursuing political equity (equal opportunity) versus individualism (enhancing choice). Another might be pursuing equity (from democratic ideals) versus economic elitism (i.e., garnering the most resources for oneself). This conflict came together in the 1970s when people had to choose whether to live in the suburbs (driven by economic elitism) and have their children bused for mandated school integration.

## EXERCISES

1. Identify a couple policy issues or recent educational policies. What value positions seem to underlie various positions taken toward them?

2. Marshall, Mitchell, and Wirt (1989) proposed a model of state educational policymaking power and influence comprised of three rings (see chap. 3). At the center are policy insiders (the most influential players), then near circle players (those with high influence, such as interest groups), and finally, far circle players (those who influence but are not crucial). Attached to this last ring are sometimes players and forgotten (or marginalized) players. Develop a similar model of policy influence in your state; that is, who are the insiders, near circle, far circle, sometime players, and often forgotten players?

3. What are some of the strengths of the cultural approach to studying policy versus its limitations?

# Chapter 5

# Punctuated-Equilibrium Theory and the Advocacy Coalition Framework

One challenge for researchers has been to explain or predict the unfolding of ideas, events, and actions that lead to policy decisions. Both of the approaches presented in this chapter, punctuated-equilibrium theory and the advocacy coalition framework, are well suited to studying how these processes evolve over considerable amounts of time. Punctuated equilibrium is a term referring to the tendency of policymaking to be generally incremental over long periods of time—punctuated with short periods of time where major policy change takes place (Baumgartner & Jones, 1993). This type of policy change often takes decades to track, as ideas move in and out of the government's policy agenda in our federalist system. In contrast, the advocacy coalition approach draws more attention to the efforts of numerous, competing groups to influence the policy development process over time by working within a particular policy domain or subsystem. Although both approaches focus on the movement of ideas and values over time, they differ most in terms of the relative importance of the general public versus policy elites—more specifically, punctuated-equilibrium focuses on the potential of the audience to become involved in policy conflicts.

Punctuated-equilibrium theory and the advocacy coalition framework focus attention on the historical or temporal context and how this contributes to patterns of policy activity that exist over time (Sabatier, 1999). They are concerned with ideas, value conflicts, negotiation, compromise, and resultant changes as more normal conditions of society (Lewellen, 1992). They pay particular attention to the manners in which groups become mobilized to pursue solutions to particular problems, devise remedies, and secure the adoption of policies in legislatures or school boards. In a democracy, the political system is a means for mediating value conflicts. As

101

Easton (1965) noted, politics is a mechanism for deciding who will get what resources or benefits from the system. Disagreements over what types of educational goals and values to pursue grow out of philosophical conflicts over the nature and goals of society, who should have power, and the proper role of government within society (Fowler, 2000).

Such deeper conflicts over who should govern and what values they should pursue may present unresolvable dilemmas for policymakers because they represent fundamental tensions in American government. Not only do these core ideological conflicts appear to recur on governmental policy agendas periodically, but features of the mechanism for dealing with them, the federalist system itself (with its separation of powers, multiple arenas, and resulting entry points for policy actors), may actually add to the controversial nature of these conflicts. As theorists have suggested, these types of conflicts appear resolved only to the point where they are compromised and redefined within the dominant political doctrine of the era (Cuban, 1990; Iannaccone, 1977). This is an important point to emphasize for it suggests that ideological trends (e.g., accountability, efficiency, individualism, choice) are a central consideration in understanding why certain types of policy issues (e.g., reforming the public education system) recur periodically—that is, the issue may reappear on the policy agenda for very different ideological reasons.

Downs (1972) pointed out three decades ago that the attention cycle of a policy issue crisis follows a relatively predictable pattern. A problem develops over a long period of time, largely unnoticed by the public. Then comes public discovery, usually triggered by some key event. After discovery, which often leads to publicity and a flurry of policy rhetoric, incremental programs—that are less disturbing to the system (e.g., lengthening the school year, upgrading standards, tightening up on assessment, providing a greater range of schooling choices)—may be created to remedy what are in fact deeply rooted structural problems. This suggests that change within the political arena is virtually constant, even though the wider system may be relatively stable.

In their analysis of efforts to reform the American educational system, Tyack and Cuban (1995) concluded that despite considerable debate and controversy over reforming the public education system, educational innovation has been more gradual and incremental. Waves of immigration during the 1800s and early 1900s contributed to public school compulsory attendance laws and child labor laws. Compulsory education laws followed the expansion of public education throughout the states beginning in the middle 1800s. By the turn of the century, child labor laws ensured that children were in school instead of toiling in factories. These helped further the ideological shift from private to mass public education, as well as subsequent attempts to Americanize students in the schools. The administrative progressives looked at rising enrollments and graduation rates, longer school years, larger school districts, growing per-pupil expenditures, and increasing differentiation in programs (i.e., kindergarten, junior high school, and then middle school) as evidence of success. During these times, reforms that were structural add-ons appeared to have the best chance of being incorporated into the existing system (Tyack & Cuban, 1995).

Whereas this regularity describes the policy system when there is relative agreement over the nature of solutions (e.g., lengthen the school year), at other times, policy seems to diverge greatly from past patterns. Less frequently, Tyack and Cuban (1995) observed that longer periods of incremental change were followed by short bursts where policy activity seemed to change direction more dramatically. One example of this latter type of change that is frequently examined was the Municipal Reform of the 1890s, which fairly quickly, and dramatically, changed the governance structure of education in the nation's cities (Plank, Scotch, & Gamble, 1996; Tyack & Cuban, 1995). To accomplish this goal, reformers enlisted the support of business and professional elites. There was considerable debate about the needed reforms. Some urban politicians fought to preserve the ward boards. Rural citizens fought consolidation of school districts. For the most part, despite the fact that the local political conditions and strategies were quite different, the governance reforms adopted were similar among the cities (Plank et al., 1996; Tyack, 1991).

Political ideology and practice may exert a major transformational influence within the political system once critical levels of support are reached (Iannaccone, 1977; Morgan, 1986; Schattschneider, 1960). At these relatively infrequent times, concern about public education becomes more widespread and intense, such that it becomes more of a national issue, debated in policy circles, and producing reform advocates who find mass audiences (Tyack & Cuban, 1995). Punctuated-equilibrium theory attributes the transformational influence to the potential for audience involvement (Schattschneider, 1960), whereas advocacy coalition theory attributes this influence to coalitions among policy elites. Trying to understand the dynamics that promote stability versus change represents a major goal of these two research lenses.

## PUNCTUATED-EQUILIBRIUM THEORY

Punctuated-equilibrium (PE) theory is concerned with explaining the relationship between policy processes that are rooted in stability and incrementalism and those occasional processes that produce large-scale departures from the past (Schattschneider, 1960; True, Jones, & Baumgartner, 1999). Changes in policy activity can occur in American policymaking as public understandings of existing problems change, even if most of the time governmental programs continue as they have previously done (see True et al., 1999 for further discussion).

PE theory emphasizes the dynamics of two parts of the process leading up to governmental policy decisions; issue definition and agenda setting.

As True and colleagues (1999) noted, when issues are defined during public discourse in different ways, and when they rise and fall in the public agenda, existing policies can either be reinforced or questioned. Reinforcement tends to create support for small changes only (i.e., incrementalism), whereas constant questioning creates opportunities for dramatic changes in policy outcomes. Although agenda setting and policymaking often proceed smoothly with only small accommodations, they are also torn by significant departures from the incremental past (Baumgartner & Jones, 1993; Iannaccone, 1977; Wong & Rollow, 1990). Building on Redford's (1969) and Schattschneider's (1960) insights about conflict within the American federalist system, Baumgartner and Jones (1993) analyzed a number of policy cases over time and found that (1) policymaking makes both leaps and undergoes periods of stability as conflicts over policy issues emerge on and recede from the public agenda; (2) this tendency toward punctuated equilibria is exacerbated by American political institutions; and (3) policy images play a critical role in expanding issues beyond the control of specialists and special interests that serve as policy insiders or monopolies. These conclusions form the major tenets of the theory.

**Understanding Political Conflict**

At the center of PE theory is the concept of political conflict. Since Schattschneider's (1957, 1960) groundbreaking work on political conflict and change in the American democracy, researchers have stressed how difficult it is to get new ideas into the established policymaking system. Conflicts represent debates over ideology and values. American political institutions tend to be conservatively designed to resist change efforts. Because formal governmental institutions cannot consider all of the policy issues in front of them simultaneously, conflicts over policy issues are generally waged within policy subsystems that consist of one or more coalitions of individuals with an interest and expertise in the policy issue under consideration. The nature of subsystem politics is typically incremental (True et al., 1999). In contrast to these incremental political activities, it takes considerable conflict, commitment, strategy, and effort toward mobilization for major policy changes to take place. At these times, debate over policy issues expand in scope and intensity, become visible, and reach the macropolitical level (e.g., legislative or executive branches). These mobilizations appear to occur periodically with the result of changing established interests. Schattschneider argued that this mobilization is related to issue expansion and contraction—that is, the socialization or privatization of conflict.

As Schattschneider (1957) noted, "the dynamics of politics has its origin in strife" (p. 935). The process and outcomes of politics depend on four dimensions that shape conflict. The first is the *scope* of conflict; that is, who and how many become involved in the conflict? When participants are added to the conflict, it tends to change the balance between combatants and alters the outcomes. Conflicts in democracies are potentially very contagious. Each consists of a few individuals who are actively engaged at the center and the audience that is attracted to the issue or debate. It is the potential for audience involvement that determines the outcome of the conflict—that is, it is determined by the extent to which the audience becomes involved.

One aspect of political strategy involves managing the scope of the conflict. The scope of conflict is affected to the extent the conflict is privatized, or settled without the intervention of public authority. For example, it may be resolved through economic competition, through negotiations, or through private sanctions. Because the combatants in private conflicts are likely unequal in strength, it is likely that the most powerful special interests prefer this manner of settling conflicts. They can dictate the outcome as long as it remains privatized. Conflicts can be managed by keeping them invisible and behind closed doors. The best time to manage conflicts is before they start, because once they get started, they may have the tendency to spread to the audience (Schattschneider, 1960). Weaker forces tend to want to socialize the conflict (i.e., mobilize support), because it is likely to change the balance of power. Because participation in government is relatively easy in a democracy, as Schattschneider (1960) noted, this "flight to government is perpetual" (p. 40). Some American ideals support the privatization of conflict—free enterprise, localism, individualism, and privacy. Others support socialization of conflict—equity, equal protection of the laws, justice, liberty, free speech, and civil rights. Democracy itself is a great source for socializing conflict because it allows the public to enter into every conflict it wants to enter. These forces tend to invite outside intervention and form the basis of appeals to the public for redress of private disputes.

Similarly, debates about the role of government at each level, federal versus state, centralization versus decentralization, can be seen as controversies about the scope of conflict. Because of overlapping boundaries, policy contestants can move freely from one level of government to another in an effort to find the level at which they may best try to get what they want (Schattschneider, 1960). This is the manner in which weaker forces try to socialize conflict. As Schattschneider noted, this is because government is never far away when a conflict breaks out.

The second dimension that shapes conflict is *visibility*. Because political systems cannot consider all of the issues in front of them simultaneously, policy subsystems are one mechanism that allows a tremendous number of issues to be considered within their own communities of experts (True et al., 1999). Often, this occurs out of the public eye. This type of routine activity favors incremental adjustments due to bargaining among interests. Some issues regularly draw attention—the economy is one of the major ones, and education is also one that draws considerable attention. Because educational issues are more often out in public discourse and have a long tradition of leading to reform-minded policies, they are more likely to draw heightened interest (e.g., from media, from policymakers). Issues that are more visible are more likely to cause controversy. They may also draw the wider audience's interest (e.g., media, public opinion polls). Therefore, because of visibility they may have a better chance of making it to the government's policy agenda.

A third dimension shaping conflict is *intensity*. American politics typically assumes public indifference on most issues. People may feel more intensely, however, about certain issues. These can include foreign policy, human rights, economic policy, and the nation's schools. These conflicts (e.g., student busing, school prayer) are fought with greater intensity.

The final dimension is the *direction* of the conflict. Conflicts arise that divide people into different factions, parties, and other subgroups. Importantly, however, these conflicts are not equal. Some conflicts displace others because they are more visible and intense. People must choose which battles to fight, and hence, the lines of conflict are drawn around high-priority issues. Those on each side of major conflicts tend to consolidate, even if they differ on lesser issues. This tends to lead to stability in politics.

The dimensions of conflict are related—that is, more highly visible and intense conflicts tend to shape the direction policy takes. Managing conflict concerns the strategies policy actors use to restrict (i.e., isolate or localize the tension on the existing decision-making system) or enlarge the conflict (i.e., spread the conflict so it is felt throughout the system). At these times private conflicts managed by a few within a policy subsystem may find their way into the more public policy arenas. Often, the opposition seeks to substitute the conflicts, by advancing other issues, raising their intensity and visibility, and splitting the dominant alliance. The substitution of conflicts alters the scope, and it may attract different people into it by shifting the direction. Once conflict intensifies, it is more difficult to manage because the audience may become involved. As conflict ascends, systems dynamics (random events with nonlinear effects) may also contribute to the mix between actors, conflicts, and strategies.

**Policy Images**

Policy images also compete for public attention. Policy images are mixtures of information and emotion. When a single image of a policy issue is widely supported (e.g., the Municipal Reform), it usually suggests a policy monopoly (True et al., 1999). In contrast, however, where there is more disagreement about how to pursue a policy problem, competing groups may adopt different sets of policy images. For example, pursuing privatization of educational services, open enrollment, vouchers, site-based management, and educational standards are all policy images about how to increase educational outcomes. These different policy images are important not only to issue definition and redefinition in policymaking, but also to the processes by which the policies are handled (i.e., within a subsystem or out in a more public policy arena). New policy images may attract new participants, which can lead to greater mobilization. If a particular policy image is stopped in one policy arena, it may achieve more success in another. This is also a part of the strategy of dealing with political conflict. Policy images may recur for different purposes and in different arenas.

## Alternating Periods of Stability and Change

The examination of how ideas and images move in and out of the policy agenda over time suggests that both stability and change are important elements of the policy process. Most policy models, however, are focused on explaining either stability (e.g., incrementalism) or change, but not both. Schattschneider (1960) concluded that the generation is the proper time period for the study of politics and change. Cycles of politicization and quiescence may unfold over 60 to 80 years. The spread of conflict in ideas (e.g., how to reform the system in a particular manner) takes a long time. Ideas must be expanded, introduced into the policy arena, shaped and reshaped in search of support for the view, and in the case of a noncoercive democracy, the majority view must be persuaded to support new ideology even after voting takes place.

A succession of fluctuations, coupled with the specific history of the policy system, forms a unique evolutionary process. In many cases, these fluctuations in the system lead only to small corrections. When the prevailing political ideology is widely supported, policymaking is incremental (Lindblom, 1968). This describes the politics of the policy subsystem. During these periods of relative quiescence, changes focus on minor, short-term solutions within the framework of existing goals and assumptions (Majchrzak, 1984).

Periodic changes in the surrounding political, social, or economic systems can trigger social turmoil and public opinion shifts (Iannaccone, 1977; Wirt & Kirst, 1989). These types of events can include crises, changes in governing coalitions, and administrative and legislative turnover. The events and actions preceding major policy change may take several decades as external conditions, policy belief systems, and policy images coalesce (Schlager, 1999). Unfortunately, however, more research is needed into the nonlinear dynamics that seem to trigger major policy changes—that is, sometimes large events lead to these changes, and at other times, small events lead to major policy changes. As True and colleagues (1999) argued, the theory can lead analysts to expect that the punctuations will occur, but it does not help us make specific predictions about particular policy issues.

## Institutional Arrangements Contribute to Policy Development

A unifying theme for PE theory is that the same institutional system of governmental organizations and rules regularly produce both small policy accommodations and a number of radical departures from the past. The nature of the federalist system (e.g., separated institutions, overlapping jurisdictions) and relatively open access to mobilizations creates an ongoing dynamic between subsystem politics and the macropolitics of Congress and the presidency—one that usually works against any impetus for change but occasionally reinforces it (True et al., 1999). Understanding debates over policy issues centers on who has access to and power within the formal policy system.

Agenda setting is important because no political system can have continuous discussion over all the issues that confront it (True et al., 1999). Only a few issues can remain on the macropolitical agenda. Instead, the majority of political issues are generally dispersed to various issues-oriented policy subsystems (True et al., 1999).Within these subsystems, the issues are generally processed in a more incremental fashion resulting from bargaining among interests and marginal moves in a way that is more shielded from the visibility associated with high-agenda politics (True et al., 1999). When a policy subsystem is dominated by a single issue, it can be thought of as a policy monopoly. It tends to develop structures that support its continued existence. Where citizens are excluded or remain apathetic, the institutional arrangement usually remains strong. Such a monopoly can thrive over a certain period of time and then collapse.

Occasionally, however, the decentralized nature of the system reinforces the impetus for change. Mobilization is required to set proposals for change in motion; however, once debate and conflict are set in motion, the diffuse jurisdictional boundaries that separate various overlapping governmental institutions can allow many actors to become involved (True et al., 1999). This socialization of conflict can lead to more widespread actions and may actually change political dynamics within the existing policy subsystem. As pressure builds up against a prevailing policy issue monopoly, it may be resisted for a time, but at this point, small changes in the objective circumstances (e.g., the involvement of the public audience, an external crisis event) may be enough to lead to a massive intervention by previously uninvolved political actors and governmental institutions. As controversy increases, the system may move further from equilibrium. Policy solutions that have worked in the past no longer seem to be sufficient. Often within the spotlight of macropolitics, some issues become widespread, dominate the agenda, and result in changes in one or more subsystems (True et al., 1999). Once the policy issue reaches the government's policy agenda, it can have an important effect on future decision making within this issue area, even after the issue has receded, as new institutional reforms are put in place in reaction to the previous policy monopoly. In his case study of the politics surrounding education for Native Hawaiians, Kahumoku (2000) found that the actual policy decision in 1896 to remove Hawaiian as the official language of public school instruction in Hawai'i was preceded by social and economic events beginning in the mid-1840s that encouraged the use of English in commerce such that by the time the actual policy was passed, only one of the islands' public schools was still teaching in Hawaiian. The symbolic nature of the gesture, however, was strong in indicating formal support for a change in ideology. It was not until 1986 that instruction in Hawaiian was formally reintroduced to Hawai'i's public schools (as part of an immersion language program).

When events surrounding a policy issue reach a crisis point, it may be quite difficult to predict the exact direction that a system will take (or how it will be transformed) before it returns to equilibrium. Punctuated-equilibrium theory offers a means of modeling the qualitative changes that lead to the crisis and of predicting how the revolution might unfold. The scope of these changes is likely to bring new perspectives, goals, and underlying ideological assumptions, as well as new governance structures to accommodate the changes. Thus, the theory provides a way of understanding why some changes are incremental and some are punctuated. During quiet periods, the particular issue is not seen as a problem. When dissatisfaction begins to arise, it advances on the agenda and macropolitical institutions may grapple with it. Major policy changes may result when one or more policy subsystems is disrupted and a new agency or program is created (True et al., 1999).

## APPLYING THE THEORY TO EXAMINE SCHOOL GOVERNANCE REFORM IN CHICAGO

There are a number of studies in educational policy that have applied concepts from punctuated-equilibrium theory to examine trends toward conflict and consensus (e.g., Benham & Heck, 1994; Heck, 1991–1992; Iannaccone, 1977; Lutz & Iannaccone, 1978; Lutz & Merz, 1992; Plank et al., 1996; Tyack, 1991; Tyack & Cuban, 1995; Tyack & Hansot, 1981). Although much of previous research on policy development has focused on incremental modifications that appear to be the norm, it is instructive to pay special attention to situations where public controversy arises over fundamental ideological assumptions and the organizational structures that have customarily managed system conflicts no longer appear capable of resolving the stress within the system (Iannaccone, 1977).

One educational policy example that illustrates some of the concepts of PE theory is the change in governance structure that took place in Chicago (e.g., Wong & Rollow, 1990) presented in chapter 3. Most research has focused on the reform efforts to introduce site-based management during the late 1980s. The governance reform that took place in large cities such as Chicago during the Municipal Reform of the 1890–1920 era and the more recent effort to incorporate site-based management are examples of policy cycles of stability and change that form bookends on the educational governance system (Heck, 1991). The city of Chicago provides an excellent case study to examine longer term policy trends, because it was at the center of the reforms during both periods.

In Chicago, the Municipal Reform process was one of pluralist politics—that is, reformers' efforts to reorganize the educational system emerged as a consequence of conflict and coalition building among diverse interests. The organized working class played an important role in the school reform politics (Peterson, 1985). The problems that led to the reform included demographic changes, overcrowding, changing job markets, and increasing financial needs for government (especially for education). The 1890s witnessed a rapid increase in controversy surrounding the lack of both quality and equity in the existing school system. Setting aside reformers' motives (which have been debated by educational historians), the focus of their attention was the intervention of political machines in the schools and the large numbers of ethnic immigrants serving on the lay boards within the ward (neighborhood organized) system. Because policy decisions were a lay function, the school boards exercised tight control over the school's day-to-day activities, including assessing students' academic progress, choosing texts, and hiring and certifying teachers (Cubberley, 1916). Local school board elections corresponded with other municipal and state elections, producing many conflicts of interest. Political corruption due to uncontrolled decentralization in governance had resulted from the ward system (Cuban, 1990). Moreover, the extreme decentralization of the system across the states (i.e., with over 100,000 school districts in the United States) had also led to a lack of consensus about the goals of education.

Feeling the need to oust political machines and consolidate control of school boards in the hands of educational professionals, financial and educational policymakers engineered a social program to produce major changes in the local educational governance system. The first step was the consolidation of small local districts into larger, centralized systems. Reformers' belief was that the professional management of education would replace a political model and would transform the educational system into modern corporate life (Cubberley, 1929). The policy image was to create a scientifically managed educational system that was separated from political influence (Tyack & Cuban, 1991). Once implemented, other districts in urban areas followed the governance change quickly (Plank et al., 1996). Thus, the development of large bureaucratic systems and scientific management (resulting from the professionals leading) changed the structure of who should govern the schools. More specifically, larger cities consolidated power in the hands of a few board members and professional administrators.

These basic assumptions regarding educational governance went relatively unchallenged for over 70 years. Eventually, however, the buffering of large bureaucracies from lay influence for decades created a contrary demand for grassroots participation in decision making (Tyack, 1991). Challenges to the basic governance doctrines of the municipal reform arose out of an erosion of trust in the professional control of the schools. Although the Municipal Reform's policy image was an elite education for all, the continued existence of racial segregation in the schools and the poor quality of student outcomes and administrators who were perceived as unresponsive to parent and community needs challenged the system's ability in its traditional structure to deliver increased social mobility through education (Cuban, 1990). Beginning in the 1960s, Chicago once again experienced major economic, demographic, and structural changes (e.g., declining population and industrialization, shifting ethnic composition, an increasing number of low-income families, a focus on downtown development at the expense of neighborhoods). During this time, demands from African Americans and other groups who had been excluded from policymaking during the previous period increased.

The increased diversity and instability in city politics led the local political system away from the politics of "selective insiders" (which had characterized the city in years past) to a broader coalition of reform-minded individuals and organizations (Ferman, 1991). Educational reform was also on the local policy agenda, but a series of legislative efforts had little success in changing the structure of the system initially. During the 1970s, Chicago, like several other large city school districts (e.g., New York, Detroit) had begun the process of decentralization as a solution to increasing demands for lay control (Heck, 1991). Chicago divided its school system into smaller districts with regional superintendents and implemented local school advisory councils (Cuban, 1990). Part of this early interest in restructuring the system, however, was sidetracked in the 1980s, as reform efforts were consolidated at the state level because of financial leverage when the district failed financially and required a state bailout (Hess, 1991). The increased state control and creation of the Chicago Finance Authority to watch over district spending (another system mechanism to manage conflict) in 1980 had the effect of keeping political conflict privatized for several more years.

As dissatisfaction with the schools increased, the competing policy images involved whether to centralize (i.e., provide more accountability and control over educational governance) or to decentralize control (i.e., provide more participation and choice). Several initial attempts at change (e.g., establishing a school report card) expanded centralized controls incrementally to improve accountability in the Chicago school system and to solve the specific problems of high dropout rates and low achievement. These attempts can be viewed as strategies to privatize the scope of conflict over who should govern by managing the debate. This initial phase of managing change culminated with the 1985 reform legislation (PA 84-126) that focused primarily on increasing early childhood education, solving the dropout problem in the schools, and enhancing elementary reading programs (Hess, 1991).

The attempt to privatize conflict through incremental management is a critical feature of systems under challenge. In Chicago, however, what began as a slowly developing (i.e., from 1970 to 1985) set of narrow reform efforts concerned with increasing participation through decentralization and accountability, quickly became socialized into a sweeping redistribution of governance power. Although existing policies were moving slowly toward improvement (i.e., shifting power away from the top), the Urban School Improvement Act (1985) and the School Finance Authority Act of 1980s had produced little real change in terms of parent participation at the site level (Wong & Rollow, 1990). The first promoted staff development and broadened principals' power, whereas the second created an oversight authority to exercise financial control over the system's schools.

Although the essential elements of the restructured governance system were already in place (i.e., a commitment to decentralization and the development of local school site councils in the early 1970s), the catalyst of transformation of the city's political and educational systems appears to have been the election of the city's first African American mayor, Harold Washington, in 1983. Moving from incremental responses to building broad support for systematic change, however, was not easily accomplished because of the stability of the political system. In this case, what moved the system toward transformation was the extent to which reform-minded leadership was able to develop a policy agenda focused on the image of change and to broaden the scope of the conflict in the public arena by developing a set of broad-based coalitions. The mobilization centered on grassroots efforts to increase parents' and community interests' local participation in school policymaking. The key was the involvement of coalitions of groups including parents, business interests, community organizations, and political leaders seeking to improve student outcomes by regaining control of the educational agenda (Hess, 1991).

A discussion of some key events of Mayor Washington's first term illustrates how the socialization of political conflict can quickly produce large effects and accelerated change. His reform agenda focused on community involvement in politics. Specifically, it included incorporating neighborhood groups into decision-making processes and holding numerous neighborhood and community forums with a goal of working together for collective benefits (Ferman, 1991). Centralized administration was replaced by community participation. The result was that neighborhoods were developed economically through bond issues, affordable housing was provided for those who were displaced, and benefits for minority and female-owned firms were promoted to break the insiders' lock on city contracts. Overall, economic redevelopment emphasized shifting investment from downtown to neighborhoods, and politically, the development of open and fair government (Ferman, 1991).

As part of this shift in ideology and corresponding political structure, the educational governance came to be viewed as community function, as opposed to a service provided by the oversized bureaucracy. The Education Summit of 1986 produced a coalition of groups interested in addressing education and employment problems among city youth. This meeting led to increased support for school reform legislation in 1987. Coupled with a teachers' strike that mobilized widespread community opposition in late 1987 and Secretary of Education William Bennett's proclamation that Chicago's schools were the nation's worst, grassroots efforts to mobilize community-based school policymaking crystallized into a coalition of supportive legislative and business and parent interest groups that cut across class and racial lines (Ferman, 1991; Wong & Rollow, 1990).

Community input in Chicago dominated the mobilization phase of the school reform effort, at least in part because it had been legitimized earlier by Mayor Washington's reform agenda (Wong & Rollow, 1990), which had begun to redefine the role of local government. In addition, school reform was able to build on numerous attempts to improve school performance over the previous years that had begun to shift power away from central bureaucracy and toward local schools. This allowed for more parent input in policymaking (Wong & Rollow, 1990). These favorable conditions within the local political system also supported the socialization of conflict about who should govern the schools.

This next phase, therefore, focused on shifting power away from the educational hierarchy state legislative control to the local community through system restructuring. Central to achieving this end, site-based management was a mechanism to increase parent participation and to decrease professional dominance (by taking power away). In part, this was a policy response to public perceptions of a growing bureaucracy marked by administrative ineffectiveness (Hess, 1991). As it created disequilibrium in the existing local political system, the mobilization of efforts to improve school quality led to a series of legislative and executive debates at the state level. Hence, the conflict became more visible and intense.

In contrast to the grassroots surge of energy toward local participation, the formal legislative process in Springfield was defined by the extent of partisan bargaining and competition, institutional constraints in the procedures of lawmaking, and conflicts between the governor (a Republican) and the Democratic-controlled legislature in a divided governing system. Mobilized community-based policy preferences were endorsed and modified by key actors in the state legislative process. For example, there were diverse proposals made that were channeled through the committee system. By introducing their own views, language, and preferences, key lawmakers set the agenda for eventual decision making on the floor (Wong & Rollow, 1990). State political leaders supported several issues that showed a clear consensus among the diverse local interests (Wong & Rollow, 1990). These included parental empowerment at the school level and shifting authority from the top of the system to the neighborhood schools. There was relatively more debate over issues that lacked consensus—an example of which was the authority at the top of the system. For example, SB 1839 was passed by 31 Democratic votes in the Senate, one more than required. The bill was subsequently passed 68 to 37 in the Democratic-controlled house (with only 4 Republicans supporting the bill). The bill was then vetoed by the governor, who opposed his own limited oversight influence and also wanted to have principals able to hire teachers without regard to seniority (Wong & Rollow, 1990).

These legislative debates also served to expand the scope of the reform conflict. Eventually, a compromise bill was reached (SB 1839). After negotiation, it was passed 56 to 1 in the Senate and 98 to 8 in the House. However, this bill was never signed into law by the governor. Instead, he submitted an amended bill to the legislature. It differed only by a few key areas—referring mainly to oversight at the top of the system (Wong & Rollow, 1990). What resulted from this amended bill was reform legislation that broadened the influence of parent and community interests throughout the school system (Wong & Rollow, 1990). Governance at the top of the system was changed by an appointed external committee to oversee reform activities and finances in the district, and citizen councils were also developed at the subdistrict level. Local school councils were mandated broad responsibilities including principal performance assessment, approval of a school improvement plan and yearly financial expenditures, and advisory power over policies and programs affecting students and instruction (Wong & Rollow, 1990). These actions suggest that as a system moves further from equilibrium, it attempts to restabilize itself by adapting to changing boundary conditions.

The reform sequence in Chicago can therefore be viewed as an integrated whole; that is, the governance and educational systems' transformation over a 20- to 30-year period resulting from public ideological changes. The redistribution of policymaking responsibilities to parents and community interests after years of control by professional educators may represent, at least in Chicago, the completion of a cycle of lay versus professional domination in educational governance, culminating in a new form of local school governance. If one goes back to the beginnings of the Municipal Reform (where lay control over school boards was replaced by professional control), the process took nearly 100 years to complete. This is consistent with Schattschneider's (1960) temporal framework for major ideological change. The resulting new governance system highlighted lay involvement in a variety of capacities at all levels of a restructured educational governance system in Chicago.

Chicago represents a case study where both the ideological assumptions about educational purposes and who should govern, as well as the structures that should manage such conflicts, were challenged and changed. The transfer of power in Chicago represents perhaps the most far-reaching solution to the erosion of confidence in professionals to govern the school over the past century. Both governance assumptions and corresponding structures were transformed because citizen groups representing new value positions that could not be met through the existing political system became increasingly politicized. Specifically, the three major tenets of Municipal Reform approach to educational governance (i.e., belief in a unitary set of values and goals, the separation of politics and education, the neutral competence of professionals to govern the schools) were changed. For example, citizen councils at various levels of the system provide a political structure to mediate value conflicts, and the composition of the councils ensures that lay interests can dominate professional interests. In Chicago, the initial fluctuations in the system, in the form of demands for participation and accountability, produced attempts to privatize the conflict through decentralizing during the late 1970s. Inability to manage these demands then led to a socialized conflict that rapidly resulted in a transformed type of educational governance where the role of who should govern was redefined and power was redistributed.

The return of political control of the schools to the local community represents the logical completion of the scientific management model held in high regard during the previous period of educational governance. The governance structure was changed largely because the population in large urban areas became more ethnically diverse and increasingly mobilized, representing new value positions that could not be represented within the ideology of a unitary community. The public demand for greater control over education is a phenomenon that extends beyond Chicago. A second part of this agenda was support for parent choice in schooling. For the second time, in about a century, it appears we are experiencing a nationwide change in the politics of education that is changing relationships within the governance system. In both cases, the causes are found in the larger political and social problems of the cities. The first crisis restructured local American government, as the Municipal Reform took power away from the city political machines and the neighborhood ward system and gave it to educational professionals. The second, beginning with cases like Chicago, promises to return more power in educational policymaking to local citizens and community interests.

## Summary of Strengths and Weaknesses of the Theory

From this case, we can derive a set of propositions that researchers can test in subsequent efforts to examine the relationship between periods of social conflict, policy debate, and their relationship to patterns of institutional change in education. These PE propositions can be summarized as follows. First, major policy changes may take several decades to unfold—for problems and policy issues to emerge, debates to ensue, and policy to be formulated, implemented, and its effects noted. By the time the actual policy change is formalized, it may be the final piece of other processes that were set in motion much earlier. Second, at the center of these debates are value conflicts about purposes and ends of education. These values appear in the statutes, rules, and regulations that are produced (Benham & Heck, 1998; Marshall et al., 1989). Policy images encapsulate the ideology and values underlying proposals for change. Third, over time, policy talk occurs much more frequently than do actual policy changes. What policy actors argue about may only be loosely connected to trends in institutional change. Fourth, institutional changes appear to be one of two types; incremental (i.e., more continuous and gradual with little disturbance to accepted educational practice) or short bursts of innovation (i.e., more radical policy alternatives departing from previous practice). Features of the policy and political system seem to either enhance or restrict changes. Fifth, features of policies themselves influence the timing and extent to which they are likely to be institutionalized. For example, Tyack and Cuban (1995) concluded that structural add-ons were most easily incorporated because they did not require fundamental change in teachers' behavior. Programs that produced influential constituencies interested in seeing them continue were more easily institutionalized. Reforms that were mandated by law and easily monitored were more likely to be implemented. Reforms that began from inside the educational system (e.g., by teachers and administrators) were also more likely to become institutionalized.

Seen from a century-long perspective, the change in governance involving Chicago can be seen as two punctuated periods that bookend a longer, quieter period. In contrast to many educational changes that seem to be incorporated more easily into practice, other policy issues (e.g., who should govern) tend to ebb and flow as different societal values and group interests are renegotiated at different levels of the system (Tyack, 1991). Such conflicts may never be settled, but are revisited within other political eras. Punctuated-equilibrium theory is useful in tracking these more complex policy situations. First, it accounts for periods of stability and change in policymaking. Incremental changes occur often, but not always. Punctuated change also happens, if not as frequently. The theory provides an explanation for both conditions. It pays considerable attention to institutional arrangements that paradoxically can support, or inhibit change. Second, in addition to the efforts of policymaking coalitions, it recognizes the potential impact of broader public participation as a critical component in the dynamics of policymaking.

PE theory has been more widely applied in public policy to understand very diverse policies than it has been applied to educational policy. The biggest problem with the theory is that it tends to work best in predicting outcomes during periods of equilibrium. It is also better at explaining policy processes in hindsight. Another problem is that the theory does not clearly define the difference between major and more routine policy change. Nonlinearity suggests predictions work in some cases, but not in other cases. Lutz and Iannaccone (1978) had some success in predicting superintendent turnover using dissatisfaction theory, which is a variant of punctuated-equilibrium theory. It appears to be much harder to predict the timing of the punctuation and its outcome. The theory helps us understand the system as a whole, but is less useful for understanding the events related to individual policies.

## THE ADVOCACY COALITION FRAMEWORK

The Advocacy Coalition Framework (ACF) also emerged out of a search for an alternative explanatory system to the stages heuristic, a desire to integrate top-down and bottom-up approaches to policy implementation, and a commitment to incorporate technical information into understanding the policy process (see Sabatier & Jenkins-Smith, 1999 for an extended discussion of the approach). Importantly, the framework challenges the implicit assumption that a policy actor's organizational affiliation is key to understanding policy behavior—that is, that legislators differ from administrative agency officials, union leaders, researchers, and journalists. ACF contends that coalitions are formed among actors across various organizations who share similar core policy values, perceptions of policy problems, and goals. The framework attends to the interactions among advocacy coalitions, suggesting that policy actions are function of both competition within the subsystem and events unfolding outside.

As opposed to policy models that focus more exclusively on the "rational behavior" of individuals, the ACF draws more heavily on their belief systems, reward structures, biases, constraints—suggesting that individuals' actions are structured by preexisting normative and perceptual beliefs. These processes contribute to individuals' use of information and strategies to achieve policy goals. ACF emphasizes that policy beliefs shared by members of different institutions are more important in explaining policy behavior than are the institutional norms and values that apply to the members of a given institution (Sabatier & Jenkins-Smith, 1999).

The framework has drawn considerable interest among researchers over the past 10 years or so, resulting in some 40 cases of research studies in a variety of policy disciplines (Sabatier & Jenkins-Smith, 1999) including at least two in education (i.e., see Mawhinney, 1993; Stewart, 1991). Mawhinney applied ACF to the process of education policy change for French-language minority education in one Canadian province. Over the past two decades, Ontario adopted and implemented a series of policy changes directed at allowing French-speaking residents the right to establish and govern their own school boards. Mawhinney used the framework to structure her examination of the involvement of coalitions over time working with a policy subsystem as they attempted to achieve goals derived from their core belief systems. Her investigative method (i.e., case study involving the content analysis of documents, newspaper accounts, interest group publications, interviews, observation of public hearings) involved identifying long-term trends as well as crises and key events in Ontario's policies for minority French-language students. Importantly, she examined several key hypotheses from the ACF approach. These involved coalition stability, the stability of their belief systems, policy-oriented learning, and the impact of changes external to the policy subsystem. These propositions were stated as hypotheses and then the relevance of each of the major framework hypotheses was examined in relation to the specific case study.

## An Overview of the Framework

Sabatier and Jenkins-Smith (1999) identified five basic premises that underlie the framework. The authors abstracted these premises from the literature on policy implementation and the use of technical information in public policy.

## Technical Information

Policymakers desire technical information concerning the magnitude and facets of problems, their solutions, and probable impacts of various solutions (Sabatier & Jenkins-Smith, 1999). Legislators often desire information about the severity of a problem and the probable benefits and costs associated with particular solutions before they create legislation. With increasing needs for fiscal accountability, there is a growing need for various types of technical policy analyses that address important policy problems that are of concern to educators and policymakers. ACF contends that the availability and use of technical information can be important parts of the policy development process, including the strategies groups use to influence the agenda setting and legislative processes. The framework emphasizes policy-oriented learning within policy subsystems, which is the process of using information to increase understanding in order to achieve policy objectives (Mawhinney, 1993).

## Policy Subsystems

A second premise concerns the most useful unit of analysis for understanding policy change. In the United States, this unit is not any specific governmental arm, organization, or program but, rather, a policy subsystem. A policy subsystem consists of individuals from a variety of public and private organizations who are actively concerned with a policy problem or issue, such as educational reform or charter schools, and who regularly seek to influence policy in that domain. An example would be the educational policy subsystem within a particular state. Because the policy process within any particular domain is sufficiently complex in terms of the laws and regulations, particular problems on the agenda, and the factors that affect development and implementation, individuals must specialize if they are going to have influence (Sabatier & Jenkins-Smith, 1999). Those intending to influence educational policy on a regular basis will have to become familiar with the various private and professional groups, legislators, and committees who occupy the subsystem.

Policy subsystems may be either existing or emerging out of a new issue or situation. Subsystems may also interact, or overlap, with each other in some situations. One of the challenges in describing a policy subsystem is that it is often not clear whether groups that interact within a policy domain across levels of government may constitute one advocacy coalition, or whether they separate into different policy subsystems by level of government. Importantly, previous case studies on the development and implementation of educational policy changes (e.g., Mazzoni & Clugston, 1987; Wong & Rollow, 1990) have consistently found that there is seldom a single dominant reform program or group at the operational level. Rather, actors within a particular policy domain are likely to initiate a number of actions within different levels of government in pursuing their own goals.

## Coalitions of Actors Within Subsystems

A third premise is that policy subsystems are comprised of a considerable number of groups including administrative agencies, legislative committees, interest groups, journalists, policy analysts, and researchers who regularly generate, disseminate, and evaluate policy ideas. The framework suggests that these coalitions are relatively stable over lengthy periods of time (e.g., a decade or so). Although policymaking normally resides within a particular subsystem, it is also the case that as conflict on a particular policy issue may widen, actors at other levels of government (e.g., governors, legislators, state superintendents, special interest groups, local superintendents and principals) can all become active in policy formulation and implementation within the same subsystem or in different subsystems simultaneously. This has the effect of socializing the conflict and making it more visible to a wider audience.

## Policies Incorporate Implicit Theories About How to Achieve Goals

A fourth premise is that policies and programs generated through interaction incorporate beliefs and theories about how to achieve policy objectives. These belief systems involve value priorities, perceptions of causal relations, the magnitude of the policy problem, and the efficacy of various policy instruments. The core belief systems of coalitions are likely to persist over time. Strategies and implementing strategies to achieve these beliefs are likely to change over time, however.

## Change Process

A fifth premise concerns the relationship between policy action and institutional change. Similar to PE theory, understanding processes related to institutional change and the role that technical information may play in policy agenda setting, action, and policy implementation require temporal perspectives that are much longer than those commonly used in policy studies.

Given the complex mix of actors, their belief systems, and changing external events, policy change is likely to take a decade or so. Longer time frames are required in order to examine policy formulation, implementation, and reformation cycles to get an accurate picture of success and appreciate the strategies actors pursue over time (Sabatier & Jenkins-Smith, 1999; Tyack, 1991). Although policymakers often work in arenas that require fast action and quick results (e.g., with average election terms of 4 years), policy changes generally require much longer time frames to achieve (Louis & Miles, 1991; Mort & Cornell, 1941; Tyack & Cuban, 1995). This suggests the importance of maintaining coalitions over time that are committed to certain policy outcomes.

ACF suggests that the internal processes of a policy subsystem are not always sufficient by themselves to alter the policy core aspects of government policy substantially. Policy change may also require external events in the socioeconomic conditions, systemwide coalitions, or policy outputs from other subsystems (Mawhinney, 1993). Rather than directly affecting change, however, external events may provide opportunities for advocacy coalitions to use them in ways that further their own purposes (Mawhinney, 1993).

**Variables in the Advocacy Coalition Framework**

From these previous premises, Sabatier and Jenkins-Smith (1999) developed a conceptual framework model. The ACF framework provides two sets of external factors. These are categorized as *stable factors* that are not likely to change over the course of a policy cycle (i.e., basic attributes of the problem, basic constitutional structure or rules, fundamental sociocultural values, natural resources) and more *changeable factors* (i.e., changes in socioeconomic conditions, changes in governing coalition, policy decisions and other impacts from other policy subsystems). Both sets of factors affect the constraints and resources of subsystem actors. Stable environmental factors also affect the degree of consensus needed for major policy change to result.

Within the policy subsystem, actors are aggregated into a number of advocacy coalitions, each composed of people from various governmental and private organizations. The key variables regarding actors in ACF is their shared beliefs and values (a type of cultural belief system) and their coordinated activity over time (Sabatier & Jenkins-Smith, 1999). At any particular time, each coalition adopts one or more strategies involving the use of guidance instruments (technical information, changes in rules, budgets, personnel, policy learning) as a means of altering the behavior of government authorities to realize its policy objectives. The goal of their efforts is to influence the decisions of government authorities. ACF attempts to understand policy-oriented learning—that is, patterns of thought or behavioral intentions concerned with the attainment or revision of policy objectives (Heclo, 1974, p. 306). As Sabatier and Jenkins-Smith (1999) argued, policy-oriented learning describes policy coalitions' desire for increased knowledge about problem parameters and factors affecting them, policy effectiveness, and perceptions of probable impact of alternative policies. Coalitions realize that they are in the policy arena for the long haul. This learning is a force that can influence policy change.

In order to accomplish their ends, policy coalitions need to develop a broad consensus to effect change. Conflicting strategies from various coalitions may be mediated by another group of policy actors called policy brokers. Their major concern is to find a compromise that reduces the conflict occurring between the various coalitions. This concern may be balanced against various constraints and resources that are associated with the various actors and their organizations that comprise the policy subsystem. The end result of the effort is often some type of program that, in turn, produces some type of policy outputs. These outputs then result in various outcomes (or impacts)—both intended and unintended. As Sabatier and Jenkins-Smith (1999) noted, based on information it receives, the policy coalition may further revise its goals and strategies.

## USING ACF TO EXAMINE POLICY

ACF also has several attractive elements as a conceptual lens for examining educational policy. These include:

1. Two primary forces of causal change—the beliefs and values of the coalition and the exogenous changes to the system.
2. Amenable to empirical testing, because it has hypotheses that can be laid out, examined with data, and modified.
3. Relatively parsimonious.
4. Can produce surprising results that allow researchers to view problems in new ways.
5. Focuses on policy processes in longitudinal settings.

Policy core aspects refer to fundamental policy position concerning basic strategies for achieving the core values. These include the seriousness of the problem, its causes, the ability to solve the problem, methods of financing solutions, and preferences about choices of action. These changes are more difficult to achieve, but they do occur occasionally. As Sabatier and Jenkins-Smith (1999) argue, major policy change refers to a change in the policy core aspects of a governmental program. These are areas that are likely to create cleavages (Schattschneider, 1960) across different coalitions. They refer to changes that affect the whole policy subsystem. A major policy change may involve the replacement of one dominant coalition by another, a surge in public concern over a particular problem, or a change in policy values (e.g., away from equity and toward efficiency). For example, a minority coalition may try to increase in importance by attempting to take advantage of opportunity provided by an external disturbance. It may use various tactics to appeal to different constituents. It may also attempt to augment its resources by short-term coalitions. In another case, if all major coalitions view continuation of the current situation as unacceptable, they may enter into negotiations to find a new compromise viewed as superior (i.e., power sharing).

In contrast, minor changes deal with change in secondary aspects. These are where most policy changes take place. Typically these deal with only a part of the subsystem. They include changes in budget allocations, a change in the seriousness of a specific aspect of the problem in some locations, a decision regarding altering a rule, or a revision of a statute. Therefore, in this framework, the topic and scope of a policy change determine whether it is major or minor. Moreover, the framework provides a way of linking change to scope; a change may be minor for one subsystem, but major for the subsystem nested in it.

## Summary of Strengths and Weaknesses of ACF

ACF provides a good example of a conceptual framework, in that it is oriented toward examining hypotheses across a variety of different types of policy cases and settings, as opposed to a theory, which is oriented toward becoming more integrated and having a denser set of relationships. The framework identifies several key variables that influence policy change. These include the interaction of opposing advocacy coalitions operating within a policy subsystem, the analysis of external factors that explain policy changes, and the examination of beliefs and core policy values that define each important coalition (Mawhinney, 1993). From the ACF perspective, significant disturbances external to the subsystem (socioeconomic conditions, public opinion, governing coalitions, or policy outputs from other subsystems) are a necessary but insufficient cause of change in the policy core attributes of a governmental program (Iannaccone, 1977; Sabatier & Jenkins-Smith, 1999). They provide an opportunity for major policy change, but as we saw with the progressive reformers at the turn of the 20th century, the system must also be skillfully exploited by the change-oriented groups. They have to develop a sufficient degree of consensus that is needed to bring about major policy change.

ACF provides a relatively clear means of distinguishing major policy change from more minor changes. At the deep core are cultural values that permeate across all policy subsystems within government. These values are related to larger cultural issues about how to prioritize basic wants, needs, and freedoms (e.g., political equality, equal opportunity, freedom of speech). These issues also identify who should receive services and whose welfare should be placed ahead of what other groups. One of the challenges in using the framework is that it does not direct attention to the processes that determine when policy changes will actually take place (generally a weakness in all policy models). This is because changes to the core values underlying formal policies are relatively rare. Therefore, they are difficult to predict. Not all exogenous shocks (e.g., economic events such as the Depression, the launch of Sputnik) and not all instances of policy learning resulting from the interactions among policy coalitions translate into actual policy change.

## APPLYING ACF: THE ROLE OF COALITIONS IN PROMOTING REFORM IN MINNESOTA

To date, ACF has not been much used in peer-reviewed educational research, although several of its basic premises undergird many case studies on educational policy change (e.g., Mazzoni & Clugston, 1987; Wong & Rollow, 1990). Mazzoni and Clugston provided a case study on the role of big business in Minnesota school reform during the mid-1980s that illustrates many of the major features of the framework. The study concerned the Minnesota Business Partnership's role as a policy innovator in K–12 school reform in the state during the 1980s. At the time the article was written, the ACF perspective did not exist, so the authors used a general political perspective that entailed many of the assumptions underlying ACF. Their political perspective proposed that state policy decisions emerge through the complex interaction of legislative processes where competing groups must mobilize influence if their demands for change are going to be heeded.

### Policy Core Beliefs of the Business Partnership

The Business Partnership was formed in 1977 as an association of executives heading the state's largest business firms. In 1982, the members formed an educational quality task force. By the end of the year, the task force decided to recommend a comprehensive review of the state's K–12 public educational system's performance and cost effectiveness (Mazzoni & Clugston, 1987). Mazzoni and Clugston identified several core beliefs were at the center of the Partnership's desire for participation in educational reform (p. 314). One belief was that the public schools were slipping educationally. A second belief was to have quality public schools available for business employees' children. A third belief was to create a competent work force. A fourth belief was that the educational system had lost its capacity to innovate. A final belief was the desire to reduce taxes, and the largest state budget item was funding for elementary and secondary education.

### Agenda Setting

One of the early features in the Minnesota case centered on the Partnership's study of the performance of the state's schools. The partnership invested over $250,000 cash and contributions and engaged an outside firm to conduct a study and to offer recommendations. The plan called for major reforms including restructuring schools, reorganizing teachers, and redistributing authority. There was also a provision for a stipend to support educational choice. The Partnership publicized the results in a number of high profile places (i.e., community presentations, favorable editorial commentary, presentations to lawmakers in legislature). Making the policy issue more public created cleavages with old groups (most notably the largest teacher union, and superintendents). Lots of coalition building was also done with meetings of several groups including a public policy and civic research organization, and other activist groups pushing for educational reform.

Disagreements arose over the priority of policy changes that would offer parents a choice of schools. At the meetings, the strategy was discussed about the role that the governor might play in advancing school reform. The strategy was to get the governor to make education a top priority (i.e., placing educational reform on the policy agenda) and then get others to buy into the plan. At the same time, the governor was also looking to cultivate the business community—as they shared many philosophical similarities. The goal was to develop a new approach to education—this one was not costly, fit with the governor's approach (strengthen education, hold educators accountable, make quality programs more widely available through choice), and it did not require extensive regulation.

As Mazzoni and Clugston (1987) found, the Business Partnership report tended to dominate the policy agenda in late 1984. The key part was the section on educational choice, which resulted in the governor's controversial plan for school district open enrollment in 1985. At this point in the policy process, further coalition building took place within various departments in the executive branch, speeches, and press releases. The report became an issue that changed cleavages between interested actors and special interests. At this point, however, the Governor's office was able to narrow the focus from a broader set of reform issues to a more narrow focus on choice. While there was overlap, each also had a separate means of attaining policy goals. The groups differed most on the scope and emphasis of their choice advocacy. Whereas the Business Partnership proposed to provide a stipend to promote choice on a more limited basis, the governor recast the issue as one of public school choice (i.e., open enrollment). As the Business Partnership was consulting with staff in the senate to prepare a bill, the governor gave a public speech promoting open school choice. At that point, the Partnership realigned with the governor on his proposal.

### Working Within the Established Policy Subsystem

The Partnership's reform proposal had to contend with subsystem politics and established interests. State K–12 policymaking was the issue domain of a subsystem within the Minnesota legislature. The subsystem was composed of legislators and staff who specialized in school finance, Department of Education officials who did the same, and representatives of K–12 lobbying groups. As Mazzoni and Clugston (1987) noted, members of this subsystem had developed a preferred strategy for acting in achieving goals—pluralistic bargaining to create lengthy omnibus bills that led to incremental outcomes. This was seen in reform laws passed in 1983 and 1984. Within this subsystem, the K–12 lobby also carried considerable influence through its major organizations (teacher unions and school board associations). Legislators saw considerable risks in going against this group's preferences.

Given the nature of the reform proposal's major policy issue, school choice, much debate ensued in the legislature over the Governor's proposal. Key advocacy opponents included the teacher unions, school boards association, and school administrators association. Officials from the rural areas were opposed because they felt school choice would lead to the consolidation of school districts. Key coalition-building efforts were central in helping the reform proposal win out in the subcommittees. These included the Governor's efforts, powerful authors of the reform bill, favorable testimony at hearings, as well as lobbying efforts by the Partnership and others (Mazzoni & Clugston, 1987). The reform proposal also received support from a postsecondary enrollment option that emerged. This allowed students in 11th and 12th grades to take courses from the state's universities and to receive funds and dual academic credit. Out of public view, the Business Partnership encouraged a key legislative leader to sponsor the bill and also contacted legislators to secure voting support.

### Are Key Premises Supported By Findings?

This case supports the first ACF premise that specialized policy subsystems, with opposing factions and coalitions, are preeminent in different policy issue domains (McFarland, 1983). Second, it provides support for the premise that under some sets of conditions, incrementalism can be superseded by deeper, and more major, policy change. The influence of outside groups, however, is mediated through public officials, constrained by established groups that have influence, and also affected by public opinion. Importantly, a larger policy change (those where the policy core is changed) occurs where the scope of conflict is broad (i.e., the belief is seen to apply to the whole subsystem), and the policy concerns a change in orientation to a basic value priority (i.e., from efficiency to choice) and is focused on a group whose welfare is of concern.

For a number of reasons outlined in the ACF, the change in Minnesota can be seen as one that involved a change to the policy core values. These are fundamental value positions concerning basic strategies for achieving policy goals within the subsystem. Before the implementation of the choice reform, the education policy subsystem was concerned with efficiency as opposed to choice. The proposed reform was viewed as a means of increasing accountability. The proposal was seen as something that could be accomplished with a minimum of regulation and money (i.e., two key elements underlying components of policy core changes in programs). Cleavages developed between proponents and longstanding groups within the policy subsystem, which widened the scope of the conflict. The scope of the reform became systemwide, in the sense that all districts in the state were affected by school choice.

The Business Partnership's greatest impact was on agenda-setting phase of policy development (i.e., sponsoring, adopting, and publicizing the plan for K–12 change). It also influenced decisions in some relatively minor areas such as postsecondary options and student testing. The proposal eclipsed other reform reports in gaining visibility. A successful strategy was to involve the Governor's office. The Partnership created new policy and political issues to get the Governor involved. After he became involved, however, he became the central actor. At that point, the Partnership became a key advocate for his plan—which focused primarily on school choice.

The Partnership's legislative clout in achieving its own agenda was limited by the rapidity of issue politicization, difficulties in gaining credible information about K–12 operations, the overshadowing of school choice with respect to its own agenda issues, shortage of funds to mount a legislative and grassroots campaign, and lack of broad ownership and commitment by business leaders to the plan (Mazzoni & Clugston, 1987). Therefore, Business Partnership can most appropriately be seen as one of many influentials within a broader coalition of individuals and organizations. The groups that gave more direction to the efforts of the members of the educational policy subsystem were political and professional in nature (Mazzoni & Clugston, 1987). It was necessary that the Business Partnership secure the backing of key politicians for proposed innovations to gain agenda status. Its efforts were also constrained by powerful educational group opposition. Moreover, the public generally gave schools high marks and was not in favor of open enrollment.

## SUMMARY

It is of interest to note that one of the key differences between PE theory and the advocacy coalition framework is the relative weight given to coalitions versus the public in moving policy debates along. In the previous ACF analysis, the role of the public is basically as a disinterested bystander. PE theory and ACF are likely to be promising additions to the set of existing theories on changes in the policy process. As suggested in this chapter, both of these conceptual lenses move researchers considerably beyond the policy stages metaphor. The PE theory is especially useful in situations where the periods of time being studied are longer. It is consistent with much previous research in educational politics and policy that examines periods of turbulence and quiescence. ACF is useful in focusing its attention on policy coalitions and how they approach policy issues over time.

## EXERCISES

1. Policy researchers have been criticized as not paying enough attention to contextual and temporal conditions leading up to policy changes. Major policy changes are often preceded by several "smaller" changes that comprise longer temporal sequences than originally thought. Try to identify some key events in the attention cycle of a particular policy (e.g., vouchers). You may find that a particular policy issue has appeared on the agenda on multiple occasions.

2. Compare and contrast some of the assumptions of PE theory and the Advocacy Coalition Framework. What might a proposed study concerning school choice look like from each perspective (e.g., purpose, research question, data collection, analysis)?

# Chapter 6

# Economic
# and Organizational Perspectives

In this chapter, a number of economic and organizational approaches for studying policy in education are introduced. Economic perspectives have dominated the analysis of social policy problems (Jenkins-Smith, 1990), but have been less frequently applied to policy problems in education (Boyd, 1992), except within the subfield of educational finance (Benson, 1988). Economic approaches to policy focus on utilitarianism (i.e., the greatest good for the greatest number), self-interest and rational decision making (i.e., people acting in ways that maximize their own interests), resource allocation, efficiency, and maximized production. The impact of various resources on productivity have often been modeled as an economic production function, or a set of economic inputs that lead to the maximization of an output.

Many of these same concepts (e.g., efficiency, utilization of resources, division of labor, control) are embedded in the classic bureaucratic theory of organizations. This theory of organizations entails several basic assumptions about the nature of work, organizations, and individuals. Underlying the theory are the concepts of goal attainment, resource allocation, rational decision making, and efficiency—which suggests that productivity is related to the optimal utilization of resources without regard to human factors. Proponents of the classical theory of organizations believed that control and accountability of workers were necessary to ensure efficient productivity. Managers, therefore, were necessary to supervise and direct the actions of workers. So pervasive has been the economic approach in guiding policymakers' decision making that some have worried about the shortcomings of economic thinking on politics in general (Schumacher, 1975; Tribe, 1972). This chapter discusses these dominant ways of thinking, some of the criticisms of their usefulness in doing policy research, and contrasts them with several alternatives.

## ECONOMIC PERSPECTIVES

Policymaking is influenced by conflict over different value positions (i.e., efficiency, equity, quality, choice). As suggested in chapter 4, these value positions tend to reinforce (e.g., efficiency, quality) or conflict (efficiency, equity) with each other. Education receives much public attention because people believe that education has a powerful effect on individuals' chances for success in society. Government support for education follows from the perception that it provides economic opportunities for the next generation; thus, the distribution of quality education across communities and states intersects with our views of liberty and social justice (Hanushek, 1997).

Broadly speaking, the economic perspective addresses the efficient allocation of scarce resources to policy problems and the determination of the most efficient solutions. Economic lenses primarily stem from the core value position of efficiency, which has been described as a "holy grail" for policymakers during the 20th century (Tyack & Cuban, 1995). Efficiency is the pursuit of value maximization (Jenkins-Smith, 1990). As DesJardins (2002) noted, economic efficiency concerns not only the exchange of goods and services, but also the way in which goods and services are produced and the extent to which they reflect the preferences of the public. Efficiency has also formed a framework for evaluating the impact of policy activity.

Increasing attention to the economics of education in recent decades has resulted from tight budgets in legislatures, pressures for greater accountability and efficiency in government, and the public's demand for higher educational productivity. Although efficiency often dominates in the allocation of scarce resources, policymakers also give attention to the other value positions. Historically, debates over efficiency and equity have been at the core of economic and social policy in the United States. As Adam Smith (1776) remarked in *The Wealth of Nations,* "No society can surely be flourishing and happy, of which the far greater part of the members are poor and miserable" (book I, chap. VIII). It is not necessarily the case, however, that efficiency and equity are mutually exclusive objectives (DesJardins, 2002). There are a number of issues, however, that make the development of a unified framework for resource allocation challenging.

It is important to understand some of the basic philosophical principles underlying various approaches to the allocation of resources both efficiently and with considerations for equity. Because educational programs compete with other social services for limited legislative dollars, policymakers need to determine how much money is needed to achieve an efficient and equitable school system and how money will be used to accomplish educational goals (Monk & Hussain, 2000; Odden & Picus, 1992). As Odden and Clune (1998) concluded, however, state school finance systems are aging and in need of substantial repair. They lack fiscal equity in remedying spending disparities across school districts, and they also fail to provide adequacy in terms of educational outcomes (Monk & Hussain,

2000)—that is, sufficient funding to support high minimum student achievement, in part because the current formulas do not promote optimal school management of resource allocation. This put considerable pressure on policymakers to find various ways to improve public education.

Over the past few decades, the equitable allocation of resources has been a concern of the courts, as they have attempted to redress inequities in the nation's practice of locally funding education through property taxes. Local funding of education through property taxes resulted in widely varying levels of state and federal resource expenditures for students across districts. Inequities in the financing of education focused primarily on unequal spending per student, or more broadly, unequal access to a uniform level of educational services (Odden & Picus, 1992). This is referred to as horizontal equity, which implies that students should receive equal amounts of educational resources regardless of the schools they attend. This view of equity is implicit in the assumption that spending levels should be equal across districts or schools.

At the same time, during the 1960s and 1970s, legislators also attempted to allocate resources to students with greater needs to enhance educational opportunity (e.g., Elementary and Secondary Education Act of 1965). Title I of the act addressed the development of compensatory educational programs to address improve the educational opportunities of students living in high-poverty communities. Considerable controversy has followed the program since its inception, however, in terms of how resources are distributed and whether supplementary programs actually work to decrease achievement gaps. In more recent years, there has been a growing recognition that students differ from each other in ways that affect the types of resources and levels of those resources that may be appropriate (Monk & Plecki, 1999). This is referred to as vertical equity. From this standpoint, the focus should be on identifying resources that are related to student learning and making sure diverse groups of students have access to the resources. To achieve vertical equity, however, likely requires the unequal distribution of resources to students (or schools and districts) with the greatest need, if they are to catch up. These issues concern both the level of funding and the use of resources to affect student learning (Odden & Picus, 1992).

As Boyd (1992) argued, disillusionment with the perceived failure of policies aimed at enhancing educational opportunity, coupled with growing economic problems of the 1970s (e.g., gasoline shortages, energy crises), led to other policy actions directed at "self-interest maximizing individuals" (Bellah, 1983; Schultze, 1977). This represented a shift from the pursuit of policy values concerned with equity, justice, and the common good to values emphasizing efficiency, quality, and liberty (choice). For example, *A Nation At Risk* (National Commission on Excellence in Education, 1983) catalyzed a perceived need to raise the quality of educational outcomes through increasing accountability and standards (e.g., upgrading standards of preparation of professionals, increasing student testing, lengthening the school year). Policy activity directed at expanding the range of choices available to parents received increased publicity beginning in the 1950s (Guthrie, 1988). This value position was represented in more recent policies emphasizing parent participation in site-based management, school choice, educational vouchers, tax credits, and market incentives to increase educational competition.

## Economic Analyses

The aim of economic analyses is to put an economic valuation on students' educational experiences. Economic analyses fall into three main categories. They can address the organizational management of scarce resources, individual and societal returns to investment in resources used to create student learning (e.g., teachers, materials, programs), and efforts to match the skills taught in education to the requirement for those skills in labor markets (Benson, 1988; Odden & Picus, 1992). This latter concern, for example, has often been expressed as the fear that the United States is falling behind other nations in terms of economic competitiveness, technology, and education. This has led to the increased demands for technology in schools as we shift from an industrial to a technological society, placing new demands on education for a different workforce.

Resources are the means of producing educational outcomes—in more recent years defined as educational performance and student learning. They include a wide variety of variables related to time (e.g., instructional time, time on task), money (salaries, class size, costs of materials, program costs), and expertise (teacher quality, staff development). Many policy questions obviously stem from resource-related questions—how effectively are dollars being used? What are the optimum sizes for schools and districts to promote optimal student learning? How can we best allocate resources, given the educational needs of groups of students?

## Educational Production Functions

Central to the pursuit of efficiency goals in education is a concern with productivity; that is, from an economic standpoint, productivity relative to cost is defined as a measure of efficiency. One important way that economic thinking has influenced educational policy is in the analysis of educational inputs and outputs. Relationships between inputs and outputs are expressed as educational production functions; that is, production functions represent the various resource inputs (e.g., per pupil expenditures, teacher characteristics, teacher–student ratios, with controls for student background) that lead to maximizing outcomes (Monk & Plecki, 1999).

In the past, considerable attention has been given to the relationship between the allocation of dollars and improved educational performance. For example, during the first part of the 20th century, the measurement of the educational system's effectiveness was the increasing numbers of elementary and secondary students who passed through the schooling process per the associated costs to educate them (e.g., teacher salaries, facilities, class sizes, periods per day). Greater efficiency could be gained by processing more students at lower educational costs (i.e., lower salaries, larger classes, more periods per day).

In the last several decades, however, researchers have attempted to relate various types of educational resources to learning outcomes (Catterall, 1997). Beginning in the 1960s, there was a policy concern in identifying factors in schools that were related to inequities in educational opportunity. This consisted of describing educational inputs (e.g., student background, resource allocation, teacher–student ratios) that might produce evidence of unequal educational conditions within schools. As Hanushek (1997) concluded, Coleman and his colleagues (1966) shifted the research orientation from locating inputs that were unequal to what mattered more—educational outcomes. The Coleman Report provided one of the first attempts to document the impact of a variety of student background and school resource inputs on student learning. The results of the study indicated that differences in students' achievement were more clearly associated with family socioeconomic status than with school-based resource variables. More importantly, it also directed the attention of researchers and policymakers toward student achievement as the primary means to assess the effectiveness of educational efforts (Hanushek, 1997). This study and subsequent research oriented researchers toward the overwhelming presence of student background in explaining achievement in comparison to school resource variables. The popular interpretation of the report, that schools "do not make a difference," subsequently led to several streams of research concerned with identifying school processes and practices that affect student learning (Reynolds, Teddlie, Creemers, Scheerens, & Townsend, 2000).

One stream that evolved from the earlier input–output studies was school effects research—that is, studies of how various school resources, structures, and processes affect student learning. Another stream led to the "effective schools" movement—that is, the identification of certain attributes and processes of schools (e.g., high expectations, frequent monitoring of student progress, strong school leadership) that were related to stronger educational outcomes. Effective school studies added a wider range of contextual and school process variables (e.g., school leadership, teacher characteristics, teacher expectations, class and school size, school climate, school socioeconomic status). Despite the identification of a broad range of indicators of effectiveness, however, it has proven much more challenging to determine precisely how manipulating these types of educational inputs might actually lead a school to increase its student outcomes. A third strand led to school improvement research, or studies that examine processes by which schools can be changed to improve their outcomes. This research is more closely associated with determining what actually works in the effort to increase educational productivity.

Production function studies have been criticized because the presence of certain resources (e.g., levels of funding, student–teacher ratios, percentage of teachers with master's degrees) does not reveal much about how resources are actually allocated and used in pursuing student achievement (Catterall, 1997; Levin, 1984). Early tests of economic input–output models tended to be simplistic (i.e., using achievement scores at one point in time, aggregated analyses at the district level). In the past, input–output studies were typically done with finance data available at the district or state levels. Student data, however, were often used in determining the impact of resources on learning (Odden & Picus, 1992).

This mismatch in organizational levels at which the data were collected created a number of problems with analyses. The analyses generally addressed resource allocations that were too far away from students to provide insights on how resource allocations affect student learning within schools. Because there tends to be much more variation in students' achievement within schools than between schools, models that examined the marginal effects of allocation of resources at higher levels (e.g., districts or school) were not well equipped to determine impact on student achievement (Catterall, 1997). Moreover, few studies have been experimental, so it is still unclear whether some identified school variables are actually causally related to student achievement or merely artifacts of statistical analyses within the individual studies (Hanushek, 1997).

Results from production function studies are therefore mixed about whether various economic input variables impact student achievement (Catterall, 1997; Hanushek, 1997; Teddlie & Reynolds, 2000). Some types of resource variables seem to matter—for example, teacher quality (as measured in a number of different ways) and teacher use of classroom time. No clear evidence exists yet on the relationship between increased spending and increased outcomes from the input–output model (Monk & Plecki, 1999). In part, this is due to the difficulty of obtaining within school data on resource allocations that can be matched with student achievement data (Heck, Brandon, & Wang, 2001).

Whereas previous analyses typically addressed the allocation of resources at the macro level (i.e., states, districts), there has been recent attention directed toward the level of educational funding that enters each school unit (Monk & Hussain, 2000). Much less is known about what happens to money inside districts and schools, and yet, these allocation decisions made by administrators at various levels of school districts can be important to concerns with equity and access because they occur at points much closer to student learning (Monk & Hussain, 2000). More specifically, some schools have greater resources at their disposal to use in educating students and use those resources in different ways. This suggests the need to make finance data available at the school level for analyses on how resources are used within the school. For example, there is preliminary evidence that funding may be related to other types of intermediate educational outcomes—achievement of general school goals, uneven distributions of resources (e.g., teacher quality, curriculum materials), and adding programs (Monk & Plecki, 1999).

There is also a growing recognition of the importance of other types of educational resources within the school and their relationship to achievement (Miles & Darling-Hammond, 1998; Monk & Plecki, 1999; Raudenbush et al., 1998). Importantly, these include curricular and instructional resources (which may be purchased through funding levels) and the capacity of human resources in and around the school (e.g., teacher preparation, teacher emphasis on various aspects of the curriculum, school leadership, parent and family factors). A number of studies have also focused on particular types of organizational arrangements that result from resource allocations. In particular, class size has been one policy alternative that has been implemented in a good number of states (Brewer, Krop, Gill, & Reichardt, 1999), although the research basis for this policy action is mixed at best. Although reducing class size alone may not be sufficient to produce consistent results on student outcomes (Hanushek, 1997), it may in fact be one facilitative condition that can allow other types of processes to emerge. Some issues related to decreasing class size include its relationship to learning for individuals and groups of students, to various educational costs, to the management of resources within the class (e.g., time, curriculum access), and to school improvement (e.g., the likelihood of teachers implementing new programs). In particular, this last issue shows promise, as it addresses how resources are used at points that are much closer to where instruction takes place than to district and school studies of resources and learning.

Of course, further research is needed on the internal allocations of resources and the types of educational process variables that serve as key resources at each level (e.g., district, school, and class) and that can have measurable effects on learning outcomes. Similarly, there is a need to examine the efficiency and effectiveness of using resources within the school site. More specifically, if it can be determined that a particular mix constitutes effective educational spending, then it might be possible to determine the extent to which states, districts, or schools diverge from these criteria (Odden & Picus, 1992). As a practical matter, however, the overwhelming majority of district budgets go to salary, so the discretionary money available to allocate to actual projects that impact student achievement may be very limited (Catterall, 1997). Schools and teachers, however, use what resources are available very differently. Where extra funds exist, researchers have found that money allocated to curriculum and instruction within the school can make a difference in improved outcomes (e.g., Heck et al., 2001).

## Studies That Incorporate Educational Costs

Production function analysis concerns the identification of factors (i.e., various types of educational inputs) that produce desired educational outcomes. However, these types of analyses are often limited because they do not typically consider the costs of inputs relative to the value of outputs (Brewer et al., 1999; DesJardins, 2002; Levin, 1983). This is one key issue that has limited the attractiveness and usefulness of economic analyses in the past. Cost feasibility, cost–benefit, and cost effectiveness analyses represent attempts to improve the analysis of educational production functions by including considerations of costs.

One primary concern of researchers has been the extent to which education systems rationally strive to allocate resources in ways that allow them to maximize clear objective goals such as increased student learning (Catterall, 1997). There are, however, few concrete examples of cost feasibility, cost–benefit, and cost effectiveness analyses in education that demonstrate their usefulness in making educational policy decisions based on the demonstrated effectiveness of particular policy alternatives. Cost feasibility studies focus on the level of resources needed to implement and operate a program (Rice, 1997). Cost–benefit analysis can be applied to a program to provide information on the degree to which investing in the program would be worth the potential benefits. To the degree that the benefit to cost ratio is high, the program would be considered desirable (Rice, 1997). Cost effectiveness focuses on integrating information on the various costs and effects of a number of alternatives to identify the option that most efficiently uses the resources to produce a desired outcome (e.g., Rice, 1994; 1997; Warfield, 1994). For a range of alternatives, estimates of costs and effectiveness are integrated into a cost-effectiveness ratio.

While analyses of alternative costs are attractive, on a practical level, they are difficult to conduct so that they provide reliable data for policymakers (Levin, 1991). Levin (1988) provided an example of a cost effectiveness study where the attractiveness of several educational alternatives (e.g., reducing class size, hiring a classroom aide) was evaluated for their cost and effectiveness in increasing learning outcomes. Even if accurate cost and effectiveness data can be brought to bear on each alternative, as a practical matter, when decisions such as reducing class size (which may require adding a teacher and obtaining more building space) are weighed against alternatives such as adding a classroom aide (i.e., putting one more body in an existing classroom), on logistics alone it is easy to see why most schools would hire an aide. It is usually difficult to assign costs and benefits within educational decisions (Catterall, 1997; Rice, 1997) . Another problem concerns the temporal relations necessary to establish cause; that is, one typically has to find evidence that the policy choice is working after the decision to implement it has already been made. Moreover, the factors chosen in one case may not generalize to others, as costs may be quite different in alternative settings. Yet, it is also obvious that some states are putting tremendous numbers of resources into projects such as reducing class size without research support that these sorts of changes will lead to improved outcomes over other potential policy options that could be considered (Catterall, 1997).

The reality is that many other issues enter into the process of educational decision making. Schools may use a variety of decision-making strategies other than a rational approach. As opposed to a rational model of decision making, Cohen, March, and Olsen (1972) described educational decision making as a "garbage can," with uncertain goals, unclear technology, uncertain outcomes, and fluid participation all entering into the decision-making mix. Educational decision makers were not as likely to act on the basis of their preferences (as rational models of organizational decision making suggest) so much as to discover their preferences through acting. Plank and colleagues (1996) noted that schools may adopt structural changes to "look" innovative, even when they don't share a particular problem with schools who first made the change. The structural changes may not actually affect educational practices. Through this structural adaptation, they manage to maintain needed levels of policymaker support.

## AN APPLICATION OF COST-EFFECTIVENESS ANALYSIS

One of the problems for policymakers is that most decisions focus on programs and resource allocations (e.g., whether to reduce class size, whether to bring a program into existence, whether to increase or decrease funding to an existing program), as opposed to decisions about the impact of such decisions on outcomes. This makes the process highly speculative. Despite some of the challenges associated with examining educational costs and their relationship to productivity, Levin (1988) provided an excellent concrete example of the potential of cost-effectiveness analysis in making policy choices among several alternatives. The costs as well as the outcomes should be considered in such analyses.

The basic technique for determining cost effectiveness involves describing what the decision problem is, identifying a range of possible solutions, deciding how to measure the effectiveness (or the impact of each on outcome results) for each alternative considered, and combining that information with the cost of each. Estimates for the effectiveness of each alternative under consideration can be derived from previous studies or evaluations that have been completed. It is obviously easier to use previous studies to obtain each measure of effectiveness; however, the usefulness of the measures that can be developed will be limited by the quality of the information about effectiveness that can be extracted from the existing studies.

Costs may be determined by identifying the particular variables that are required for each alternative (e.g., personnel, facilities and equipment, materials), assigning a cost associated with each variable, and adding the costs to determine the total cost associated with each alternative. Costs must then be expressed in terms of the effectiveness measure used (e.g., achievement gains per student). Cost-effectiveness ratios are typically based on the average effects and costs per student (Levin, 1988). Levin suggested four further considerations in actually making decisions based on cost-effectiveness ratios. These are as follows:

- Make sure the scale of use on which the cost-effectiveness ratio is based is pertinent to the decision-making context (i.e., some average costs might be high if implemented on 30 students and much lower if implemented on 1,500 students).
- The impact of cost per student on the outcome should be consistent across the ranges represented in the study (i.e., if $20 produces a certain level of effectiveness, then $200 should generate an additional 10 units of effectiveness).
- Decisions should be based on results that suggest a substantial difference in cost effectiveness (i.e., if the differences are small across the alternatives, then on the basis of their cost effectiveness, there is little basis for choosing among them).
- Decisions should consider the quality and appropriateness of the effectiveness studies and criteria on which they are based (e.g., if measures of effectiveness are poor or inappropriate, or there are confounding problems with the studies, then the reliability of the cost-effectiveness ratio will suffer).

Levin and his colleagues (Levin, Glass, & Meister, 1987; Levin, 1988) provided an instructive demonstration of cost-effective analysis applied to a decision concerning the cost and effectiveness of several within-school alternatives for improving student achievement. In this application, the decision consisted of four possible alternatives. These included a computer-assisted instruction (CAI) intervention (i.e., 10 minutes of daily drill and practice), smaller class sizes (considered in increments of five), a longer school day (i.e., lengthened by one hour and consisting of 30 minutes each of math and reading instruction), and peer tutoring (i.e., 15 minutes of tutoring of 2nd-grade students by 5th- and 6th-grade students).

They developed measures of effectiveness for each alternative using a number of different published studies (see Levin et al., 1987; Levin, 1988). Next, costs for each intervention were estimated on a yearly per-student basis. The least costly interventions were reductions in class size of five students and lengthening the school year. The most costly was peer tutoring. CAI was relatively inexpensive compared with peer tutoring or large decreases in class size (i.e., reducing from 35 to 20 students). In terms of effects, peer tutoring was the largest (resulting in nearly a year gained in math and a half year gained in reading). Lengthening the school day and making class reductions by five students were the smallest in terms of effects. CAI was associated with middle-range results on student learning.

The next step after estimating cost and effects is to create the cost-effectiveness ratios by showing the estimated annual cost to obtain an additional month of student achievement per year of instruction. For example, a longer school day cost $61 per student and resulted in .30 months of achievement gain. Therefore, the estimated cost to obtain an additional month of student achievement per year of instruction would be $203 ($61/.30). In contrast, peer tutoring cost $212 per year but resulted in 9.7 months of gain, so its cost effectiveness was much better at $22 ($212/9.7). In contrast, CAI cost $119 per student and resulted in 1.2 months gain in achievement, so its cost effectiveness was $100 ($119/1.2). So, in this comparison, implementing peer tutoring requires about 1/9 of the resources to obtain the same added month of achievement as lengthening the school year.

The cost analysis of various policy alternatives is a relatively new type of analysis in education. It can yield answers to whether it is more efficient to utilize resources in one manner or another. Despite several considerations regarding difficulties with estimating costs of variables associated with alternatives and of the effectiveness of alternatives across various settings, the approach has promise. Obviously, the usefulness of the analysis depends on the quality of the data that can be brought to bear on the estimates of costs and effectiveness. As more data are made available about educational costs within schools, they should aid analysts in conducting cost-effectiveness analyses. For interested readers, Rice (1994) and Warfield (1994) have provided excellent applications of educational cost-effectiveness analysis.

## ORGANIZATIONAL PERSPECTIVES

Organizational theorists have advanced a number of different theories to explain regularized patterns of action and interaction (referred to as formal structures). These patterns of behavior may be explained by alternative "logics" that organizations employ (Ogawa, Sandholtz, Martinez-Flores, & Scribner, 2003). These logics fall into a few dominant categories. One category is often referred to as the rational perspective, whereas the other is referred to as the institutional perspective (Ogawa et al., 2003). The rational perspective includes theoretical orientations such as rational systems theory (e.g., bureaucratic model of organizations), rational choice theory, and structural functionalism. The institutional perspective includes orientations such as natural systems theory, social constructivist theory, and symbolism, myth, and ceremony (Ogawa et al., 2003). These theoretical orientations provide alternative ways to explain how goals and mission, norms and rules, roles, and other work-related processes bind organizations, their members, and the surrounding environment together.

For much of the 20th century, the dominant view of organizations was grounded in a modernist perspective (Sackney & Mitchell, 2002). Modernity emerged in an economic environment that relied on efficiency in the production of goods within factories. This orientation was derived from Weber's bureaucratic and rational model of organizational life.

Rational models emphasize that organizations are formally structured collectives oriented toward the pursuit of specific goals. The formal structures include a strict division of labor, well-defined and differentiated roles for leaders and workers, clear technology to perform necessary tasks, a hierarchy of communication and control, and clear organizational rules, policies, and procedures to guide worker behavior and organizational activity (e.g., stating goals, implementing standard operating procedures, using data in evaluating the achievement of goals). The presence of these structures contributes to the cohesion of the organization and the efficiency with which goals are attained (Ogawa, 1992; Ogawa et al., 2003). Managers develop or alter these formal structures in ways that facilitate goal attainment (e.g., setting priorities, allocating resources, coordinating and supervising work, maintaining order and discipline, evaluating the attainment of outcomes). Decision making within rational frameworks tends to be concentrated at the top of the organization, based on the consideration of criteria (e.g., cost, efficiency) in relation to the selection of the best option among alternatives.

In contrast, the institutional perspective describes behavior in organizations that lack conditions (e.g., clear goals and technology) necessary to demonstrate the efficiency and effectiveness of their operations (Ogawa et al., 2003). The absence of clear goals and technology describes schools as organizations (Cohen et al., 1972). In these organizations, the concern is more with protecting the organization (i.e., making sure it continues to exist over time) than with the attainment of specific goals. As Ogawa and colleagues noted, to maintain the organization, it develops formal structures that reflect institutional logic—that is, that enhance the chances of survival. This can include adopting cultural norms and patterns of behavior consistent with the wider society. For example, an organization may adopt innovations that make it look innovative to its external stakeholders (e.g., parents, community interests, policymakers), as opposed to improving its ability to achieve its formal goals. To illustrate, implementing a new staff development program within a school could reflect rational (i.e., improve outcomes) or institutional (i.e., look innovative) logic.

Although rational approaches have been much employed in policy analysis in the past, there have been a number of criticisms raised about their usefulness in the examination of educational policy. First, they generally focus on examining events within a limited time frame (i.e., because they view the system as more static) and ignore historical antecedents and evolving conditions that pose various challenges for policymakers. Whereas policymakers are supposed to make rational decisions that maximize their self-interest and benefits, it is generally the case that due to constraints of time, resources, and external conditions, they "muddle through" decision making, because it is seldom the case that there are adequate resources and time to make optimal choices.

Second, rational views of educational policymaking imply more conservative social positions on the nature and purposes of education, the relationships between educational institutions and their environments, and the study and solution of educational problems (Angus, 1996). For example, they tend to focus on the behavior of those in formal positions of authority and view the purposes of policymaking as maintaining equilibrium and stability, where conflict should be managed before it spreads. Thus, they have not been very useful in examining the policy process—which itself has been described as disorderly and dynamic.

Third, the emphasis on particular models (e.g., bureaucracy, rational decision making) and methods of examining policy processes tends to accept certain texts, discourses, social groups and individuals, while it excludes others. The pattern of inclusion and exclusion is accepted as foundational and unquestioned (Marshall, 1993; Sackney & Mitchell, 2002). This unarticulated foundation is established over time through a complex process of legitimization within educational communities (e.g., research agencies, journals, professional meetings, professional training) and policymaking communities (e.g., cultural values, rules, norms of behavior).

Finally, the notion of rationality also underlies the belief that policy analysis based on the application of scientific principles can contribute to the solution of important social problems. Many of the tools of policy sciences (e.g., fiscal planning, cost-benefit and cost effectiveness analysis, input–output analysis) have not been widely applied or produced satisfactory results to educational policy problems. Whereas the policy analytic framework derived from Lasswell's work in the early 1950s was supposed to contribute to a science of policy that would inform governmental decision making, researchers have concluded that it has many shortcomings (Sabatier, 1999; Schon & Rein, 1994).

## INSTITUTIONAL RATIONAL CHOICE

Rational choice theory is an explanatory theory used in economics and sociology. It suggests that individuals make decisions based on a cost–benefit analysis of a set of alternatives (Beekhoven, De Jong, & Van Hout, 2002). Individuals' analyses of potential choices, however, are bounded by the social structures in which they operate (Elster, 1986). Variants of this theory used in policy research include institutional rational choice (which focuses on how institutional rules alter the "rational" behavior of self-interested individuals) and the multiple streams framework (based on the "garbage can" model of organizations), which views the policy process as composed of various streams of actors and processes. These include a problems stream, a policy stream involving solutions to proposed problems, and a politics stream consisting of elections and elected officials.

## Overview of the Framework

Institutional rational choice (IRC) is an extension of rational choice theory. IRC is a general framework that stresses how institutional norms, rules, and strategies affect the internal incentives confronting individuals and their resulting behavior (Ostrom, 1999). *Institutions* in the context of the framework refer to the shared concepts used by actors in repetitive situations organized by rules, norms, and strategies (Ostrom, 1999). Examples of institutions include concepts such as property rights, due process, and equal educational opportunity. Institutions define the goals, meaning, and actions of individuals who are interacting within a particular policy subsystem or other social setting. For example, increasing educational opportunity may underlie the efforts of individuals trying to influence policymakers to increase funding for a particular educational program.

When individuals interact in repetitive settings, there are operational rules that govern how they can interact. Rules are shared understandings that refer to what actions are required, prohibited, or permitted (Ostrom, 1999). Within policy subsystems, the existence of these rules influence who will share in what services or benefits, how decisions will be made, how people will behave in delivering those benefits, and how outcomes will be monitored and reported. Working within arenas that have rules governing interactions, policy actors are viewed as rational decision makers who make choices to advance their own welfare (Boyd, 1992). IRC assumes that individuals seek to realize a few goals efficiently, but they must employ various strategies to overcome a variety of environmental, political, and organizational obstacles to attain their goals (Sabatier, 1999).

IRC is an appropriate framework to use to examine the relationship of educational organizations to the broader context surrounding them. For example, Brewer, Gates, and Goldman (2002) suggested that despite voluminous research on various aspects of higher education, very little attention has been paid to the strategies universities pursue in obtaining their goals. Strategies refer to the means used to set goals, the plans for achieving them, and the set of indicators examined to assess the achievement of goals. An important part of the analysis is identifying the underlying institutions that are embedded in policy decisions. Universities make a number of strategic decisions about which markets to serve and which services to offer within each market. One recent example is the processes by which university presidents decide to change conference affiliations in sports.

IRC can be a useful conceptual lens to apply in situations where the policy problem and choice options are relatively well defined; however, determining the constraints and consequences of the alternatives are more problematic (Sabatier, 1999). One of the important aspects of the IRC framework is that it is multilevel. The IRC framework suggests that policy decision making is at least three-tiered; constitutional, collective choice, and operational. Analyses can be concerned with policy processes and decisions within any particular level or among several levels simultaneously. The lowest level of analysis is referred to as the microlevel, with all higher levels of analysis called the macrolevel.

A second assumption of the framework is that there are fundamental elements within the framework that can be used to analyze outcomes and their evaluation at any of the three decision-making tiers (Ostrom, 1999). Decisions made at any level are usually made within a structure of rules existing at a different level. The problem could be at an operational level, where individual actors interact in light of the incentives they face to generate particular types of outcomes. Studies at the microlevel focus on individuals within an identifiable group (e.g., a group of coaches, superintendents, university presidents) who may share certain properties—for example, socialization patterns, traditions, attitudes, and work goals, and must make operational decisions in competition with each other. The problem could also be at a policy (collective-choice) tier—for example, a situation where decision makers have to make choices within the constraints of a set of collective-choice rules and pressures from a variety of constituents and external constraints (Ostrom, 1999).

Often, the interest in an IRC analysis is on how individuals at the microlevel respond to policies that are implemented at levels above their normal operating arenas. More specifically, the IRC framework suggests that changes in environmental conditions affect the action arenas where individuals are making operational decisions. An arena refers to the space where individuals interact, exchange goods and services, compete, and attempt to dominate one another (Ostrom, 1999). The focus of the analysis is on the resources (e.g., finances, support, expertise, prestige) brought to bear on the situation, the valuation the actors assign to particular actions, the ways actors acquire and use information, the strategies and processes they use to select courses of action, and the costs and benefits they assign to outcomes.

## Conducting An IRC Analysis

A first step in conducting an IRC analysis is to identify a conceptual unit called an action arena that can be used to analyze and explain behavior within institutional arrangements. The action arena refers to the social space where individuals interact with each other. The action arena itself is affected by the first set of structural variables related to the environment—that is, the rules used by participants to order their relationships, the attributes of states of the world that are acted on in these arenas, and the structure of the more general community within which an arena exists (Ostrom, 1999).

Analyses using institutional rational choice should identify the major types of structural variables that are present in all institutions but whose values differ from one type to another. These include (a) the action arena (i.e., a conceptual unit that is used to analyze, predict, and explain behavior within institutional arrangements); (b) the variables affecting the action arena (e.g., attributes of the community within which a particular arena exists, physical and material conditions in the environment that are relevant to a particular arena, and rules that are used by participants to structure relationships); (c) the patterns of interaction and outcomes; and (d) the evaluative criteria used to determine the effectiveness of interactions and outcomes (Ostrom, 1999).

After identifying an action arena, it is important to identify the set of variables (i.e., rules, environmental conditions, community conditions) that shapes behavior in the action arena. Individuals use working rules in making decisions. The rules are important to the ways individuals structure their relationships, how they view physical and material conditions in their environment, and how they interact with their larger community. These sorts of value systems affect the ways individuals interact and how they interpret the outcomes of their actions. Once the rules are known, it may be possible to learn where they come from as well as how they influence subsequent patterns of interaction and outcomes. The concept is similar to Marshall and colleagues' (1989) notion (see chap. 4) of identifying the assumptive worlds that policymakers use in constructing policy decisions. There may also exist a nested structure of rules within rules, within still further rules (Ostrom, 1999). The same set of rules may lead to different action situations depending on the types of events in the world on which individuals are acting (e.g., availability of resources at a given time). The attributes of the community (sometimes referred to as the culture of the community) and conditions in the environment (e.g., changing economic conditions, political demands) also affect the structure of the action arena (e.g., norms of behavior accepted within the community).

**The Action Arena**

The essential elements of the action arena include the action situation and the relevant actors in the situation. Both components are needed to diagnose, explain, and predict actions and results (Ostrom, 1999). An action situation can be characterized by a common set of seven types of variables including the participants, their positions, the set of allowable actions and their linkages to outcomes, the potential outcomes that are linked to individual sequences of actions, the level of control participants can exercise, the information available to actors about the structure of the action situation, and the costs and benefits they assign to the outcomes. It is important to identify this set of variables before the analysis begins.

The actors may be thought of as individuals or groups functioning as a team. The analyst must make assumptions about what actors value—the resources, information, and beliefs they have; what their information processing facilities are and what mechanisms they use to devise strategies (Ostrom, 1999). The choice of strategy is related to the classical economic view that actors weigh the benefits and costs of various strategies and their likely outcomes. Four sets of variables are related to actors; the resources that they bring to the situation; the valuation they assign to states of the world and actions; the way they acquire, process, and use knowledge contingencies and information; and the processes they use to select certain courses of action. It is likely, however, that individuals do not always have access to the same information others have within the arena. Some may have greater opportunity to apply particular strategies that maximize benefits. When the researcher is explaining the actions and results within the framework of an action arena, these are the givens that one works with in describing the structure of the situation.

## Patterns of Interaction and Outcomes

Depending on the structure of the situation (e.g., constraints, patterns of relationship, external factors), the analyst makes strong or weak inferences about the patterns of interaction and results. In tightly constrained, one-shot action situations where actors have complete information, and where they are motivated to select a specific strategy that leads to stable equilibria, the analyst can often make strong inferences and specific predictors about likely patterns of behavior and results (Ostrom, 1999). In contrast, in most situations, participants cannot make independent decisions and may be embedded in communities where norms of action (e.g., equity, fairness) may force them to use a wider range of strategies. They may change their strategies over time as they learn about the results of their past actions. Here, the analyst will have to make weaker inferences over interactions and outcomes and may suggest that a particular type of outcome is likely to result from a particular situation.

## Evaluating the Outcomes

In addition to predicting likely outcomes, the analyst may also evaluate the outcomes that are achieved. Criteria may be applied to both the outcomes and the processes individuals use to achieve those outcomes. The criteria could include economic efficiency (did the situation increase net benefits?), equity (e.g., did the set of actions tend to level the playing field, or benefit targeted groups?), accountability, adaptability (i.e., how well they adapted to a changing environment), and conformance to general ethics (e.g., did the situation increase cheating, were promises kept?).

## Assessing the IRC Framework's Value and Challenges

The IRC framework is useful in studying how rules, material conditions, and community culture structures the actions and outcomes of participants within an particular policy arena. It thus appears to be adaptable to a wide variety of policy problems. It appears to be useful in presenting several theoretical premises that can be examined in specific research instances. Thus, it has been helpful in organizing empirical research in a number of policy areas (e.g., see Ostrom, 1999).

It also presents a number of challenges. The term *institution* has a number of meanings including both organizations and the shared concepts (e.g., rules, norms, strategies) used to structure interactions within and across organizations. To study institutional arrangements (markets, hierarchies, firms, families, national governments, universities, schools) requires flexibility in inputs and concepts drawn from a number of disciplines. This represents a challenge to develop a coherent framework that can be used for diverse problem situations. The different levels of decisions require a more complex analysis that can take in the multiple levels.

## AN APPLICATION OF INSTITUTIONAL RATIONAL CHOICE

Takahashi (2002) used institutional rational choice to examine the effects of Proposition 48 on the recruiting practices of Division 1-A football programs. Proposition 48 was a policy implemented by the National Collegiate Athletic Association (NCAA) in 1986 to upgrade the entrance requirements for student athletes playing intercollegiate sports. The intent was to upgrade the academic quality of incoming freshman with a goal of increasing athletes' graduation rates. The policy was therefore developed at the collective-choice tier. Although the policy's intended outcome was to increase graduation rates, Takahashi hypothesized that it would also have an unintended effect on coaches' operational decisions in the action arena where they compete to recruit football talent. More specifically, because the policy was expected to affect programs by reducing the size of the pool of available freshmen athletes (due to the higher test scores required to gain entrance into universities), it would likely alter the recruiting strategies used to obtain football players.

### The Action Arena

The action arena in this situation was the competition that takes place among Division 1-A football coaches regarding the pool of available freshman and junior college athletes each recruiting year. The decision-making process concerns coaches' strategies to secure the top athletes available in any given year. Having a successful recruiting record translates into on-field success and higher institutional prestige. Regarding rules in use that affect the action arena, major universities use various strategies to enhance their reputations and prestige. Student quality, research, and sports are seen as three generators of prestige (Brewer et al., 2002). Many of the nation's most familiar universities have prestige because of a combination of achievement in research, student quality, and sports. Prestige in higher education appears to be built over a long period of time. Moreover, as a rival good, it suggests that each university's maintenance or increase in prestige is related to others' expense in terms of the opportunity to maintain or build their prestige—that is, when one institution rises in ranking, another falls in the same rankings, at least for the short term (Brewer et al., 2002).

Universities have several choices in pursuing a strategy in each prestige generator. For sports, there are several considerations, including at which level to compete (e.g., Division 1-A), with which conference to affiliate, which teams to field, which players to recruit, and which bowl games to accept. Men's football and basketball programs can confer prestige, especially if the teams rank high in national competition, yet it is expensive to maintain a high-quality program (Brewer et al., 2002). Community expectations in this situation concern the culture (norms, values, expectations, traditions) regarding the university's football program. For example, the norms and expectations are very different at Notre Dame, Michigan, Miami, and Nebraska from other Division 1-A programs. Institutional prestige, therefore, likely interacts with the recruiting strategies schools use to secure athletes for their programs. The relevant set of variables that define the action situation in Takahashi's (2002) study were as follows. The set of participants was the set of universities that have Division 1-A football programs ($N = 108$). The positions variable was head football coaches (who make decisions about player recruitment). The set of allowable actions in this case included the continued recruitment of freshman student athletes (in a shrinking pool of athletes) versus the recruitment of junior college student athletes, who in the context of 1986 represented a largely untapped potential source of players. The potential outcomes refer to how the participants affected the allowable actions. In this case, it is assumed that individuals acted in ways that they thought would increase the on-field productivity of their programs. The level of control over choice refers to the amount of control coaches had over the respective pools of available students. For example, it was assumed that higher prestige schools (i.e., ones with established traditions, resources, and on-field success) would have greater control over the premier freshman athletes. The information available concerns how well programs scouted particular athletes, recruited effectively, and established a record of securing athletes in the various pools of talent. Finally, the costs and benefits of actions and outcomes refers to the costs associated with recruiting in each pool, and the benefits derived. For example, freshman athletes are said to provide more revenue to programs over their 4-year careers than junior college transfer students, who may only be available for 2 years.

The individual's choice of strategy in an action situation depends on a particular combination of these variables (e.g., level of control, information, weighing of costs and benefits). In highly competitive environments, such as intercollegiate sports, individuals who survive tend to maximize a key variable associated with survival in the environment—that is, good coaches and programs acquire good players who tend to perpetuate their programs' success. From this perspective, observed changes in the operating procedures of Division 1-A football programs may be viewed as a function of both competition among and within the action arena and events outside. Individuals operating within an action arena need to be able to respond to ever-changing policy environments.

Program managers (e.g., coaches) have to make operational decisions within the constraints of a changing set of rules. The choice of strategy in a particular situation depends on how the decision maker perceives and weighs the costs and benefits of various strategies and their likely outcomes. Trade-offs are often necessary in selecting from alternative choices (e.g., such as recruiting freshmen versus junior college students). In a relatively limited action situation, where participants are motivated to select particular strategies or chains of actions, the analyst may be able to make specific predictions about likely patterns of behavior and outcomes (Ostrom, 1999). From an analysis of the data, one may be able to confirm decision strategies used before and after Proposition 48 was introduced.

## Explaining Patterns of Interaction and Outcomes

Depending on the structure of the particular action situation and the assumptions made about the actors, the analyst can make either strong or weak inferences about results. In a tightly constrained situation where there are limited choices, where complete information is available, and where participants are motivated to select particular strategies or actions, it is possible to make specific predictions about patterns of behavior. In other situations, however, the results are not as easy to predict. Given more uncertainty, participants may use a broader range of strategies. They may alter strategies over time as they learn about the results of past actions. In these more open situations, less can be said in terms of the predictability of outcomes. Takahashi (2002) hypothesized that because the pool of freshmen athletes would shrink in the aftermath of Proposition 48, coaches would adopt an alternative recruiting strategy. They would compensate by increasing the number of junior college transfer students they recruited. He also hypothesized that institutional prestige would interact with recruiting strategies; that is, the recruiting practices of higher prestige universities would be less affected by the policy's introduction.

In his analysis of the data, Takahashi (2002) found that the number of freshmen student athletes being recruited into football across Division 1-A schools in the 3 years prior (1983–1985) to the implementation of Proposition 48 was already slightly declining. The average number of entering freshmen student athletes in Division 1-A universities declined from about 22 students to 21.5. After Proposition 48 was implemented, the number of entering freshmen student athletes recruited continued to decline, but more sharply, culminating with an average of 17 during the last year that the data were collected (1991). Thus, on average, about 4.5 fewer freshmen student athletes were recruited in 1991 as opposed to 1985, the last year before the implementation of the policy. Conversely, during the initial year of the implementation of the policy (1986), an average of about four junior college transfer student athletes was recruited across the programs (no records were kept on numbers of transfer students before the policy was implemented). This number steadily rose over the data collection years, reaching a peak average of about 12 junior college transfer students, an increase of about 8 transfer student athletes over the course of the trend. These contrasting trends are summarized in Fig. 6.1.

Based on these results, it is clear that there was a considerable decrease in the number of freshmen student athletes that were recruited corresponding with a significant increase in the number of junior college transfer student athletes that were recruited after the implementation of the policy. Thus, it appears that the implementation of Proposition 48 did affect the recruiting practices of Division I-A football coaches in general by causing a significant reduction in the number of freshmen student athletes recruited and a significant increase in the number of junior college transfer student athletes recruited.

In a changing environment surrounding recruiting, therefore, coaches had to draw on a different source of potential players to make up for the shrinking pool of freshmen. This finding is consistent with institutional rational choice, which suggests that actors will make choices based on the set of allowable actions and their perceived linkages to outcomes, the level of control they have over their choices, and the perceived benefits or costs associated with their actions and outcomes. Where coaches would have less control over the shrinking pool of available freshmen, they would have greater control over the recruiting of junior college players.

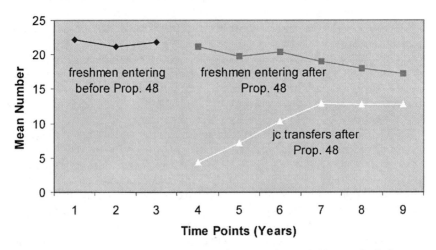

FIG. 6.1.   Entering freshmen and junior college transfers in division I-A football programs.

Figure 6.1 shows visually that during the first 3 years after implementation (i.e., 1986, 1987, and 1988) there was a considerable gap between numbers of freshmen entered and numbers of junior college players entered into Division 1-A football programs. One interpretation of this pattern is that the fluctuations experienced during the first 3 years of the policy could be attributed to transition to the new environment. As the actors became more familiar with all of the intricacies of the policy, they were better able to adjust their recruiting practices to meet their needs. By the end of the trend (1990 and 1991), the numbers of freshmen and junior college transfer students recruited each year were much closer (i.e., an average 12 junior college transfers and 17 freshmen).

Takahashi (2002) further hypothesized that programs with higher program prestige (e.g., established on-field success, stronger financial support) would be able to continue their pre-Proposition 48 strategy of recruiting freshman student athletes, even with the pool of potential athletes shrinking. In contrast, lower prestige programs would be likely to have to shift their recruiting strategy away from freshman to junior college student athletes. He found considerable support for this hypothesis from the data trend before and after the policy was implemented. More specifically, after Proposition 48 was introduced, coaches in high prestige schools continued to recruit more freshmen student athletes than their counterparts over the course of the trend. However, these numbers also declined over time after the introduction of the policy (i.e., from 22.0 in 1986 to 18.50 in 1991, on average). During the first year of implementation, high prestige and other schools entered almost the same numbers of junior college transfer student athletes (3.31 to 4.58, respectively). By 1991, however, high prestige schools accepted 8.81 junior college transfer students on average, whereas less prestigious schools accepted 13.75. Although even higher prestige schools had to recruit more junior college transfer student athletes over time after the introduction of the policy (i.e., from 3.3 to 8.8), these numbers were still considerably lower than their counterparts in less prestigious programs.

## Evaluating the Outcomes

In an IRC analysis, outcomes can also be evaluated in a variety of different manners. Some of the criteria include their efficiency (i.e., their magnitude of change in the net benefits associated with an allocation or reallocation of a resource). For example, in the case presented on Proposition 48, the researcher could examine whether programs' won–lost records or number of bowl appearances were affected by changes in recruiting strategies after the implementation of Proposition 48. A redistributional equity view of outcomes might examine the extent to which changing recruiting practices tended to equalize programs. Accountability might focus on the extent to which programs complied with the rules of the policy. Programs' adaptability could be assessed by examining the extent to which they were able to successfully adapt to the policy change by continuing (or increasing) their on-field success.

## INSTITUTIONAL THEORY

Institutional theory is an emergent set of theoretical arguments about the influence of broader sets of societal values, cultural theories, ideologies, perceptions on organizational structures and practices. Although more often applied to organizational studies, the theory offers an alternative lens through which to view the behavior of actors in policy situations, as well as the behavior of organizations in adopting policy changes. Institutional theory stresses the cultural theories, ideologies, and other social rules that define patterns of appropriate political activity. This focus makes institutional theory similar in some ways to the IRC framework. The main difference, however, is that in institutional rational choice, individuals' behavior is assumed to be directed toward maximizing internally derived benefits in meeting prescribed goals (i.e., acting rationally to maximize self-interest). More specifically, institutional norms often alter the "rational," goal-oriented behavior of self-interested individuals. Ogawa and colleagues (2003) concluded that schools face organizational dilemmas reflecting the presence of both rational and institutional elements.

Institutional theory focuses on the influence of institutions rather than on internally derived benefits in explaining behavior. From the institutional perspective, policy action results from the enactment of institutional norms and rules as opposed to individuals' choices (Ogawa, 1992), and policy implementation refers to the extent to which organizations adopt structures consistent with these broad values and ideological positions. Institutional theory is actually more focused on groups than on individuals, as it seeks to identify "the impact of the institutional environment on a particular type of organizational action; the adoption of structural features" (Ogawa, 1992, p. 16). From an institutional view, organizations adopt structures not so much for the purpose of maximizing their efficiency in attaining goals (i.e., which is more of a rational, economic explanation) but, rather, for the purpose of aligning with their external environments. They mirror other organizations' actions in order to gain social legitimacy (Ogawa, 1992). For example, schools might adopt particular policy changes (e.g., curricular standards, modular scheduling, year-round schooling) to look innovative if this is a community expectation.

Institutional theory attends to the hierarchical nature of social systems, suggesting that behaviors of social units (including individuals, organizations, states, and nations) are affected by cultural rules that prescribe appropriate behavior. More specifically, as Ogawa (1992) argued, the institutional perspective suggests that an understanding of actions taken at any level in a hierarchy is contingent on actions at levels both superordinate and subordinate to the level of interest. This perspective is potentially quite useful in examining policy development and implementation, as well as the impacts of policy outcomes on the organizations that they often target—schools, districts, or state educational structures.

**Major Components of the Theory**

The institutional perspective is useful in explaining why organizations in very diverse settings often end up looking quite alike. As Meyer, Boli, and Thomas (1987) described this, "Institutions define the meaning and identity of the individual and the patterns of appropriate economic, political, and cultural activity engaged in by those individuals" (p. 12). Political behavior can be understood as the enactment of broader institutional (or cultural) scripts (Ogawa, 1992). From this type of perspective, the environmental context may be seen as impacting a particular type of action taken—such as the change across the nation's school districts to decrease the size of school boards and increase the size of administrative staff at the turn of the 20th century, or the shift of decision-making authority from districts to schools in the 1990s.

DiMaggio and Powell (1983) argued that both competitive and institutional factors contribute to the structural similarities seen among organizations such as school systems. A first premise is that organizations facing similar problems may respond in similar fashions, as this can enhance survival and growth. The adoption of institutions (i.e., altered practices), however, may have less to do with efficient operation, despite the rhetoric, than with conforming to wider cultural rules and myths that confer social legitimacy. Organizations that fail to adapt to changes in their environment face becoming obsolete. Because institutions embody widely endorsed beliefs, organizations can ensure social legitimacy by adopting the appearance of innovation as a means of getting stakeholders to continue to invest resources in the organization.

A second premise is that organizations may also adapt similarly to environmental pressures because legal and ideological norms of practice and accountability require them to employ professionals who share similar backgrounds and common values (e.g., Plank et al., 1996). For example, the professional requirements for teachers and administrators are similar across the states, as are the socialization processes. Both these premises help explain why districts and states tended to follow suit in mandating teacher tenure, attendance policies, kindergarten, similar yearly schedules, comprehensive high schools, lengthened school years, and stronger accountability policies during the 1980s, and choice and charter school policies during the 1990s. From the institutional perspective, policymakers act as implementers of widely endorsed cultural norms. These norms represent boundaries for accepted policy behavior. In education, policymakers' actions reflect tinkering with the system for the most part, and widespread social and educational change, while part of the rhetoric, is seldom pursued (Tyack & Cuban, 1995).

DiMaggio and Powell (1983) identified three ways that organizations adopt institutional structures. First, coercive adoption results from pressures by other organizations on which the organization is dependent. For example, in education, this might explain typical school responses to pressures exerted by local businesses that depend on graduates. Second, organizations tend to mimic successful changes made by other organizations— for example, when several companies downsize, this can become a much wider trend. Finally, organizations may use normative means, that is, adopting norms because of the influence of professions (or others higher on the social scale) surrounding them (as members within the profession aspire to that social standing). For example, in education, this might explain much of the rhetoric over the past couple of decades about "professionalizing" teaching and building "career ladders" for teachers.

Because of these three means of adoption, a third premise of the theory is that over time, organizations can become more homogeneous within their particular field. For example, through several means of adopting cultural institutions, over time, schools have become rather homogeneous in structure (Tyack & Cuban, 1995). Institutional theory, therefore, is a lens that is useful in explaining why many of the educational reforms identified in local settings tend to mirror those in other settings, despite the existence of different local politics and political culture. The educational changes that appear to follow such periods of reform may also be more symbolic than substantive. For example, as Ogawa (1992) noted, school-based management was one popular governance reform in the 1980s and 1990s that was largely a symbolic action—that is, shifting decision-making authority and accountability from districts to schools did little to alter how or what teachers teach in classrooms. Yet, in many places, school-based management was enthusiastically endorsed by administrators, parents, and teachers as providing opportunities to participate in policymaking. School-based management can be seen as an organizational response to changing environmental demands. Through using several means of adopting wider social and political values, including symbolic reform, schools can become rather homogeneous in structure over time. Ogawa and colleagues (2003) provided a similar case study of the implementation of standards-based curriculum in a school district, suggesting that whereas the rhetoric suggests standards are to improve accountability and improve outcomes, they may actually serve more symbolic purposes that actually work against the stated aims.

Institutional theory seems to have grown in conception and application in recent years (Willower & Forsyth, 1999). Importantly, however, it still exhibits little consensus or definition of key concepts, measures, and methods because of its lack of attention to processes of institutionalization (Tolbert & Zucker, 1996). It has not been widely applied to educational policy situations; however, it has potential because of its flexibility in explaining changes in policy outcomes over a variety of situations and its adaptability to multilevel analysis (Ogawa, 1992). Future research using institutional theory should pay attention to identifying the propositions that can be derived from the theory.

## AN APPLICATION OF INSTITUTIONAL THEORY

Plank and colleagues (1996) provided an excellent application of institutional theory to the explanation of administrative changes in education that took place across the United States at the turn of the 20th century (e.g., size and composition of boards, numbers of administrators vs. teachers). They concluded from their review of the literature that case studies were the primary research design to investigate these changes. From this literature, the researchers determined that at least four different conceptual models were used to explain the decreases in school board size and increases in school bureaucracy that took place over a short period of time.

In the first explanation, the progressive reformer elite (i.e., middle and upper class reformers) gained political control from the immigrant working class and was successful in asserting its own control in taking over public institutions (e.g., school boards) and public resources (Tyack, 1974). This view explained the reform in some cities. In other cities, however, reform politics were more open and pluralistic. A second view, therefore, suggested that changes emerged out of conflict and bargaining among a diverse array of interests, as opposed to in response to an agenda set by a single elite. Indeed, in some cities, local elites played an important role in school reform politics (e.g., Chicago), but as one among several powerful interests (Plank et al., 1996). In contrast, a third view was one of limited pluralism. In these cases (e.g., Atlanta), the changes were the result of struggles between two local elites, representing only a small class cross-section of the population (i.e., middle and upper class whites). A final explanation noted that in some large cities (e.g., Denver, Seattle), and also in many smaller cities, school administrations were highly centralized from the onset, and no major changes were made in the size of the board or in other administrative arrangements during this time. Instead, changes that were made proceeded incrementally, within existing administrative structures.

Plank and colleagues (1996) argued that none of these conceptual views was completely adequate in explaining the wide range of changes that took place during this period of time. In fact, the reforms adopted ended up making the school structures look quite similar, but the political processes that led to the reforms were quite different (Plank et al., 1996). In order to explain some of the discrepancies in the literature, they designed a different type of study, one that focused on collecting data over a wide range of cities, as opposed to focusing on a small number of cities.

## The Theoretical Propositions

Plank and his colleagues (1996) focused on two theoretical propositions embedded in institutional theory to explain the tendency of schools to reduce the size of their boards of education and increase the size of their administrative staffs during the Municipal Reform. The propositions, which were outlined by DiMaggio and Powell (1983), suggest that both competitive and institutional factors contribute to structural isomorphism among organizations.

- Regarding competition, organizations facing similar problems and opportunities typically respond to them in similar ways. Organizational responses that enhance effectiveness and claims on resources in a changing environment ensure survival and growth. Less successful innovations may lead to decline. Hence, over time, organizations appear more similar because innovations that are not adaptive to changing conditions are selected out.

- Organizations in a common domain also come to resemble each other because of institutional factors that may have little to do with effectiveness or efficiency. They may model themselves after one another because of legal and ideological norms requiring employment professionals who share similar backgrounds and common values. Conformity to rules and rationalized myths increase the likelihood of survival, not by making them more effective, but by enhancing their power and legitimacy. These mechanisms make organizations look similar in terms of structure and activities.

Plank and colleagues (1996) devised a quantitative analysis of existing data to test whether the Progressive Era reforms implemented by big-city school systems could be better explained by a political view (e.g., local city political conflicts, efforts of local politicians) or by an institutional view (e.g., as an adaptive response to changes in their economic, social, and political environments). In the institutional view, population growth, increasing school enrollments, and changing labor markets all created challenges for public school systems in large cities. This environmental complexity suggested the need for increased resources to run larger school systems. Securing increased resource allocations might result from adopting institutional structures such as changing the size and composition of school boards and imitating the practices of large corporations by becoming more efficient and scientifically run (Callahan, 1962).

Plank and his colleagues (1996) used decennial census data from 1890, 1900, 1910, and 1920 to test out institutional and political explanations for changes in the size, rate of growth, and numbers of teachers and administrators employed in each of the cities whose populations were among the

100 largest in any of the 4 decades covered during the era. Their data set, therefore, focused on a relatively large number of cases, as opposed to a small number of cases or a single case (as was often the focus of previous research). They also compiled data on the changes in school board size during the time. While the data were not ideal because they were not fine-grained enough, they allowed a unique type of analysis of historical data. Plank et al. focused on two changes; reductions in school board size from 1890 to 1920, and the ratio of school administrators to teachers in 1920, as a measure of bureaucratization.

## The Hypotheses

Plank and colleagues (1996) linked the theoretical propositions to a set of hypotheses that would be expected to result if the interpretation of change was due more to local politics or to institutional (cultural) factors. A first set of hypotheses distinguishing political and institutional interpretations concerns the political context in which the changes took place. In the political view, political conflict variables, which they defined by proxy indicators of ethnicity (i.e., the percent of the population born outside the United States) and social class (i.e., the share of the labor force employed in industry), should exert effects on the size of school boards. In the institutional view, changes in the size of school boards should be unrelated to the presence of political conflicts.

A second set of hypotheses distinguishing the political and institutional explanations had to do with the social processes that affected cities in similar ways. In the institutional view, Plank and his colleagues reasoned that change in the size of school boards should be related to factors that affected all cities in the same way—primarily growth in urban populations and school enrollments—and should be unrelated to factors associated with political conflict. In the institutional explanation, therefore, indicators of the population size and increase in school enrollments should negatively affect the size of school boards (because they would tend to produce administrative structures that were unwieldy, inefficient, and in need of change). In contrast, in the political view, the size of the urban population and school enrollments would be of little concern, whereas the composition of the population (social class, ethnicity) would be of great concern.

Another reform of the era involved the progressives' desire to use scientific management (and bureaucratization) to run schools more efficiently. The outcome variable used in this part of their analysis was the ratio of administrators to teachers. Institutional theory suggests the size of the population would have a negative effect on the ratio of administrators to teachers because of the operation of institutional rules defining the appropriate complement of administrative roles; that is, larger school systems still have only one superintendent regardless of the number of students enrolled (Plank et al., 1996). Rate of population growth, however, was hypothesized to have a positive effect on the ratio of administrators to teachers—as cities attempted to look innovative by adding administrators. In the political view, the population size and changes in the population size would be inconsequential, although as Plank and colleagues (1996) cautioned, one could argue that increased city size might lead to greater conflict over resources. On the other hand, indicators of political conflict should have positive effects on the ratio of administrators to teachers (i.e., to increase control).

## What Plank and Colleagues Found

First, regarding school board sizes, the researchers found considerable support for the institutional view. As hypothesized, population size was related to reduction in school board size. This suggested that larger cities moved to adopt structures that were believed to be more efficient in dealing with growing enrollments. Neither ethnic composition nor class (which might indicate greater political conflict) was influential. Contrary to the institutional interpretation, however, rate of change in urban population was not significantly associated with reductions in school board size. This result can be partially explained by considering regional differences. Some of the fastest growth took place in cities in the South and West. Reducing school boards was not an issue in some of the cities within these regions, because the school boards never grew to be large (Plank et al., 1996). Most of the boards considered to be too large were in the Northeast. In contrast, however, school boards were reduced in size in all regions, which was consistent with the institutional view that they adopted the change to look innovative.

Second, regarding the bureaucratization of urban school systems (as implied by changes in the ratio of administrators to teachers), they also found some support for the institutional view and weaker support for the political view. As predicted by the institutional view, population size had a negative effect on the ratio of administrators to teachers. It was the single strongest predictor. They also found that administrator/teacher ratios were smaller in cities where a larger proportion of the population was enrolled in public schools and where the percentage of the population enrolled in public schools increased most rapidly. Rate of population growth, however, was not related to increases in the ratio of administrators to teachers, as the institutional perspective suggested. Regional differences were also observed—suggesting that cities in other regions were imitating the modal patterns of bureaucratization defined in the Northeast by adding administrators.

Overall, Plank and colleagues (1996) concluded that the institutional perspective better explained urban school reform during the Progressive Era. The changes in institutional structures represented adaptive responses to the changes in environments (e.g., increasing population) surrounding large-city school systems. The pattern of results suggested that large, northeastern cities reduced the size of their overgrown school boards and expanded the size of the administrative staffs in response to the growth in size and complexity of their school systems. These innovations were soon adopted elsewhere in smaller cities and in other regions. The size of school boards soon converged on an institutionalized norm between seven and nine members (Plank et al., 1996).

The study provides evidence that institutional factors are related to the types of educational policy reforms that reach the agenda and become an accepted type of solution to educational problems. The complex interplay of demographic, economic, and organizational factors that accompanied the industrialization and growth of large American cities led to a common set of school adaptations. The institutional perspective provides a useful explanation about how these types of reform can become widely endorsed and quickly adopted. From a methodological perspective, the study is also exemplary. It provides a rare example demonstrating the testing of competing theoretical explanations with one data set. The authors took great care to lay out the competing conceptual models, to identify the major theoretical principles, and to link them to variables through a set of logical hypotheses, and to present the results in a manner that suggested whether they tended to support or reject the two possible interpretations of the data.

## SUMMARY

The economic and organizational lenses presented in this chapter provide diverse perspectives to analyze policy problems. Readers are invited to examine the tenets of each, the strengths and weaknesses of each, and the ways in which authors in the examples employ them in analyzing policy problems. The key to using any of them in empirical work is whether they provide useful ways to organize the analysis and whether they lead to new discoveries and better explanations of policy phenomena.

## EXERCISES

1. Describe some of the central components of economic perspectives on policy. Why do you think economic arguments have often dominated policy debates? What are some of the ways that economic considerations influence policy processes?

2. School effects studies have been conducted for the past 30 years. In what ways might they reflect economic conceptual underpinnings and a rational view of organizations? Are there differences in the conceptual and methodological underpinnings of school effects and school improvement studies? If so, what might some of those differences be?

3. How do schools as organizations embody both institutional and rational organizational perspectives? How might these theories be useful in explaining the tendencies of schools to support or resist policy changes?

# Chapter 7

# Going Against the Grain: New Approaches

Some conceptual lenses presented previously have focused on a more technical and rational, or functionalist, view of institutions—they are predicated on identifying individuals' rational behavior in pursuit of clearly defined organizational goals. Broadly speaking, these lenses (e.g., policy stages, rational choice theory, production functions, cost-effectiveness analyses) have their roots in a positivist construction of knowledge. In recent decades, however, much dissatisfaction has been directed at dominant methods of studying political, organizational, and educational processes. Criticism suggests that these lenses have not been entirely satisfactory in explaining policy activity or in resolving social problems.

There is no denying the bias toward dominant perspectives that has characterized social policy research and analysis since its early days. In the past, policy-oriented research often focused on using rational argument as a means of confirming theories already held. Commonly accepted approaches used in studying policy in education from the 1960s through the 1980s were largely defined by systems theory (i.e., demands become inputs to the system, which translates resources into outputs and outcomes) and a rational view of organizational behavior. Researchers using these more accepted approaches tended to view the process of knowledge generation as more objective and separated from the subjects providing information about the phenomenon under study.

The theory movement, which was a prominent intellectual influence in educational administration, borrowed largely from social science theory and methods. It suggested that educational organizations could be best understood and improved by applying theories and research methods from the social sciences. Some of the underpinnings included an objective notion of scientific truth, hypothesis testing, rationality embedded within the systems analysis of variables (e.g., structural functionalism), quantitative analysis, and generalization of results. Within the historical context of higher education, some of this thinking made sense. Educational administration was a new field trying to gain a foothold with the more established social science fields within universities, with little consensus about its knowledge base, research methods, and preparatory studies and skills for administrators or professors. Earlier generations of professors tended to move into university settings after long careers as administrators in the public schools. Their undergraduate background training was typically in the humanities or history, and their advanced course work was in education or educational psychology.

The rejection of dominant ways of thinking about organizations and policies was originally a reaction to the force of a singular notion of truth in creating knowledge and the impact of this manner of thinking on creating a type of "privileged" research account (Sackney & Mitchell, 2002). Foucault's (1970, 1973) examinations of power and knowledge suggested that discourses about truth were historically situated, politically charged, and as a result, it was difficult to establish a single objective truth. Derrida (1976, 1977) argued that the meaning of particular ideas depends largely on the ways in which language is used to discuss them. Because meaning relies on specific language, it cannot be established by the use of the same general concept; that is, different language yields different meanings relative to the same general concept. Generalizations, therefore, become suspect because they are heavily influenced by language and their existence excludes competing and equally plausible explanations and interpretations (Boje, Gephart, & Thatchenkery, 1996; Sackney & Mitchell, 2002).

In this chapter, an overview of several new and promising alternative approaches for examining policy activity is presented. These alternative perspectives have their roots in several socially critical theories of knowledge and, as such, require considerable change in thinking about political institutions and educational organizations. This is because many theories that have dominated past research were constructed from assumptions about the world that grew out of an industrial economy and hierarchical social and educational order. Because of globalization, these conditions no longer reflect the reality of many people now (Sackney & Mitchell, 2002). Permeating the critiques of dominant research paradigms is the growing recognition of important intellectual blind spots in accepting one particular approach over other approaches (Heck & Hallinger, 1999; Marshall, 1997). The influence of alternative theories of knowledge, human cognition, research methodology, and the relationship of theory to practice have markedly influenced the fields of administration and policy (Evers & Lakomski, 1996). One of the strengths of alternative views is that they can help researchers, policymakers, and practitioners think about the policy process in more expansive and diverse ways.

Although criticisms of existing research approaches imply empirical inadequacies in supporting proposed theories, it is important to realize that the criticisms may leave unanswered the question of why some theories are more useful in addressing policy problems than others (Feuer et al. 2002; Heck & Hallinger, 1999; Sabatier, 1999). Diverse epistemological perspectives and methodologies can bring exciting new possibilities for thinking about and resolving policy problems. They also bring challenges for organizing findings and drawing conclusions (Heck & Hallinger, 1999; Maxcy, 1995). At one end of the spectrum, positivist research traditions have delineated narrow conditions that must be present for a study to be accepted as policy research. At the postmodern other end, there are no common foundations for creating knowledge.

We have only begun to learn about educational policy processes from alternative conceptualizations and methodologies. Alternative perspectives often focus on reflexivity as a means for understanding how language helps construct reality (Sackney & Mitchell, 2002). This preliminary work has detailed important issues dealing with the description, analysis, interpretation, and writing of research texts. Readers are therefore encouraged to read in depth about particular approaches that they believe might be useful in framing policy research problems. They should also discover for themselves whether empirical studies from each particular lens are useful in illuminating policy problems and solutions in new ways.

## PERSPECTIVES THAT CHALLENGE

Traditional policy analysis has often studied those who hold power within formal political arenas. Dominant lenses (e.g., rational theory, systems analysis) may imply conservative social positions on the nature and purposes of education, educational institutions, and the study and solution of educational problems (Angus, 1996). They tend to see conflict as something to be managed and institutional relations as relatively stable and homogeneous in culture. Contrasting views of institutions suggest that they are arenas for conflict and dispute (Meek, 1988). As opposed to a concern with formal structures and authority, these newer perspectives help provide an understanding of human endeavors from a relational standpoint—that is, how contextual conditions impact on sets of social actors involved in social discourse with respect to interpreting their world (Sackney & Mitchell, 2002). In education, this research is characterized by a multiplicity of views; disillusionment with conventional solutions, new political coalitions around issues such as school choice, racially exclusive schools, and vouchers for religious schools, to name a few examples (Marshall, 1993).

Critical approaches to social analysis entail a critique of inequities in existing social and political relationships (i.e., often due to class, race, and gender) and, subsequently, an advancement toward desired ones (Fay, 1987; Keith, 1996; Lather, 1991; Marshall, 1997). They include a variety of

theories and perspectives including critical theory, feminism, neo-Marxism, cultural studies, critical race theory, postmodernism, and post-
structuralism. Socially critical approaches have been largely ignored by the
positivist stance because of the different manner in which the research questions are posed and the more varied role the researcher can assume in investigating the phenomenon under study and in presenting the research
text. Some critical perspectives may focus more on the critique of existing
social relations, whereas others may focus on advocacy, action, and the re-
construction of social processes. Although there is certainly a certain
amount of overlap in the various lenses that critique dominant social processes, it would be a mistake to suggest that they all can be lumped under
the same socially critical umbrella, because each approach has its own underlying assumptions, research goals and traditions, and empirical literature (Blackmore, 1996).

Policy is inherently value laden because the language used to construct
policies includes certain ideas, concepts, and processes—while excluding
others. Because policy involves the allocation of values, if the process is not
open, it creates power and privilege. Often, the paradigms framing most theories concerning research and practice in educational policy have fallacies including the superiority of the bureaucratic organizational structure, a focus
on the actions of policy elites or powerful individuals, and little concern with
the experiences of those affected by policies. Critical theory focuses attention
on structural, ideological, and cultural features in order to understand why
certain individuals and groups are favored in the distribution of power and
resources. The explanations for existing school inequities are often found in
the persistence of certain meaning systems that influence the social construction of educational policies and practices. Schools help construct social
meanings because they reinforce what counts as knowledge (Angus, 1996).

The feminist perspective on social analysis originated in women's experiences and suspicions about male-dominated theories and organizational
structures (Lather, 1986). Within the general perspective, however, there
are several different types including liberal, Marxist, socialist, existentialist,
radical, and postmodern feminism (Tong, 1989). While they may overlap
and build on each other, they also have varying assumptions and epistemological strengths and weaknesses (see Tong, 1989 or Blackmore, 1996 for
further discussion). Critiques of liberal feminism, for example, suggest that
it infers that many educational solutions (e.g., increasing access of females
to athletics, academic disciplines in higher education, educational leadership positions) can be worked out within existing social relations (Bensimon
& Marshall, 1997; Blackmore, 1996). Radical feminists have brought new
concepts about how power, institutional arrangements that are dominated
by men (e.g., colleges and universities), and political, cultural, and social
traditions may work to silence women.

Although feminist thought shares some similarity with critical theory,
there are some key differences. Feminist critiques of critical theory focus

largely on how critical theorists' concept of generalized oppression fails to address the specificity of how different oppressions work in particular contexts and in relation to each other (Blackmore, 1996). As Kenway and colleagues (1994) concluded, critical theory has largely focused on critiquing and understanding what is, as opposed to new possibilities, action, and change. More recently, feminists and critical theorists have incorporated elements of postmodern and poststructuralist theories of culture based on a common identification with and interest in certain social movements (Kenway, Willis, Blackmore, & Rennie, 1994; Lather, 1991). The various approaches thus share a concern with power, language, communication processes, and voice (Blackmore, 1996).

Postmodernists examine constructions of reality as situated in specific times and places, with particular power structures and accepted discourses about policy problems, solutions, and activities. As Sackney and Mitchell (2002) argued, "language is not seen as a reflection of the real, but rather, instead it gains its signification and meaning through social discourse inasmuch as every experience results in some form of text and meaning that is both written and read through the interplay of various social actors" (p. 887). Power structures are not viewed as fixed, but rather, as relational and held together by discursive practices that are accepted within prevailing historical and cultural traditions. Because there should be no clear center of power, concepts such as empowerment, diversity, collaboration, participation, and voice are important in ensuring that individuals are able to actively participate in policymaking processes.

Power resides in the capacity to define what counts as knowledge—both in terms of what is accepted practice and how to study social processes. As opposed to a focus on formal roles in constructing policy and the presentation of a singular view of what works across large numbers of often faceless subjects (i.e., undefined by ethnicity, gender, class) in terms of desired policy activity, a postmodern approach might attempt to find local, situated understandings of the policy and acceptance of multiple language forms (Sackney & Mitchell, 2002). The analysis could focus on how the targets of educational policy "make sense" out of policies—that is, how they read and interpret, and how they incorporate the meaning of such policies into their experiences (e.g., Blackmore et al., 1993). The purpose of this kind of self-reflection and text analysis is first, to expose our points of view and prejudices and, second, to recognize that through language, discourse, and content, particular views and ways of knowing are affirmed or denied in ways of which we are seldom aware (Sackney & Mitchell, 2002). Research examining such meaning systems often questions the legitimating role that policymakers and administrators play in endorsing existing social arrangements within society, as well as the role of research in defining, maintaining, or changing those relationships.

As suggested previously, in their roles, policymakers learn unstated institutional rules that limit the range of possibilities for finding solutions, that dictate acceptable values, that define the boundaries of policymaking, and that teach how they must conform their behavior to the particular policy subsystem (Marshall et al., 1989). Because of this socialization, educational policy has tended to favor incrementalism, standardization of practices, and stability (Tyack & Cuban, 1995). Schools, as targets of educational policymakers, have been viewed as politically neutral institutions that pursue a set of interests and values that are shared by society. A major impact of these policymaking traditions has been to legitimate policymakers' and administrators' (as implementors of policy) respective functions as allocators of social values, for example, in the institutionalization of inequities within schools (e.g., grouping, tracking, access to quality teachers and other resources). In much research on educational policy, for example, contextual conditions have been regarded primarily as a backdrop to the school, as part of the environment beyond the school, or as a source of inputs to which the school must respond (Angus, 1996).

In socially critical analysis, however, schools are seen as being in constant interaction with multiple contexts as both causes and effects of social and educational concerns. The goal is to understand the implicit social, political, and educational causes and effects of educational policy and educational practices (Angus, 1996). Anderson (1990, 1996), for example, called our attention to how current constructions of social reality are created (or reinforced) in schools. As he argued, rather than places that pursue mythical sets of values endorsed by society, schools should be viewed as arenas of cultural politics in which the educational outcomes are always a function of the daily political struggles that take place within and around them. Minority groups have always had to battle government-sponsored public schools to try to gain educational opportunities. Wealth and privilege have led to understandings of race and ethnicity as a permanent part of the psyche of everyone in the nation (Bell, 1992). Cultural background, religion, and gender all help develop particularized views of schooling (Banks, 1993; Dillard, 2000).

As Anderson (1996) noted, examining the cultural politics of schools draws our attention to how power is exercised not only in politics, but also in the cultural realm through the manipulation of language and other types of symbols. One goal of socially critical analyses is to understand the political and cultural struggles within schools as a way of producing changes, as opposed to merely managing them. Anderson (1990) proposed that researchers must find ways to study the invisible and unobtrusive forms of control exercised in schools in order to address the problems of the underprivileged clients who attend them. The focus of this work is often how sets of relational conditions and dominant discourses, such as policies, serve to silence or to give voice to women and minorities—those who have often been outside of the mainstream policy and research processes.

When the mainstream structures filter out the voices and experiences of some, then the resulting policy processes and outcomes will lack the diversity that is present within the society. Policy analysis that focuses on race, gender, class, and multiculturalism represents a diversity of perspectives and disagreements about what major problems are, their causes, their solutions, as well the ways in which problems should be studied (Marshall, 1993). These "discourses of resistance" (Fine & Weiss, 1993) form a type of challenge to traditional policy structures, analyses, and problem solutions. Researchers adopting these perspectives seek to understand how policies have often impacted those on the margins of the educational system and to express their subjects' dissatisfaction with conventional solutions to the politics of race and gender (Marshall, 1993). This focus suggests that multiple interpretations of data are not only probable, but also desirable because each person reading the data will analyze and interpret from a different social, political, or organizational location. By bringing into the open individuals' needs, aspirations, and experiences with educational policy, alternative perspectives uncover and seek to change various types of institutionalized racism and sexism present in the educational system. Importantly, a focus on formal policy structures presents a type of bias and therefore an incomplete picture of the experiences of those who are not included in the process of setting policy agendas. Policy, therefore, becomes a powerful means of exerting social control.

Although the database is not large yet, a number of these alternative theoretical frameworks have been applied to understanding educational policy problems and activity (e.g., Anderson, 1990; Dillard, 2000; Marshall, 1997; Marshall et al., 1989). These provide an openness and questioning of established ways of analyzing policy problems. As suggested in the last chapter, institutional theorists identify the tendency of schools to adopt innovations to "look" progressive in order to gain social legitimacy and to maintain policymakers' support. Alternative approaches that challenge existing paradigms focus on biases inherent in conventional policy studies that tend to obscure institutional structures that produce power differentials between policymakers and the targets of their policies (Marshall, 1997). Concurrently, a wider array of methodological approaches (i.e., philosophical frameworks for generating knowledge) and methods (ways of collecting data) provide new opportunities to examine policy environments, the complex organizational and governmental relations that envelop the educational policy system and its actors, and the particular design and subsequent "lives" of educational policies during and after their implementation. Just as policymaking has an historical context, so too does scholarship on assessing educational policy.

## CRITICAL THEORY

In this section of the chapter, some of the assumptions underlying newer approaches are presented. The critical perspective draws attention to broad issues concerning culture, power, economics, history, exploitation, and the limits of rational perspectives in understanding institutional dynamics (Blackmore, 1996; Fay, 1987). Thus, it shares many concerns with feminism and postmodern/poststructural thought. Its origins were in Marxism and phenomenology (Blackmore, 1996). For critical theorists, hierarchical arrangements in education are a direct reflection of macro social and cultural arrangements and historical conditions. These can produce differentials in decision-making power, control of resources, and resulting equity.

One of the primary assumptions underlying the critical approach is that educational policies can implicitly institutionalize societal inequities by reinforcing dominant social values. These wider societal structures are reproduced in institutional relationships; that is, ruling groups maintain influence by imposing repressive structures on key organizations such as educational institutions (Benham & Heck, 1998; Corson, 1996). Dominant groups protect their stature by controlling key organizational processes and shaping them to suit their interests. The critical stance questions the legitimating role that policymakers and school personnel play in endorsing and reinforcing existing social arrangements (e.g., power differentials, class differences, unequal access to educational resources).

Another assumption is that traditional policy analyses represent incomplete explanations of the practical realities and problems in education. As Marshall (1997) argued, policymakers and analysts need to recognize how issues of gender, class, and race/ethnicity should be included in policy solutions aimed at improving educational opportunities within schools that lead to successful and productive lives for groups that have been marginalized. Those who are often the targets of well-meaning policy in the past have been locked out of discussions of the problems, proposed solutions, and implementation strategies. Critical theorists often take a problem such as tracking or the gap in achievement between minority and majority students as a starting point for constructing a larger picture of the whole in which the initially identified problem is one component. The analyst then seeks to understand the processes of change in which both the parts and the whole are involved (Cox, 1981).

A third assumption is the concern with changing existing social arrangements. Critical theory is supposed to focus on how to transform existing social inequities identified in schools. Some have argued that because schools are constrained by various political, economic, and social relationships, they are particularly difficult organizations to transform in a systematic way. Despite the usefulness of critical theory in identifying oppressive social arrangements, there is some debate over the extent to which it actually entails advocacy and change—that is, a commitment to challenging existing relationships and using research to reach a certain end (Blackmore, 1996; Lather, 1992; Robinson, 1996). Feminist researchers have commented on the tendency for critical theory to be more focused on identifying oppressive processes than actually changing them. Lather, for example, argued that critical theory is more concerned with disclosure as opposed to prediction or prescription.

Robinson (1996) concluded that weaknesses in the way critical theory addresses change limit its usefulness in actually transforming educational institutions. Critical theory incorporates both a theory of change and purposes to which change should be directed—reconstructed social arrangements that enable individuals who have suffered under those previous arrangements to determine collectively what constitutes their self-interest (Fay, 1987). After understanding the reasons behind existing social arrangements, a social action phase takes place where individuals redress the problems that were the subject of the analysis (Robinson, 1996).

Given the practical commitment of critical theory to changing social relations, Robinson (1996) suggested that it is appropriate to determine how well it produces resolutions to the social problems it addresses. Although the theory has been relatively successful at critiquing social relations, few critical theorists in education have been able to lay the theoretical basis for changing modes of practices in policy and administration and actually implementing such practices (Anderson, 1989; Robinson, 1996). Because critical theory tends to widen the analysis from part to whole, it may stretch our limits to provide the types of analyses that need to be conducted to influence policy (Robinson, 1996). As Weick (1984) reminded us, however, many social reform efforts fail because they are too large in scale.

A second possibility has to do with how researchers and practitioners frame problems and solutions. Robinson (1996) argued that often research meant to uncover oppressive practices in schools (e.g., tracking, achievement gaps) frames the studies in ways that do not suggest to practitioners how to change these practices. She suggested that researchers view the problem in one set of terms (e.g., Why do tracks persist; What are the effects of tracks on students?). In contrast, practitioners focus on how to organize students of varying interests and abilities in ways they believe are effective and efficient, given resource constraints and large numbers of students to be educated.

For policy research conducted from a critical perspective to make a difference in changing school practices, it will be necessary for researchers to understand the values, beliefs, and theories underlying how policymakers and practitioners attempt to solve problems. They must then learn how to intervene in the systems that are the subjects of their analyses (Robinson, 1996). Moreover, it will also be important to have the means to evaluate proposed practices against each other. Critical theory may leave more open the problem of how to decide among competing policy solutions (Robinson, 1996). Robinson suggested that involving stakeholders in a problem-solving discourse over problem causes, methods of inquiry, information, and solutions may assist in solving long-standing problems.

One way to begin to bridge these different discourses about critical theory, change, and policy problems is to focus on a smaller scale on aspects of the policy process that are more hidden within traditional, larger scale analyses (Marshall, 1997). These areas could include the successful implementation of social changes as school case studies; the cultural values embedded in policies; the deconstruction of the language and intent of existing policies; the analysis of policy effects on silenced groups (e.g., women, minorities); the micropolitical aspects of policy; and the policies, programs, and political stances that represent neglected needs in schooling. These are fruitful areas for future research.

## FEMINIST THEORY

The feminist perspective directs attention to the personal dimensions of educational policy, focusing on the perspectives of women. Feminist studies are concerned with historically embedded structures that focus employment around males or that exclude females from pursuing certain careers, with a critique of the assumptions of these policies and structures. If the study included an advocacy stance for redesigning the structures and practices to be more supportive of women, then it would entail feminist critical analysis (Bensimon & Marshall, 1997). Even though a wide variety of analyses are spoken of as feminist, in reality there is no single theory regarding feminist analysis (Tong, 1989). Instead, there are a variety of feminist ideological positions that inform the research questions posed, the decisions made about research design, and the conclusions and recommendations that are made about change (see Bensimon & Marshall, 1997, for further discussion). Bensimon and Marshall outlined some of the differences underlying liberal feminism (i.e., a more accepting version grounded in conceptions of individuals' civil rights and emphasizing equal access to domains where men traditionally dominate), cultural feminism (i.e., a version that suggests women and men are different because of socialization to different roles in society), power and politics feminism (i.e., identifying the range of structural, overt, and subtle ways through which men retain power and control and suggesting that alternative means must be constructed that recognize the differences), postpositivist feminism (i.e., using language at center of analyses to understand existing power relations and to identify strategies for change), and critical theory (i.e., examining how domination occurs at the intersection of sex, race, sexual orientation, and class, and focusing on how individuals can resist oppression ).

There are several common characteristics of feminist studies (Bensimon & Marshall, 1997). First, feminist perspectives put the social construction of gender at the center of the inquiry within which meaning and value are assigned to organizing social relations (Harding, 1986). Gender is viewed as a basic organizing principle that shapes the conditions of subjects' lives (Lather, 1992). More specifically, gender structures experiences, relationships, processes, practices, and outcomes. This is found within many occupational structures that focus on men's work and women's work (e.g., academic life, school administration, the practice of law). Second, most feminist perspectives suggest that equity cannot be attained without critical and gender-based appraisals of structures, practices, and policies (e.g., including language) that create patronizing, indifferent, or hostile workplaces for women (Tierney & Bensimon, 1996). Third, more recently, postmodernist feminism during the 1990s has developed from realizations that women are not a universal class; that is, politics of difference arose as African American and "third world" feminists challenged the dominant voice of White, middle class feminists (Blackmore, 1996).

Feminist policy analysis involves a critique of knowledge gained from mainstream policy analysis and the design of feminist policy studies. It concerns the analysis of differences, local context, and specificity (e.g., regarding not only gender, but also race and class). The data in feminist studies are the experiences of women. Feminist theorists, for example, pointed out the androcentric bias in the theories, policies, and methodologies in educational administrative research that result from focusing on the behavior of males (and particularly White males) universally (Shakeshaft & Hanson, 1986). As Marshall (1993) noted, feminist studies are characterized by disillusionment with conventional liberal political solutions to fix schools (e.g., lengthening the school year, pay incentives, staff development) and interest in pursuing more radical solutions (e..g, single-sex schools, schools for African American males, community control, community investment).

Feminist theory suggests that one of the ways that mainstream policy analysis has failed is apparent in studies that are not sensitive to the nature of groups (e.g., gender, class, ethnicity). This is an area where technical–rational policy analyses have had little success. For example, rationalist studies on gender might describe demographic differences between women and men in terms of salary, job satisfaction, or demographic trends in entrance to universities. Differences between men and women on these variables would be explained in terms of existing organizational relations (e.g., enhancing communication and understanding), as opposed to underlying assumptions about how structures and processes may operate within various settings to marginalize or silence women. In rationally based analyses, proposed solutions for these problems might focus on providing greater equity for women by raising their salaries, providing programs to increase women's awareness of and entry into management positions, or delineating ways to increase their job satisfaction within present organizational systems (e.g., see Tong, 1989). As some have suggested, rational analyses (i.e., including liberal feminism) tend to focus on changing women to become more like men, rather than on changing organizations and their cultures (Blackmore, 1996).

In contrast, more radical variants of feminist analysis (e.g., radical feminism, poststructural feminism) attempt to provide explanations about political, social, and organizational phenomena from the perspectives of women. As Blackmore (1996) noted, earlier feminist critiques often focused more on leadership (e.g., women's ways of leading) than on power, viewing power in negative terms and characterizing women as powerless. Fundamental to these newer feminist critiques is the redefinition of power and its exercise, as well as the recognition of the relationship between power and knowledge construction. Bensimon and Marshall (1997) argued that the feminist analysis of policy focuses on an awareness of how gender bias is embedded in disciplines, theories of knowledge, and research designs that are at the base of conventional policy analyses (which are supposed to be neutral).

Poststructural theories of power, which have been incorporated into feminist thought, suggest the struggle against male dominance in many organizational settings is fundamentally different for different women (Blackmore, 1996). Increasingly, informed by radical feminists, feminist inquiry also examines the powerful shaping forces of contextual organizational factors, race, class and sexual orientation, examining the interaction of such social forces in the construction of subjects' lives (Lather, 1991; Robinson, 1996). An analysis of this dominance for different women involves considering the extent to which mainstream techniques fail to take into account their experiences that may not be typical of men and also other women—that is, their experiences are made marginal or invisible.

Ultimately, most types of feminist analyses are interventionist and seek to transform institutions. Importantly, whereas conventional analyses of policy and institutional processes often aim to promote equal access and equity, feminist analysis seeks to change structures that disadvantage women, as opposed to merely ensuring that women have equal access to outcomes. As Blackmore (1996) argued, much mainstream policy knowledge has been framed by reactive theories (e.g., policy stages, systems theory, elite theory). For example, policy is viewed as resulting from more static and regular processes—environmental demands are made, inputs are presented, turned into policies, with largely predictable outcomes. It has not been informed to any great extent by theories of action (e.g., change theories). Therefore, the aim of feminist scholarship is not only to have women's diverse views included and incorporated into mainstream policy discussion, but further, to dismantle systems of institutionalized power and replace them with more preferable ones (see Marshall & Anderson, 1995).

## POSTMODERN AND POSTSTRUCTURAL PERSPECTIVES

Postmodernism also represents a shift away from the assumptions of the rational frame of scientific thinking and progress directed at a narrow description of "objective truth" that represented modernist thought (Lather, 1992; Sackney & Mitchell, 2002). In recent years, traditional social and organizational arrangements (e.g., bureaucracy, social class) have been called into question as representing boundaries against the full expression of human existence. Postmodernism actually represents several streams of social theory in which there is little agreement about the meaning of key terms, concepts, and constructs (Sackney & Mitchell, 2002). With this caution in mind, postmodernism can be seen as both a cultural form or social era that follows modernism (i.e., its historical context) and as an epistemology or method that centers on reconceptualizing how we perceive, experience, and understand the empirical world (Sackney & Mitchell, 2002). Setting aside its historical context, a first characteristic of postmodern thought is that it represents a rejection of the Enlightenment dualities such as rationality and emotion, rights and responsibilities, subjective and objective, male and female, and universal and particular (Blackmore, 1996; Lather, 1991). It is directed at examining the historical processes, complexity, power, and various contingencies in constructing knowledge.

A second characteristic is the rejection of generalizations (called *grand narratives*), which usually formed the basis of privileged research accounts (Anglo, male-centered). This concern, however, has subsequently evolved into a search for contextualized understandings, often focusing on how language is used to construct text and how various texts are read and understood by social actors (Sackney & Mitchell, 2002). Because of the role language plays in constructing reality, truth cannot be seen as static and objective. This is because meanings are shifting, language is understood differently by individuals, and knowledge is constantly changing. Hence, reality is replaced by its representations, making it ultimately difficult to distinguish between them (Sackney & Mitchell, 2002). This set of conditions tends to diminish rational attempts to know.

A third characteristic concerns power and how it influences discourse surrounding the construction and dissemination of knowledge. If some individuals are more powerful than others, their particular accounts and views take on greater significance in the construction of knowledge. For postmodernists, there should be no static power centers, because as knowledge and meanings shift, so does power (Sackney & Mitchell, 2002). Postmodern analysis therefore focuses on multiple sources of data and interpretation, such that no particular source receives greater privilege than others.

Poststructural refers to the working out of cultural theory within the postmodern context—especially with regard to theories of representation (Lather, 1991). In particular, poststructural approaches to the construction of scientific knowledge have called attention to the use of language in the research process (Grant & Fine, 1992). This placed the researcher at the center of how research is conducted and the text of the research written. Issues of language are salient to data collection, analysis, and interpretation. The intellectual roots of this work are the analysis of verbal and nonverbal behavior, communication within and across different groups, conversational analysis, and discourse analysis (Gee, Michaels, & O'Conner, 1992). The analysis can focus on the structure of language and features of texts, or on how texts relate to social, cognitive, political, and cultural constructions.

The interpretation of the research text is influenced by the text's structure and the social circumstances surrounding its production (Gee et al.,

1992). How readers read and interpret the research text is at the core of textual concerns. Readers' own backgrounds may differ from those of researchers. This in turn can influence their interpretations of the text. The subject's language may also differ from the researcher's language (Gee et al., 1992). Research results, therefore, are always a construction because the researcher puts herself or himself into the process of collecting, analyzing, and interpreting the data. It is important to recognize that this is the case, regardless of the extent to which the researcher has or has not participated in what is being studied. More specifically, postmodern and poststructural approaches deconstruct the scientific knowledge base of traditional theory.

Importantly, rather than focusing on a particular lens or paradigm for understanding, postmodern and poststructural approaches imply that there is no clear window into the inner life of subjects. Our attempts to describe and understand actors' belief systems, motivations, and behavior are always filtered through lenses of gender, class, and ethnicity. These affect the analyst or researcher's construction of the study's text. For these reasons, multiple perspectives are desirable because each reader will tend to analyze and interpret information from a different personal, social, and organizational location (Sackney & Mitchell, 2002).

Because differences abound, postmodern and poststructural views lead scholars to examine the research process and the role of the researcher, subjects, and readers in this process. They also suggest that there is much worth studying that lies "in the cracks" after systematic categorizations have been made (Lather, 1992; Lecercle, 1990). The relationships between researcher and subjects impact the research, no matter if the intended stance is to remain neutral or a variety of biases is acknowledged.

From a postmodern perspective, policy processes and institutions are viewed relationally as sets of actors involved in interpreting their world (Sackney & Mitchell, 2002). These interpretations are related to the contexts within which they work and the activities that they conduct. This places the research emphasis on bringing their stories to light in ways that reduce privilege and power (i.e., of both certain subjects such as policymakers, administrators, and the researcher). Concerns with textual issues have led some researchers to examine how they construct their research texts. Some could argue that any attempt to explain subjects' accounts would result in a researcher's grand narrative. This influence has been much felt in other perspectives such as feminism (Blackmore, 1996). As Blount (1994) suggested, feminism offers strong theories for social critique and political action aimed at dismantling oppressive systems, whereas postmodernists and poststructuralists offer theoretical tools for challenging feminist tendencies toward a limited grand narrative involving the experiences of women.

The concerns expressed over the construction and presentation of texts have led researchers to consider the nature of their analyses and texts in different manners. One attempted solution to this dilemma has been to present the participants' texts with little or no analysis from the researcher, or to allow the participants to construct and interpret their own texts. This implies a type of reflective, collaborative, and conscious process to develop the text. The blending of researcher and subject suggests ways in which both engage in the process of interpreting their lives and work within various political and cultural contexts. Personal experience methods such as biography and narrative uncover subjects' beliefs and perceptions and articulate them more directly to readers.

It is important to consider that these types of studies may be quite opposed to policymakers' notions about discourses concerning school reform (e.g., holding schools accountable, improving test scores). This can be challenging in using this approach to examine policy problems. There are few guidelines governing the methodology. On the plus side, however, the approach is unique in raising questions about language and power, as well as relationships among policymakers, practitioners, targets of policy, and researchers.

## SUMMARY OF STRENGTHS AND WEAKNESSES OF THESE APPROACHES

Empirical studies that illustrate these newer approaches in the area of educational policy are still rather limited. To date, a good number of examples are chapters in edited volumes, which do not go through the same extensive peer review and revision process. For this reason, there is a need for more exemplars that can help new researchers think about how to approach this type of work in K–12 policy analysis (e.g., see Kenway et al., 1994). There are a number of examples in higher education (e.g., Moore & Sagaria, 1993; Park, 1996; Rich, 1993; Townsend, 1993). Moreover, the various theoretical perspectives are not as developed yet compared with some of the other frameworks—that is, what premises underlie each theory, how the research is framed, what elements characterize an analysis, and what each illuminates about the structure of K–12 and higher education. As Blackmore (1996) suggested, often researchers and policymakers frame problems in different ways, and this can obscure or diminish the influence of the research in actually changing educational practices.

Similarly, with most of the newer analytic frames, there are few guidelines regarding methodology. For example, currently there are few norms for how to present data and construct the text within the context of examining educational policy. Researchers have identified a number of concerns with the construction of research texts. These concerns include how to approach the researcher–subject relationship, how to write up field notes, and how to present holistic accounts of experience. The intention is to reduce the intrusion of researchers' own biases by letting subjects construct their own narratives of their experiences.

Despite the shortage of literature illustrating these newer approaches for examining educational policy, there is obvious value in these types of analyses that goes against the established grain. Besides raising questions about methodological issues, they also highlight substantive concerns in educational policy such who has access to the policy system, who is served, and how well they are served by various educational policies. They also question the logic of continuing to use rationalist-economic frameworks on school reform (i.e., what is the result on outcomes if we increase this particular input variable) in the face of evidence that studies of inputs and outputs have not led to blueprints that can be used to improve schools successfully.

The coming decade is likely to see greater flexibility, experimentation, and eclecticism in terms of philosophical stances and methodologies used to study educational policy. These new orientations will require considerable demonstration, application, and further discussion among policymakers, researchers, and practitioners. So far the approaches have illuminated important blind spots in previous analyses. Critique and exposition of relevant philosophical frameworks have served a useful purpose to date. However, systematic empirical inquiry must follow. There is also a need to continue conversations about philosophical foundations and methods in academic, policymaking and practitioner forums.

## BLACKMORE, KENWAY, WILLIS, AND RENNIE'S (1993) STUDY OF GENDER POLICY

Blackmore, Kenway, Willis, and Rennie (1993) provided an excellent analysis of a gender equity policy in Australian schools from a feminist (and poststructural) perspective. In Australia, there was a major effort for gender reform in the schools beginning in the mid-1970s. Much of the effort centered on increasing career opportunities by increasing women's access to math and science courses and by using methods of instruction that would be more gender inclusive. As Blackmore and colleagues suggested, the dominant gender policy reform model in Australia followed a liberal feminist approach. More specifically, the model assumed a linear relationship between policy interventions and outcomes, largely ignored different cultural contexts, gauged the success for women in male terms, left unchallenged unequal power relations and biases embedded in organizational structures, and assumed that the policy would be received uncritically and accepted by the targeted population.

The assumptions underlying the model implied that schools' curricula were appropriate, but that males made well-informed choices about what courses to take and what careers to pursue, whereas females made ill-informed choices. From this perspective, the policy problem reduced to one of changing the choices that girls made. Therefore, the basic reform program was based on the assumption of girls' underachievement in identified curricular areas. Over the years, however, several reviews of the policy's implementation determined that despite the various policy initiatives, there had been no substantive changes in the pattern of girls' postschool choices of education or training.

## Intents of the Study

This lack of change suggested a reexamination of the assumptions underlying gender reform policies in Australia (i.e., their content and focus), the manner in which they had been studied previously, and whether the overall change process was itself different when dealing with gender (Blackmore et al., 1993). The authors suggested that the actual intents of policymakers in the case of gender reform were not clear, nor were the conventional ways of examining policy implementation adequate; that is, although various gender policies had been implemented, previous analyses did not address how they were being received within school sites. More specifically, existing literature viewed the teachers, parents, and students as passive "recipients" of policies who either implemented them without problem or resisted them (Blackmore et al., 1993). As the authors argued, the lack of extensive empirical literature on the policy's implementation and the failure of what research did exist to provide adequate theoretical frameworks were largely due to a lack of empirical investigation about how actors at the school level (i.e., administrators, teachers, students) received the gender reform initiatives.

## Analyses

To accomplish their research goals, the authors examined ways in which the policy was read, interpreted, and acted on within the specific contextual settings of two schools (e.g., their structures, cultures, and individuals). The authors used a variety of data collection techniques (interviews, observation of classes, attendance at meetings, informal and formal meetings, shadowing, staff and student evaluations, and writing) to capture the dynamics of policy implementation within the contextualized school settings. These varied data sources allowed the researchers to get an up-close view of how both teachers and female students read and responded to the policy's text.

The analysis also demonstrated the importance of considering policy implementation within specific organizational contexts—because each setting had a profound influence on how the policy was understood, implemented, and interpreted. In one school, for example, the policy was perceived as more of an "add on" to the school's curricular program; that is, it was a mostly marginalized approach to gender reform that included some relatively standard programs—girls-only math, science, and computer classes—and additional policies concerning sexual harassment and equal opportunity. The second school had these same basic programs and policies. In addition, however, the authors found it also had more breadth and innovation in gender equity programs that included community-oriented activities (e.g., self-defense, TV and publicity programs in the press, multilingual community nights, girls into science career nights, school–industry links) and work transition for girls, girls-only summer camps, and special curricular programs.

As a lens to analyze the implementation of gender policy, the authors drew on feminist poststructuralism and culture studies. Feminist post-structuralism suggests that ideas about meaning, the way in which meaning is made, the way it circulates, the impact it has, and finally, the connections that are made between meaning and power are shifting rather than fixed (Blackmore et al., 1993). For example, these differences among women may arise from race, ethnicity, and class. It suggests that policy is interpreted in highly differential ways in specific contexts by those it is expected to assist in a homogeneous way. Through this lens, the authors examined how social and cultural practices impact the production of a policy's text (e.g., assumptions and traditions underlying how the policy is developed and implemented) and its reception—that is, the way it is read and used in defining social relations in people's daily lives (Kenway, 1992).

One aspect of this type of analysis is the relationship of the policy document to larger cultural issues that influence its development. Another aspect is the actual reading and understanding of the document itself by both policymakers and recipients. Policymakers thus are both producers and consumers of these texts, as they draw on several often contradictory discourses (Blackmore et al., 1993). Moreover, the consumers of written policy interact with the texts in various ways based on their own perspectives. Individuals and groups may read and interpret the text selectively. This suggests that policymakers do not necessarily control the ways in which their policies are "read" into practice. At the same time, however, certain readings of the text may be privileged by both students and teachers; the privileged status of some readings may constrain the possibilities of other readings.

## Findings

In the first school, researchers found that there was a schoolwide discourse of equal opportunity focused on integrating gender equality into the entire school. At the same time, there were several different groupings of teachers according to how they positioned themselves with respect to the policy in general. For example, a minority of the staff was more vocal about feminist viewpoints, involved in extraschool activities and postgraduate studies, and interested in feminist literature. Another group of teachers was less vocal, but prepared to teach the gender-inclusive curricula. A third group, "the silent majority," rarely stated their positions publicly. They adopted the interconnected view that girls were disadvantaged in mixed classes because boys monopolized teacher time; girls benefitted from entering nontraditional subject areas such as math; and girls lacked self-esteem. Finally, there was a group comprised of teachers who were active opponents to changes and gender reform in particular. They were predominantly men and had little inclination to change their teaching practices or curriculum with respect to girls, unless forced to do so.

The researchers found that successful integration of the gender policy into the curriculum at the school level was also related to other reforms that were taking place simultaneously in the school. The gender-inclusive curriculum and teaching practices had to be legitimized by other discourses—that is, those surrounding the nature of good teaching practice. Gender reform was "piggybacked" on other reforms that required that gender be addressed (e.g., curriculum frameworks and the introduction of a certificate of education). This whole-school approach favored producing policies and then implementing them throughout the entire school. Adopting this overall approach to reform meant that change took longer than initially anticipated. Consequently, staff not directly involved with the initial policy writing and activities to raise awareness saw the first years of policy implementation as unsuccessful. These school members suggested that too much emphasis was placed on writing policies and not enough on actually doing (i.e., producing the classroom materials). Finally, many of the initiatives created by the reform-minded group of faculty were subverted or distorted in a variety of ways by others. These efforts had to do with attention given to changing male faculty and boys' perceptions of women.

The researchers found that most staff read the policy text in a noncritical manner. They believed in gender equity and the well-known strategies (i.e., girls-only math, group work in science). This allowed the silent majority group to look for a quick fix to the "girl problem," in a sense not having to evaluate the more subtle beliefs, attitudes, and aspects such as language practices (Blackmore et al., 1993). Most staff accepted gender-inclusive curriculum as good teaching practice, yet girls-only activities were still seen as favoring girls by many students, staff, and parents, and therefore were perceived as unfair. Equality was interpreted as meaning equal treatment—not treatment according to the different needs of girls. Others suggested that students needed different treatment, but according to their individual needs and not because they were male or female. These latter positions tended to shift away from the assumption that girls had been systematically disadvantaged and therefore needed different or additional programs and resources as a group—which was the original message of the policy writers. Thus, the policy was selectively read in ways that changed its initial intentions.

In the second school, the activities resulting from the policy's implementation tended to be add-on or marginal to the mainstream curriculum (e.g., improving physical facilities for females, purchasing gender-inclusive materials, offering self-defense classes for females, providing videos about unequal classroom participation by boys and girls, increasing career advice). The responsibility for specific projects constantly shifted among individuals. The equity discourse was subordinate to other more significant reform discourses, like curriculum reform. More radical views of feminists were totally dismissed. However, the policy was superficially accepted as addressing females' disadvantage. Therefore, single-sex classes were seen as recipes for resolving females' problems, and hence, this did not require teachers to reflect on or alter their own teaching practices (Blackmore et al., 1993).

At this school, a female math class was created, and the coordinator convinced a number of better achievers among the women in math to take an additional two-period extension. Most of these women also took a two-period science class during their next year. Females saw this class as directed toward them out of concern that women should have more career choices because more young women drop out of school than do young men and because women don't like math. Through self-selection and teacher selection, this group was highly motivated to continue with math and science. Within this group, there were three basic positions toward the gender policy. Females drew upon these positions differently, depending on their positioning within the school culture as well as the various discourses of feminism, liberalism, and cultural pluralism (Blackmore et al., 1993).

The feminist position was voiced by those young women who felt women's disadvantage within the dominant notions of equal opportunity. This was expressed as liking single-sex classes because they were more supportive environments for women. Females in this group felt males disrupted classes and called females names, which impacted females' capacity to learn. They also felt that males do this because they are more likely to go into a trade (e.g., carpenter) or family business, whereas females have to pursue further education to break out of their traditional secretarial work.

A second group was labeled the "strong girls." This was the most widely espoused view. This group saw the feminist view as "anti-male" and did not wanted to be associated with that extreme position. Young women in this group were likely to oppose differential treatment of females as unfair to males, arguing that females as a group were not disadvantaged, because they as individuals did not feel disadvantaged. This group maintained that females can be just as good in math and science as males, so they don't need separate classes. Yet, these young women accepted the separate classes as generally increasing their options for work in the future.

They drew largely on the view of liberal feminism, emphasizing equal access and merit, rather than that of social justice or cultural difference. As one young woman suggested, having a girls' council was unfair because if they had a boys' council, it would be labeled as sexist and a big uproar would result (Blackmore et al., 1993). Those in the group tended to feel that equal opportunity meant that all are treated equally. Any different treatment would be unfair to males. The strong girls accepted males' teasing and jokes because they "are used to it … and know the boys don't mean it. You get used to it as you know they are mucking around" (p. 196). They tended to blame other females as not being able to cope with the boys or lacking in confidence and being weak. This put them in opposition with feminist teachers who tended to try to protect girls from harassment; that is, the strong girls saw sexual harassment policies as necessary only to assist weak girls (Blackmore et al., 1993).

The third group consisted of non-Australians and "nerds." Those not born in Australia tended to feel that Australia offered equal opportunity and acceptance of many different ethnic groups. One young woman felt whatever harassment she experienced was largely because of cultural and language differences, suggesting that when "you come from another country, when you are black or not white, they tease you. They tease you because of your colour or accent" (p. 198). In this case, gender was not seen as the cause of the treatment so much as racism was. As one female expressed it, "Some guys will pick on girls ... who aren't normal. They are nerds or non-Australian. Boys direct attention to that" (p. 198). Ironically, in this group some saw the problems as due to the young men's lack of self-esteem and ability.

As the authors noted, the responses to the policy were quite different across the groups. In the case of the strong girls, who actually opposed the policy in principle because it was unfair for females to get special treatment, this interpretation suggested that equal opportunity should be equated with equal treatment. This was based on the feeling that they as individuals were not disadvantaged, so other females (described by default as weaker) were not deserving of this intervening type of policy. In contrast, the women in the non-Australian and nerd group actually read the policy text in an entirely different way than it was intended (i.e., their mistreatment being the result of racism or demonstrating the weaknesses of males). Moreover, the policy did not necessarily translate into more equitable practices in other areas; that is, sympathy or even claims for gender equality did not mean sympathy for claims for race or class equality (Blackmore et al., 1993).

## How Policies Are Understood and Acted Upon

From their investigation, the Blackmore and her colleagues (1993) drew several important conclusions for examining how policies are understood and acted on by those who are the targets of the policy. First, it demonstrated the power of the policy to legitimate the beliefs and activities of those faculty committed to create an environment that is more accepting of women's needs. Second, it demonstrated the limitations of large-scale policy initiatives that do not consider the multiple types of readings of the policy text within different types of settings. Some determinants of these readings were the level of gender awareness and receptivity in the school, the beliefs and practices that become embedded in the school's culture and organization, and the class, racial, ethnic, and sexual composition of the school's students (Blackmore et al., 1993). This finding implies the need to consider the level of receptivity to particular policies, working with those interpretations that have more legitimacy, while also seeking to shift the interpretations in more desired directions and reconstructing new interpretations that agree with the experiences of students and teachers—that is, reformulating and reconceptualizing key terms in ways that do not reproduce inequitable practices (Blackmore et al., 1993).

Overall, the study illuminated how the intents of policies are constrained at the school level, in that only certain activities may be legitimated, and the policy text itself is limited by the selective readings of the majority of students. This finding suggests challenges for implementing policies created at the macrolevel (e.g., state) in terms of how they are interpreted and practiced at the microlevel within individual schools. For example, regarding gender, it indicates that relational aspects of gender should be taken into account. As the authors noted, because masculinity is deeply ingrained in the schools, focusing gender equity programs on women made masculinity problematic (Blackmore et al., 1993), because the two are interrelated. These programs often have little relevance to males, so the key strategy issue becomes how to direct attention to gender relations and masculinity without shifting attention away from women.

## SUMMARY

One of the blind spots in many policy analyses is that single results are often assumed for all intended targets. The focus in traditional analyses is generally on the macro level, and the tone of the analysis is more neutral and disinterested. The approaches presented in this chapter ask different types of questions and examine the way the policy documents are being read and interpreted by various groups within the school. Issues of gender, culture, language, power, and privilege are at the center of their questions, their analyses, and their conclusions. They tend to turn traditional approaches sideways—that is, they look between the cracks, focus on microanalysis where the focus is on results that are contextualized as opposed to generalized, and employ methods of analysis (e.g., interpretive, critical) that allow them to get up close.

Importantly, they provide analysis that is not directed toward the problems and solutions of those who create the problems, so much as they are directed at those who are silenced, declared irrelevant, or ignored (Marshall, 1997). They demonstrate ways to think about policy questions differently, to expand analytic lenses to include critical and feminist lenses, and are directed toward uncovering sources of oppression, domination or marginalization, and examining how such policies are received, and can be reinterpreted, in ways that are more attentive to the needs, aspirations, and values of those at the margins of the policy process (Marshall, 1997).

## EXERCISES

1. Describe some of the ways in which alternative lenses mentioned in the chapter challenge traditional views of the policy process. In what ways do they shift the attention of our policy analyses?

2. Suppose a policy researcher is interested in studying reasons for differences in science achievement among various groups of students (e.g., gender, socioeconomic background, culture or ethnicity). How might the research be framed (e.g., focus, purpose, research question) from the perspectives of liberal feminism, critical theory, and poststructuralism? What might be the criticisms of each perspective from the standpoint of some other lenses?

3. Do you believe that policy researchers have a social responsibility to advocate for, or become actively involved in seeing their recommendations for policy changes implemented? Why or why not? What might be some of the implications of their involvement or noninvolvement?

# *III*

# *POLICY RESEARCH METHODS*

Calls for improving schooling through diverse reforms (e.g., charters, site-based management, vouchers, standards, accountability) have focused attention on the role of research in providing definitive answers about the relative merits of educational innovations. Many of these reforms, however, have not been adequately evaluated to determine whether they actually result in improved outcomes. Both policymakers and researchers have concluded that there is a need for stronger conceptual frameworks and methods for conducting rigorous scientific research that has implications for producing educational policies (e.g., Feuer, Towne, & Shavelson, 2002). There is considerable debate among various stakeholders, however, about what constitutes rigorous and scientific.

Policy scholars have acknowledged that relatively narrow views on conceptual models and methods have dominated past policy research (Boyd, 1988; Marshall, 1997). As suggested in chapters 4 through 7, alternative theoretical orientations about educational policy derive from a broader range of epistemological views, raise different research questions, and lead researchers toward more diverse methods of empirical study. Critics argue that past research has primarily been limited by an overreliance on quantitative analytic methods and hypothesis testing (i.e., both closely identified with positivism), a trend that was established from early years in policy analysis and the result of the requirement of policymakers for facts (Bulmer, 1982). Criticisms of a narrow, positivist approach to past policy research imply empirical inadequacies in supporting proposed theories. Of course, the overreliance on one particular research approach can lead to "blind spots" in the field related to the types of questions asked, the manner in which studies are conducted, and the ways in which data are analyzed and presented. For example, although critics suggest quantitative research has been overutilized in educational policy research (e.g., primarily utilizing correlational and causal-comparative, nonexperimental designs), it is also the case that experimental designs (i.e., randomized field trials with random assignment of subjects to treatment and control groups and the manipulation of a treatment variable) have been little used. This occurs despite the acknowledged superiority of this type of design for drawing inferences about the impacts of planned change compared with other types of research designs (Cook, 2002; Feuer et al., 2002; Slavin, 2002).

The federal education mandate No Child Left Behind Act of 2001 (Public Law 107-110), which amends the Elementary and Secondary Education Act of 1965, became law in January, 2002. This mandate represents the latest attempt to improve poorly performing schools by holding educators accountable for outcomes. The law has a number of standards-setting, testing, and accountability provisions that require changes in the practices of many states (Linn, Baker & Betebenner, 2002). Importantly, No Child Left Behind (NCLB) and other recent federal policy developments also call for a renewed emphasis on educational research to document practices that have an impact on educational improvement. In numerous passages, NCLB details that rigorous educational research on improving educational practices should equate with the use of experimental designs (i.e., randomized, controlled field trials). This preference for a particular type of design has also translated into proposed criteria for federal funding of future educational policy research. The passage of NCLB has therefore generated a tremendous amount of interest and discussion among practitioners, policymakers, and researchers about the nature of scientific research and the appropriate use of the methodological perspectives of various research designs in conducting policy-related research. It has also stirred up the political question of who should define the nature and conduct of educational research.

Progress in a field of study occurs when headway occurs simultaneously on substantive, theoretical, and methodological fronts (Hallinger & Heck, 1996). The time to think about substantive issues, theoretical lenses, and methodology is before the study is conducted. The first two sections of the book present several different conceptual frameworks and theories that have been used in framing studies that examine educational policy issues. The political turbulence surrounding the nature and usefulness of policy research for resolving critical educational problems such as the improvement of school outcomes and the closing of achievement gaps between minority and majority students reiterates the importance of conceptual underpinnings and research methods in framing the scientific study of policy problems.

In the next section of the book, our attention turns to research methods for conducting policy research. Currently, there are few research methods texts directed at conducting policy research. Moreover, policy research methods are typically not discussed in existing research texts. Most quantitative texts in education present methods and techniques appropriate to using experimental designs (e.g., $t$ tests, analysis of variance, multivariate analysis of variance, regression) in relatively limited settings (e.g., a treatment and control groups with a small number of subjects), whereas qualitative texts often center on participant observation (fieldwork), interviewing strategies, and analysis (e.g., content analysis, constant comparative method). Policy researchers, therefore, typically have had to adapt the methods they use from a variety of other sources including psychology and educational psychology texts, studies they have seen in journals, and their own research experience.

Chapter 8 provides an overview of policy methods, focusing in particular on several research designs that can be used in pursuing particular types of policy research purposes and questions including experimental and quasi-experimental, nonexperimental, case study, and historical designs. Chapter 9 presents an introduction to the use of qualitative methods in conducting case studies and historical studies. In chapter 10, basic issues in using quantitative methods for policy research are discussed—with a focus on nonexperimental designs and the use of multilevel modeling—because these are necessary tools in the investigation of how policies impact schools and students. Chapter 11 provides an introduction to the use of longitudinal data in studying changes in policy activity or student growth over time. These techniques can be used with experimental, quasi-experimental, and nonexperimental designs. For chapters 10 and 11, some sample data are also provided in the appendix, so interested students can recreate or extend some of the analyses using the appropriate multilevel modeling computer software.

# Chapter 8

# An Overview of Method
# in Policy Research

The object of policy research is to understand the policy world in terms of its patterns and idiosyncracies and to formulate explanations of our observations. Policy knowledge is constructed from the commonly used theoretical and conceptual frameworks, the constructs included in them, and the accumulated knowledge from previous studies (Smart, 2002). As developed in previous sections of the book, conceptual frameworks, theories, and models are beneficial to the design of studies in several ways. They provide a structure to the research process by identifying important constructs to be included in the study and by suggesting relationships among the constructs. Conceptual lenses help contribute to the accumulation of knowledge by providing a basis for comparing the results of a current study with previous findings within a logical and consistent framework (Smart, 2002)—in short, they help frame the way the researcher will approach the research study. To the extent that conceptual frameworks and theories are applied to important policy issues, they can also generate further research because they provide a useful structure for understanding policy problems and the usefulness of solutions.

It is important that researchers work to integrate their conceptual frameworks or theories with their procedures of scientific inquiry. Methodology concerns the process by which we construct knowledge. It is the description, explanation, and justification of research methods (Kaplan, 1964). Methodology concerns the underlying theories about how we construct knowledge (epistemology) and also the analytic frameworks that guide the research process. Where methodology refers to the philosophical underpinnings and assumptions embedded in how researcher's construct knowledge, method refers to the "moves," or logic that the researcher uses in conducting the study (e.g., how research questions are stated; sampling strategy; data collection procedures; ways of structuring, analyzing, and interpreting the data). Techniques are the specific means used to gather information (e.g., survey, interview, observation). The aim of methodology is to detail the study's methods—how it is conceptualized and designed; how the data are collected, analyzed, and interpreted; as well as the theoretical and technical justifications for the scientific procedures used (Everhart, 1988). Methodology, therefore, is concerned not only with the products of scientific inquiry, but also with the underlying assumptions, and processes associated with the construction of knowledge from a particular scientific approach. As suggested throughout this volume, contextual conditions and historical traditions can exert a powerful, and often unacknowledged, influence on the way scholars think about theoretical, epistemological, and methodological issues.

The interplay between the conceptual underpinnings and methodology employed in the investigation of a research problem will determine its scientific quality. As Feuer and colleagues (2002) reminded us, it is the appropriate application of the approach to a particular problem, rather than the approach itself, that enables judgments about a study's scientific merit. The political controversy that can brew over the conduct and results of a study suggests that researchers should exercise care in conceptualizing and conducting policy-related research that is of a high scientific standard. Only studies that meet this standard will be useful in crafting effective policy solutions. The intent of this chapter is to provide an introduction to several issues to consider in the conceptualization and design of policy research—that is, the methodological justification for the research approach taken toward a particular policy problem.

## HOW DOES POLICY RESEARCH DIFFER
## FROM OTHER RESEARCH?

Policy research differs from basic social research or technical research in a number of ways (Majchrzak, 1984). First, policy research focuses on problems that have drawn considerable political attention, and it generally seeks a higher utility of results to generate greater understanding of policy issues, actions, and impacts in resolving social problems. The aim is to produce results that provide a diverse audience with an increased understanding of a policy problem's context and issues, processes, intervention strategies, and their demonstrated effects. This information can be used to generate implications and recommendations that can ultimately lead to future policy actions that reduce or alleviate the problem.

Some authors form their implications for policy action as a more concrete set of recommendations and their likely effects. Often, options are considered in relation to the availability of resources. Other policy researchers stop short of telling policymakers what they ought to do. These decisions are mostly a matter of style. The results of studies, therefore, help contribute to a knowledge base on how particular approaches work (or don't work) in alleviating a problem. As evidence mounts for or against particular approaches, it can influence how people think about the issues, the problem, and the viability of potential solutions. The extant research may enable policymakers to identify underlying assumptions and to inspect critical links that must hold if a particular strategy is to work in solving a problem (Malen, Croninger, Muncey, & Redmond-Jones, 2002). Research can help policymakers assess promises of a particular approach against various costs that accompany particular policy options. For example, here is how Desimone and her colleagues (2002, p. 105) summed up their longitudinal study of the effects of professional development on teachers' instruction:

> ... in the absence of increased resources, the federal government, states, districts, and schools still have to make difficult choices whether to sponsor shorter, less in-depth professional development that serves a large number of teachers or to support more effective, focused, and sustained professional development for a smaller number of teachers. The results of this study support the idea that districts and schools might have to focus professional development on fewer teachers in order to provide the type of high-quality activities that are effective in changing teaching practice.... The longitudinal study reported here indicates that much of the variation in professional development and teaching practice is between individual teachers within schools, rather than between schools. This finding provides evidence that schools generally do not have a coherent, coordinated approach to professional development and instruction, a least not an approach that is effective in building consistency among their teachers.... Nevertheless, districts and schools could go a long way in developing high-quality professional development activities. To develop meaningful professional development plans, districts and schools would have to ... [a set of specific recommendations follows].

Second, because issues, actions, and solutions can be politicized, there can be great interest in the results of policy studies that address policymakers' aims. There are a myriad of persistent and complex social and educational issues that affect students that should be of concern to the American public, educational policymakers, and researchers (Tillman, 2002). Many of these issues go right to the core of what it means to live in a democracy (e.g., tracking, testing, school choice, access and retention in higher education, economic and racial segregation in educational institutions). It is important to realize, however, that in policy domains, research findings are only one of many inputs into decisions (Majchrzak, 1984). Because the whole process of identifying policy issues, developing policy actions, and implementing policies is politically driven (Marshall, 1997), it should come as no surprise that the conduct of policy research relevant to these activities may also have a political component (e.g., priorities for problems to be researched, guidelines for methods used to study problems, decisions about what research gets funded). Exemplary policy research should make clear what the results are and how the results are linked to either an increase in policy options (i.e., they give expanded ways to look at a problem and its solution), or a narrowing of options (i.e., they focus the range of options to make clear that only one or two options are likely to work) that will bring a desired resolution to the problem.

Third, temporal issues and the observation of change are also central to research on educational policy. Policy develops, is implemented, and produces impacts over a considerable period of time. A key consideration in the design of policy studies is how time will be incorporated. As Tyack (1991) suggested, "Almost everyone who thinks about educational policy uses a sense of the past either consciously or unconsciously. A picture of where we have been shapes our understanding of where we are and where we should go" (p. 2). The researcher will likely have to decide what period of time is appropriate to bound a study examining policy development and implementation, or the time that is needed to observe subsequent changes in behavior that result from policy activity. Although time figures into the design of the study, change is often the object of the researcher's interest—changes in behavior, changes in policy values, growth in student learning, changes in institutions, or the relation between periods of policy reform rhetoric and actual institutional changes (Tyack, 1991).

## Examining the Relevant Literature

One way to start thinking about the design and conduct of policy research is to consider how others in the field study policy problems. Researchers often begin to conceptualize a study by assessing the empirical literature that exists on a particular policy problem. Published research and conference presentations provide up-to-date sources of information about policy problems. Studies that are not grounded in the appropriate research literature lack substantive and methodological guidance—that is, they do not contribute to growing evidence about a policy problem. Systematic, accumulative knowledge emerges over time as a result of collective studies (Smart, 2002).

As suggested in the introduction, policy scholarship has evolved considerably over the past 35 years. In education, the policy field is sufficiently large, such that any comprehensive review of the literature must address a number of subfields (e.g., school effects research, resource allocation, educational tracking and ability grouping, dropouts, professional development and teacher instruction, charter schooling). This presents considerable challenges in trying to organize a discussion of the scientific properties of the research. Several broad assessments of the field have concluded that the knowledge gained from the volume of work on educational policy has been uneven (Boyd, 1988; Fowler, 2000; Mitchell, 1984; Teddlie, Reynolds, & Sammons, 2000). Reviewers have noted that educational policy research has not always done justice to the complexity of policy topics in terms of theoretical and methodological sophistication (e.g., Boyd, 1988; Fowler, 2001; Hallinger & Heck, 1996; Marshall, 1997; Ouston, 1999;

Teddlie & Reynolds, 2000). Reviews have also acknowledged that educational policy processes and the impacts of educational policies need to be studied through more diverse conceptual and methodological approaches. Yet, it is also true that in some subfields of educational policy (e.g., tracking, grouping, course taking) we know much more than we did previously through sustained inquiry over many years.

A review of the research in a particular policy area should be conducted with a particular purpose in mind—that is, to assess the studies' contribution to knowledge and evolving policy scholarship. The first step is to identify a set of studies that are relevant to a particular policy problem. Studies should be identified through establishing identified criteria (i.e., relevant to the problem, are scientifically rigorous). For example, the researcher may want to identify empirical studies that demonstrate a policy's impact and that are conducted with scientific rigor (i.e., they follow prescribed methods of design, data collection and analysis, are published in blind-review scientific journals). For this specific research purpose, scientific journals with high criteria for acceptance would be favored over chapters in books, presentations at conferences, unpublished papers, and doctoral dissertations.

The analysis of a set of studies that meet the established criteria should focus on both the philosophical underpinnings and theoretical concepts in each study, as well as on the processes of scientific inquiry used to generate the results. Researchers may have to deal with what appears to be contradictory or conflicting findings in individual studies and reviews of the literature. For this reason, it is important to consider issues of design and methods of analysis, as the underlying assumptions of alternative designs and methods are critical to the credibility that can be placed in the results of studies. Sometimes, apparent contradictions may be explained by differences in the theoretical and methodological assumptions of studies or by the criteria for selection in reviews (Hallinger & Heck, 1996). In the past, researchers have often given little or no attention to the philosophical and theoretical underpinnings of their studies and how these affect research questions, design, methods of data collection, and analysis. Researchers may define some facets in detail, whereas others are vaguely acknowledged, or even remain unstated.

## Deciding on a Research Design

The intents of the proposed research and the relevant previous literature can be useful in helping to decide on an appropriate research design. Research design is actually a broad term that can refer to a number of different aspects of the research process including the research questions, theoretical formulations, study setting, the unit of analysis (e.g., an individual, a group, a school, a policy subsystem), measurement of variables, sampling, data collection, the logic linking the data to the propositions, and the criteria for interpreting the findings (Pedhazur & Schmelkin,

1991; Yin, 1989). Design therefore concerns the assumptions underlying the manner in which the study is constructed to pursue inquiry about the phenomenon. These assumptions include the researcher's beliefs about the nature of science, the "proper" conduct of the study given the researcher's definition of science, the analysis and interpretation of facts, as well as the construction of the research text.

Decisions about the focus and conduct of a study are at the core of what it means to do science and produce scientific knowledge. Hence, the study's design underlies whether or not the research questions can be answered through the manner in which the data are collected. If the design is incomplete, it is likely that the data will not provide answers to the questions posed initially. A study's credibility, therefore, is largely a function of its conceptual underpinnings (e.g., theoretical approach, design) and methods used to conduct the study. As the National Research Council (NRA) 2002 report on scientific research in education emphasized, it is not the particular designs or methods themselves that make a study scientific. Rather, judgments about the scientific merit of a particular method can only be made with reference to its ability to address the particular research questions at hand (Feuer et al., 2002).

It is a common misconception to assume that there is a type of hierarchy of design approaches with some approaches only being appropriate for exploratory purposes, or for describing data, whereas only experimental designs can be used for explanatory or causal inquiries. That said, however, some designs are better suited for answering particular types of research questions than are other types of designs (Feuer et al., 2002). Recently, the National Research Council (2002) committee on the status of educational research developed a typology based on the questions commonly framed in educational research. These questions fall into three general classes: (i) What is happening (description); (ii) is there a systematic effect (cause); (iii) and why or how is it happening (process or mechanism)? As researchers (Feuer et al., 2002; Yin, 1989) argued, a range of designs and methods can legitimately be used to address each type of research concern. The choices should be made after considering the particular purposes and circumstances of the research and the strengths and limitations of each approach. Importantly, the research questions and purposes should drive the selection of research design and methods of inquiry—not the other way around (Feuer et al., 2002). The relative control the researcher has over actual events (e.g., whether a policy treatment can be introduced, whether extraneous events can be controlled) and the focus on contemporary versus historical phenomena can be useful criteria in selecting a research design (Yin, 1989).

The decisions the researcher makes in conceptualizing and conducting policy research vary not only with the problem being addressed, but also with her or his creativity, style, and judgment (Majchrzak, 1984). If policymakers, practitioners, and other researchers are to have faith in the credibility of findings, however, policy studies must be conducted with scientific rigor (e.g., see Feuer et al., 2002), no matter what particular conceptual lens and methodological approach are being used to frame the study. Maximizing the strengths of a particular design within the focus of a study, while minimizing its weaknesses, helps to reduce or eliminate alternative explanations.

## Types of Designs

One of the problems in thinking about design in conducting policy studies is there is very little guidance provided in statistical texts for this type of research. Basic statistical texts, typically written from an educational psychology perspective, often focus on experimental designs (i.e., with individuals nested in treatment and control groups) and the use of $t$ tests or analysis of variance (ANOVA) for examining the variability within and across groups. Books on research design may cover basic issues such as variables and hypotheses, sampling, instrumentation, as well as a number of different types of designs (e.g., experimental, single-subject, causal-comparative, correlational, survey, historical) and qualitative and quantitative methods of analysis (e.g., Fraenkel & Wallen, 2000). In her book, *Methods for Policy Research*, Majchrzak (1984) concluded that no comprehensive methodology for policy research exists, so researchers must know a variety of different methods in order to apply them to particular research questions.

Majchrzak (1984) noted three broad differentiations in the field including policy "think pieces" that synthesize existing information from a variety of sources in support of a particular argument, empirical studies that involve the direct analysis of data, and cost–benefit or cost-effectiveness studies that weigh alternative policy options. Majchrzak referred to think pieces as focused synthesis (i.e., assessing available information, constructing a focused argument, and providing policy recommendations). In contrast to policy think pieces are a number of empirical approaches including secondary analysis (i.e., using existing data to examine policy questions), field experiments or quasi-experiments (i.e., developing and implementing an intervention on a target population to alleviate a social problem), surveys, case studies, and focus groups. All of these involve manipulating data. In the third group, cost-feasibility, cost–benefit and cost-effectiveness analyses provide data related to the choosing of an optimal policy alternative among several evaluated alternatives. Some of these appear to be designs, whereas others are methods of analysis. Thus, there is no "neat" way to organize policy research designs.

For our purposes, we limit the discussion to empirical research. There are actually several different designs that are appropriate to use in doing empirical policy-related research. These may be broadly classified as nonexperimental (e.g., surveys or secondary data sets, where there is no treatment that has been manipulated and subjects have not been assigned to control and treatment groups), experimental designs (i.e., where there is a treatment and subject assignment to control and treatment groups), quasi-experimental designs (i.e., where there is the presence of a treatment, such as a policy that has been implemented, but no random assignment of subjects to treatment and control groups), case (i.e., where the focus is on studying a contemporary phenomenon within its real-life context and where the boundaries between the phenomenon and context are not clearly evident), and historical (i.e., where the phenomenon and context are also entangled but the focus is on past events). Although there is certainly over-lap among the approaches, each type of research design has some distinc-tive characteristics. For example, a nonexperimental study to describe factors influencing teacher turnover may also be a case study design, if it is limited to studying teachers in one school district. It is therefore appropri-ate to view designs as pluralistic (Yin, 1989); that is, to be used for a variety of research purposes ranging from exploratory and descriptive to causal (explanatory and predictive) and process oriented (uncovering how and why something occurred).

The different research design approaches are briefly outlined in Ta-ble 8.1. Each design is then discussed in more detail in the remainder of the chapter.

As summarized in the table, nonexperimental designs are often used for descriptive research purposes (e.g., to identify a set of relationships, deter-

**TABLE 8.1**

**Policy Research Approaches**

| Design | Research Questions | Control Over Events | Contemporary | Analysis |
|---|---|---|---|---|
| Nonexperimental (e.g., survey, cross-sectional data) | Descriptive (What, How many, How often) | No | Yes | Quantitative |
| Experiment/ Quasi-experiment | Casual (Is there an effect?) | Yes | Yes | Quantitative |
| Case Study | Descriptive (What) | No | Yes | Qualitative Quantitative |
| | Process (How, Why) | | | Qualitative Quantitative |
| History | Descriptive (What, How many) | No | No | Qualitative Quantitative |
| | Process (How, Why) | | | Qualitative Quantitative |

mine how many, how often something occurs). These include research questions directed more at answering "What is the case?" or "What is happening?" Descriptive studies may suggest hypotheses for further study about why a particular situation exists. Most descriptive studies provide a snapshot of a situation at a particular point in time, although it is also possible to describe trends over time.

The goals of descriptive research are summarized quite well in Lankford, Loeb, and Wyckoff's (2002) quantitative case study on the variation in teacher qualifications and how this variation is influenced by attrition and transfer of teachers, as well as by the job matches between teachers and schools at the start of teaching careers. They also examined how differences in teaching salaries across schools contribute to or alleviate inequities in teacher resources. To construct their case, Lankford and colleagues linked several data sets and other information characterizing districts, communities, and labor markets in New York state over a 15-year period to yield detailed data characterizing the career history of individual teachers. As the authors indicated, the purpose of the study "describes the sorting of teachers across schools and does not test hypotheses for why this sorting exists" (p. 38). They go on to suggest that although several hypotheses may be plausible explanations for teacher sorting, "in fact, we know very little about sorting or the causal relationships that lead to sorting. In this paper we provide an empirical foundation on which to build models of teacher and school district behavior" (p. 39). As the authors concluded in their recommendations:

> Policies that aim to improve the achievement of low-performing students but ignore teacher labor market dynamics are unlikely to impact the sorting of teachers that appears to strongly disadvantage poor, urban students. This analysis provides a foundation for further work by documenting the extent and nature of teacher sorting. However, there is much to learn.... What factors are most important as individuals choose to become teachers and decide in which school to teach? Can changes in the structure of salaries alter the current sorting of teachers? Universally, what policies can be employed to attract and retain high-quality teachers in low-performing schools? (p. 55)

The sentences on further research demonstrate the usefulness of descriptive studies in providing information about the scope of a policy problem. The recommendations section ends by raising several questions that are important to the further study of teacher sorting and its impact on students (e.g., determining how new teachers move into their schools, looking at the function of salary to affect teacher sorting, seeking retention policies).

Another purpose of nonexperimental research may be to determine the association between a particular variable, or set of variables, on an outcome. Descriptive and associational research (e.g., correlational, causal-comparative) can be important for building theory and suggesting subsequent variables to include in actual randomized field trials (Slavin, 2002).

In some policy situations, where experiments are not feasible to implement, nonexperimental designs may be sufficient in answering policy questions. For example, the researcher may set out to find an association between an outcome (or dependent variable) such as students' learning and several explanatory (or independent) variables that have policy relevance (e.g., the presence of a particular type of classroom grouping practice or instructional technique). Relevant research questions might be "What are the key individual and school variables that affect student learning?" or "What are the effects of teachers' practices of grouping children for instruction on student learning?"

In nonexperimental research, the researcher has no real control over the actual events. They have already occurred. The researcher cannot manipulate the student's motivation, the quality of his or her teacher, the grouping practices used in the student's class, or his or her socioeconomic background in trying to determine how these variables affect student learning. The researcher actually needs to work backward from the outcome to uncover relevant associations. Because of this, inferences about causality are weak at best. Nonexperimental designs, therefore, are not as well suited for causal purposes (e.g., to determine an effect) compared with experimental designs, especially when the data used are cross-sectional. As critics have suggested, cross-sectional data are not sufficient for determining causal relationships, because the data are collected at one point in time (Davies & Dale, 1994). This muddies the water for determining which variables are actually "causes" and which ones are "effects." Moreover, nonexperimental designs also are not particularly well suited for investigating processes (e.g., determining why or how something occurred).

Causal studies are used determine the impact of a key variable (e.g., a policy or program) or set of variables on an outcome. This research goal can lead to the use of experiments or quasi-experiments (Cook, 2002; Feuer et al., 2002). As Feuer and colleagues noted, where well-specified causal hypotheses can be developed and randomization of subjects to treatment and control conditions is ethical and feasible, experiments are the best design for determining the effects of policy interventions. Researchers would do well to seek opportunities to use these types of design more often than is currently the case in policy research for questions concerning the impact of various types of policy interventions or programs on school outcomes. It can be somewhat more difficult, however, to implement these types of designs (e.g., high costs, often not practical within the normal ways schools operate, school and district officials may be reluctant to approve various interventions). Whereas experiments have not been much used in examining the impact of educational policies and pedagogy in schools (e.g., effective school practices, site-based management, charter schools), as Cook (2002) indicated, they have been more frequently used in school-based prevention studies (i.e., designed to improve student health, reduce use of tobacco, drugs, or alcohol).

Quasi-experiments are similar to experiments in purpose and many structural details. The defining difference is that they are used where subjects are not able to be randomly assigned to treatment and control groups. As Cook (2002) argued, quasi-experiments use design controls, rather than statistical controls, to create the best approximation to the missing random assignment of subjects to groups. Some of the possible controls are matched comparison groups, a series of pretest measures before the treatment begins, an interrupted time-series, the assignment of the treatment to different groups at different times, and the inclusion of multiple outcomes into the study—some influenced by the treatment and others not (Cook, 2002). Quasi-experimental designs, therefore, are often practical to use where there are naturally occurring groups available to study and where they are available before and after a policy has been introduced. Although there have been considerable advances in the design and analysis of quasi-experiments, however, there are few examples of interrupted time-series studies, regression discontinuity studies, and nonequivalent control group designs with more than one pretest measurement on matched cohort samples in the educational policy research literature (Cook, 2002).

Although nonexperimental designs using quantitative analysis have dominated policy research in the past, more recently other epistemological perspectives (e.g., interpretive, phenomenological, critical, poststructural) have broadened the ways in which researchers examine educational policy. Terms such as *deconstruct, multiple realities, contextualized, unique, holistic,* and *grounded theory* have entered the vocabulary of social science researchers. From these alternative lenses, research design is considered as a more flexible endeavor. The design may proceed from identifying the phenomenon to be studied (with limited or no use of formal theoretical lenses) and may lead to decisions about setting and participants, but in less formal ways. Where the concern is with the interplay between cultural contexts and policy activity, change over time, or how individuals and groups make sense of their evolving beliefs and actions, the researcher may have to choose a design that allows more flexibility in framing the research and in collecting and analyzing the data.

These types of methodological concerns often are best suited to case study designs (e.g., a single case or multiple cases) that use qualitative methods of data collection and analysis, even though it is also possible to use quantitative methods in doing case study (Sabatier & Jenkins-Smith, 1993). As suggested in Table 8.1, in case study designs the focus is often more on the process involved (i.e., how a policy developed or was implemented, discovering a process that explains a chronology of events), as opposed to describing the behavior of individuals or the impact of a particular treatment on individuals (Merriam, 1988). As Cook (2002) suggested, case studies are particularly useful for determining why findings come about because close attention is paid to social processes as they unfold at different stages in a policy's development and implementation.

Where the concern is with policy that happened in the past, the researcher may need to use an historical design. What sets historical analysis apart from case studies is that historical analysis focuses on periods of time in the past, often where the subjects are no longer available to be interviewed. In case and historical designs, the focus is more on policy activity within natural settings as it unfolds (or as it unfolded in the past). As Yin (1989) indicated, case studies and histories can be used for descriptive and exploratory purposes (What is the situation?) or for explanatory purposes (how and why questions). Examining processes leads to research questions that deal with operational links that need to be traced over time. For example, if a researcher wanted to know why a particular policy was passed, she or he would likely have to conduct a case study to examine relevant events and participants' perspectives.

## EXPERIMENTAL DESIGNS

For some types of policy questions, especially those concerning the effects of planned interventions, the randomized experiment is acknowledged to be superior to other types of research designs across diverse fields such as medicine, public health, agriculture, psychology, and criminology (Cook, 2002). As suggested, however, this has not necessarily been the case in education. In experimental designs, issues related to rival explanations are dealt with by randomly assigning subjects to treatment or control groups (which tends to eliminate differences among subjects). Subsequently, the researcher manipulates a treatment variable (such as an intervention) and examines resultant differences between groups. Sometimes, statistical controls are also used (i.e., the effects of extraneous variables on a dependent variable are eliminated by equalizing subjects on a particular variable). The goal is often to determine whether the treatment (e.g., a particular policy) had an impact on some outcome of interest (e.g., how it changed behavior, whether it resulted in improved services or outcomes for targeted students).

The notion of experiment is very ingrained in thinking and writing about science, such that many, including policymakers, may consider them as synonymous (Pedhazur & Schmelkin, 1991). Causal inferences are made from an independent variable that is manipulated (e.g., a policy or program is introduced) prior to observing its effects on the dependent variable (i.e., the effects that are made after the independent variable is introduced). Hence, there is a temporal element in the underlying logic of the design that is related to a causal connection; that is, the treatment was introduced before the effect was observed—time lapse between measurements of variables increases the claim of causality. By randomly assigning subjects to groups and properly maintaining the experiment over time, therefore, observed group differences at the end can be reasonably attributed to the intervention (Cook, 2002), as opposed to other types of rival explanations (e.g., selection, maturation, history). For example, the differences observed would likely not be due to selection biases (e.g., differences in the subjects within each group), as the assignment process renders these differences as unlikely.

A number of different experimental designs can be employed, depending on the particular policy problem. Most popular are two-group designs (i.e., a treatment and control group), with random subject assignment (R) to treatment (X) or control groups. Changes in the groups may be observed (O) after the treatment has been implemented:

$$R \quad X \quad O$$

$$\overline{\phantom{R \quad X \quad O}}$$

$$R \qquad O$$

or before and after the treatment has been implemented:

$$R \quad O \quad X \quad O$$

$$\overline{\phantom{R \quad O \quad X \quad O}}$$

$$R \quad O \qquad O$$

More complex experimental designs can include multiple treatment and control groups, some of which may have pretesting and some of which may not (see Campbell & Stanley, 1963, for further discussion). Various forms of subject matching may also be used under some conditions to increase the likelihood of equivalency among the groups of subjects.

Although a number of researchers have argued that only randomized experiments will work for evaluations of educational interventions and policies (e.g., Cook, 2002; Mosteller & Boruch, 2002), they have been rarely used in education (i.e., Cook estimated the number of randomized experiments to be below 1% of dissertation studies and studies abstracted in ERIC). In studies of the prevention of negative behavior conducted in schools (e.g., to improve student health, reduce student use of tobacco, drugs, and alcohol), however, there are many more instances of the use of experimental designs. This suggests that it is possible to conduct experiments within school settings under some sets of conditions (e.g., see Nye, Hedges, & Konstantopoulos, 2002, for one recent example).

There may be political, disciplinary, and training issues that underlie the lack of use of experiments in education, compared with the use of experiments in other fields such as the health sciences (Cook, 2002). Cook proposed several possible reasons for their lack of favor among educational evaluators and policy researchers. Philosophical arguments focus on the limits of positivism (e.g., hypothesis testing, measuring) to explain social behavior. A case in point was the large-scale studies in the 1970s on educational innovation associated with the Elementary and Secondary Education Act of 1965. As quantitative evaluations began to demonstrate that programs had uneven implementation and impact across different sites and conditions, critics focused on the limitations of design and methods of analysis to provide adequate explanations for the failure of these interventions. In response, researchers shifted their emphasis from determining policy impact to identifying the supports and barriers to change at the local school level associated with the implementation process. Correspondingly, ethnographic studies were used to examine the dynamics of change implementation processes (Firestone & Corbett, 1988).

Experimental designs have also been criticized as not providing unbiased tests of causal hypotheses because researchers' values and judgments may enter into the scientific process. Cook (2002) argued that when experiments produce negative results, their advocates may be likely to make methodological and substantive changes that affect the results (e.g., use a different outcome measure, conduct the study in a different setting). Experiments are often seen as costly, time consuming, or impractical in schools because of the existence of many established practices, such as the process of assigning of students to courses and teachers. These practices are rarely done in a random fashion. Where it is possible to assign students to different groups for study, this can result in differential types of student attrition, depending on the nature of the treatment and control groups. Although federal policymakers are now supporting the use of experiments in educational research, it is uncertain whether this will lead to changes in behavior among educational researchers.

Experiments have also been criticized as resulting in undesirable trade-offs such as sacrificing external validity (i.e., generalizability to other settings) for internal validity (eliminating rival explanations). In fact, however, it is more important to determine whether something works than to determine whether it will work across other contexts. Replication of study results in other settings is another important way of ensuring that external validity may be increased. Finally, some have argued that experiments won't be used in schools because they are favored by federal or state policymakers, who are not major actors in educational policy. Legislation such as No Child Left Behind leaves little doubt that the federal role in education has been expanding. School personnel are also often characterized as only interested in their own school results. There are, however, also many questions of interest to local school personnel (e.g., about programs or specific types of instructional strategies) that could be answered definitively through these types of designs. Finally, some suggest that experiments are not necessary because better alternatives exist (e.g., case studies, quasi-experimental designs and causal modeling with longitudinal data). Case studies have been viewed as superior in having more flexible research purposes, as opposed to the more narrow purpose related to determining cause. The broad purposes of case studies can be particularly illuminating in determining why particular types of findings occur, because attention can be paid to a variety of social processes as they unfold at different stages in a program or policy's progress (Cook, 2002). The biggest limitation of case studies, however, is that there is generally a single group under consideration, which makes it difficult to determine how a group receiving the policy or program would have changed in the policy's absence.

Despite the limitations of experimental designs in many educational settings (costs, ethics), there are a number of policy situations where they might be profitably employed. For example, it is clear that experimentation is a powerful design approach for determining the relationship between policy actions and outcomes (Feuer et al., 2002). Although this approach is much favored in funding circles today in Washington, it is important to emphasize, however, that this is over a relatively small subset of policy research purposes—that is, determining the effects of policy or programmatic interventions. There are many policy research situations where experiments may not be desirable or feasible to use.

## QUASI-EXPERIMENTAL DESIGNS

Quasi-experimental designs include the presence of some type of treatment effect (such as the introduction of a policy) but without random assignment of individuals to groups. In situations where it is not possible to achieve random assignment of subjects to treatment and control groups, it still may be possible to manipulate a treatment variable (e.g., the implementation of a policy or some type of program) and observe its impact. As Cook (2002) suggested, quasi-experimental designs attempt to make up for the lack of random subject assignment by using one or more design controls (matching, time-series data collection, assigning the same treatment to different groups at different times) to create a design tailored to the specific research problem and resources available. In these situations, using a quasi-experimental design allows the researcher to make use of some of the features of experimental designs—in particular, their ability to get at systematic relations between actions and outcomes (Feuer et al., 2002).

It is important to note, however, that quasi-experiments each have certain limitations that may influence the validity of the results when compared with their experimental counterparts. The wide variety of quasi-experimental designs and analyses are not equal (Cook, 2002). Although there have been recent advances, not all of these advances have been incorporated into educational research (Cook, 2002). Cook noted that a number of quasi-experimental designs are "generally causally uninterpretable." One of these is the nonequivalent control group design with one pretest, which has been much favored among educators. This design suffers primarily from the interaction of selection and the treatment—

that is, one can never be certain the groups were equivalent to begin with—that makes it exceedingly difficult (i.e., impossible) to disentangle treatment effects from subject effects. There are a number of ways in which this can be improved, however (e.g., adding a series of pretests, using matched cohort samples). Hence, the potential weaknesses of each type of quasi-experimental design should be considered carefully before it is used in a research study. Some may not be well suited to determine causal relationships (Cook, 2002). Even with stronger designs, as Cook argued, it may take a number of replications to arrive at a trusted conclusion, so the results from quasi-experimental designs should be viewed more tentatively than the results of experiments.

That said, however, a number of quasi-experimental designs may be useful in examining policy problems (e.g., time-series, regression-discontinuity, nonequivalent control groups with more than one pretest and matched cohort samples). One of the common types of quasi-experimental designs is the time-series design. The essence of a time-series design is the presence of periodic measurements and the introduction of an experimental change into this time series of measurements. The time-series design is applicable to situations where data are routinely collected over time. The key is knowing the specific point in the series when the treatment (e.g., a policy being implemented) was introduced. The purpose of the analysis is to infer whether the treatment had an impact (Cook & Campbell, 1979). If it did, the observations before the treatment would likely be different from the ones after it.

The series of measurements before and after the policy was introduced might differ in a number of ways. First, there might be a sharp discontinuity at the point of the interruption (Cook & Campbell, 1979). This might be observed as a change in the level of the means (intercepts) comprising the series. For example, after the policy is implemented, the means for each successive occasion might rise or drop sharply compared to their levels before the policy was introduced. Second, the slope of the series of measurements taken after the policy was introduced might be different from the slope of the measurements taken before it was introduced. For example, if the slope prior to the policy were one unit of Y per unit of X, and afterward it was three units of Y per unit of X, this increase in slope would indicate a considerable change.

The posttreatment scores might also be affected by the length of time the treatment exerts an impact. A discontinuous effect is one that does not persist over time. There may be an initial change in the level and slope of the trend that over time returns closer to pretreatment levels. In contrast, in other situations, policy interventions are not implemented very rapidly. They may take considerable time to diffuse through a population or system. Policy effects might be delayed in either predictable or unpredictable ways following the policy's implementation. It is obviously easier to interpret an instantaneous effect. Complicating the interpretation of results is that there may be little theoretical specification about how long an intervention might take to be implemented or what type of delay should be expected (Cook & Campbell, 1979).

The most basic type of research design concerned with the effects of an intervention is the one-group pretest–posttest design. This design has been described as very weak, since it offers few controls against internal validity problems (Campbell & Stanley, 1963). Researchers often attempt to remedy this flaw by adding some type of comparison group that is not affected by the intervention. As suggested previously, the weakest part of the nonequivalent control-group design is the possibility of selection interacting with the treatment. Important for conducting policy research, both of these designs do not allow the assessment of trends (i.e., multiple occasions) before and after an intervention has been introduced; that is, they depend on single measurement occasions before and after. In these types of design, it is not possible to disentangle the subject and treatment effects from each other. For example, if the pretest measure were atypically low (e.g., due to measurement error), the difference between the pretest and posttest attributed to the intervention would be inflated (Cook & Campbell, 1979).

A time-series design requires a series of measurements taken before and after a treatment is introduced. This allows a check on the plausibility of the pretest measures and the determination of trends before and after the treatment is introduced. The design may be diagramed as follows:

$$0_1 \; 0_2 \; 0_3 \; X \; 0_4 \; 0_5 \; 0_6 \; 0_7 \; 0_8 \; 0_9$$

where the three 0's preceding the X represent a yearly trend of practices prior to the introduction of the treatment. The results are indicated by a discontinuity in the measurements recorded in the time series (Campbell & Stanley, 1963). Consider an example such as the introduction of a policy to raise academic standards for entering freshmen. The policy's impact would be determined by examining the fluctuations in the data over the years prior to the policy being introduced with the years following its implementation. More specifically, the researcher would examine the equality of the pattern of intercepts and slopes before and after the policy was introduced.

The basic time-series design with measures taken before and after the introduction of a policy is a sound design, provided certain threats to internal validity can be successfully argued away (Campbell & Stanley, 1963). The argument concerns the consideration of plausible competing hypotheses that offer possible alternate explanations for any shift in the time series other than the introduction of the policy (Campbell & Stanley, 1963). The major threat to the internal validity of the single group, time-series designs is history; that is, the possibility that something else other than the intervention was responsible for the change in trend observed (Cook & Campbell, 1979).

In some cases, history might be dealt with by minimizing the time intervals between measurements or by adding a no-treatment comparison group (Cook & Campbell, 1979). Although this rival explanation may be reduced (at least partially) by adding an appropriate comparison group, one of the problems in trying to use quasi-experimental designs in policy research, however, is there may not be appropriate comparison groups available to study. In other cases, it may be possible to increase the validity of the design by collecting data on some other variables that should be affected by the policy (i.e., in addition to the outcome of interest) and some that should not. Then, if all variables behave as expected, it lends support to the policy's effects. To deal with history as a rival explanation, it is important for the researcher to specify in advance the expected relationship between the introduction of the treatment and the manifestation of an effect (Campbell & Stanley, 1963); that is, how soon the effect would be seen. As the time between implementation and resultant effect increases, the effects of extraneous events become more plausible. To examine trends in an optimal manner, it is important to have sufficient data to examine the trend before the policy is introduced, as well as data at several time points after the policy is introduced.

Another possible threat is instrumentation. A change in administrative procedures can lead to a change in the way records are kept. It is important to check for these possible types of changes; for example, to note whether the data being collected are related to the same construct over time, as well as to note how the quality of the data collected may have changed. A point of caution, however, is that it may not always be possible to obtain data before a policy was introduced, because the development and implementation of a policy itself may lead to the necessity of collecting data about it. In such a case, the comparison of trends before and after the policy was introduced is precluded. Of course, this would significantly weaken any inferences that could be made about the policy's impact, as opposed to possible rival explanations.

A third possibility to consider in some situations is selection; that is, the possibility that the composition of the group under consideration may have changed in important ways over the course of the measurements taken. In many cases, data are collected from samples of a population over time (e.g., K–12 students in a state, third-grade students in a school). If the population changes over time (e.g., in background composition), it may not be possible to disentangle the effects of the treatment from the selection problem of having different individuals being in the time series at various points (Cook & Campbell, 1979). As Cook and Campbell noted, the simple solution to the selection problem is to restrict the analysis to the subset of units that were measured at *each* time point (e.g., where increases in student learning would be assessed using the same individual students, as opposed to different students each interval). This is not always possible, however, in cases where the researcher might be looking at changes in test scores over time at particular grade levels within schools. In this situation, it is more difficult to deal with the problem of selection (because students may differ in various ways year to year). One possible solution involves examining the background characteristics of students (or other sampled units) to determine whether there is a sharp discontinuity in their profile after the treatment was introduced (Cook & Campbell, 1979). If there is not, then selection is not likely to be a serious threat, unless the background characteristics were poorly measured or were not the appropriate ones to consider with respect to the dependent variable in the time series.

A final threat to consider is the presence of cyclical influences over the course of data collection. In policy interventions directed at schools, one example of a cyclical effect might be that students' absence rates generally fluctuate over the academic year as a function of weather. This could lead the researcher to interpret this cyclical influence as a policy effect. The observational series can be arranged to hold this type of cyclical event relatively constant (e.g., by collecting data at the same time intervals over a relatively long period of time to establish the cyclical trend). This lessens the possibility that some other corresponding extraneous event would produce the expected trends other than the implementation of the policy.

The discussion of some of the problems involved with using time-series data suggests careful consideration of the goals of the research, the availability of the data, its validity and reliability, as well as the sequencing of the data with respect to the introduction and implementation of the policy and the time frame for observing its effects. At one end of the spectrum, in economic forecasting, it is recommended that the researcher have longer data series (i.e., often 50 observations are recommended for estimating the structure of correlated errors in the series). There are, however, many situations in practice where the desired (or available) time frame of study is much less. Policymakers work in time frames requiring much faster results. Therefore, fewer observations may be available (i.e., comprising perhaps 4 to 10 time intervals), but the advantages are many for having additional measurements beyond a single pre and posttest measure, even if the time series is relatively short (Cook & Campbell, 1979).

Time-series designs also present a number of challenges in terms of their correct analysis. The types of analytical methods used for longitudinal data are different from the types of statistical analyses with which most educational researchers are familiar. Some of these challenges are discussed further in subsequent chapters. Basically, they deal with the limitations of ordinary least squares (OLS) regression for longitudinal analysis and the discussion of some of the methods that are more appropriate for the analysis of change over time.

## NONEXPERIMENTAL DESIGNS

In many cases, policy researchers are not interested in establishing the effects of a policy intervention on an outcome. Other types of policy research studies involve various types of correlational or causal-comparative designs (which primarily differ from each other in terms of the scaling of variables) that have been labeled as nonexperimental research (Pedhazur & Schmelkin, 1991). Aside from descriptive purposes (i.e., to determine how many teachers are teaching outside their field of teaching preparation), the goal of nonexperimental research is generally explanation—for example, to explain variation in students' test scores as a function of their backgrounds, their classroom experiences, and the school's instructional and curricular processes. This is accomplished through finding sets of independent variables that are associated with (i.e., or explain variation in) the dependent variable of interest.

## Limitations in Establishing Causality

In conceptualizing nonexperimental policy studies, it is also important to keep in mind the extent to which proposed studies may suffer from inherent weaknesses in their design. These types of issues are often not given much attention in planning studies. Through careful planning, however, some of these weaknesses may be reduced. Researchers need to address three necessary conditions for establishing cause and effect. First, the two variables must be associated. Second, the proper time condition must be established; that is, if a school condition affects student learning, then the school condition must occur prior in time to the observed change in learning. Third, the observed relationship must not be due to a confounding variable. Randomized experiments are strong on all three conditions.

In contrast, however, nonexperimental designs are weaker in establishing time order and in ruling out alternative explanations (Johnson, 2001). Whereas inferences in experimental designs are made from the cause (an intervention) to the effect, as suggested earlier in the chapter, in nonexperimental designs, inferences are typically made in the opposite direction. In reality, the independent variables and the dependent variable may all be collected at the time. Therefore, although there may be an assumed "causality" in the model, such as how students' backgrounds affect their test scores, the researcher does not actually observe the effects of students' backgrounds prior in time to determining their effects on students' achievement in the same way that she or he might observe a treatment's effects on the subsequent achievement gains of group of subjects. Nonexperimental studies do not preclude the collection of data over time, however. Such studies may make a stronger claim toward causality, if it can be established in the theoretical model that changes in other key variables (e.g., school processes, resource levels) were in fact made prior to the changes in learning observed over time. For example, one might begin by measuring changes in independent variables first and then by measuring changes in the dependent variable and assessing how changes in the former are related to changes in the latter.

Because independent variables are not manipulated as they are in experimental designs nor are subjects randomly assigned to groups, nonexperimental designs are not as strong for controlling extraneous variables. As Cook (2002) argued, although there is no doubt that nonexperimental studies can reduce some of the uncertainty surrounding cause, perhaps even all in some instances, it will usually be difficult to know when this has actually occurred. The major threat to validity in nonexperimental research, therefore, is from uncontrolled or confounding variables. Empirical research grounded in overly simplistic conceptualizations is unlikely to yield results that are of use from practical or theoretical standpoints (Hallinger & Heck, 1996). One must recognize the need to include all *relevant* independent variables to specify the model correctly. As Smart (2002) cautioned, throwing 30 or more predictor variables into a regression analysis is clear evidence that the study is not guided by a sound theory. Moreover, it suggests the researcher has not used theory to distinguish between important and unimportant variables.

### Sampling Issues

Sampling issues are a second set of concerns in nonexperimental research. Sampling is a process aimed at obtaining a representative subset of a population, with the intent of making inferences about the population from the subset of subjects. A sample is usually used because it is less costly to draw a sample than to study a whole population. Moreover, in some situations (e.g., survey research) it is actually easier to obtain greater accuracy when a sample is scientifically drawn and monitored (with follow-up reminders to complete the survey) than when one attempts to study a whole population and cannot implement adequate monitoring. Sampling is therefore a key component of nonexperimental designs.

The manner in which the sample is obtained is central to the validity of the results. Samples are broadly of two types; nonprobability samples, which are based on convenience or accessibility; and probability samples, where assumptions are made about the criteria and procedures for obtaining them. Probability samples are preferred because they provide much better protection against various kinds of selection bias. In some cases, a researcher may focus on a single school system or complex of schools and include all schools and their personnel within that population. Where populations are used, it is not necessary to use statistical testing, because the researcher is not generalizing findings from a sample to a population.

Decisions about sample size are relatively complex and subject to a number of issues. These can include the sampling strategy, economic, and practical considerations. For some policy problems, researchers can obtain large data sets that are collected at the national level. One example is the NELS:88 data (i.e., a longitudinal study of almost 25,000 eighth-grade students). The sample size in this type of large-scale study is not a problem. It readily allows analyses of subsets of the data that still have sufficient numbers of individuals. It is important to recognize, however, that large data sets can lead to situations where almost every variable is statistically significant, because significance testing is in part a function of sample size. Where almost every small effect is significant, the researcher has to make judgments about the substantive importance of the effects. This is referred to as determining the "effect size," which implies an interest in the strength, or importance, of the findings. Calculating the effect size (i.e., the extent to which a phenomenon is likely present in a population) is one way the researcher can compare an effect across several studies (known as meta-analysis).

Sample size also plays a role in establishing whether hypothesized effects are present in the population. In many studies that attempt to examine school effects on student outcomes, for example, it is likely that the size of the effect (i.e., effect size) for most variables will be relatively small (e.g., school size, teacher quality, school climate). To detect small effects implies the need to have a large sample available to study. Otherwise, one may fail to reject the null hypothesis (called a *Type II error*) because the research was not designed with sufficient ability to detect the effect in the population if it were present, due to the small sample size. An important step in designing a study, therefore, is to consider the size of the effect one anticipates finding in relation to the sample size that would be needed to have confidence in detecting the effect, should it exist. Statistical power refers to the ability of the statistical analysis conducted to detect the presence of an effect, should one exist, given various effect sizes, levels of significance, and sample size (Cohen, 1988). Other things being equal, small samples are only capable of detecting relatively large effects in the population.

Much of the discussion of sample size also depends on the purposes of the research, the unit of analysis, and the analytical techniques used to investigate the data. The best time to think about these issues is before the study is conducted. In the absence of preferred methods of sampling, however, replication across educational settings (i.e., with varied samples, instruments, and analytic techniques) becomes an important means of increasing confidence in findings. This is an important role that meta-analysis (i.e., the analysis of observed effects on an outcome across a set of studies) plays in policy-related research.

**Overreliance on Cross-Sectional Data**

A third set of concerns in the use of nonexperimental designs is related to the overreliance on cross-sectional data (i.e., information collected at one point in time). Recently, much criticism has been raised about the limitations of research comparing schools in terms of their outcomes where the data are cross-sectional (Teddlie & Reynolds, 2000). First, as suggested previously, cross-sectional data are unable to resolve the ambiguity inherent in correlations and other measures of association about the direction of causality (Davies, 1994). Second, with cross-sectional data, one cannot characterize the inertial properties of possible reciprocal relationships, because it is often implied that policy effects, for example, will only become apparent after the passage of time. Thus, to specify such models properly, longitudinal data are preferred. Third, the impact of the school is likely underestimated in cross-sectional designs during the process of adjusting schools for differences in their students' backgrounds. Making statistical adjustments for student composition within schools (which is commonly done to make the schools more equal before comparing their student outcomes) greatly diminishes the between-school variance in outcomes (Hill & Rowe, 1996). Because the differences in outcomes are diminished, there is little variance left to be explained by school process variables. The impact of process variables such as leadership, expectations for students, curriculum standards, teacher quality, and opportunity to learn will therefore be underestimated in determining their relationship to school effectiveness (Hill & Rowe, 1996; Teddlie et al., 2000; Willms, 1992). As Willms (1992) concluded, "A preferable indicator of a school's performance ... is the distribution of the rates of growth of its pupils, rather than the distribution of pupils' scores on one occasion" (p. 34). Fourth, cross-sectional designs are also not sensitive to differences in school effects that may occur over time.

These issues are often important in research directed toward the appropriate comparison of schools. Correctly modeling changes in school outcomes has often been problematic in previous research. One of the pertinent issues is the current practice in many states of testing each year's third-grade students, as opposed to examining growth in the same students over time. There is no foolproof means of determining that this year's third graders are like last year's third graders in known and unknown ways—thus, a potential selection problem exists from the beginning in this type of analysis. Often, schools rated high in achievement one year may be rated low the next. This can result in some schools being labeled as outstanding or in need of improvement based only on random fluctuations in scores from year to year (Linn & Haug, 2002). Although there are problems associated with longitudinal analyses (e.g., student turnover, separating "natural" growth from growth attributed to the school), they provide a more accurate assessment of the school's contribution to student learning. When the same students are monitored over time, there is likely to be more stability in the effects of schools, which makes this a more valid way of determining school accountability (Heck, 2003).

### Appropriate Analytic Techniques

Finally, the appropriateness of analytic techniques researchers use affects the substantive conclusions that can be drawn from a nonexperimental study (Hallinger & Heck, 1996). Certainly, more rigorous analyses may lead to uncovering relationships in the data that are not revealed in more simplistic analyses. At the same time, however, they are also more likely to lead to fewer findings of substance than have often been claimed in studies that employ more simplistic analytical methods (Pedhazur & Schmelkin, 1991). It is important in nonexperimental designs, therefore, to give considerable attention to both the relationships implied in the theoretical models under consideration (e.g., Is it an individual level or a multilevel theoretical model? Are there directional or reciprocal relationships implied?), as well as the strengths and limitations of various analytic techniques that will be used to test the relationships implied by the model or models under consideration.

## CASE STUDY

Another type of design used extensively in policy research is the case study. Case studies focus on an in-depth understanding of complex social processes up close within their natural contexts and holistically. A strength of the case study approach is that it brings together a wealth of information from a variety of sources that can be used to examine a situation (see Yin, 1989, for an introduction to case study methods). Case studies have a variety of different potential applications to policy research. These include examining policy implementation processes (e.g., how was a policy action changed as it was interpreted and adapted by different groups) that are often too complex to get at through survey data. Case studies are useful in describing the context and the behavior in which policy processes take place. For example, case studies make up the bulk of research on policy implementation and change. They might also be employed to determine the impact of a particular policy on groups within a specific setting.

One of the essential features of case study is its flexibility of purpose. Merriam (1988) outlined three general purposes. Descriptive case studies present detailed accounts of phenomena under study. These types of studies are neither guided by theoretical propositions (although they may be informed by previous literature) nor by a desire to develop general hypotheses. They may chronicle a sequence of events, such as a process through which a policy perspective becomes law. They are useful in illuminating processes where little research has been previously done. Interpretive, or explanatory, case studies use rich description to develop support for, or to challenge, theoretical propositions that may be held prior to data collection (Merriam, 1988). They may make use of a particular policy lens in order to support or challenge an existing set of theoretical propositions. For example, Flyvbjerg (2001) defined critical case study as "having strategic importance in relation to the general problem" (p. 78). One type presents conditions that are most likely to confirm theoretical propositions (Ogawa et al., 2003). The analytic strategy then relies on the interplay between case description and the theoretical framework. The researcher derives a set of theoretical propositions and then tests the propositions against the case description (Ogawa et al., 2003). As Merriam noted, the level of abstraction in explanatory types of case studies may range from suggesting relationships among key concepts identified to constructing a theory. Explanatory case studies are differentiated from descriptive case studies by their complexity, depth, and orientation toward theory (Shaw, 1978). Finally, evaluative case studies can involve description, explanation, and judgment about the worth of a particular policy, program, or intervention (Merriam, 1988).

Selection of the different types of case approaches depends on the research purposes, the types of research questions asked, the amount of control a researcher has over actual events, and the degree of focus on current versus historical events (Yin, 1989). For example, the research questions often relate to operational links that need to be traced over time (i.e., how something occurred, a sequence of events detailing why something developed). Cases are typically used in situations where the researcher has little control over events (such as through manipulating a treatment variable in an experiment).

After determining the purposes of the research, another key activity in conceptualizing a case study is "bounding" the case, or establishing how it is to be framed (e.g., with respect to setting, subjects, or some other factor such as events before and after a key policy is developed). In a policy case, for example, key elements may be the actors in a policy subsystem, a particular policy, or a particular reform period. These decisions will have an impact on how the data will be subsequently collected and analyzed.

To describe a phenomenon, or to figure out how and why it occurred, case studies largely rely on a wide range of evidence such as direct observation, interviews with participants, documentary records (e.g., documents detailing actions, legislative documents, election results, media reports), artifacts, and secondary analyses of others' research (Sabatier & Jenkins-Smith, 1993 ). Case study, however, should not be confused with qualitative research methods in general, even though the design often utilizes a number of related qualitative methods of data analysis (Yin, 1989).

Cases studies can also be quantitative in nature. For example, quantitative data can be developed from documents expressing policy beliefs and preferences of those in the center of such situations. In one example quantitative case study, Jenkins-Smith and St. Clair (1993) used content analysis of roughly 400 testimonies before the Congress spanning two decades to create a data set reflecting the expressed beliefs of an array of groups in the energy policy subsystem dealing with petroleum leasing on the outer continental shelf of the United States. After assembling this data, it was then possible to test hypotheses concerning the stability of coalitions over time, their belief systems, and the effects of external events. This technique of data acquisition and analysis can be used where governments publish the testimony presented at public hearings. The general strategy is to use qualitative methods to establish the overall policy context and then use quantitative methods to examine specific trends in greater detail. This approach can provide more systematic tests of theories of policy change (Sabatier & Jenkins-Smith, 1993).

Because of the emphasis on how events unfold over time, the case study is an excellent design for reporting results occurring in natural settings. Case studies can be used to explain causal links in real-life interventions that are more complex than can generally be studied with surveys or other strategies (Merriam, 1988). The analysis may also reflect the dynamic nature of events being examined. Thick description may be used first to develop tentative hypotheses about what works. These hypotheses may be checked against subsequent data collected. This round of observations may lead to revisions in the hypotheses until, finally, explanations are reached that are grounded in the data. The process of examining the case thus lends itself to making decisions based on judgments that are grounded in the experiences of people in the setting.

Case studies have a number of limitations that should be acknowledged. One limitation is the potential time and cost of conducting the study. The research methods most often used in case study research (e.g., archival, fieldwork, interviews) can be very labor intensive and, therefore, generally preclude the possibility of conducting research on more than one setting at a time. Even the most ambitious types of work have to limit their investigations to a few cases. A second issue is ensuring rigor in the scientific investigation. If the methods used are sloppy (e.g., purposes not well delineated, data collection and analytic techniques not explicated), there will be little credibility in the findings and conclusions. The case may oversimplify the situation. A third issue stems from difficulties in replicating the results of case studies. Cases studies focus on the particular. Different scholars examining the same data sources can arrive at quite different conclusions (Sabatier & Jenkins-Smith, 1993). This can limit the usefulness of the case study approach in reducing (or eliminating) the uncertainty surrounding cause (Cook, 2002).

In some research situations, multiple cases may be part of the design to understand some of the similarities and differences that may occur from different contextual settings. While any one case is likely to be limited in its ability to provide an adequate test of a theory of policy change, there is a potential benefit in using several cases, as each case added begins to illuminate different aspects of a theory. Multiple case studies can be useful in presenting a more compete (or contrasting) view. This approach could include, for example, the use of multiple cases to examine continuities and discontinuities in policy activity over time (e.g., see Benham & Heck, 1994).

Even as case studies accumulate, however, they leave something to be desired for building or testing theories (Plank et al., 1996). When filtered through individual lenses of each researcher, the idiosyncratic nature of the case can make it difficult to transfer the results to other settings. It may be difficult to decide whether the case is a typical example (and would replicate elsewhere), or whether it is more of an anomaly. As Sabatier and Jenkins-Smith (1993) concluded, part of the problem in evaluating theories of policy development, implementation, and change is related to the difficulty in collecting data over a sufficient range of cases to provide adequate tests for a theory's hypotheses. Researchers often argue that generalizability of findings is not a key concern in case studies, but it is important to realize that in the field's overall construction of knowledge about policy problems and processes, it is important to be conscious of the potential limitations of research designs and settings. Whereas some policy researchers are cautious in interpreting findings from very limited settings, others readily extend their conclusions over the full population.

## HISTORICAL RESEARCH

Similar to case study, historical research examines questions related to how and why phenomena occur. The phenomena studied in historical research need to be traced over time (Yin, 1989). The primary distinction between case and historical research is the temporal setting of the study. Case studies generally focus on more contemporary events (Yin, 1989), whereas historical research concerns the more distant past. The two research approaches begin to overlap, however, if the past events under study are more recent. An example of this latter blending of strategies is the evolution of "oral history" studies (Yin, 1989).

Historical analysis can have a number of different purposes. One purpose is descriptive. Historical research is useful in identifying and tracking trends over long periods of time. It can be used to trace debates over educational purposes as well as progress in attaining selected actions. A subfield of historical research (known as historiography) also focuses on the development of causal explanations (Yin, 1989). Hypotheses may be tested concerning various relationships or trends. It is important to note, however, that claims of causal connections or generalizations made about the past are rarely beyond dispute.

There is no single definable method of inquiry associated with historical research. Both qualitative and quantitative methods are used in examining historical data. Although qualitative methods are used more often, Plank and colleagues (1996) provided an excellent illustration of a quantitative analysis applied to test hypotheses about school reform with data collected at the turn of the 20th century.

There are a number of problems with the data that can arise in doing historical analyses. Disputes over interpretation of past events tend to result from the interaction between fragmentary evidence and the values and experiences of the historian (Kaestle, 1988). One issue concerns the availability, completeness, and reliability of the data. Finding what is available, gaining access to it, and then locating the variables that one wants to examine can be troublesome (Cook & Campbell, 1979). Because the people who witnessed the events are typically not available to be interviewed, there are seldom any contemporary sources of evidence, such as direct observations of a phenomenon or interviews with key participants (Yin, 1989). To cover a substantive area adequately, data may have to be assembled from a number of different sources. Historical researchers depend on the interpretation of documents (e.g., letters, memos, statutes, policies, newspapers, governmental statistics) and other available archival artifacts as primary texts, as well as other researchers' previous writing (called secondary sources). They may also make use of available descriptive statistics. A major difficulty with the data is their inflexibility. Relevant data may have only been collected at 10-year or yearly intervals, may be incomplete, or inaccurate. The data may not permit disaggregation by variables.

Once the data are located, there may be systematic bias in their content. As Cook and Campbell noted (1979), because most data that are collected and stored are used for purposes of monitoring, the available variables are likely to be outcome oriented, as opposed to process oriented. Definitions of the variables may shift over time. It can be difficult to determine exactly what shifts in definition have taken place and when. Data may be missing for periods of time, or may have been interpolated. Fortunately, there also other more powerful means of dealing with missing data currently. As Cook and Campbell (1979) suggested, with sufficient ingenuity and perseverance, it is possible to assemble a data set that one would not expect to find from the historical record.

A final issue to consider in historical research is how to bound historical phenomena in time. As Tyack (1991) suggested, metaphors are sometimes used to characterize historical trends such as a cycle, pendulum, or wave. These metaphors may refer more to the debates about reform, however, than actual changes in institutional practices. The time frame for historians to observe policy changes is much longer than the quick fixes policymakers often demand. For examining policy trends and resultant changes, historical researchers can frame their studies in years, decades, generations, or even centuries (Tyack, 1991).

The key problem is determining what time frame is most appropriate for the topic and the data one is investigating (Tyack, 1991). Periods seem to have appeal to historical researchers because they are perceived to have some internal integrity and causal significance (Tyack, 1991). As Tyack suggested, historians may argue about the meaning of historical periods, but they tend to assume their existence and importance. These periods often parallel the chronology of important political or economic shifts. Larger political, social, or economic events, however, may not actually signal changes in educational practices. Inappropriately framing a period for study may obscure more than it illuminates. In his discussion of historical methods, Tyack used the example of the Depression and New Deal, which produced many changes in American society, but had little impact on public schools. In doing historical research examining institutional changes, one key to identifying the proper time frame is first to discover good evidence of change and then attempt to work backward to find appropriate explanations (Tyack, 1991).

## SUMMARY

Currently, there are expanded methodological perspectives to use in examining policy problems. This chapter covers some of the basic issues regarding research designs that are used in conducting policy research and policy analysis. Choosing a design is an important part of the research process, as each design will lead the researcher in particular directions in terms of framing the study's purposes and research questions, the techniques used in data collection, and the manner in which the data are analyzed. The major emphasis is that each design has certain features that lend themselves to particular research purposes and questions. This overview sets the stage for more extensive discussion in the chapters that follow about how to analyze data.

## EXERCISES

1. Construct a matrix where you can summarize the designs discussed in the chapter. For each of the five designs, list a research purpose or two for which it would be well suited, the type of data collection it would entail, a couple of strengths, and perhaps a limitation.

2. After reading the introduction, you may have taken some time to write a short statement of a research problem and a way of studying it. Using that initial short proposal (or another), think about a research design or two that would be well suited to use in the investigation of the problem you defined. Additionally, you might consider how the investigation would proceed from the perspective of different conceptual lenses (e.g., a critical theorist, institutional, or rational lens)? How might the designs and conceptual lenses alter the purposes, research questions, and data collection?

# Chapter 9

# Qualitative Methods in Policy Research

In the past, quantitative methods of analysis were almost used exclusively in conducting policy research—often addressing questions related to determining efficiency of delivering services or monitoring the impact of a policy in bringing about some desired outcome. More recently, however, policy scholars have been interested in examining a broader range of research questions and, hence, have employed alternative analytic methods to conduct research. This diversity of research interests has led to expanded views about the nature of policy problems, processes, and methods of investigation.

Over the past two decades, there has been an increase in the use of qualitative research methods in applied policy research (Ritchie & Spencer, 1994). Broadly speaking, qualitative research is a general category that refers to a number of different orientations used to describe and explain processes occurring within natural and everyday settings. Ritchie and Spencer (1994) noted researchers' interest in describing and understanding complex systems, cultures, and political and social relationships has led to the wider use of qualitative methods of inquiry. More recently, qualitative research methods have also been shaped by the influence of critical theory, postmodernism, and feminism. These lenses direct attention toward oppressive structures, power relationships, the dynamics of change, and the uses of language to construct knowledge. In this chapter, some of the general uses of qualitative methods in conducting policy research are introduced, with a focus primarily on conducting case studies and historical research.

## ESSENTIAL FEATURES OF QUALITATIVE INQUIRY

Numerous discussions across the social sciences have identified differences between qualitative and quantitative methods of inquiry (e.g., Bernard, 1994; Fraenkel & Wallen, 2000; Smith, 1983; Smith & Heshusius, 1986). Some of the differences concern assumptions about the nature of scientific "truth" and the construction of knowledge, the goals and purposes of the research, the methods used to investigate the research phenomenon, the collection and analysis of data, and the presentation of the study's claims within the scientific text.

"Qualitative" methods is actually a term for a wide variety of approaches, methods, and presentations that can be used to conduct social research. Some of these include traditional fieldwork or ethnography, naturalistic inquiry, phenomenology, constructivism, discourse analysis, and personal experience (Blackmore et al., 1993; Keith, 1996). Qualitative methods can refer to the construction of knowledge (what counts as research), the evidence collected (what types of evidence and how they are collected), and the ways in which the evidence is presented and interpreted (e.g., the construction of research texts). Qualitative research may be interpretive at an epistemological level (i.e., focused on the social construction of processes), open-ended in terms of data collection, or may involve "grounded theory" in the analysis of the data (i.e., where theory is constructed from the results as opposed to imposed on the data prior to the analysis).

Bogdan and Biklen (1998) described several essential features of qualitative inquiry. One feature is the focus on the social construction of reality by participants. The setting that surrounds subjects is the direct source of data. The social construction of reality is sometimes referred to as "sense making"; that is, how people make sense of, or construct, their social world. Policy activity is a socially constructed endeavor; therefore, policy actions both shape and are shaped by the assumptions, values, beliefs, and goals of those who develop, implement, and are affected by them. This focus on sense making puts the concept of culture at the center of many different types of qualitative inquiry, in that culture concerns the process through which individuals such as policymakers develop, transform, and ultimately reproduce aspects of their past through their everyday lives (Everhart, 1988; Marshall et al., 1989). It is important, therefore, to understand the cognitive processes of participants as they interact within policy arenas to produce policy actions. As Everhart suggested:

> The essential quality that emerges from analysis of phenomena from the actor's perspective, as those phenomena develop within a context emphasizing multidimensionality, can emerge only as the researcher participates in the ongoing events characteristic of that setting.... perhaps a strong criterion for choosing it over other forms of research, lies in its emphasis on construct va-

lidity (Rist, 1977)—the meaning of events or situations to those individuals who engage in them. (p. 704)

The focus of qualitative inquiry on understanding the meaning of events from those individuals who engage in them is unsurpassed for purposes of doing policy research (Everhart, 1988). For example, Blackmore and colleagues (1993) examined ways in which gender reform policy was being implemented in Australia and how it was affecting secondary school girls. To achieve this research goal, they described the necessity of examining how subjects make sense out of policies:

> For us, as researchers, the problem has been how to get into the girls' and teachers' heads.... It also has led to a focus upon discourse and the "productivity of language in the construction of the objects of investigation" (Lather, 1990, p. 13, as cited in Blackmore et al.). This research, therefore, has focused upon eliciting some understanding of the gender reform texts and other discourses (such as equity) that have informed teachers and students. (p. 187)

Often, the goal of qualitative research is to describe a phenomenon in great detail, emphasizing holistic description of the phenomenon, as opposed to testing hypotheses about relationships. It would be a mistake, however, to think of qualitative methods as used merely to describe phenomena in rich detail.

A second feature of qualitative research is that it is heavily process oriented; that is, it attempts to examine events and meanings as they unfold and to understand the contingencies that influence the manner in which such events evolve (Everhart, 1988). Because actors construct meanings within a social context, understanding the context in which a policy is developed and implemented is essential to understanding its particular implementation—that is, how the policy may be interpreted and acted on by people in that setting. The goal is to produce results that are contextualized (e.g., in terms of their social, historical, and temporal contexts), as opposed to generalizable to other settings.

As a practical matter, the concern with examining events up close tends to limit the scope of the study to one particular case, or perhaps, a few cases. Researchers doing qualitative policy research can spend considerable time in the setting (e.g., school board meetings, in schools, at legislatures) observing, interviewing, and writing field notes. The concern with particular settings also tends to put the focus on theory building (as opposed to theory testing). Qualitative research design therefore favors a flexible approach, such that the inquiry can evolve as contextual situations change.

Third, in qualitative inquiry the data collected are typically analyzed inductively; that is, qualitative researchers do not tend to develop hypotheses first and then test them. Instead, it is more common for the researchers to begin organizing and analyzing the data while they are being collected.

Through the exploration of the data, patterns and interrelationships begin to become apparent. The preliminary relationships can be checked and refined through further data collection. The difficulty for beginning researchers is to know when enough data have been collected or that enough time has been spent such that the phenomena has been adequately described or explained.

Finally, in qualitative research the data are collected in words as opposed to numbers. The data come from such sources as interview transcripts, field notes, video and audiotapes, records, minutes of meetings, and other such sources that describe people's actions and words. Because qualitative research concerns participants' sense making and the understanding of social processes holistically, the role of the researcher in collecting, analyzing, and presenting the data becomes an important consideration in the research process. Because of this, it is important for researchers to acknowledge the choices that have been made about the methods underpinning the study (e.g., decisions made about setting, collection of data, analysis, and interpretation), possible researcher-related biases (e.g., relationship to subjects, role in the data collection, researcher's gender, social class, and cultural background), and other factors that might affect the construction of knowledge.

Recently, for example, qualitative researchers (e.g., Grant & Fine, 1992; Wolcott, 1994) have paid considerable attention to the use of language in the research process (as part of data collection, analysis, interpretation, and text construction). The intellectual roots of this concern are found in the analysis of verbal and nonverbal behavior, communication within and across cultural groups, conversational analysis, and discourse analysis (e.g., Gee, Michaels, & O'Conner, 1992). The interpretation of research texts is influenced by the text's structure and the social circumstances surrounding its production. Readers' own language and backgrounds may differ from those of the researchers. This, in turn, can influence their interpretations of the text. Research, therefore, is always a construction because the researcher puts herself or himself into the process of collecting, analyzing, and interpreting the data. This is the case regardless of the extent to which the researcher has or has not participated in what is being studied. Concerns with textual issues (e.g., how to present the researcher–subject relationship, how to write up field notes, how to present holistic accounts of life in school) have led some researchers to examine the construction of the research text more closely. Researchers can approach the construction of their analyses and their texts in different manners. Empirical studies that illustrate these newer approaches are not fully refined yet, however. There are few guidelines governing the methodology and few concrete examples that can serve as exemplars.

Issues about the researcher's role in the collection, analysis, interpretation, and construction of the research text affect the credibility of the study's findings. Credibility of the findings refers to the confidence that can be placed in the research, the text, and the interpretations that arise from the analysis. Much of the argument about credibility falls back on the researcher; that is, decisions that were made in entering and observing in a setting (length of time, meetings that were attended, key policy actors that were interviewed), particular biases that might enter into the analysis, and issues in constructing the text. All of these components contribute to the presentation of an accurate portrayal of the phenomenon.

## QUALITATIVE METHODS IN CASE STUDY RESEARCH

As discussed in the previous chapter, case study as a research design focuses on understanding contemporary phenomena within their real settings where the boundaries between the context and the phenomenon are not evident (Yin, 1989). Multiple sources of evidence are used to provide an in-depth, contextualized understanding of the phenomenon. Although as Bernard (1994) suggested, case study data can be used in a positivist manner (i.e., focusing on an "objective" reality), it is generally associated with an interpretivist, or phenomenological, approach—that is, where the concern is with sense making, or the social construction of reality. Case study, however, should not be confused with ethnographic methods (which is one type of method that can be used in conducting case studies). Case studies can consist of either quantitative or qualitative data, as well as combinations of both. As Yin (1989) noted depending on the nature of the topic under investigation, one could also do a high-quality case study within the library, without ever going into the field.

### Developing the Case

The case starts with the problem, its definition, and the rationale behind the selection of the design. It is important to have a clear understanding of the policy problem and the issues involved, because decisions will have to be made during the course of data collection and analysis as the study proceeds. One of these first considerations is to define the study's purposes (i.e., What do I want to find out?) and research questions.

A second consideration is the scope and boundaries of the study. Researchers should make decisions that narrow the study; otherwise, one is likely to end up with data that are too diffuse and often unrelated to what he or she is doing (Bogdan & Bilkin, 1982). "Bounding the study" refers to considerations about the setting and data collection, so that the study will be manageable and the types of information collected will maximize the investigator's time (Merriam, 1988). Bounding the study initially is an important consideration, because time and resources are limited. One way that a case may be considered as bounded is when it is identified as a particular instance that is drawn from a broader class of instances (Adelman, Jenkins, & Kemmis, 1977). These decisions reflect what is the proper unit of analysis of the case. In some instances, the case may be the individual (from a broader class of individuals), as in a particular actor who plays a key role within an organization or policy subsystem. A case might also be a particular site, such as a school, or a particular policy decision reached within a policy subsystem. The identification of the unit of analysis as a rule will relate to the way the research questions have been defined (Yin, 1989).

Another way a case can be considered bounded is when the issues are indicated, discovered, or studied so that a full understanding of the phenomenon is possible. This often occurs in the process of determining the relevant policy subsystem, the actors, organizations affected by a policy, the geographic location, the type of evidence that should be collected, and the priorities in doing the analysis (Yin, 1989).

Time is another important consideration in bounding the case. Time relates to the relevant length of time that is appropriate for studying the case (e.g., several months, years, a decade or more), or for which the data are to be collected. The length of time for data collection may also be dictated by political situations; for example, there may be pressures from agencies that need answers more quickly to influence their planning or policy decisions. Time considerations may also be central to comparisons made across a number of cases. As Tyack (1991) noted, this can be related to the periods of time that are appropriate to observe policy change. Considerations of time are therefore important in constructing a view of the way the phenomenon under study operates with sensitivity to a number of specific contexts.

A final consideration in bounding the study is determining the type of case study that will be conducted given the research purposes—descriptive, exploratory, explanatory—and whether it will involve a single case or multiple cases. *Descriptive* cases focus on describing a policy phenomenon, such as the manner in which a policy was developed or implemented. This type of study is a viable alternative when theoretical propositions are not a foundation of the study's purposes (Yin, 1989). *Exploratory* studies may seek to identify a process and make some initial guesses about how it works. In contrast, *explanatory* cases have as a goal the explanation of why a certain set of events may have occurred—perhaps even identifying a set of causes and effects. Often, the analyst may pose competing explanations for the same set of conditions and may attempt to determine how such explanations may apply to other situations (Yin, 1989).

The researcher should also consider whether (and how) previous research and existing theory should be used prior to actual data collection. In some situations, researchers use existing empirical studies (e.g., their conceptual lenses, data collection procedures, and methods of analysis) to help them frame the study. Previous studies can also help guide the data collection and strategies to use in data analysis (Yin, 1989), although some analytic approaches favor allowing data categories, themes, and concepts to emerge from the data, as opposed to being structured by previous analyses. The researcher may also decide to frame the study in a way that is different from previous studies (e.g., in terms of conceptual lenses or methods of inquiry). The lenses outlined in the first part of the book might be useful in helping the researcher refine what aspects of the phenomenon will be studied, how they will be studied, and what is to be learned from the study.

It is desirable to have some clear ideas about these issues, because it is likely that the case will take some twists and turns during the investigation. The researcher should keep in mind the original purposes of the study but be able to adapt procedures as needed if unexpected events occur (Yin, 1989).

## Single and Multiple Case Designs

Single case designs are appropriate in situations where the focus is on describing how a process works in a particular instance (such as the development of a policy). The case may also involve the observation of a particular institution up close (e.g., such as how a school board makes policy) or a policy subsystem. One of the important steps in designing a single case is determining what the unit of analysis is. This will determine how the data will be collected. Some cases have only one unit of analysis (e.g., such as a policy subsystem), whereas others may have more than one unit of analysis (e.g., groups comprising coalitions within a policy subsystem).

This latter type is called an embedded case study (Yin, 1989), which may focus on several different aspects of the same case. Examining several subunits within a case can be one way to guard against the tendency of the case to evolve over time, such that what is being studied at the end is not what was proposed in the beginning. In other words, often the problem with choosing a single unit of analysis within the case is that the situation may not turn out to be what it was thought to be at the onset (Yin, 1989). For example, one may start out to describe the range of interactions within a policy system, but end up focusing on the individuals within one or more coalitions. In contrast, the problem with examining subunits in too much detail is that the researcher may not return to the larger unit of analysis (e.g., the policy subsystem) and, hence, may lose the holistic (and contextual) aspect of the case. Hence, as Yin noted, one should not commit to a single case study until the major concerns have been addressed.

A multisite case study involves selecting more than one case for cross-case comparisons (Burgess, Pole, Evans, & Priestley, 1994). Studies consisting of multiple cases are appropriate when there is a need to bring together a sufficient range of cases to provide a comparison across cases where the research goal is to provide validation of important parts of a theory (Yin, 1989). One attempts to build a general explanation that fits the individual cases, although there will be variation in the details of each case. These types of analyses are often seen as more compelling because the data are collected from several different sites. On the other hand, they do not address the same purposes as the single case design (Yin, 1989).

Studies of multiple cases are becoming more widely used in policy and organizational research. The key concern is likely how to identify the criteria that should be used to select the cases. It is important to develop the criteria first and then find the cases. Finding cases first and then developing criteria would likely compromise the findings in known and unknown ways. Criteria need to link back to the purposes of the study, what the researcher wants to find out, and any possible underlying theoretical propositions guiding the study. Keeping an eye on one's purposes should make the development of criteria to direct the selection of appropriate cases easier. As Yin (1989) argued, the logic underlying the use of multiple cases should be that they are selected to produce similar results (across several cases), as in the notion of replication of findings, or that they produce different results, but for predictable reasons (theoretical replication). When there is uncertainty about external conditions that may produce different results within the set of cases, it is likely that the researcher will need to articulate these relevant conditions more explicitly at the beginning of the study and expand the number of cases to be included. Of course, another consideration in determining the number of cases to include is the amount of resources available for conducting the study.

This logic of developing multiple cases in qualitative research contrasts with the notion of sample representativeness (i.e., how one would select a sample from a population) in quantitative research. There would seldom be a situation where selecting three or four cases could be considered as representative of a population. Limitations would seldom permit one to select enough cases that would represent the whole population. Given the purposes and needs of the study, criteria can be developed and the units can be selected with an eye toward the criteria.

Sampling in qualitative studies involves selecting information-rich cases for study (Patton, 1990). Information-rich cases are those from which one can learn a great deal about the issues of central importance to the research. Criteria for selecting cases can include the extent to which the case is likely to yield information that adds another dimension to multiple perspectives, that it fits within the overall objectives of the research, that it fits the study's initial research questions, and that it fits the study's evolving analytical questions. Theory-based strategies of sampling suggest selecting cases that provide the greatest potential for manifesting the theoretical propositions being studied as they apply to the overall study. It is also important to keep in mind that designing a research study is often a compromise between the need to do a rigorous assessment coupled with the fact that funds are limited (Burgess et al., 1994).

The key is to decide early on in the study's conceptualization that the cases will be used for cross-case comparisons, as opposed to conducting separate case studies. Sometimes the data might be collected at multiple sites simultaneously (Bryman & Burgess, 1994). In contrast, sites could be studied sequentially, where one case might build on a prior one. The researcher should also give some preliminary thought to some common elements that will be included across the cases to facilitate comparisons. For example, there may be some common units of study and a common interview set of questions that would be laid out ahead of time.

## COLLECTING THE DATA

Yin (1989) suggested three important principles guiding the collection of data in case studies. These include focusing on multiple sources of information, creating a database for the case (or cases), and maintaining a chain of evidence. These are strategies used in qualitative research to ensure the credibility of the analysis.

*Multiple Data Sources.*    One principle is to focus on collecting multiple sources of data. A strength of the case study is the ability to bring multiple sources of evidence to bear on a phenomenon, so it is important to include several sources and to corroborate the data from one source with other sources. This allows one to "triangulate" the data, or arrive at converging sources of information. Unfortunately, researchers often do not get training in collecting, interpreting, and triangulating data from several different sources. Triangulation is the process of obtaining information from multiple data sources, cross-checking, and verifying sources of information. Member checks refer to taking the data and interpretations back to the subjects and asking them if the results are plausible (Merriam, 1988). Peer examination refers to asking colleagues to comment on findings as they emerge. In some studies, participants may be involved in various parts of the research process from conceptualizing to writing up the results (Merriam, 1988).

It is important to give adequate attention to the quality of data collection that goes into the construction of the research findings. There are generally great differences in the amounts of time researchers spend in collecting data within qualitative research. At one end of the spectrum, researchers may interview subjects for an hour or so. At the other end, the may spend several weeks or several months in the field at a particular site. There are obviously no specific rules covering the length of time in the field or the description of the method. Of course, these differences may be related to the purposes of the research, but time in the field is important for developing credibility in the results of a study. It is important, however, for researchers to give sufficient attention to methodological issues such as the quality of their data collection procedures, the presentation of sufficient data (e.g., in the form of tables, matrices, quoted material) within the research text to develop and illustrate their arguments. One point about researchers' use of quantitative designs and analysis is that they are frequently put to critique in reviews and meta-analysis. It is important that advocates of newer approaches for examining policy problems also demonstrate the rigor of their methods within the texts of their research (Heck & Hallinger, 1999).

*Creating a Database.* A second principle for collecting data in case studies has to do with building a database from the various sources of data used. Currently, there are few norms associated with the practice of assembling the data used in qualitative studies. Typically, the data in such a study are the information contained in the text of the report produced. It is important to make sure that the report has enough evidence presented so that readers can follow the researchers' main method steps and how the conclusions were drawn. Beyond that, however, it is also important to provide evidence about where the information was obtained. One reading the report has no way of actually checking what evidence was used in constructing the narrative.

Often, researchers can keep this information on hand, if others might be interested in examining the data. This might consist of a journal of case notes, a box of interview tapes or notes, and a bibliography of documents analyzed. Information sources can also be provided more extensively through a set of endnotes (e.g., identifying information sources, locations of documents and reports such as libraries, and assessing the quality of the information obtained) referring to key interpretations and conclusions. It is possible to do this and still maintain the confidentially of subjects.

*Maintaining a Data Trail.* A third important aspect of data collection involves creating the data trail, or chain of evidence. This consists of careful notations about where the information that was used is located. This can help others understand how various interpretations and conclusions were arrived at by allowing them to go back to where the data can be accessed directly (e.g., tapes, field notes, primary and secondary data sources, dated meeting minutes, locations of documents). This can be an important aspect of linking the individual pieces of information back to the study's purposes and research questions. It allows outside individuals to examine the credibility of the study by examining the actual data against the investigators' descriptions of methods, findings, and their interpretations.

## A Protocol for Data Collection

There are a number of important analytic strategies for handling case study data (see Yin, 1989, for further discussion on these approaches). It is important to develop a framework, or strategy, for analysis to deal with the amounts of information that can be collected. When possible, it is recommended to access primary data sources first, while using secondary data primarily as a means of triangulation. It is often useful to develop several analytic questions to give focus to the data collection and help with the initial organization of the data as one proceeds. As Yin (1989) concurred, some of the issues on which to focus include why the study is being conducted, what types of data are being sought, what type of variations might be expected (and what should be done if it occurs), and what would constitute supportive and contrary evidence of a given proposition.

Yin (1989) suggested developing a protocol for the case (or each specific case, if multiple cases are used), which is a type of map of the topics and activities that will be covered in the investigation. Developing the protocol is similar to laying out the purpose and scope of an evaluation study. It is a document that guides the course of the investigation and the collection of data. It is especially important if there will be several people involved in collecting data and managing various aspects of the project.

There are a number of sections that the protocol should have. It should include an overview of the project (the purposes of the case or cases, the issues, the background and literature), the case study questions, the identification of the site or sites, the tasks that are to take place during the investigation (i.e., the site visits, writing the case, reviewing and approving drafts), necessary training (e.g., how to do fieldwork, interviewing, observation), the assignments that various investigators and staff will have, the schedule of contacts (names, organizations, phone numbers), the procedures to develop the data trail when collecting and cataloging data (lists of participants, notes, tapes, other types of data), and the audience for the written report. Documenting the data is important because it may be necessary to provide access to this information in the report (e.g., by providing a bibliography that details the documents used from the study's database).

The development of the protocol is an important step, because it helps identify potential flaws in the design and the initial definition of the study's problem (Yin, 1989). It helps identify (or modify) theoretical propositions that will be tested, and allows the researchers to make modifications to the protocol as needed. The protocol also becomes a type of contract about what is to be done and a means of knowing when the job has been completed. For example, the protocol gives guidance to handling the volume of data that will typically be collected. As Bryman and Burgess (1994) noted, it is important to detail the manner in which the data were collected, entered into a database, and how the collection of data will be linked to their analysis.

## Data Sources

Case study designs make use of multiple sources of data. Some of these include interviews, focus groups, direct observations, documents, archival records, and physical artifacts (Yin, 1989). Participant observation (ethnography) and narrative are other types of data collection approaches that are intertwined with methodology.

*Interviews.* Interviews are a primary source of case study information. There are several types that are typically used including structured, where the subjects are asked a constant set of questions, as in a survey, semi-structured, where a time schedule and set of questions may be followed, but the interviewer also may probe as needed for additional information, and open-ended, where the interviewer may engage the subject in conversation, asking about events, perhaps even opinions and insights.

*Focus Groups.*    Focus groups are a data collection technique that involves interviewing several subjects at once. They are usually conducted in a semi-structured manner, where the researcher has a particular purpose and a set of guiding questions. Focus group settings allow for a type of verbal interchange between participants about the issues that they or the researcher may feel are important. This setting may cause them to think about issues in ways that they might not if they were interviewed alone. Of course, this cuts both ways, because being in a public setting may also cause subjects to temper their remarks. One advantage of focus groups is that they allow the researcher to gather multiple perspectives about research issues in one sitting. Another is that they are relatively economical, in that the researcher can perhaps gather information from 30 to 40 people in three or four focus group meetings.

*Direct Observations.*    Observations, such as those taken at formal meetings, informal conversations, and of people doing their routine work, can be another source of important information about a situation under study. They can provide important information about the extent to which something is actually being implemented, or is in use during the course of a day within a school, for example. Observation can be a useful part of the empirical process of putting together what people say they do (such as through interviews) and what they actually do (as an observation of their behavior). This process of checking often turns up considerable discrepancies between what participants do and what they say they do. This represents a good example of what researchers call "espoused theory" versus "theory in use" (Everhart, 1988). Of course, putting this together also depends on the researcher's interpretation (with potential bias) of a subject's words and actions. In the case where there are multiple observers, it becomes possible to get an assessment of the reliability of their observations.

*Documents.*    Documents are written material that are relevant to the development of case studies. Documents can provide another important indication of the organization in action. The organization's culture leaves its imprint on most of the printed material that is produced. Relevant documents might include memos, letters, meeting agendas and minutes, written reports and evaluations, and newspaper coverage. Getting access to them, finding where they are kept, and verifying their authenticity and accuracy are important parts of the data collection process regarding documents (Merriam, 1988). Documents are typically not produced for research purposes; hence, they may be fragmentary, may not fit the purposes of the research, or may be difficult to authenticate (Merriam, 1988). It is important to remember that such items have a definite "slant" to them, so the investigator should be aware that it is evidence about the organization or group as seen through its eyes. For example, minutes of meetings are often edited to present them in a concise manner. They may not indicate the full range of debate, and perhaps anger, that may be displayed at hearings over policy disputes. It is important, therefore, to seek clarification and corroboration of documentary evidence from other sources.

**Archival Records.**    Related to documents are various types of archival records. These might include personnel records, records of budgets, particular types of survey data, maps, and various organizational charts. These may be relevant in some cases and much less so in others (Yin, 1989). It is important to determine the accuracy of the evidence. It is quite possible that they are incomplete and inaccurate, and therefore, may have little relevance to the situation at hand. As Tyack (1991) noted, in attempting to use statistics collected previously, the researcher may determine that they were not collected before a particular policy was introduced. It is the support for the policy that often legitimates the collection of data about it.

**Artifacts.**    Artifacts are another type of data that may be relevant to an investigation. These might include the types of computers or technology used, instruments, art, sayings or common expressions used, and other types of physical objects with some type of meaning to members of a particular group or organization. The use of the artifacts by the group may also have particular relevance to the investigation. For example, if a researcher is investigating the implementation of a technology policy, an important source of information might be the number of computers in classrooms, the time they are used, the manner in which they are used, and what is produced with them.

**Ethnography/Participant Observation.**    With its roots in anthropology, ethnographic methods have the longest track record of the qualitative methods in use today. Consequently, researchers have had more time to refine the tools of ethnographic observations and interviews into a cohesive and articulate methodology (Heck & Hallinger, 1999). Ethnography involves a set of methods used to collect data, and the written record is the product of using the techniques. Ethnography represents a strategy of data collection focusing on interviewing, documentary analysis, life history, investigator diaries, and participant observation (Merriam, 1988). Hence, as Merriam noted, an ethnography is a sociocultural interpretation of the data. Its goal is to reveal the context and the social reality (e.g., shared norms and values that guide people's behavior) within a particular setting. For example, in a phenomenological approach, the focus is on the activities and the meaning those activities have to the actors who engage in them (Everhart, 1982). Concern with the cultural context is what sets this type of case study apart from other types of research. This makes it somewhat unique from other fieldwork, or direct observation techniques (Merriam, 1988).

Ethnography involves immersion over a substantial period in a single setting and detailed, descriptive evidence from observation and interview (Yin, 1989). Ethnography is generally conducted through participant observation, which involves getting into a setting and getting up close to the members of a group or organization such that the researcher can observe and interview them to determine how they participate in and make meaning of their social and cultural situations. Participant observation allows the researcher to note participants' behavior in actual settings, as opposed to what they might say in retrospect on a survey or what they might intend to do. Ethnography can be used to observe people as they attend meetings and to interact with them about important and sensitive issues. Everhart (1988) provided a comprehensive rationale and description of how one might use fieldwork in the analysis of educational policy problems.

*Critical Ethnography.* A related approach, critical ethnography, carries a social concern for power inequities into the field setting. This agenda enters into the construction of text about the social relationships studied and highlights the further responsibility of the researcher, after identifying and studying inequities, to promote social justice through the writing and dissemination of the research (e.g., see Anderson, 1990). Its approach is to examine invisible and unobtrusive forms of control that may result in schools from policies. These types of analyses can illuminate how policies and schools may fail to address the problems of the underprivileged (Anderson, 1990). The critical approach to ethnography focuses on the concept that social reality is constructed from ongoing social interaction; therefore, it examines the often invisible ways in which social interaction is structured, power exercised, and privileged interests protected within organizational contexts (Anderson, 1990). Policymakers and administrators often play key roles in legitimating social allocations of values. This tends to privilege some, and may help reinforce the marginality of others.

Critical (and poststructural) approaches have called attention to the use of language in constructing texts in the research process (Grant & Fine, 1992). Concerns about the language used, research texts emerged as researchers gave greater attention to how subjects construct meaning in social relationships and activities. This attention places the researcher at the center of how research is conducted and the text written. Issues concerning language are salient to data collection, analysis, and interpretation. Interest in the dialogue of subjects stems from attempts to reveal ordinary life through the routine actions and sense making of individuals. The roots of this work are the analysis of verbal and nonverbal behavior, communication within and across cultural groups, conversational analysis, and discourse analysis (Gee et al., 1992). For example, discourse analysis focuses on the structure of language and the features of texts. It also delves into how texts relate to social, cognitive, political, and cultural constructions. The interpretation of texts, therefore, is influenced by the text's structure and the social circumstances surrounding its production (Gee et al., 1992). This type of analysis in policy is related to the values embedded in statutes (e.g., Benham & Heck, 1994) as well as the interpretation of policy texts by the implementers and targets of policies (Blackmore et al., 1993).

Critical approaches raise textual issues about how the research is conducted, analyzed, written, and presented to practitioners and policymakers. This has led to a range of experiments intended to enlarge the range of possibilities available for expressing "voice" in the research text. Personal experience methods uncover subjects' beliefs and perceptions and articulate them directly to readers. The intent is to reduce the intrusion of researchers' own biases by letting subjects construct their own experiences. How readers read and interpret the research text is at the core of textual concerns. Readers' own backgrounds may differ from those of the researchers. This in turn can influence their interpretation of the text. The subject's own language may also differ from the researcher's language. Researchers often create texts that are meant for other researchers. Research, therefore, is also a social construction because the researcher puts herself or himself into the process of collecting, analyzing, and interpreting the data. This is the case regardless of the extent to which the researcher has or has not participated in what is being studied.

*Narrative.* Narrative and personal history are other types of qualitative inquiry. Narrative has evolved out of ethnographic concerns with presenting subjects' constructions of their worlds. It is philosophically aligned with experiential philosophy, critical theory, and anthropology. Narrative functions as both phenomenon and method (Connelly & Clandinin, 1990); commonly, the method is referred to as story and the inquiry as narrative. It is well suited to examining the inner lives of subjects. Although narrative has been used to examine the lives of administrators, its application to policy to date has been rare.

Narrative presents numerous difficulties in terms of construction and presentation. Much needs to be learned about the range of purposes and variants of this method. For example, subjects may differ in their understanding of the method and in their ability to use sources for data collection (e.g., such as written accounts of their experiences). Recollections or attributions concerning how one has experienced a policy are by definition highly subjective. The developmental stage and personal style of the subject can influence the trustworthiness of the narrative. Processing subjects' accounts therefore becomes an important consideration. Subjects may also alter their narratives in various ways—leaving out details that may be controversial or overly revealing. Because stories that serve as data are created by the teller, researchers must use care in moving from individual cases or stories to comparisons across several narratives. Finally, in personal experience forms, there are few norms yet on how to analyze and interpret the data (Grant & Fine, 1992). Some do not analyze the stories, arguing that this would impose their own biases on the narrative. Others attempt to find emergent categories across several narratives (using the comparative method). This diversity suggests the need for developing guidelines to assess research efforts.

Researchers are still left with an unsolved dilemma—they may intentionally acknowledge (or unintentionally overlook) how the researcher–subject relationship impacts the research. One solution has been to present the participants' texts with little or no analysis from the researcher. Another is to allow the participants to construct and interpret their own texts. This can be very problematic, especially in conducting personal experience research, because subjects' own thoughts and accounts are of unknown scope even to themselves. They may reconstruct their accounts over time. How they perceive the researcher may interact with how they interpret the data collection process (e.g., giving voice, counseling, spying). There are, however, few norms yet for presenting such oral histories as policy research. The blending of researcher and subject suggest ways in which both engage in the process of interpreting their lives and work. Thus, the method used in narrative studies provides a sharp contrast to the traditional (presumed) objective stance of the researcher presented in most policy studies.

### Establishing a Data Filing System

As suggested, during data collection it is important to develop a data base, or filing system, where the various pieces of data are deposited. In addition, a comprehensive and detailed audit trail should be maintained. For example, a journal can be used to record daily research activities including the location of material, the logistics of obtaining the data, decisions regarding the selection of data, what pieces of data led to other exploration, emergent themes, new research ideas, problems in data collection and analysis, and decisions that were made to resolve research and writing problems (Benham, 1993).

As Benham (1993) noted, much of the information may be primarily of use to the researcher. Some of the information, however, is also instructive as to how decisions were made about data, the trustworthiness of sources, and the coding of information. The process provides an important check of the researcher's initial versus evolving perspectives and the subjectivity of the research process, data, and solutions.

### ANALYZING THE EVIDENCE

Data collection and analysis in case study research are ongoing processes that can extend indefinitely (Merriam, 1988). As suggested, the case study's protocol is important to the collection of data as well as to their analysis. As opposed to being separate phase (as in a quantitative study), analysis unfolds both during and after data collection. Some researchers prefer to do much of the analysis primarily in the field (i.e., during data collection), whereas others carry out the analysis portion of the research after a substantial amount of data have been collected. This issue should be visited frequently in the early stages of the case's design before the data collection begins. If that is done, it greatly facilitates working through the analysis phase.

The raw data first have to be prepared in some fashion—placed on index cards, put in an information retrieval card system, or entered into a computer program designed to store and sort qualitative data (Merriam, 1988). Coding (or indexing) the various data sources is a process that serves to organize the notes, transcripts, or documents that have been collected. The term is a broad one, and as such, carries a number of different meanings to quantitative and qualitative researchers. At times, coding refers to assigning numbers, so that text can eventually be analyzed quantitatively. At other times, it may refer to the retrieval of text (Bryman & Burgess, 1994). Importantly, however, there is a risk, in that when information is removed from its surroundings, much can be lost. Coding the data, however, represents an important first step in the conceptualization of the data (Bryman & Burgess, 1994).

## Linking Data to Propositions

Linking the data to propositions is the core of data analysis. This step has to do with generating concepts that can form the foundations of a theory (Glaser & Strauss, 1967). In some ways, linking data to propositions has been least well developed in case study research (Yin, 1989). As suggested, the coding of the data is integrally related to their conceptualization. Conceptual categories become more abstract and, hence, further from the data.

There are several ways to approach this part of the research process. There is considerable debate about whether conceptual categories should be to some extent "imposed" on the data (e.g., from previous research), or whether they should "emerge" from the data. Using previous research may reinforce blind spots (i.e., findings that have been missed previously due to shortcomings of the conceptual underpinnings and analysis). On the other hand, a classification scheme that works for the data may not manifest itself. Issues to consider include how to make a credible presentation of the evidence, the extent to which the evidence may or may not fit with various theoretical propositions stated initially, and the consideration of alternative explanations.

*Pattern Matching.*    One way to link data to propositions is through "pattern matching," or linking information from the case to an existing theoretical proposition (Yin, 1989). This consists of comparing an empirically based pattern with a predicted one (or with several alternative ones).

The predicted pattern should, of course, be defined prior to the collection of the data. Predicted sequences can be compared against the unfolding process that takes place within the case. Ogawa and his colleagues (2003) used pattern matching to examine institutional and rational explanations for a school district's development and implementation of a standards-based curriculum.

Chronological sequences are often used in presenting qualitative data within case studies (Yin, 1989). The analysis of chronological events, which is frequently employed in case study, can be seen as a special type of time-series analysis (Yin, 1989). In this type of situation, the case approach allows the researcher to trace the development of events over time. This can allow the investigator to determine causal events over time, because the basic sequence of a cause and its effect cannot be switched (Yin, 1989). The goal would be to compare the chronology with that which would be predicted by some type of explanatory theory (see Heck, 1991–1992 for one example of this type of analysis). The theory would have to suggest that some events occur before others, with the reverse being impossible, that some events are always followed by other events on a contingency basis, that events can only follow other events after a prespecified passage of time, or certain time periods in the case study may be marked by types of events that differ from those events in other time periods (Yin, 1989). If the events in the case follow a predicted sequence as opposed to a rival sequence, it can provide the basis for causal inferences.

***Explanation Building.*** Another strategy that can also be applied to explanatory cases concerns developing causal links from the study to various known aspects of the policy process (called explanation building). This can occur, for example, in examining regularities that occur across a number of individual cases. In this way, a number of individual studies may help to build theory.

The particular use of theory to guide data collection and analysis suggested in these first two strategies has typically been overlooked in case study research (Yin, 1989). Students are typically encouraged to bypass theoretical propositions initially and proceed to data collection. This is a risky proposition, however, if the researcher has little prior experience in dealing with the management of qualitative data. One can spend lots of time collecting mounds of data but then be overwhelmed with how to begin to make sense out of what has been collected. It should be obvious that there are places in the research process where previous theory and empirical work can be important guides in helping the researcher structure what to observe and how to make sense of the data being collected.

***Emergent Categories.*** In contrast, other researchers favor the creation of new categories from the data, as opposed to imposing existing ones from previous research (Bryman & Burgess, 1994). This suggests that concepts should be extracted from the data. Researchers favoring this approach prefer to spend less time "theorizing" up front and, instead, move more quickly to data collection and having the theory emerge from the data, a process known as "grounded theory" (Glaser & Strauss, 1967). Although researchers may argue that categories and concepts should emerge from the data, they are not always exactly clear how that is supposed to happen.

The actual analytic process consists of manipulating the data in various ways (e.g., placing similar pieces of information in a pile) such that a classification process begins to take shape. Emergent categories should reflect one classification scheme. The number of categories that emerge from the data will depend on both the data and the purposes of the research. Objects within categories should be similar, whereas categories should be heterogeneous, unambiguous, and exhaustive. Categories should also be plausible, given the purposes of the study. In general, a large number of categories is likely to express an analysis based primarily on description, whereas fewer categories permit a greater level of abstraction (Merriam, 1988).

Once a preliminary set of categories is developed, this set should be further scrutinized and refined against the data to determine whether there might be alternative ways of organizing the data. Bryman and Burgess (1994) noted that there seems to be a lack of certainty about the degree to which theory is actually generated in the process of conceptualizing the patterns in the data. Theory generation is usually seen as a desired end, as opposed to a guide to a method for handling data (Richards & Richards, 1994). In reality, it is often necessary to make various statements about the focus and purposes of a study before the data collection. Of course, these statements will have some influence on the data collection and results of the study.

No matter which way the researcher chooses to proceed in structuring the analysis of the data, it is important to keep in mind that the focus of the case study is to produce evidence about how and why something is the way it is. The goal is to contribute to knowledge and theory building about policy processes, social processes, and organizations. Analytic generalization (as opposed to statistical generalization from a sample to a population) refers to the comparison of empirical results against previously developed theory, or the contribution of results to the building of theory through the case. In this sense, analytic generalization refers to the abstracting of results, and in this way, several individual case studies can provide strong evidence in support of theory, because the theoretical propositions are supported in several different settings, as opposed to the statistical notion that the sample represents a population (Yin, 1989).

## Making Comparisons Across Cases

Comparisons across a number of cases can produce evidence that is more compelling than a single case, because it is based on more instances. The goal of a comparative analysis is to produce a general explanation that fits across the individual cases, even though they may differ in their contextual details (Yin, 1989). It is important to establish the reliability and integrity of each case first. Then the researcher can identify similarities and differences across the cases that help build a comprehensive, unified explanation. Differences across the cases, for example, suggest the theoretical explanation that must be qualified based on the presence of contextual factors that may be acting in expected (or unexpected) ways. In contrast, similarities allow the analyst to extend the theoretical explanation across a variety of situations.

*Comparative Method.*   Researchers conducting analyses of multiple cases often use the comparative method (Glaser & Strauss, 1967). This is an inductive process whereby the data gradually evolve into some type of theoretical framework that guides the further analysis of the data. This process involves refining the emergent categories and their properties, developing a theoretical base for making comparisons among cases, and formulating hypotheses (Merriam, 1988). The theoretical base should be relatively parsimonious (i.e., have a clear formulation with limited number of interrelationships among concepts), and its scope should be broad enough to allow it to be applied to a variety of situations. For example, if the researcher has three cases that will be compared, each case has to be constructed separately first, but in a way that also permits subsequent comparison.

Next, a theoretical basis for comparing cases (e.g., format, criteria for comparison, essential information about each case) has to be devised. This is a means for displaying the relevant data from each case simultaneously. It often helps to sketch out a preliminary scheme on a piece of paper. It is likely that the analyst will have to go through several iterations of this process until she or he is satisfied with the criteria for comparison. This conceptualization is an important step because the way the data are partitioned will dictate what the analyst sees in the subsequent analysis.

Finally, the analyst proceeds to make comparisons among the cases. Keeping in mind the study's purposes, the analysis begins by looking for patterns, or regularities, that occur across most or all of the cases. One can begin by jotting down notes about salient information that appears across the cases, or by filling in cells within the comparison framework that has been developed. After identifying several similarities, the analyst may also make note of any important differences and speculate about what might explain these differences (e.g., contextual conditions, temporal conditions). Eventually, the analyst begins to make inferences based on the comparison—that is, she or he derives theoretical propositions that provide a general explanation of the phenomenon that is grounded in the individual cases. These propositions emerge simultaneously as a result of comparing cases against each other.

*Case Survey.*   Another analytic strategy for comparing multiple cases is to examine how a set of existing empirical cases might fit together according to a conceptual framework or theory (Miles & Huberman, 1984; Sabatier, 1999; Yin, 1989). This is referred to as a case survey, or secondary analysis across cases. The idea is similar to a meta-analysis of existing empirical studies about a particular phenomenon in quantitative research. Secondary case analysis is a relatively sophisticated type of analysis and interpretation, as it involves tying findings together into overarching propositions (Merriam, 1988). On a practical level, the approach necessitates developing a coding system that can be applied to each case. Collective data are then analyzed (Yin, 1989). This type of analysis is more difficult to accomplish, however, because the researcher has little control over how each of the cases was presented in the literature (e.g., purposes of the research, description of the case, what data were included, findings, and interpretations).

## PRESENTING THE CASE

Once the data are organized, the next step is to construct the case. A good place to begin is by revisiting the initial research goals and purposes. It is possible that the study will have evolved away from the initial purposes. In beginning to construct the case, it is likely that the researcher will cross-reference the protocol of the case study (Yin, 1989). The researcher will also examine the organized data several times, taking note of major ideas and features (Merriam, 1988). Developing categories and other useful ways of displaying the data should be guided by the study's purposes, the ideas expressed by the participants, and the researcher's knowledge and experience. Categories are typically refined through successive iterations. It is also a process that relies heavily on content analysis (Merriam, 1988).

A number of different techniques of organizing the data can facilitate the overall presentation. These techniques include putting information into different arrays, developing a matrix of categories and placing the evidence within the categories, creating data displays (e.g., flow charts) to examine the data and note relationships between variables, building logical chains of evidence, tabulating the frequencies of certain events, or placing the information in chronological order using some type of temporal scheme, and making metaphors (Miles & Huberman, 1984). Computer programs for qualitative data analysis can also facilitate the organization and display of data.

These various methods of displaying the data become a way of organizing and presenting the case analysis. The goal of the analysis is to link the data together in a narrative that makes sense to the reader (Merriam, 1988). It is likely that the writing will undergo several revisions as the data need to be continually cross-referenced against the text. This results in a more complete description and explanation of the phenomenon being studied.

In presenting the analysis of multiple cases, there are a couple of additional considerations. First, it is necessary to present a succinct narrative of each individual case, so that comparisons across cases can be conducted. It is important that readers can observe similarities (and differences) across the cases sufficiently, so they can verify the analyst's assertions. Second, the analyst then has to make the comparisons across the cases based on the theoretical framework that has been developed to facilitate the analysis. The evidence presented from the comparisons should be easy to follow, logically consistent, integrated, and yield overall explanatory power about theoretical propositions. A useful way to present this type of analysis for readers is to construct a matrix to display the cases, comparison scheme, and relevant information that supports the explanatory power of the analysis. Finally, the interpretation of the analysis should lead to some sort of empirical explanation about the phenomenon under study and its likely transference to other situations.

Initial drafts of the study can be shared with colleagues. They may suggest aspects of the study that need to be clarified, point out alternative interpretations, and identify important omissions of information.

Yin (1989) suggested several features that make an excellent case study. First, the case should address a significant policy problem or issue (i.e., it represents a policy problem that is of interest to policymakers). Second, it must be complete (i.e., the boundaries are given significant attention in framing the study and are shown to be the correct ones). Within the boundaries, it must involve a thorough investigation of the evidence. Third, it must consider alternative perspectives. Fourth, it should display sufficient evidence to enable readers to see how conclusions were drawn. Finally, it should be written in an engaging manner for readers.

## APPLICATIONS OF QUALITATIVE METHODS
## TO HISTORICAL RESEARCH

Historical research is a second type of policy research that most often employs qualitative methods of investigation. One way to think about historical research is like a case study where the focus is on past rather than contemporary events. For this reason, rather than present the same issues related to case study research, this section focuses on some of the additional design issues that are salient to historical investigations.

Similar to case study, historical research has diverse purposes that range from describing to explaining past events through systematic inquiry. More specifically, historical studies have several goals (Windschuttle, 1996). First, they attempt to uncover the truth about past events. For example, an historical study may provide evidence that leads to new claims. Second, they attempt to build explanations of past events through disciplined investigation, using research techniques and data sources that are accessible to others. An historical study may provide a synthesis about past events; that is, it may order what is already known in a way that provides a new perspective on the past (e.g., by refuting the evidence for completing claims). Third, they contribute to building a knowledge base about the past. Fourth, the may test hypotheses about past relationships and trends. Fifth, they seek to inform present discussions of policy problems by building theory about how past policy practices have evolved.

Historical research involves the investigation of a phenomenon over time. At the center of historical analysis is time, which is one of its defining characteristics (Windschuttle, 1996). Historical analysis focuses on change over time in events that, by their nature, do not repeat (Windschuttle, 1996). Hence, the focus in historical studies is on specific circumstances, as opposed to generalizations about data patterns. Therefore, it is not oriented toward prediction, as some other designs might be. This makes the underlying logic of historical research quite different from some other types of designs that we might use in studying policy change (e.g., time-series studies). Historical studies cannot separate context (or outside forces) from the phenomenon under study. Therefore, historical research concerns the description and explanation of unique events.

One of the challenges for the researcher in conceptualizing an historical study is how to bound the period of time under study appropriately (e.g., identifying natural bookends to the study). Historical researchers use decades, generations, and even centuries to bound their studies. The researcher should present a rationale for why the study was bound in the particular manner chosen (see Plank et al., 1996; Tyack, 1991). The key is finding the time period that is most appropriate to the data and the interpretation of the topic one is examining (Tyack, 1991). It can be a challenge, however, to find periods of reform, as opposed to periods of reform rhetoric. If historical periods follow other social or political movements, they may provide parallels in thought, but not necessarily result in actual changes.

## COLLECTING THE DATA

Historical research depends on the collection of primary data sources (Merriam, 1988). Primary sources are first-hand information provided by individuals who were participants or witnesses to the event being studied. Finding and using primary sources can be a challenge. This is because the available documents often are not very complete.

Critics of historical data collection suggest this can be problematic in several ways (Fraenkel & Wallen, 2000; Windschuttle, 1996). First, it is important to determine whether the documents are in fact genuine. If they are genuine, it is important to determine when they were written, why, and under what conditions they were written. Second, it is also important to determine whether the documents are accurate. The writers may have incomplete or inaccurate information about the events. They may also attempt to persuade or mislead through their writing. Statistical information available may be of very poor quality. Third, data that exist may be the results of others' efforts to influence the historical record. The actors of the era can play a potentially large role in determining what documents are left behind. On the other hand, many other documents that exist are not stored with any particular interest in what future generations may think. Fourth, the process of analyzing the data rests largely on interpretations of the existing material. Accounts are written by individuals holding a variety of political and social perspectives. They may also reside in very different positions in relation to the events they are describing (e.g., political insiders, reporter, disinterested bystander). The researcher must read, interpret, and evaluate the text. Finally, the researcher's own views and biases can introduce an amount of subjectivity into the analysis if the method is applied in a sloppy fashion. For these reasons, it is important to corroborate documents with other sources (and viewpoints) where possible.

Various types of documents and archival evidence are the primary sources of historical data. These can include government documents and reports, statutes, numerical records, oral statements, letters, personal diaries, essays, photo collections, newsreels, films, school records, records of court cases, board of education minutes, textbooks, and other types of artifacts. The advantage of evaluating this type of data is that people cannot really change their behavior (such as if they observe you watching them). The data sources are relatively inexpensive also. One just has to be able to find where the data are located and how they can be accessed. Often, it is difficult to determine the effort various researchers go to in order to locate relevant documents, as well as their skill in evaluating the evidence. On the other hand, researchers are also limited by what data exist and their accuracy. Hence, there may be considerable gaps in the evidence that can be assembled to answer a research question.

In addition to primary sources, researchers may also access secondary data sources. Secondary sources are materials written by other individuals who received their information from participants and witnesses. Secondary sources should also be approached with caution because they are constructed from others' interpretation of data. Their value depends on the skills, credibility, and biases of those writers. It is preferable not to use secondary sources as data, yet sometimes this is unavoidable due to a lack of primary data sources. Secondary sources are often helpful in leading researchers to primary data sources. They may be useful in helping the researcher interpret events from multiple perspectives (i.e., by offering a variety of contrasting views). To assess policy events from an historical perspective, therefore, requires researchers to examine varied data sources in putting together a puzzle of the past.

## ANALYZING THE DATA

Examining past trends in policy requires probing what historians do to try to make sense of the past, or "historiography" (Tyack, 1991). Historical researchers use many of the same procedures as case study researchers to establish a protocol, a database of evidence, an audit trail of where the material was found, and a means of coding the data for retrieval. Exercising care in searching for and assembling the data will greatly facilitate its organization for analysis. Historical research focuses on developing a narrative explanation of what are likely causal events grounded in the data (Windschuttle, 1996). Of course, there is the likely possibility that debate may occur over various interpretations of past events. This is because the data about past events are always incomplete. The explanation, therefore, rests on the logic of a plausible argument presented (based always on incomplete evidence) that can be evaluated against rival claims. To understand a past policy event involves examining the context of the event, the ideological assumptions behind it, and perhaps the event's impact on participants and institutions (Benham & Heck, 1998).

The goal of the analysis is to construct the historical case. The case should be constructed accurately and without going beyond the data that are present. The analysis proceeds in several steps. First, the researcher must determine what evidence exists about the phenomenon. Second, she or he must analyze the existing evidence. Analyzing the evidence means assessing its authenticity and its relevance and significance in relation to the situation under study. The key is finding the appropriate evidence, establishing its authenticity, and then linking the significance of the evidence to the explanation (Windschuttle, 1996). Third, after searching through and evaluating the evidence, the researcher constructs an account of what happened. The analysis relies on disciplined inquiry, especially in handling the evidence that is used to construct the explanation of the event.

## Content Analysis

Content analysis is the most frequently used method of analyzing historical data. Content analysis is a phrase that actually represents a range of different techniques for extracting patterns and making inferences from text. The data can be any chunk of text, such as a memo, an newspaper editorial, an advertisement, a photograph, cartoon, or a song. One type of content analysis is to code information by assigning numbers so that it can be categorized and counted (e.g., frequencies). It can then perhaps be compared with other information quantitatively (e.g., through correlation). A second way examines the text of documents themselves. The researcher may wish to develop a description of a particular event through the eyes of the person who witnessed it. In contrast, the researcher may wish to determine whether particular ideas or concepts, words, phrases, and types of speech patterns are present in the text (e.g., by circling key phrases, identifying particular words). This can lead to a type of analysis of the language and thought used. Hence, content analysis represents a type of blend between qualitative and quantitative analysis (Bernard, 1994; Sabatier & Jenkins-Smith, 1993).

The approach begins with the text. It is important to determine what will be the unit of analysis (e.g., particular words, concepts). The researcher may make hypotheses about what type of patterns or information are in the text. Next, it is important to develop some type of sampling plan for the content analysis, because it may not be possible to examine every written instance. This will depend on the amount of data available, its accuracy, and its relevance. After obtaining the data, some type of systematic coding must be applied (e.g., assigning numbers to the data or developing various ways to identify and differentiate among key words or phrases).

After organizing the data, the researcher will perform either a type of quantitative or qualitative analysis. For example, if the analysis is quantitative, the analysis might range from descriptive data presentations such as frequency counts to correlations between variables, to attempts to cluster the data according to patterns (Satatier & Jenkins-Smith, 1993). If the analysis is more qualitative, the text can be screened for emergent categories and patterns. For example, computers can be used to build dictionaries of words that are indexed with the same code word (Bernard, 1994). Content analysis can also proceed from categorizing schemes suggested by theory and previous research.

Suppose a researcher wishes to study whether a policy developed to improve school performance is having any effect on schools' curricular improvement plans. The goal of the research might be to uncover evidence of principals' attention to student performance (e.g., improving the learning of students). If the researcher obtains the improvement document for each school over several years, an analysis of the content of the documents can be conducted. A coding system can be devised to identify particular words that are related to school effectiveness and improvement (e.g., effectiveness, efficiency, skill, competence, productivity, high test scores, increased learning) and to track the words used over time. The analysis might then focus on whether schools that indicate stronger commitment to improving learning through their improvement documents actually produce higher outcomes (e.g., see Heck & Crislip, 2001).

Content analysis has several cautions, however. First, the databases constructed can be problematic in several ways. For example, they depend on the extent to which the data have been adequately sampled, decisions about their accuracy and relevance, and other possible researcher biases that entered into their collection in known and unknown ways. Second, the actual coding of the text is also critical to credibility of the content analysis. It is important to consider a number of possible sources of error (e.g., subject error, observer error) that might have affected the recording of the data (Bernard, 1994). If the researcher is only analyzing text and perhaps coding information, there is no possible check on the reliability of the coding decisions. A single coder may tag words consistently, but may make systematic errors in deciding what concepts to use in relationship to certain words. Using more coders generally improves reliability, because it is possible to establish the level of interrater reliability. These limitations have to be considered in relation to the crafting of the case and its conclusions.

## CONSTRUCTING THE CASE

Although historical analysis facilitates the investigation of many problems that cannot be studied through any other means, its primary limitation is the incomplete and likely biased (in known or unknown ways) nature of the data. The limitations of data make historical studies very difficult to conduct. Unfortunately, the researcher may not uncover these problems until considerable time has been invested.

One of the important aspects of constructing the case is the linking of the data back to the study's original purposes and propositions, as well as any new propositions that have arisen during the course of the analysis. The researcher likely will have a particular goal in mind of supporting a particular theory or interpretation. It is often the case, however, that in evaluating, organizing, and presenting the evidence, the original approach must be modified. Flexibility, therefore, is the second important aspect of examining historical evidence. Unexpected evidence often leads to alternative arguments, interpretations, and conclusions (Windschuttle, 1996).

Presenting a credible explanation, therefore, rests heavily on providing ample citations and discussion of the data (e.g., how they were selected and evaluated, their accuracy, relevance) to ensure that others can access and examine the evidence on their own and reach similar conclusions about the explanation provided. Footnoted references and proper documentation are necessary to produce credible presentations of results (Windschuttle, 1996).

### Strengths and Weaknesses of the Historical Approach

Developing a credible historical study is difficult. The major strength of historical research is its great flexibility and creativity in looking in windows to the past. The incentive is to identify something previously unknown about the past or to provide a new explanation of past events. To do this, historical research rests on the collection and evaluation of varied artifacts. The source of its strength also turns out to be its greatest potential weakness. More specifically, the major disadvantage is the considerable difficulties that can occur in collecting the existing documents, evaluating their accuracy and relevance to the research, and coding them. Historical analysis depends on content analysis, which is subject to some important limitations. While the data assembled may appear to be reliable, there may be lots of errors in them. There are also numerous ways that researcher bias can enter into the analysis.

## SUMMARY

In this chapter, a number of different means of examining policy problems within case and historical designs were presented. Qualitative methods of analysis represent a diverse set of analytic techniques that can be used to examine a wide variety of policy problems, research questions, and purposes. They have the advantage of getting researchers up close to the ways in which meaning is made in social situations involving educational policy.

## EXERCISES

1. Discuss several strengths of qualitative analysis in policy research. What types of research purposes are well suited to qualitative analyses? Identify several conceptual lenses that would lend themselves to framing qualitative analyses and provide a rationale for your selections.

2. Identify some of the steps that researchers should take to demonstrate the scientific rigor of their qualitative analyses? Why are these steps important to address in communicating a study's results?

3. The analysis of historical data presents a number of challenges for researchers. Describe two to three challenges and ways that you might address them in conducting your own research.

*Chapter* **10**

# Multilevel Methods for Conducting Policy Research

Many examples of educational policy research involve the analysis of hierarchical, or nested, data structures. These data structures are prevalent in research on educational organizations (i.e., where students are nested in classrooms, schools, districts, and states) and policy systems (i.e., where individuals are nested in various policymaking groups). Because of the limits of statistical model techniques, until recently, researchers had to make choices about whether to ignore the groupings and analyze the data on individuals, or whether to ignore the individuals and analyze the data for groups only. Neither solution took full advantage of the complexity of the data structure. Concerns in various fields with how to analyze hierarchical data properly led to the development of multilevel models as extensions of linear models over the past few decades.

Multilevel modeling is fast becoming the standard analytic approach for policy research on schools due to its applicability to a broad range of research situations, designs, and data structures (nested data, cross-sectional and longitudinal data). Multilevel modeling is referred to by a variety of names; random coefficients models, multilevel regression models, hierarchical linear models, mixed-effects models, and multilevel covariance structure (or structural equation) models. This diversity of names is because the statistical theory for multilevel models developed out of methodological work in several different fields. Despite a growing recognition of its importance, however, the assumptions and uses of various multilevel modeling approaches have not yet been fully integrated into research and statistics textbooks. Similarly, multilevel modeling techniques are not an integral part of the analytic techniques available in most commonly used statistical software programs. Although a number of methodologists have led the way in developing multilevel models for the social sciences, there is a need to introduce a wider audience to an overview of the techniques and their applications in conducting policy research.

This chapter introduces two basic approaches to multilevel modeling. The material is challenging because the models are more complex than the general linear model, with which most readers are familiar from their statistics courses. Like everything else, however, one has to start somewhere. The general concepts do become more familiar as one reads more research that makes use of the techniques. It is assumed that readers have some familiarity with basic statistical concepts (e.g., mean, standard deviation, analysis of variance, multiple regression). In addition, a working knowledge of some multivariate techniques (e.g., factor analysis, multivariate analysis of variance) is helpful. After first reviewing some basic concepts of the single-level, multiple regression model, the multilevel regression model is introduced and illustrated with several examples. Next, an overview of multilevel structural equation modeling is similarly presented.

The intent is to develop the rationale behind the specification of these models in a relatively nontechnical manner (while still providing some of the mathematical discussion for interested readers) and to illustrate their use in policy research. Further information about the use of these methods and specific software programs can be obtained from sources referenced throughout the chapter. The methods and examples presented in this chapter should help readers discover the possibilities of applying these techniques to their own research interests.

## BASIC MULTIPLE REGRESSION CONCEPTS

Linear models (e.g., analysis of variance, analysis of covariance, multiple regression, multivariate analysis of variance) have had a long tradition in the social sciences for analyzing data from experimental, quasi-experimental, and nonexperimental research designs. Univariate analysis (e.g., multiple regression, analysis of variance) is concerned with examining the variability in a single outcome (or dependent) variable from information provided by one or more predictor (or independent) variables. Multivariate analysis (e.g., multivariate analysis of variance, discriminant analysis) is the more general case of univariate analysis; that is, it facilitates the examination of multiple independent and dependent variables in one simultaneous model. A commonality between these univariate and multivariate approaches, however, is that they are confined to single-level analyses; that is, either individuals are the unit of analysis, or groups are the unit of analysis.

It turns out that many of the distinctions made between the various types of linear models are largely artificial, resulting from differences in terminology, how the independent variables are measured (e.g., categorical, continuous), and historical traditions within various social science disciplines (e.g., whether subjects were studied in their natural settings such as schools, or whether they were placed in experimental settings). Multiple regression (also called ordinary least squares regression) is the most widely used statistical technique in social science research.

Multiple regression requires a continuous (i.e., measured on an interval or ratio scale) dependent variable (e.g., salary, writing test score) and can handle both continuous and dichotomous (e.g., gender) independent variables. It cannot handle categorical variables (as analysis of variance does) without recoding them in some way. Applied to the same design and data, however, multiple regression and analysis of variance (ANOVA) yield identical results (Pedhazur & Schmelkin, 1991).

Broadly speaking, multiple regression is used for both predictive and explanatory research purposes. One purpose is to make predictions about an outcome based on values of predictor variables. The linear regression model assumes that a unit increase in the independent variable is related to an expected constant change in the dependent variable. For example, we might want to predict someone's likely starting salary in a new job if she or he has a certain level of education and experience. For the linear model to hold, it is assumed that an increase in each year of education (or experience) added will bring an expected similar change in starting salary, regardless of where someone starts in terms of education. For this type of research purpose, the focus of the analysis is primarily on the efficiency of the prediction and the parsimony of variables included in the prediction equation.

A second purpose is to determine how a set of independent variables affects a dependent variable and to estimate the magnitude of the effects for each independent variable. For example, existing research may suggest that a particular model (i.e., consisting of identified market processes, individual background, and perhaps organizational factors) interact in a way that influences beginning salary. The focus in this type of study rests more on the correct specification and testing of a theoretical model that is under consideration. In this case it is important to include in the model the sets of variables identified as important by the theory and previous research. More specifically, the researcher formulates a model from theory, tests the model against the data, and determines how well the empirical test of the model confirms the proposed theory.

Of course, the two goals are not mutually exclusive. The distinction between the goals is important, however, because in predictive studies, variables might be retained in an analysis only because they are statistically significant and dropped simply because they are not (Heck & Thomas, 2000). In other words, theory would not enter into decisions about model efficiency. In contrast, in the explanatory approach to modeling, the specification of the theoretical model should be carefully considered, and subsequent changes (e.g., whether to add or drop variables from the analysis) should be made sparingly and also with regard to theory. Otherwise, it may be difficult to attach any substantive meaning to the final model.

Consider the relationship in a sample between a predictor (X) such as student socioeconomic status (SES) and an outcome, Y, such as a writing test score. We might hypothesize that socioeconomic status is positively related to the subject's score on the writing test. The relationship between the two variables may be expressed mathematically as

$$Y_i = \beta_0 + \beta_1 X_i + e_i,$$ (1)

where $Y_i$ is the predicted score of individual $i$ on the test, $\beta_0$ (beta) is the Y intercept (or value of Y when $X_i$ is 0); $X_i$ is a predictor (SES); $\beta_1$ is the slope, or the average change in Y associated with a one unit increase in X, $e_i$ is a random error term for individual $i$. Note that $\beta$ refers to a population parameter and not a standardized regression coefficient.

From a scatterplot of 100 students' SES information and their test scores, the goal is to determine what the best fitting line is that describes the relationship between SES and test scores for this sample. This is accomplished by estimating values for the intercept ($\beta_0$) and slope ($\beta_1$). Of course, once we estimate the predicted values for each subject on the two variables, there will be a discrepancy between the predicted values (which would lie on the line) and subjects' actual values on the SES and writing test measures. The difference between observed and predicted values is represented as error. The intercept coefficient represents the average level of student scores when SES is zero (i.e., which represents a mean adjusted for SES), and the slope represents the average effect of SES on the writing scores across the sample of students. These values become "fixed" for the entire sample; that is, because individuals are randomly sampled, it is assumed that the values represent population averages.

Fixing the values of the intercept and slope results in the regression line in Fig. 10.1 that summarizes the relationship between SES and writing scores. The principle of "least squares" states that the correct regression line is the one that best fits the data points. Fit is assessed by summing the squared distances of each observed value from its predicted value that rests on the regression line. The line that minimizes the sum of these squared distances (i.e., they are squared to cancel out positive and negative errors above or below the line) is said to fit the data best; hence, the term *least squares* regression (Heck & Thomas, 2000). In the regression model, the error term, $e_i$, is a random source of variation which we assume is zero on average and normally distributed, varies independently of $X_{1i}$, and that it has constant variance across all levels of $X_{1i}$.

We can add other continuous or dichotomous variables to the equation:

$$Y_i = \beta_0 + \beta_1 X_{1i} + \beta_2 X_{2i} + e_i.$$ (2)

It turns out that adding a dichotomous variable like gender, which can be dummy-coded (e.g., coded 0 = reference group, 1 = female), or another categorical variable (e.g., a series of groups) that has been recoded into a series of

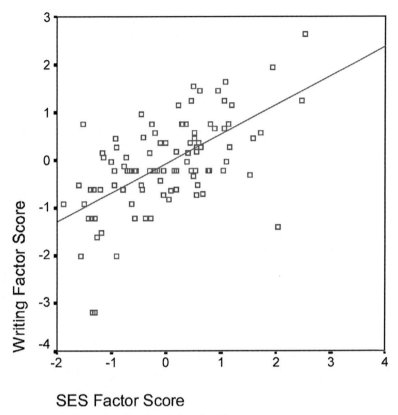

**SES Factor Score**

FIG. 10.1.   Scatterplot of student SES and writing scores.

dummy-coded variables, produces a special type of model with separate re-gression lines (summarizing the relationship between SES and the writing score) for each variable category. For a dummy-coded variable, the test of the parameter's significance (i..e., summarized as a $t$-ratio by dividing the parame-ter by its standard error) represents a test of the difference in the group means. If the gender variable is significant, for example, it suggests the intercepts of the male and female regression lines are different (i.e., where they intersect the Y axis). In this hypothetical arrangement, the slopes (i.e., representing a con-stant effect of SES on writing) would be fixed at one value, but the intercepts would be different across the two groups. These can be visualized as a set of parallel regression lines crossing the Y axis at different places.

We can also begin to capture variation in slopes by examining whether there is a possible interaction effect that is due, for example, to the categorical variable (e.g., gender) and SES (similar to interactions in ANOVA). The slope of the line representing the relationship between SES and the writing scores of males might be much steeper than the slope of the line for females. By adding an interaction effect to the model, we can test whether males or females get better writing test results for their added levels of SES. Testing for an interaction is actually a test of whether the slopes of the set of regression lines are parallel. The model with interaction can be represented as follows:

$$Y_i = \beta_0 + \beta_1 X_{1i} + \beta_2 X_{2i} + \beta_3 X_{3i} + e_i, \tag{3}$$

where $X_{3i}$ represents the interaction between gender and SES for individual $i$. The interaction term can be created by computing a new variable where gender (coded male $= 0$, female $= 1$) is multiplied by SES. Once again, the $t$-test of the new coefficient (i.e., the ratio of the parameter to its standard error) determines whether the two slopes differ significantly. If the interaction is not significant, it suggests the slopes of the lines are parallel and, therefore, there is no SES-writing test interaction effect present between males and females.

If the slopes describing male and female writing scores for added levels of SES are significantly different (i.e., the lines are not parallel), as the lines in Fig. 10.2 appear to be, the presence of the interaction term may make the other coefficients in the model look different from previous models. When slopes vary across groups in this manner, it becomes more difficult to interpret the intercepts. The interaction coefficient can be interpreted as the additional effect of SES when the person is female (i.e., because by definition, multiplying the SES values by the coded value of 0 for males will result in an overall added effect of 0). It is possible that at times, however, using this type of approach will produce multicollinearity among the dichotomous variable (e.g., gender), other predictor (i.e., SES), and the slope interaction variable.

Importantly, the assumptions necessary for multiple regression models to yield the best, unbiased estimates are most realistic when the data have been collected through simple random sampling. Random sampling assumes that subjects in a study are independent of each other. As groups are added to a study, however, this assumption becomes more tenuous. In large-scale educational research, simple random sampling is rarely used. Instead, various types of complex sampling strategies are employed to select students, classrooms, and schools. These can include, for example, multistage sampling strategies where individuals may be sampled within various groups, and the likely oversampling of some groups.

Clustered data, therefore, result from the sampling strategies used in large-scale databases, as well as natural groupings of students in educational institutions. The single-level regression model cannot take into consideration that the students may be clustered within a number of schools with other students having similar writing scores and SES backgrounds. Because the single-level linear model assumes that prediction errors are independent for each individual student, this assumption will likely be violated

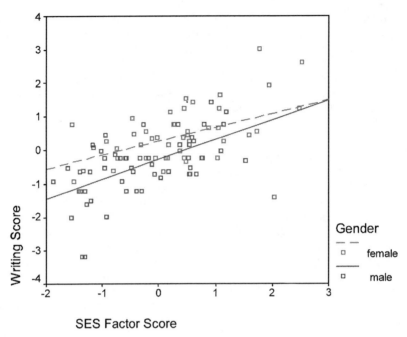

FIG. 10.2.   SES and writing score regression lines by gender.

when students are actually grouped within schools. Where data hierarchies exist (i.e., either from sampling strategies or the natural clustering of individuals), the school intercepts (e.g., writing means adjusted for SES) would likely vary across the sample of schools in the study. Moreover, there might be some schools where the effects of student SES on writing achievement (represented by the slope coefficient, $\beta_1$) are greater than or less than the average (or fixed) effect. There might also be some schools where there is no effect at all. In other words, where there are clustered data, it is likely that there is a distribution of both intercepts and slopes around their respective average effects. In this situation, we might wish to investigate the "random" variability in intercepts and slopes across the sample of higher level units in the study (e.g., classrooms, schools).

## MULTILEVEL MODELING IN POLICY RESEARCH

Although there are many educational policy problems that lend themselves to analysis with multiple regression, research on schools presents many opportunities to study phenomena in hierarchical settings. Recently, much policy research has focused on the analysis of existing, large-scale databases, because the data are more readily available. Because of the costs involved in collecting data, existing databases can provide a unique opportunity to investigate a variety of policy issues. Of course, their limitation is the sampling strategy used and the variables assembled within the data set. The data may be cross-sectional (collected on subjects at one point in time) or longitudinal (collected at several points in time). More specifically, the use of longitudinal data in a variety of different designs presents another research situation where a series of measurements is nested within the individuals who participate in the study, who are also likely nested in classes and schools (Hox, 1998).

Given the increased availability of many quality data sets, it is important to use analytic methods that are most appropriate to the data collection strategy. In the past, however, researchers have had considerable difficulty analyzing data where individuals are nested within a series of hierarchical groupings. Applying the single-level linear model to hierarchical data produces several analytic difficulties. These include a forced choice over the proper unit of analysis (i.e., the individual or the group), trade-offs in measurement precision, limitations in ways in which the model's parameters can be examined (i.e., because intercepts and slopes are considered as fixed), and violations related to errors in the prediction equation (e.g., errors should be independent, normally distributed, and have constant variance). The random error components of hierarchical data structures are more complex because the errors within each unit are dependent, as they are common to every individual within the unit.

Where similarities among individuals are present (i.e., clustering effects), multilevel or random coefficients models are acknowledged to provide more accurate assessments of the properties of schools than are single-level multiple regression. This is primarily due to their greater efficiency in calculating standard errors for each model parameter. Because tests of significance (e.g., a $t$-test) for variables' effects on an outcome are calculated as the ratio of each estimate to its standard error, ignoring the presence of hierarchical data structures can lead to false inferences about the relations among variables in a model (due to biased standard errors), as well as missed insights about the social processes being studied. It is important to emphasize, therefore, that conducting an individual-level analysis implies that no systematic influence of group-level variables is expected and, therefore, all group influence is incorporated into the error term of the model (Kreft & de Leeuw, 1998).

Multilevel analysis therefore provides both conceptual and technical benefits—that is, it reflects the way in which the data were collected and therefore allows researchers to partition the variance in an outcome into several components (e.g., an individual component, a class component, a school component). The general multilevel modeling framework allows the formulation of several useful submodels that can subsequently be used to explain the outcome's variance components at different levels. In this way, it is possible to avoid problems related to choosing the unit of analysis (i.e., the need to aggregate or disaggregate data to a single level of analysis). The presence of these submodels also allows the analyst to define explanatory variables at their correct theoretical levels. For example, variables related to the school (e.g., size) should be estimated with respect to the number of schools in the study, as opposed to the number of individuals. Similarly, class size should refer to information about classes within schools, not to individuals or to schools.

Multilevel modeling encourages researchers to ask more complex questions about the data. One specific example is examining the distribution of slopes (which summarize effects) across schools. If variability in slopes is present, it may also be explained by a number of group-level variables. This type of analysis is often referred to as examining "slopes as outcomes." (Bryk & Raudenbush, 1992). For analyses concerned with changes in student learning over time, it is possible to provide a multilevel analysis of growth. The shape of the growth curves could be explained by various types of school and contextual variables. In some schools, for example, students might show greater improvements in learning outcomes over several years. In other schools, there might be little relationship between subsequent measures of student progress.

## THE MULTILEVEL REGRESSION MODEL

In multilevel regression modeling, the values of the intercept and slope coefficients for individuals, which were fixed in the single-level regression model, can be treated as randomly varying about their averages. Consider the previous example involving student SES and writing scores. Suppose now that the previous scatterplot of 100 students measured on SES and writing outcomes represented data collected from students within five schools. We can estimate a separate regression equation for each school. Each school would have its own intercept (describing the level its students outcomes adjusted for SES) and a slope (describing the relationships between SES and writing within that school). The intercept for each school can be described visually as the point where each regression line crosses the Y axis. In a multilevel model, the level of writing outcomes produced would be expected to be different in each of the schools. It is also possible that the slopes (i.e., defined as the change in Y per a unit change in X) might also vary across schools. It is important to note that in some research situations, we might be interested in explaining the slope variation (i.e., if it is hypothesized that performance assessments in writing are more equitable for low SES students), whereas in others, we might just want to accept those differences as fixed across the sample of schools.

The separate regression lines are shown in Fig. 10.3. The figure shows considerable variability in intercepts the slopes of the lines (i.e., an extension of the two-group model represented in Fig. 10.2).

From this data structure, one can use multilevel modeling to specify a hierarchical system of regression equations that take advantage of the clus-

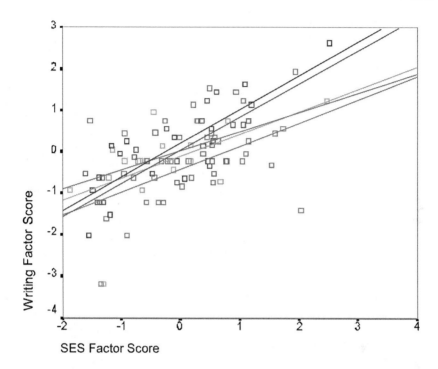

FIG. 10.3.   Scatterplot of regression equations across 5 schools.

tered data structure (Heck & Thomas, 2000). Multilevel regression involves first estimating a level-1 model within each higher unit (e.g., schools) and then estimating a series of between-unit models using the within-unit estimates (i.e., intercepts or slopes) as dependent variables. In contrast to a single-level regression model, where the impact of a variable like SES is assumed to be fixed (i.e., the same) across all individuals in the sample, with multilevel regression modeling, one can specify a single-level regression equation that can be estimated within each school (as shown in Fig. 10.3). This allows the effect of SES on writing to vary randomly across the number of schools in the sample. In this way, the researcher can determine whether the effect of SES on writing is stronger or weaker in some schools.

In its basic form, the level-1 model is equivalent to a least squares regression model, except that instead of estimating the model's parameters across all $N$ cases in the data set, the level-1 model is used to produce estimates within each level-2 unit. To represent the hierarchical nature of the data, the subscript $c$ is added to represent the cluster (group) component and $i$ can be used to represent the individual component. The multilevel model yields a potentially different set of estimates for each level-2 unit. The level-1 model can be written as

$$Y_{ci} = \beta_{0c} + \beta_{1c}X_{ci} + e_{ci} \qquad (4)$$

where $Y_{ci}$ is the observation for the $i$th individual in the level-2 unit $c$, $\beta_{0c}$ is the level-1 intercept within unit $c$, $X_{ci}$ is a predictor (such as SES), $\beta_{1c}$ is a level-1 slope within unit $c$, and $e_{ci}$ is the error for individual $i$ in unit $c$. If sufficient variation exists across the set of groups in the sample, the model will yield a different set of estimates of the intercept and slope for each unit. Each of the $c$ within-unit models is an ordinary regression model, where the regression coefficients indicate the effects of level-1 characteristics on the level-1 outcome within each unit.

Rather than considering all of these regression equations separately, instead we treat them as a system of estimates with an overall mean and variance averaged across all level-2 units. Because the intercept and slopes are allowed to vary across the level-2 units, researchers can attempt to explain this variance by incorporating various level-2 variables in an intercept model and a slope model. More specifically, the level-1 intercept and slope may be treated as outcomes in level-2 equations, perhaps explained by school-level variables such as size, curricular processes, or teacher quality. As suggested previously, in situations where there is little variation in slopes present across the units (or no specific research hypothesis proposing that a particular slope is likely to vary), the analyst may decide to fix the slope across the sample (i.e., as in single-level regression) and only examine variability in the intercepts.

In the case where there is one predictor at level 1 ($X_1$), the level-2 models to explain the intercept ($\beta_{0c}$) and slope ($\beta1_c$) can be written as

$$\beta_{0c} = \gamma_{00} + \gamma_{01}Z_c + u_{0c}, \qquad (5)$$

and

$$\beta_{1c} = \gamma_{10} + \gamma_{11}Z_c + u_{1c}, \qquad (6)$$

where $\gamma_{00}$ is the mean value of the level-1 outcome, controlling for the level-2 predictor $Z_c$; $\gamma_{01}$ is the slope for a level-2 predictor $Z_c$; $u_{0c}$ is the error for organization $c$; $\gamma_{10}$ is the mean value of the level-1 slope, controlling for the level-2 predictor $Z_c$; $\gamma_{11}$ is the slope for the level-2 predictor $Z_c$; and $u_{1c}$ is the error for organization $c$. In contrast to the level-1 outcomes, which are based on $N$ individual-level observations, the level-2 estimates are based on $c$ unit-level observations. It is important to note that the level-2 estimates for the intercept and slope are not observed; that is, they need to be estimated from the level-1 data.

By considering the level-1 and level-2 models as a single system of equations, all of the information necessary for estimation of the parameters at both levels is provided (Heck & Thomas, 2000). This is shown through substitution in the following equations:

$$Y_{ci} = (\gamma_{00} + \gamma_{01}Z_c + u_{0c}) + (\gamma_{10} + \gamma_{11}Z_c + u_{1c})X_{ci} + e_{ci} \tag{7}$$

$$Y_{ci} = \gamma_{00} + \gamma_{10}X_{ci} + \gamma_{01}Z_c + \gamma_{11}Z_cX_{ci} + u_{1c}X_{ci} + u_{0c} + e_{ci}. \tag{8}$$

As with ordinary regression models, $Y_{ci}$ is generated by two components: the linear relationship defined by the model (referred to as the deterministic part), and the random error terms (or stochastic part). The random component is comprised largely of specification and measurement error. Two differences, however, should also be noted. First, the term $\gamma_{11}Z_cX_{ci}$ in Equation 8 is a cross-level interaction between the level-1 variable (e.g., SES) and a level-2 variable ($Z_c$). This represents the moderating effect of the level-2 variable on the relationship between a level-1 predictor and the outcome $Y_{ci}$. Second, the random component of Equation 8 consists of the more complex error term $u_{1c}X_{ci} + u_{0c} + e_{ci}$. This accommodates the relationship between $u_{0c}$ and $e_{ci}$, which is common to every level-1 observation within each level-2 unit—a dependency that violates the assumption in OLS regression of independent errors across observations.

The relationships proposed in the theoretical model are then tested through the use of an iterative fitting function such as maximum likelihood (ML). In a multilevel analysis, the parameter coefficients can be more appropriately weighted by considering the more complex covariance structure among the errors (i.e., because the errors within each unit are dependent). The consideration of this more complex error structure affects the precision of the structural coefficients between groups, because the amount of data available in each organization will generally vary (Bryk & Raudenbush, 1992). In this way, units from which more information is derived are given more weight in determining the model's final parameters.

The basic two-level model can also be expanded to three or more levels, depending on the type of research question being addressed and the nature of the data set. For example, one might examine the impact of a policy across a random sample of schools in districts within a state, or across the 50 states. The multilevel regression model can also be extended to examine multivariate models with latent variables, by defining a measurement model at level 1 that corrects observed indicators of the underlying constructs for measurement error (Bryk & Raudenbush, 1992). Individual (level 2) and group-level (level 3) predictors and mediating variables can be added to this type of model to explain variation in the latent constructs.

**Steps in the Analysis**

There is a logical set of steps to conducting a multilevel regression analysis (Heck & Thomas, 2000). Determining the extent to which the clustering is present is typically the first step in deciding whether random coefficients modeling will offer an improvement in the precision of estimates over single-level techniques. Partitioning the variance in an outcome into its variance components allows the researcher to determine how much of the total variance in the outcomes lies between groups. This can be determined by calculating the intraclass coefficient (ICC). If there is little variation present at the group level, there would be no need to use multilevel techniques. Where variability due to clustering is present across levels, however, multilevel analyses yield better calibrated estimates of population parameters (intercepts, slopes, standard errors) than analyses conducted at a single level without adjustments made for clustering effects.

*Null Model.*    To determine whether there is variation present at higher levels, the researcher typically begins by defining a model (sometimes called a null model) that has no predictors:

$$Y_{ci} = \beta_{0c} + e_{ci}, \qquad (9)$$

where $Y_{ci}$ is an outcome defined by an intercept ($\beta_{0c}$) and an error term ($e_{ci}$). Each level-1 error term is assumed to have a mean of 0 and a constant variance ($\sigma^2$). Simultaneously, a companion level-2 equation is fitted to complete the partitioning of the variance in the level-1 outcome into its within- and between-group components:

$$\beta_{0c} = \gamma_{00} + u_{0c}. \qquad (10)$$

Through substitution of equation 10 into equation 9:

$$Y_{ci} = \gamma_{00} + u_{0c} + e_{ci}, \qquad (11)$$

where $e_{ci}$ is the level-1 effect and $u_{0c}$ is the level-2 effect, and $\gamma_{00}$ is the grand mean of $Y_{ci}$. This model partitions the variance in $Y_{ci}$ into its within-group and between-group components. The partitioning creates two variance components, one at level 1 ($\sigma^2$) and another at level 2 ($\tau_{00}$). From this, the variance of the outcome $Y_{ci}$ can be rewritten as:

$$\mathrm{Var}(Y_{ci}) = \mathrm{Var}(u_{0c} + e_{ci}) = \tau_{00} + \sigma^2. \qquad (12)$$

**TABLE 10.1**

**Sample Estimates of SES and Writing Outcomes**

| Fixed Effect | Standard Coefficient | Error | Approx. T-ratio | P-value |
|---|---|---|---|---|
| Average School Mean, $\gamma_{00}$ | 0.007 | 0.031 | 0.215 | 0.83 |
| Mean Low SES, $\gamma_{10}$ | 0.554 | 0.020 | 28.230 | 0.00 |

| Random Effect | Variance Component | df | Chi-square | P-value |
|---|---|---|---|---|
| School Mean, $u_0$ | 0.122 | 163 | 905.88 | 0.00 |
| SES slope, $u_1$ | 0.027 | 163 | 288.84 | 0.00 |
| Level-1, $e_{ci}$ | 0.501 | | | |

The information is now sufficient to determine the proportion of variance at each level for the outcome, $Y_{ci}$. These proportions are determined by calculating the intraclass correlation $\rho$ with knowledge of $\sigma^2$ and $\tau_{00}$:

$$\rho = \tau_{00}/ (\tau_{00} + \sigma^2). \tag{13}$$

The intraclass correlation provides an estimate of the degree to which differences in the outcome $Y_{ci}$ exist between level-2 units. It helps determine whether the data are clustered, and by extension, suggests the development of helpful level-2 models to explain the variance in Y.

*Level-1 Models.* If there is sufficient variance to be explained across level-2 units, the researcher may first develop a level-1 random-intercept model by adding sets of predictors (X) only at the lowest level of analysis. Initially, the variables should be modeled with fixed slopes (i.e., where the variance components for each coefficient are constrained to 0) in order to assess the importance of each in accounting for variance in $Y_{ci}$.

$$Y_{ci} = \gamma_{00} + \gamma_{10}X_{ci} + u_{0c} + e_{ci}. \tag{14}$$

The researcher may also decide to treat a level-1 slope as randomly varying. The decision to consider parameters as randomly varying depends both on whether there is sufficient variance in the slopes across the level-2 units (which can be determined empirically) and on the re-

**TABLE 10.2**

**Example Multilevel Model With Random Intercept and Slope**

| Fixed Effect | Coefficient | Standard Error | T-ratio | P-value |
|---|---|---|---|---|
| Model for School Means | | | | |
| Student stability | 0.022 | 0.006 | 3.78 | 0.000 |
| Model for SES-writing Slope | | | | |
| SES | 0.555 | 0.020 | 28.50 | 0.000 |
| Student stability | 0.006 | 0.004 | 1.74 | 0.082 |

| Random Effects | Variance Component | df | $\chi^2$ | P-value |
|---|---|---|---|---|
| School mean, $u_0$ | 0.10877 | 162 | 762.319 | 0.000 |
| SES-writing slope, $u_1$ | 0.02517 | 162 | 284.106 | 0.000 |
| Level-1, $e_{ci}$ | 0.50910 | | | |

searcher's conceptual framework. For example, she or he may have hypothesized that the effect of SES on writing outcomes is different across schools and may wish to explain those differences, by adding the random slope component.

$$Y_{ci} = \gamma_{00} + \gamma_{10}X_{ci} + u_{1c}X_{ci} + u_{0c} + e_{ci}. \qquad (15)$$

To illustrate this situation, let's examine students' scores on a performance based writing test (standardized with a mean of 0.0 and a standard deviation of 1.0). In this analysis summarized in Table 10.1, the writing mean of 3,300 students nested in 164 elementary schools averages 0.007 and the average slope is .55 (i.e., which suggests that as a student's SES goes up 1 standard deviation, the student's writing score goes up .55 of a standard deviation). The slope coefficients for the first ten schools in the sample varied from 0.18 to 0.86. This suggests that there may be significant variation in slopes present across the entire set of schools. Table 10.1 provides estimates of the variances of the random effects and tests of the hypothesis that the variances are null. In this case, the evidence suggests there is significant variation in achievement intercepts ($\chi^2 = 905.88$, $p = .00$) and in slopes ($\chi^2 = 288.84$, $p = .00$) across schools.

In addition to investigating random variation in school means, because there is considerable variation in slopes present ($u_1$), it would make sense to let the SES-writing slope vary at random across schools and subsequently try to explain this variation with a set of level-2 predictors.

*Level-2 Models.* Next, one or more level-2 models might be estimated with predictors that are hypothesized to explain the variation in school outcomes and slopes. Table 10.2 summarizes the coefficients for the example model with random intercept and slope. Student stability (defined as the percentage of students enrolled for the entire school year) is added at the school level to explain variability in the level of school writing and the impact of student SES on school writing. In building final models, hypotheses are tested on the basis of significance tests for individual parameters, changes in the initial variance components, and changes in the overall fit of the model against earlier models (see Bryk & Raudenbush, 1992, for further discussion of these steps).

As the table summarizes, student stability affects the level of writing outcomes at the school level. Student stability, however, did not explain variability in SES-writing outcome slopes ($p > .05$). The table also suggests that adding student stability to the model decreases the school mean variance ($u_{oc}$) component (i.e., from .122 in the first model to .109). These changes in variance components can be used to calculate the amount of variability accounted for at the school level. In this case, student stability accounts for about 10.7% (i.e., calculated as $.122 - .109 = .013/.122$) of the between-school variability in writing scores.

### Cautions in Using Multilevel Regression

There are also a number of cautions to be considered in conducting multilevel regression analyses (de Leeuw & Kreft, 1995; Teddlie et al., 2000). These include technical issues such as sampling, required sample sizes for efficient estimation, methods of estimation under various conditions, the proper measurement of variables (e.g., measurement errors on observed variables, variability of parameters and errors across units), and the amount of variability in outcomes due to successive clustering in the data hierarchy (i.e., students within classrooms within schools). For estimating model parameters and standard errors, it appears that having a sufficient number of groups is more important than having a large number of individuals in each group (Mok, 1995). In most situations, there are sufficient numbers of individuals within groups, so that estimates of random and fixed parameters and standard errors at the individual level are accurate. Group-level parameters (especially standard errors and variance estimates), however, become increasingly biased when the number of groups is much below 50 to 100 (Hox & Maas, 2001).

Another consideration is the accuracy of estimating slopes. Estimating slopes (e.g., in representing growth in achievement) is generally less reliable than estimating means, because the accuracy of the slope's estimation depends not only on the sample size of the group (as does the estimation of the mean), but also on the variability of the explanatory variable within the group. If the true variance in slope coefficients across the schools is much smaller than the true variance in means, the slope's measurement will be less reliable (Bryk & Raudenbush, 1992). Moreover, in making statistical adjustments for student composition within each school, the residual coefficient (i.e., the observed minus the predicted score) will always include an amount of error, and estimates of the error are greater for smaller schools (Willms, 1992).

To compensate for differing reliability of measurement across groups, some multilevel regression software programs make adjustments for these errors by borrowing information from the data set as a whole. Schools with smaller numbers of students in the sample have their results "shrunk" to the overall mean to a greater extent than do schools with large numbers of students. From a statistical perspective, the advantage of taking shrinkage into consideration is generally greater efficiency of predictions over single-level analyses. A disadvantage, however, is that the estimates are often unrealistic for units with only a few observations (Kreft & de Leeuw, 1998). As a practical matter, a small school in a specific type of setting that is doing particularly well may be penalized by having its results adjusted downward toward the overall sample mean. In sharing the results with practitioners, this could be an important concern for the principal in this school who is held accountable for achievement outcomes.

These issues highlight the difficulty in presenting the results of rather complex statistical analyses to practitioners and policymakers. In thinking about the utility of results from policy studies, it is important to keep in mind that multilevel models are necessary only to the extent that the data being analyzed provide sufficient variation at each level. In the absence of multilevel features in the data (i.e., observed similarities among students in classrooms or schools), there is little benefit to using a multilevel model. In these instances, single-level and multilevel techniques will yield much the same result, and, hence, less complicated techniques like multiple regression often provide a clearer picture for practitioners and policymakers (Teddlie et al., 2000). There is no fast "rule of thumb" here about what is sufficient. This depends on theoretical concerns and the structure and quality of the data. It is always important, therefore, for researchers to consider choices (and their implications) in how they deal with both technical and practical issues associated with clustering effects (similarities among students), design effects (over or underrepresentation of certain types of schools in the sample), and analysis in examining how schools affect student learning (e.g., Muthén & Satorra, 1995; Teddlie et al., 2000).

## COMPARING THE EQUITY AND UTILITY
## OF WRITING ASSESSMENTS: AN EXAMPLE

In the following example, multilevel regression is used to demonstrate how multilevel techniques may be applied to policy problems. The illustration presents a simplified set of model tests comparing the utility and equity of performance-based and indirect (i.e., defined as a standardized test consisting of grammar, sentence structure, mechanics in multiple-choice format) tests of writing (see Heck & Crislip, 2001, for the complete analysis). Over the past few years, the use of performance-based assessments in large-scale testing has dramatically increased as an alternative to the multiple-choice format for assessing student learning and monitoring school progress. Proponents argue that performance tests assess a broader range of skills (problem solving, critical thinking) than do standardized tests, and because of this, are more closely matched to the curriculum that is taught. Because they are more closely linked to the curriculum, performance tests are also thought to provide greater utility than multiple-choice tests in helping school personnel improve their curriculum and instructional practices. Performance assessments may also be a more equitable testing format, if they reduce differences in scores associated with student composition (e.g., gender, ethnicity, socioeconomic status) that are normally observed on standardized tests (Darling-Hammond, 1994). Few tests of these propositions about the utility and equity of performance assessments exist, however (e.g., see Supovitz & Brennan, 1997).

Given the various policy issues surrounding the use of performance and standardized tests, the focus of the example is on their equity and utility in assessing the impact of state policy directed at school improvement and in providing an assessment format that is more effective across various groups of students. More specifically, a first concern might be to determine whether schools are directing staff energy toward improvement (as required by state policy to improve schools) of their writing curriculum and, if so, whether their efforts over time result in any measurable effects on school writing levels. To do this, schools' improvement plans were content analyzed to determine the extent to which they had committed school energy to improving writing over time.

A second concern might be whether performance-based writing is more equitable (in relative terms) than standardized tests of writing knowledge in terms of assessing what the school taught, as opposed to picking up differences in students' backgrounds (e.g., due to gender, socioeconomic status, or language ability). Equity in terms of individual comparison focuses on the performance outcomes achieved by various groups of students within schools (e.g., females, low-SES students, students with different language backgrounds). Equity in terms of school comparison focuses on how differences between schools in student composition (e.g., school SES) and other school context variables may affect the school outcomes produced. The utility of performance tests would be enhanced if they could be shown to be less sensitive to variables that schools cannot control (e.g., student composition), while being more sensitive to schools' curricular and instructional processes.

These propositions were tested with a sample of 3,300 third-grade students randomly selected from within a sample of 165 elementary schools. In order to compare the influence of the different groups of variables (controls, equity indicators, school improvement process) on the two sets of scores, a particular type of random coefficients modeling with multivariate outcomes was used (see Bryk & Raudenbush, 1992). The procedures for setting up the model tests are detailed because they illustrate the capability of multilevel techniques to provide many other interesting tests beyond the typical way the techniques are used (i.e., to summarize the effects of individual and group variables).

In a multivariate, multilevel formulation (required when one wishes to examine multiple outcomes), the two sets of test scores are entered for individuals at level 1 of the data hierarchy. This formulation allows the incorporation of a true-score estimate of each individual's performance on each assessment—that is, the estimate after other sources of influence (e.g., measurement error) have been removed. Tests of the differential effects of the predictors on the two scores for the same sample of students can only be conducted within a single, multivariate model (see Supovitz & Brennan, 1997, or Heck & Crislip, 2001, for further information about how to specify the model). After defining the multivariate outcomes, individual background variables can then be added at level 2 and school variables at level 3 of the data set. The data were then analyzed with a three-level hierarchical linear model and the HLM computer program (Bryk, Raudenbush, & Congdon, 1996).[1]

The analysis consisted of developing a series of successive models (i.e., a null model, a model consisting of demographic controls and equity variables, a model adding the school-level writing improvement variable) and making several comparisons between the two assessment formats using multivariate hypothesis tests. Model 1 (the null model) contained no predictors, but the variance components could be used to calculate the amount of variance that was accounted for by the sets of predictors included in each successive model. For the writing performance model, the intraclass correlation (i.e., the proportion of variance in the outcome that lies between schools) was .24, suggesting there was considerable variability in student writing performance that might be explained by school-level variables. In contrast, for the indirect (multiple-choice) writing model, a smaller amount of variance (.16) was found to lie between schools. The true-score correlation between the writing performance and indirect writing assessments for individuals was moderate (i.e., .56), whereas at the school level, the correlation between school means on the two assessments was somewhat stronger (.71).

The first type of comparison made is an omnibus hypothesis test that can be used to determine whether added sets of variables in successive models

**TABLE 10.3**

**HLM Coefficients for a Model Comparing Student Performance
on Direct and Indirect Writing Assessments**

| | Direct Writing Coefficient | SE | Indirect Writing Coefficient | SE | Multivariate Tests $\chi^2$ (1 df) |
|---|---|---|---|---|---|
| **School-level Variables** | | | | | |
| *Controls* | | | | | |
|   Sped% | −0.339* | 0.131 | −0.353* | 0.122 | 0.01 |
|   Student Stability | 0.216* | 0.068 | 0.044 | 0.044 | 7.16* |
| *Equity Predictors* | | | | | |
|   Slep% | −0.165* | 0.071 | −0.136* | 0.056 | 0.20 |
|   Low SES% | −0.059* | 0.019 | −0.068* | 0.018 | 0.25 |
| *School Proecess* | | | | | |
|   Writing Curricular | 1.036* | 0.509 | 0.266 | 0.308 | 3.91* |
|   Focus | | | | | |
| **Student-level Variables** | | | | | |
| *Equity Predictors* | | | | | |
|   Low SES | −2.860* | 0.327 | −4.093* | 0.346 | 13.59* |
|   Female | 2.639* | 0.279 | 2.417* | 0.037 | 0.55 |
|   Slep | −8.327* | 1.061 | 7.622* | 0.656 | 0.64 |

*Note.* Writing SAT reliability estimate = .86; language SAT reliability estimate = .79.
*$p < .05$

have a differential impact on the variance accounted for in each set of writing scores. Model 2 added the set of controls (i.e., percent special education, student enrollment stability) and equity variables [i.e., low SES, female, limited English speaking (Slep), percent low SES in school, percent Slep in school] to the null model. In actually conducting a series of model tests, it might be useful to separate the controls from the equity predictors. For writing performance, Model 2 accounted for 4.5% of the variance in writing scores at the student level and 43% of the variance in writing scores at the school level. The indirect writing model accounted for a similar 5% of the variance at the student level and 67% of the variance at the school level. The difference in variance accounted for in the two sets of scores attributed to the variables in the model was also significant, $\chi^2 ( = 7, N = 165, 3{,}300) F$

= 403.82, $p < .001$). This suggests that the performance assessment of writing may be more equitable in comparing scores across schools because it is less affected by school-level composition variables. Finally, Model 3 added the school improvement variable to the model. Adding this variable, however, did not result in further differences in variance accounted for across the two sets of scores.

## Examining Individual Model Parameters

The second type of comparisons involves conducting a series of specific tests on each predictor separately to determine whether it affects students' performance within each assessment format. While there was a clear difference in variance accounted for by the set of controls and equity predictors across the two types of assessments, the results regarding the relative equity of each assessment format must be qualified when each student background variable is examined separately. The parameter estimates for the complete model (Model 3) are presented in Table 10.3.

To facilitate the comparison of coefficients, the student scores on each assessment were adjusted to have true-score variance equal to 100 ($SD = 10$), so the coefficients are readily interpretable in terms of standard deviations.[2] For example, a coefficient of 5.00 on a dummy variable (female, Low SES) would represent a one-half standard deviation achievement difference between the two groups.

*Student Background.* For the student-level variables, the gap in performance on both assessments was rather strong for limited English speaking (SLEP) students. More specifically, students receiving language support services scored significantly lower than their non-SLEP counterparts on the performance writing assessment ($\gamma = -8.327$) and on the indirect assessment ($\gamma = -7.622$). Girls had significantly higher predicted writing scores than boys on both the direct assessment ($\gamma = 2.639$) and the indirect assessment ($\gamma = 2.417$). Low SES students scored significantly lower on both assessments; for the writing performance model the coefficient was $-2.860$ and for the indirect model the coefficient was $-4.093$.

*School Variables.* For the school-level model, percent of special education students ($\gamma = -.339$), percent of SLEP students ($\gamma = -.165$), and percent of low SES students ($\gamma = -.059$) were all significantly negatively related to performance writing outcomes. In contrast, student stability was positively related to direct writing outcomes ($\gamma = .216$). This latter finding suggests that schools having higher percentages of students enrolled throughout the entire school year had higher writing outcomes. For the indirect writing assessment, the pattern of school-level effects was similar, except that student stability was found to be unrelated to indirect writing outcomes.

Finally, the school's stated commitment to planned improvement in writing was significantly related to the performance writing scores ($\gamma = 1.036$), but not to the indirect scores. This finding provided preliminary evidence that the school's planned curricular improvement in writing/language arts was related to its subsequent higher direct writing outcomes.[3] This hints at the performance assessment's utility in monitoring the planned efforts of school personnel to improve their curriculum and instruction.

*Tests of Differential Parameter Impact.* The third type of comparison concerns possible differential effects of variables across the two assessment formats. This provides information about the formats' relative equity. It is possible to test for possible differences in the size of the individual effects across the two sets of scores. This can be accomplished by constraining one parameter at a time to be equal across the two models and then examining the resulting difference in chi-square from a model where the parameter was not constrained to be equal (see Raudenbush et al., 2000, for further discussion). An insignificant chi-square coefficient indicates that there is no difference in the size of a variable's effect across the two assessments. These results are also summarized in Table 10.3.

Several parameters were significantly different across the two assessments. First, for low SES students, the achievement gap in their performance writing scores was significantly smaller than the gap in their indirect writing scores, $\chi^2 ( = 1, N = 165, 3,300) = 13.59, p < .05$. Second, student stability had a significantly stronger impact on the performance writing scores than on the indirect scores, $\chi^2 ( = 1, N = 165, 3,300) = 7.16, p < .05$. Third, the impact of the writing curricular focus variable was significantly stronger on the performance assessment scores than on the indirect scores, $\chi^2 ( = 1, N = 165, 3,300) = 3.91, p < .05$.

## Implications For Studying Policy

As this example illustrates, multilevel modeling techniques can be quite useful in examining policy issues involving the utility and equity of different types of student assessments. First, it provided evidence that the school's deliberate focus and energy directed toward writing curricular and instructional improvement was related to higher school writing scores. This provides preliminary evidence of the relationship between schools' intended efforts to reform their educational practices and actual impacts on outcomes. The relationship between reform efforts and achievement impact has often been hard to demonstrate in studies due to the substantial relationship of context and composition variables to student outcomes. From a practical perspective, the finding is encouraging because it provides evidence supporting the view that schools can undergo a specific, purposeful improvement process that helps them become more effective. This correspondence also supports the view that the writing performance assessment likely measures what students learn in the school as opposed to what inequities they bring from the home.

Second, if writing performance assessments provide a more equitable testing format, the set of controls and equity variables should account for lower proportions of variance at both the student and school levels on the writing performance assessment than on the indirect assessment. In this example, this finding was not supported at the student level, amounting to a difference of less that 1%. At the school level, however, the difference in variance accounted for across the two assessments was more substantial. About 67% of the school-level variance in indirect writing scores was attributed solely to factors outside the school's control (e.g., student composition, student stability, percentage of SLEP students). This suggests that after the student composition and school context variables were added to the indirect model, there would be little variation in outcomes left to be explained by school variables that might be expected to explain school performance (e.g., academic press, teaching quality, curricular improvement emphases). In contrast, only slightly more than 40% of the variance in direct writing scores was attributed to the student composition and school context factors included in the model.

## MULTILEVEL MODELING WITH SEM

In recent years, researchers have worked to integrate multilevel regression, or random coefficients, modeling with structural equation modeling to provide a general methodological approach that would account for clustered sampling (i.e., students nested in classes and schools), population heterogeneity, measurement error, and simultaneous equations (Bryk & Raudenbush, 1992; Kaplan & Elliott, 1997; McArdle & Hamagami; 1996; Muthén, 1991, 1994; Muthén & Muthén, 1998–2001; Muthén & Satorra, 1989, 1995; Raudenbush & Bryk, 2002; Willett & Sayer, 1996). There are considerable similarities between the two basic approaches. To date, however, multilevel SEM has only rarely been applied to research on schools (e.g., see Kaplan & Elliot, 1997; McDonald & Goldstein, 1989; Muthén, 1991, 1994). In part, this was due to a lack of available software and the associated difficulty with correctly estimating multilevel data with SEM techniques. Currently, however, a growing number of SEM software programs are capable of analyzing multilevel data structures.

In this part of the chapter, multilevel structural equation modeling (MSEM) is discussed and illustrated with another policy example. Some of the features of SEM make it an attractive way to investigate policy problems and an approach that is likely to generate much high quality theoretical and statistical work concerned with the effects of schools on students over the next few years (Teddlie, Stringfield, & Reynolds, 2000). There are a number of reasons for this optimism.

First, one of the key features of SEM is its two submodels. The first model (called the measurement model) relates observed variables to their underlying (latent) constructs. This model corrects the latent constructs for errors in their observed measures. The second model (called the structural model) examines relations between the constructs in the model. Correcting for measurement error allows a more accurate estimate of the model's structural parameters. For multilevel modeling, this latter point is especially important, in that most previous multilevel regression models in research on schooling assume that predictors at all levels were measured without error.

Second, the SEM approach readily allows the modeling of separate sets of structural relationships within and between groups involving direct effects, indirect effects, reciprocal effects, and multiple outcomes. Whereas previous multilevel SEM studies were limited to the examination of randomly varying intercepts only, the method has been expanded technically to also allow the investigation of randomly varying slopes as outcomes at the group level (i.e., for observed variables only). Incorporating the benefits of factor analysis (defining latent constructs through a set of observed indicators to account for measurement error) and path analysis (including direct and indirect effects of variables) can provide more complete tests of multilevel conceptual frameworks (Muthén, 1994; Raudenbush & Bryk, 2002).

Third, the method opens up some new opportunities for investigating complex relationships involving repeated measures (i.e., growth or change) in school settings. Measurements on individuals can be collected at varying time intervals or can be missing for some occasions. When students are changing academically over time, they may be changing simultaneously in several domains. SEM allows the investigation of whether the changes in mathematics, reading, and language achievement themselves are mutually interrelated (Willett & Sayer, 1996).

## The Multilevel SEM Model

The general statistical model for multilevel SEM is complicated and difficult to implement as a practical matter because of the inherent complexities in computing separate covariance matrices for each unit (Hox, 1995; McArdle & Hamagami, 1996). This is because SEM techniques depend on large sample sizes for efficient estimation. Instead of developing a separate covariance matrix for each unit, however, one way to simplify the analysis of multilevel data using SEM techniques is to assume that there is one population of individuals who are clustered in groups. The goal of the analysis is to decompose the variation in a set of dependent variables into variance components associated with each level of a hierarchical data structure and explain the variation present at each level simultaneously using sets of predictors (Muthén & Muthén, 1998–2001).

In the multilevel SEM approach (also called disaggregated modeling), the total score for each individual is decomposed into a within-group com-

ponent (the individual deviation from the group mean) and a between-group component (the disaggregated group means). This decomposition is used to compute separate within-groups and between-groups
covariance matrices. Following Muthén and Muthén's (1998) discussion,
the general two-level model considers a vector of observed variables that
can contain cluster-specific (group level) variables $z_c$ (c = 1, 2, ... , C) and
individual-specific variables ($\mathbf{y}_{ci}$ and $\mathbf{x'}_{ci}$) for individual $i$ in cluster $c$, where

$$
\mathbf{v}_{ic} = \begin{pmatrix} z_c \\ y_{ic} \\ x_{ic} \end{pmatrix} = \mathbf{v}_c^* + \mathbf{v}_{ic}^* = \begin{pmatrix} v_{zc}^* \\ \upsilon_{yc}^* \\ v_{xc}^* \end{pmatrix} + \begin{pmatrix} 0 \\ \upsilon_{yic}^* \\ \upsilon_{xic}^* \end{pmatrix}.
$$
(16)

The asterisked components are independent between and within components of the respective variable vector (Muthén & Satorra, 1995). The between-group matrix contains the between-group predictors ($\mathbf{z}_c$), group-
level variation in intercepts ($\mathbf{y}_c$), and group-level variation in the individual-level predictors ($\mathbf{x}_c$). Note that the within-group matrix contains the intercepts and individual-level predictors and zeros (0) for the group-level
variables (i.e., because they have no within-group variability).

The multilevel model can be translated into a between-cluster model
with observed and latent variables and errors (representing measurement
errors in defining factors and errors in structural equations):

$$
\mathbf{v}_c^* = \upsilon_B + \Lambda_B \eta_{Bc} + \varepsilon_{Bc},
$$
(17)

$$
\eta_{Bc} = \alpha_B + \beta_B \eta_{Bc} + \zeta_{Bc},
$$
(18)

and a similar within-cluster model

$$
\mathbf{v}_{ci}^* = \Lambda_W \eta_{Wci} + \varepsilon_{Wci},
$$
(19)

$$
\eta_{Wci} = \beta_W \eta_{Wci} + \zeta_{Wci}.
$$
(20)

Readers familiar with SEM methods will recognize that Equations 17 and
19 represent the measurement models linking observed variables to underlying factors for each level, whereas Equations 18 and 20 represent the structural models relating latent variables to one another for each level. Using the
familiar parameter arrays for the measurement model and structural model
in SEM at each level results in the following general mean and covariance
structure model for two-level data (Muthén & Muthén, 1998–2001):

$$\mu = \upsilon_B + \Lambda_B (\mathbf{I} - \mathbf{B}_B)^{-1} \alpha_B , \tag{21}$$

$$\Sigma_B = \Lambda_B (\mathbf{I} - \mathbf{B}_B)^{-1} \Psi_B (\mathbf{I} - \mathbf{B}_B)'^{-1} \Lambda'_B + \Theta_B , \tag{22}$$

$$\Sigma_W = \Lambda_W (\mathbf{I} - \mathbf{B}_W)^{-1} \Psi_W (\mathbf{I} - \mathbf{B}_W)'^{-1} \Lambda'_W + \Theta_W . \tag{23}$$

## Developing the Within- and Between-Group Covariance Matrices

SEM methods depend on the construction of covariance matrices from raw data. The decomposition of variables into their within- and between-group parts is used to compute the between-groups covariance matrix $\mathbf{S}_B$ (the covariance matrix of the disaggregated group means $Y_B$) and the within-groups covariance matrix $\mathbf{S}_w$ (the covariance matrix of the individual deviations from the group means $Y_w$). The covariance matrices are orthogonal and additive:

$$\mathbf{S}_T = \mathbf{S}_B + \mathbf{S}_W . \tag{24}$$

Muthén (1989, 1994) demonstrated that the pooled within-group sample covariance matrix $\mathbf{S}_{PW}$ (referred to as $\mathbf{S}_W$) is the unbiased estimate of the population within-groups covariance matrix ($\sum_w$). This is calculated in a sample as

$$\mathbf{S}_W = (n - C)^{-1} \sum_{c=1}^{C} \sum_{i=1}^{n_c} \left( \mathbf{y}_{ci} - \overline{\mathbf{y}_c} \right) \left( \mathbf{y}_{ci} - \overline{\mathbf{y}_c} \right)' . \tag{25}$$

This equation corresponds to the conventional equation for the covariance matrix of individual deviation scores, with $N - C$ (i.e., the number of individuals minus the number of groups) in the denominator instead of the usual $N - 1$ (Muthén, 1994). Importantly, analyzing the pooled within-group matrix instead of the total covariance matrix provides one correct strategy that researchers can use to correct for the bias resulting from cluster sampling (Muthén, 1989), even if the researcher is not interested in between-group relationships. Analyzing the total covariance would be incorrect, because it is based on a sample size of $N - 1$ (for individuals) as opposed to a sample size of $N - C$. Because the pooled within-group covariance matrix is an unbiased estimate of the population within-groups covariance matrix ($\Sigma_W$), we can estimate the population within-group structure by constructing this matrix.

The between-groups covariance matrix $\mathbf{S}_B$ for the disaggregated group means for the sample is written as

$$\mathbf{S}_B = (C-1)^{-1} \sum_{c=1}^{C} \mathrm{n}_c \left(\overline{\mathbf{y}_c} - \overline{\mathbf{y}}\right)\left(\overline{\mathbf{y}_c} - \overline{\mathbf{y}}\right)', \tag{26}$$

with $\mathbf{y}$ denoting the overall sample mean vector (Muthén & Satorra, 1995). It is important to note that $\mathbf{S}_B$ is not a simple estimator of the population between-groups covariance matrix ($\Sigma_B$). It turns out that $\mathbf{S}_B$ is a consistent and unbiased estimator of

$$\Sigma_W + s\Sigma_B, \tag{27}$$

where the scalar $s$ is the common group size for balanced data (Muthén, 1994; Muthén & Muthén, 1998),

$$s = [\mathrm{n}^2 - \sum_{c=1}^{C} \mathrm{n}^2_c] [\mathrm{n}\,(C-1)]^{-1}. \tag{28}$$

For unbalanced data and a large number of groups, it is possible to proceed as if the group sizes were equal and calculate the scaling factor $s$ as a combination of the observed cluster sizes similar to the mean (Muthén, 1994). The maximum likelihood (ML) estimate of $\Sigma_W$ is $\mathbf{S}_W$. Because the population counterpart of $\mathbf{S}_B$ ($\Sigma_B$) is a function of both $\Sigma_W + \Sigma_B$, as Muthén (1990) indicated, it is estimated as

$$\hat{\Sigma}_B = (\mathbf{S}_B - \mathbf{S}_W)/s. \tag{29}$$

It is important to note that different SEM software programs (e.g., LISREL, Mplus) that can handle multilevel data may print different between-group covariance matrices. For example, LISREL 8.54 (Jöreskog & Sörbom, 2003) prints the estimates of $\Sigma_B$ for the between-group covariance matrix in its output, while Mplus 2.13 (Muthén & Muthén, 1998–2001) prints $\mathbf{S}_B$.

### Model Estimation With Balanced and Unbalanced Groups

It is also important to keep in mind that model estimation techniques such as maximum likelihood (ML) depend on large sample sizes, preferably at both levels, for the estimates to have desirable asymptotic properties (e.g., Bassiri, 1988; Fotiu, 1989; Muthén, 1989). With balanced group sizes, ML estimation can be used to estimate the model's parameters. With unbalanced group sizes, however, in the past it has not been practical to use conventional SEM estimation techniques such as maximum likelihood because the fitting function involves terms for each distinct group size, including information on the mean vectors (Muthén, 1990, 1994). The new version of LISREL (8.54), however, has implemented full information maximum likelihood to estimate the model's parameters.

In contrast, Mplus uses a slightly different estimation method for multi-level models with unbalanced groups sizes. Muthén (1990, 1991) developed a quasi-likelihood estimator that can be used to estimate the model's parameters. This estimator is similar to a conventional two-population covariance structure analysis using ML estimation under normality, even though it makes use of less information than ML (Hox, 1995; McDonald; 1994; Muthén, 1990; 1994; Muthén & Muthén, 1998–2001). Muthén (1991) demonstrated that this fitting function is a consistent estimator of the population between-group covariance matrix (see Equation 29), when sample sizes are sufficiently large and group sizes are not extremely different. Muthén's quasi-likelihood estimator (called MUMLM in the Mplus software program) contains the Muthén-Satorra (1995) rescaling of chi-square statistic and standard errors, which produces corrected estimates for unbalanced group sizes (Muthén & Muthén, 1998–2001). Researchers should note that in my preliminary experimentations with these two software programs, I have found that they produce very close (but not exact) estimates of parameters, standard errors, and fit indices with unbalanced group sizes.

There are several other issues that should be considered in designing studies using SEM. First, similar to the cautions with multilevel regression, the researcher should carefully consider the number of units available in the study (because SEM estimation depends on having larger sample sizes available for efficient estimation). A number of studies on sample size have determined that various conditions (e.g., small number of groups and varying intraclass correlations) can have a considerable impact on the correct calculation of parameter estimates, standard errors, and fit indices (e.g., Hox & Maas, 2001). The number of units available can also affect the statistical power associated with the model (i.e., the probability of finding a significant effect if it indeed exists). Second, the methods of estimation may differ slightly across software programs, as can the procedures for standardizing parameter estimates. These may produce discrepant results. Finally, because multilevel modeling with SEM tends to be more complicated to implement than is multilevel regression modeling (i.e., because of the presence of observed indicators, direct and indirect effects), there are occasions where we are likely to encounter problems in setting up and testing the whole model first. In these cases, it sometimes helps to build the model a step at a time (e.g., defining a latent variable and its indicators, or estimating the individual level separately before adding the group level) in order to simplify the computations and identify where possible sources of misspecification are. It is sometimes difficult to determine exactly where the problem lies, so remember that patience is a virtue!

## A MULTILEVEL SEM EXAMPLE

An example may help to illustrate the multilevel SEM approach. Assume that we wish to examine variation in student achievement (defined by scores on reading, math, and language subtests) that can be explained by several variables within and between schools. The proposed model is summarized in Fig. 10.4. Between-group variables ($z_c$) include school socioeconomic status (CSES); school quality (conceived of as a latent variable measured by perceptions of the school's leadership, academic focus, expectations for student progress, monitoring of student progress, climate, and home–school relations collected from parents, students, and staff surveys); and the group-level intercepts ($y_c$) for the observed measures of academic achievement (i.e., reading, math, and language subtests)

Within-group predictors are female (coded 1) and low student socioeconomic status (coded 1). In this case, these variables are defined as varying only within groups ($x_{ci}$). In other situations, we might want to decompose an individual-level predictor into its own within- and between-group components ($x_c$ and $x_{ci}$). For example, the researcher might want to consider a between-group SES component (defined for a dichotomous variable as the percent of low SES students in the school). In this example, however, this would probably not be useful, because we already have a separate school SES variable.

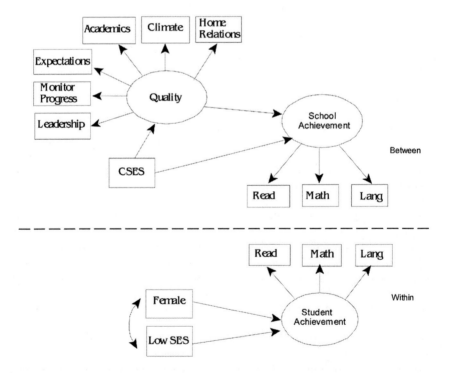

FIG. 10.4.   Proposed multilevel model.

The model was tested with Mplus 2.13 on a data set consisting of 6,970 sixth-grade students in 123 elementary schools. The first step in the analysis was to determine the percentage of variation in outcomes that lies within and between groups. Larger intraclass correlations (which describe the percentage of between-group variation) suggest greater similarity among members in each group. The unadjusted intraclass correlations (ICC) were .17 for reading, .21 for math, and .15 for language, suggesting sufficient variability between schools on the outcome measures to proceed with the analysis.

SEM software programs provide maximum-likelihood estimates of model parameters by iteratively minimizing a fitting function based on observed data and the implied model. The model is defined through writing the model's equations in matrix form (McArdle, 1998). The models are often represented using path diagrams, which facilitates the specification of the mathematical relationships. A proposed model is then tested against the data and its fit against the data may be assessed by examining a number of statistical and practical indices. One common way of assessing the discrepancy of fit between the hypothesized model and the data is through the chi-square distribution. Because the chi-square test of fit examines a very rigid hypothesis of perfect model fit (and is also dependent on sample size), however, researchers often use other indices as well.

We can also make use of several other fit indices to determine whether the model is a plausible representation of the data. For example, the Comparative Fit Index (CFI), which compares the fit of the model against a baseline "ill-fitting" model, was .98. Values above .95 are often accepted as providing evidence that the model fits the data adequately. The root mean square error of approximation (RMSEA) measures the discrepancy in fit per degree of freedom in the model. RMSEA has the advantage of providing a statistical test of model fit (i.e., that RMSEA is smaller than .05). In this case, the coefficient was small (0.026) and nonsignificant ($p = 1.00$). This result suggests the model should not be rejected on statistical grounds alone. Finally, the standardized root mean square residual (SRMR) provides an overall summary of the magnitude of the residuals. Values of .05 or smaller also indicate good fitting models. In this case, the SRMR was .01 for the within-schools model and .06 for the between-schools model. Although in theory it is always possible to find better fitting models, they might make little sense substantively. On the other hand, achieving an acceptable fit, however, does not guarantee that the model is the "best," or only, model that fits the data. Because other models might fit the data as well or better, it is generally the case that theory should be a guide in deciding whether or not a model should be accepted.

Once the model is determined to fit the data adequately, we can examine the parameter estimates. Figure 10.5 provides a summary of the standardized estimates and highlights several important findings. First, the indicators of achievement measure the latent achievement factors well both within and between schools. The factor loadings range from .82 to .98. Second, the

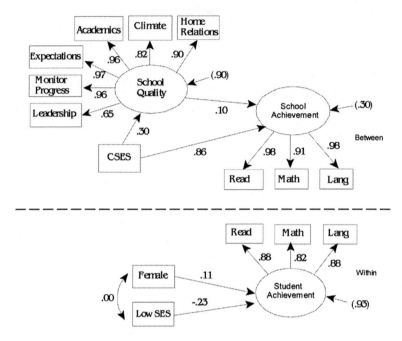

FIG. 10.5.    Multilevel model of variables affecting school achievement.

school quality latent factor is also well measured by the observed indicators (with coefficients ranging from .65 to .97). It is important to point out that multilevel analyses with latent variables provide results that correspond to those that would be obtained from perfectly reliable measures of the observed variables (Muthén, 1994). Correcting the model for measurement error, therefore, is an important step in obtaining more accurate estimates of the structural relationships between the latent variables. Third, we can see that school quality has a small (.10), but positive, relationship with school achievement; however, this relationship is much weaker than the relationship between school SES and school achievement (.86). Fourth, school SES affects school quality positively (.30), suggesting that schools with higher SES also have higher perceived school quality. Overall, the model explains about 70% of the variance in school-level achievement (due primarily to the influence of CSES), with unexplained variance for each latent variable indicated in parentheses (i.e., .30).

We can also extend the previous model by adding a previous achievement latent variable at each level. This change can be used to assess the stability of school effects over time (see Heck, 2003, for further discussion). In the past, the inclusion of measures of previous achievement in multilevel modeling, especially at the school level, has been more problematic and, therefore, not adequately studied (Teddlie et al., 2000). Most multilevel studies have focused on learning at one point in time. Studies of student learning over time (requiring the collection of longitudinal data on the same students) put the attention more squarely on students' experience in attending a particular school over an extended period of time (e.g., 3 to 6 years), as opposed to their experience over the course of a year with a particular teacher in the school (Teddlie et al., 2000). The effects of the quality of the school's entire educational program and processes are likely to accumulate over time.

The flexibility of the SEM approach makes it an ideal modeling strategy for researchers to use in examining changes in school achievement over time after adjusting for measurement error. The model formulation may be thought of as a longitudinal, multilevel model with two or more measurement occasions, so that the second and subsequent sets of achievement indicators (e.g., reading, math, language) are repeated measures of the first set of indicators.

Once again, the model fits the data well (i.e., CFI = .98, RMSEA = .034, $p$ > .05). The model's standardized parameters are displayed in Fig. 10.6. The strong relationship between the achievement factors at the school level (.85) suggest that school achievement effects are relatively stable over time for this set of schools. In this case, the between-school model was specified slightly differently, to indicate the small relationship between school quality and third-grade achievement (.10). Actually, this was not surprising because the survey described conditions at the school during the cohort's third-grade year. The direct effect, however, of school process on sixth-grade achievement is negligible (.01, not shown in the figure).The flexibility of the multilevel SEM formulation, however, allows the calculation of a small indirect (.1 x .85 = .085) effect between school quality on the sixth grade outcomes.

Within schools, the figure summarizes a strong relationship existing between students' third-grade achievement and sixth-grade achievement (.90). Notice, also, that student composition variables also exerted small direct (and indirect) effects on the student achievement factors. For example, the strongest negative direct effect on third-grade outcomes was for special education students (–.27). Moreover, minority students scored substantially below nonminority students on third-grade outcomes (–.17) and with a smaller direct effect (–.05) also present on sixth-grade outcomes. The same pattern was evident for low SES status. Given the pattern of direct (and several indirect) effects in the model, we can conclude that the effects of some student demographic variables accumulate over time (low SES, minority status, gender, SPED status).

### Examining the Policy Concerns

One of the policy issues embedded in this analysis concerns the stability of school effects over time and how the relative stability of school quality mea-

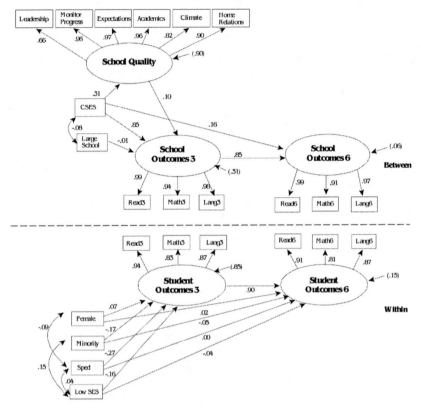

FIG. 10.6.  Multilevel model of stability of achievement over time, controlling for student and contextual influences. *Note*. Correlations between predictors smaller than .04 are not shown.

sures and school achievement measures might impact on school effectiveness criteria. Concerns have been raised over the extent to which schools identified as effective at one point in time remain effective on successive measurements. If schools are to be evaluated as effective, they should produce consistent results across time and multiple types of outcomes (e.g., subject areas, attendance, behavior). Without reliable and valid measures, policymakers and can have little confidence in evaluations of school progress for accountability purposes. The multilevel SEM approach illustrated in this example provides positive evidence regarding the stability of school effects over time. Multilevel SEM can control for many of the rival sources of influence that have plagued previous research examining school effectiveness over time (e.g., measurement error, confounding influence of composition and context). It has been a challenge to adjust for many of these influences adequately in order to estimate school effectiveness.

Another policy issue concerns the use of school process indicators in examining school outcomes. Multilevel indicator systems provide a more refined means for making school comparisons for accountability purposes by examining relevant variables that influence student outcomes, after controlling for student composition within schools. The measures of school quality (important to policymakers) were found to be related to differences in third-grade school achievement (and indirectly with small differences in sixth-grade outcomes). This provides evidence that schools rated as having higher quality processes do actually score higher in terms of school achievement. This has often been difficult to demonstrate in school effects studies. The flexibility of the SEM approach would make it possible to also monitor changes in school quality over time and to determine how those changes might affect changes in outcomes.

## SUMMARY

The examples provided in this chapter provide a glimpse of the ways in which multilevel modeling can be used to investigate various policy issues. The benefits of doing multilevel analyses are many—including greater conceptual clarity in defining relationships among variables and greater precision of estimates where there are clustering features present. It is important to consider, however, that their appropriate use depends on guidance from strong theory to explicate relationships and the collection of quality data. One of the drawbacks of using multilevel models is the challenge of learning how to use the software appropriately. Another concerns how to best communicate the results of multilevel analysis to practitioners and policymakers. As the techniques continue to become more readily available, however, their use in policy research should expand rapidly.

## EXERCISES

1. Compare and contrast some of the major assumptions and considerations involving the use of single-level and multilevel analyses in policy research.

2. Using some of the constructs of the policy model presented in Fig. 3.2 (e.g., environmental processes, policy-belief systems, interactions, outcomes), develop a simple policy study that would involve a multilevel type of analysis.

## ENDNOTES

1. Following Supovitz and Brennan's (1997) notation, for this particular use of multilevel modeling, the level-1 model represents the measurement model for the two outcomes used in the study. It is represented as

$$Y_{ikj} = \pi_{1kj}\, a_{1ikj} + \pi_{2kj}\, a_{2ikj} + e_{ikj},$$

where $Y_{ikj}$ is the observed score for assessment i for individual j in school k; $\pi_{1kj}$ is the true-score estimate for the direct measure of writing for individual j in school k; $\pi_{2kj}$ is the true-score estimate of the language standardized test score for individual j in school k; $a_{1ikj}$ is a dummy variable coded 1 when the assessment is writing and 0 when it is not; $a_{2ikj}$ is a dummy variable coded 1 when the assessment is language and 0 when it is not; and $e_{ikj}$ represents the error for student j in school k for assessment i. Note that the equation contains no intercept and that the scores are entered into the model as uncentered.

The level-2 model includes the sets of student-level predictors of each outcome in the parallel models. The interest is in the parameters representing the two outcomes ($\pi_{1kj}$ and $\pi_{kj}$). The models may be represented as follows:

$$\pi_{1kj} = \beta_{10k} + \beta_{11k}\, X_{1jk} + \beta_{12k}\, X_{2jk} + \ldots + \beta_{1Qk}\, X_{qjk} + r_{1jk}$$

$$\pi_{2kj} = \beta_{20k} + \beta_{21k}\, X_{1jk} + \beta_{22k}\, X_{2jk} + \ldots + \beta_{2Qk}\, X_{qjk} + r_{2jk}$$

In this set of equations, $\beta_{10\kappa}$ and $\beta_{20k}$ are the intercepts for each of the two true-score estimates, $\beta_{1Qk}$ and $\beta_{2Qk}$ (q= 1, 2, ... , Q) are student-level coefficients predicting each of the true-score estimates, $X_{qik}$ are predictors for individual j in class k; and $r_{1jk}$ and $r_{2jk}$ are the level-2 random effects for individual j in school k for each of the assessments.

At level 3, school predictors for each of the student-level intercepts ($\beta_{10k}$ and $\beta_{20k}$ ) are included. The two relevant models are

$$\beta_{10k} = \gamma_{100} + \gamma_{101}\, W_{1k} + \gamma_{102}\, W_{2k} + \ldots \gamma_{10S}\, W_{sk} + u_{10k}$$

$$\beta_{20k} = \gamma_{200} + \gamma_{201}\, W_{1k} + \gamma_{202}\, W_{2k} + \ldots \gamma_{20S}\, W_{sk} + u_{20k}$$

At this level, $\gamma_{100}$ and $\gamma_{200}$ are the school-level intercepts for each outcome, $\gamma_{10S}$ and $\gamma_{20S}$ (s = 1, 2, ... , S) are coefficients predicting $\beta_{10k}$ and $\beta_{20k}$ for each of S school predictors ($W_{sk}$), and $u_{10k}$ and $u_{20k}$ are the school-level random effects. The level-3 equations predicting the level-2 intercepts are also parallel.

2. I am indebted to Robert T. Brennan for advice on how to rescale the true-score variance for each assessment. First, it is necessary to create a weighting variable to be used in the HLM analysis. This is computed as

$$\text{Weight} = 1/(1 - \text{reliability}) * \text{variance}.$$

Second, a standardized unit of comparison must be created for conducting the hypothesis tests between the two assessments. This involves obtaining the original variance estimates for the two outcomes and then adjusting them to be equal. In this case, we set the true-score variance for each outcome to be equal to 100, with a mean of 50 and a standard deviation of 10.

3. It is possible that the writing improvement variable might be significant on the direct writing assessment because there was a greater proportion of variance left unexplained after the other control and equity variables were entered into the model. This possibility was checked by examining other models where we changed the order of the writing improvement variable's entry into the models. Although its influence was similar when its entry order was changed (e.g., entered before the student-level variables, entered before the school controls), it had to be entered into the model after school SES was controlled.

# Growth Modeling Methods for Examining Policy Change

As we have seen in the last chapter, in many studies of schooling that examine processes and outcomes, the outcome and process variables are only measured on one occasion (i.e., using cross-sectional data). A limitation of static, cross-sectional data, however, is that they are not well suited to investigations of processes that are assumed to be dynamic. This is because it is difficult to establish the proper time ordering necessary to address causal relationships in cross-sectional analyses. It therefore becomes more difficult to rule out alternative explanations. Analyses based on cross-sectional data may only lead to a partial understanding of processes at best, and misleading interpretations at worst (Davies & Dale, 1994). As suggested in the chapter on qualitative methods (chap. 9), time is a key factor in understanding how policy processes unfold, as well as how their impacts may be observed. Limitations of data and method have in the past restricted the quantitative analysis of policy processes. Increasingly, however, both the concepts and methods are becoming available that can provide a more rigorous and thorough examination of longitudinal data. Although there has been considerable development of longitudinal data analysis techniques for use with experimental, quasi-experimental, and nonexperimental research designs, there is still a need to make the techniques more accessible to those interested in conducting policy research.

This chapter presents an introduction to quantitative methods that can be used to examine changes in individuals and institutions over time. It represents an extension of the multilevel methods introduced in the last chapter. First, it outlines some of the various ways of collecting longitudinal data. Next, two approaches for examining changes within individuals and groups over time are developed. The first approach focuses on estimating growth or change from the perspective of random coefficients (multilevel) regression modeling, once again using the HLM 5 software (Raudenbush, Bryk, Cheong, & Congdon, 2000). The second approach provides and overview of how structural equation modeling (SEM) can be used to examine longitudinal data, using the Mplus 2.14 software (Muthén & Muthén, 2001). Once again, readers may find some of the technical aspects of the analyses a challenge to understand. A number of examples are provided to help you think about different ways that longitudinal data analysis can broaden the conceptual possibilities for designing studies to answer policy questions.

## COLLECTING AND STRUCTURING LONGITUDINAL DATA

### Repeated Measures

There are a number of different ways to collect and analyze data over time. A first type of longitudinal data collection is referred to as repeated measures. Repeated measurements are used in research examining growth processes in individuals and groups. Where individuals are measured at successive time points, it is possible to investigate how outcomes of interest are related to the earlier circumstances of the same individuals. The analysis of the successive measurements allows researchers to identify individual growth patterns as well as between-individual similarities or differences in growth processes. This allows the researcher to build a causal model that explicitly takes into account the earlier circumstances that might have effects at later points in time.

Because the data are nested (i.e., measurement occasions within individuals), strong temporal dependencies may be created (Davies & Dale, 1994). To analyze repeated measures with least squares regression, therefore, would violate an important assumption underlying the method; that is, individuals' responses at different time points are not independent of each other. As we observed in the last chapter, when data are nested, a more complex error structure must be added to account for the dependencies among observations. One way to incorporate a series of observations nested within individuals into a growth model is to view the observations as multilevel data. We can approach the analysis of individual growth as a multilevel (random coefficients) regression model. In a random coefficients growth model, the series of repeated measures within each individual forms the lowest level (level 1). The individual measures (e.g., outcomes on achievement tests) are hypothesized to vary as a function of time. This relationship produces a random intercept and slope (describing the steepness of the growth over time) that vary across individuals. Similar to the multilevel regression model where a separate regression line is produced for each unit, in the random coefficients growth model, the relationship between the repeated measures outcomes and time produces a separate growth curve or trajectory for each individual. Time is usually considered as discrete in this type of model (i.e., subjects' conditions or characteristics are recorded to reflect particular points in time), with measurements taken at fixed or varying intervals. Time-varying covariates can be added at level 1, because they affect the successive measurements for each individual. For example, data on students' motivation could be collected at each successive time point before they take an achievement test.

At level 2, time-invariant covariates describing individuals (e.g., gender, socioeconomic status) can be incorporated to explain variation in individual growth patterns. If needed, a third level can be added to incorporate the nesting of individual growth trajectories within groups (e.g., classrooms or schools). At this level, differences in group growth patterns can be investigated.

Another way to treat the repeated measures data is as parameters in a latent variable (or structural equation) model. As demonstrated in the last chapter, latent variable modeling is a general framework that is widely adaptable to examining statistical concepts such as direct, indirect, and reciprocal effects; fixed and random effects; measurement errors; variance components; and missing data. Because latent variables are unobserved, they must be defined by measuring multiple observed indicators. In this way, it is possible to define latent factors through the observed repeated measures data representing the level of growth (i.e., an intercept factor), as well as the shape of the growth (e.g., a linear, and perhaps, a quadratic factor). Because the successive observations are treated as loadings on underlying factors describing the growth process, in the SEM approach, individual growth can be represented as single-level data. A second level can then be added (as in chap. 10) to examine differences in growth between groups (e.g., classrooms or schools).

Repeated measures data are most often used where subjects participate in some type of experiment and the data are collected within a fairly confined time—for example, before, during, and after the treatment is introduced. For example, successive measurements might be taken on individuals in treatment and control groups and their growth trajectories compared. In other situations, cross-sectional information might be collected on several occasions for the same individuals through surveys. The length of time between data collection points might vary from several weeks to several years.

We may also study individual growth over time in situations where students have not been assigned to treatment and control groups. One example of repeated measures in a nonexperimental design is a study to determine the effects of school inputs and processes on student academic growth. Achievement data would be collected at specific time intervals on the same individual students. The analysis might focus on determining how various types of school inputs (e.g., teacher quality, resources) and processes (e.g., grouping alternatives, instructional techniques, student expectations) influence student growth over time, after controlling for various individual background variables (e.g., gender, socioeconomic status). In this case, the researcher might view inputs and processes as time invariant (i.e., measured at only one point in time), with only achievement outcomes varying over time. Alternatively, it would also be possible to examine how changes in inputs and processes over time might affect changes in outcomes. Although this type of data collection would allow more complex examinations of how inputs, processes, and outcomes are related through time, this type of data collection does not frequently occur. More commonly, predictor variables are seen as static, whereas outcomes may be seen as dynamic.

**Repeated Cross-Sections**

Another way to collect data over time is through repeated cross-sectional surveys that are given to different random samples of a population at particular time intervals (e.g., every year, every 10 years). One example is the United States Census. Where surveys are repeated over time with a high level of consistency between items, sequences of measures may be created in discrete time, and these can be used to approximate changes that occur in a population. These types of analyses are often referred to as trend studies. Although this particular data structure does not allow individual change to be modeled, it can also be useful in describing changes in the population over time (see Johnsrud & Heck, 1998, for one example). Importantly, however, it is more challenging to determine the causes of these changes (e.g. by including variables that can help eliminate rival explanations). Within educational settings, for example, trend analyses of test scores are frequently conducted to describe and compare the academic achievement of successive cohorts of elementary, middle, and high school students. Yet, it is difficult to attribute any type of cause for why the scores go up or down year to year (Linn & Haug, 2002).

There are several alternatives for organizing this type of repeated cross-sectional data for analysis. For example, if the variables measured are consistent across occasions, the researcher could pool them into a larger database and designate a time-related variable to indicate when each interval of data was collected. Usually, this interval represents a year. Pooling the data across years has the benefit of adding considerable data to an overall database where the collection at each time interval might be too small. The time-related variable that designates the interval of data collection can be used in the analysis to describe changes in the population that occur over time.

If there are sufficient data for each year, a second alternative is to consider each year's data separately and to conduct a multiple group analysis across the successive years. The researcher constructs a theoretical model that examines key relationships within a baseline year and then compares the similarity of the models across years. These types of model comparisons are referred to in the SEM literature as tests of model invariance. They are conducted by specifying a theoretical model for the first time interval and then comparing the fit of this proposed model across the other time-interval models. If the structure and measurement qualities of the models are similar (e.g., factor structures, item loadings, relations between factors, errors), then the researcher can describe changes in outcome means that occur over time. This allows the charting of a growth trend over time.

A third possibility is to aggregate data collected within repeated cross-sectional surveys, so that each aggregate measure represents a single case within a larger data set (Davies & Dale, 1994). Economists often use this type of data structure to model time trends and to produce economic forecasts. One of the aims is to model temporal dependencies in the data and then use this information to predict changes in the future. An application of this type of aggregated cross-sectional analysis is when researchers examine historical or archival data (e.g., enrollment, staffing, achievement data) collected over a period of time to identify trends or to test theories about the impact of political and social changes on educational practices (e.g., see Plank et al., 1996, for one example study).

Within school districts and schools, many data are routinely collected each year. Data on individual students' test scores, attendance information, and their graduation status might be aggregated to represent a single score on each variable for a particular year. One should, however, carefully consider the assumptions underlying decisions about data collection. Aggregating data to a macro (grouped) level eliminates micro level (i.e., individual) variability. Although aggregating data on individuals eliminates the possibility of examining individual change, it does provide a relatively accessible way of incorporating a time dimension that allows the examination of trends, on the assumption that other things are equal (Davies & Dale, 1994). This may allow the researcher to uncover relationships that would not be observed in examining each cross-section separately. This potential benefit must be weighed against the caution that with only one measure at each time point, and typically strong correlations between time points, it can be challenging to test hypotheses.

Time-series data therefore present some complex and distinctive methodological challenges for researchers. One example is determining whether the introduction of some treatment (e.g., the implementation of a policy) produces a change in behavior. It may be possible to assemble a database that has information on a key behavior the policy is intended to affect before and after a policy is introduced. Assembling the data itself can be challenging, because as Tyack (1991) reminded us, the implementation of the policy itself may legitimate the collecting of data about it. In time-series designs, the impact of the treatment is indicated by a discontinuity of measurements recorded in the time series. Time-series data are useful in testing hypotheses about trends; for example, determining whether a trend before a policy is introduced is similar to a trend afterward, or determining whether policy changes might be dependent on certain temporal conditions or external disturbances (e.g., changing economic conditions, crises). As an example, current policy choices may be dependent on other choices made on previous occasions (e.g., how policymakers voted in the past). Particular types of social, community, or economic ties may create dependencies that affect policymakers' choices among policy alternatives. Moreover, external factors may also act in such a way as to influence their choices at later times.

## Continuous Time

A third way to collect information about processes over time is through what researchers refer to as "continuous" time data. In recent years, there has been growing interest in recording life-course events, such as work histories. In contrast to discrete time data, where information is recorded at particular points in time (e.g., repeated measures, repeated cross-sections), continuous time data are typically collected retrospectively, for example, by asking people on surveys to respond to certain conditions in their lives after the events have happened. The events must be dated so that they can be sequenced. In these types of "event history" studies, the focus is often on the number, sequence, and duration of particular events of interest. The relationship of one event to another can then be analyzed.

Continuous time data collection can aid researchers in discovering factors that influence particular outcomes, as well as factors affecting the timing of the outcomes (Davies & Dale, 1994). Decisions have to be made about when data collection should begin; for example, the respondent's first teaching position or administrative position. For interested readers, modeling these types of event histories are often accomplished though hazard models, where the event of interest is the "hazard," and one models the "survival" or "failure" time until that event and the variables that affect the survival time (see Davies & Dale, 1994). The terminology derives from biomedical sciences.

## ANALYZING LONGITUDINAL DATA

One of the obvious benefits of longitudinal data is the increased ability to disentangle causal relationships. As previously suggested, cross-sectional data are unable to resolve the ambiguity in correlations or other measures of association. On the other hand, the development of proper methods to examine change has challenged researchers for many years. There have been inadequacies in the conceptualization, measurement, and design of change studies (Bryk & Raudenbush, 1992).

*Repeated Measures ANOVA.* Traditionally, repeated measures analysis of variance (ANOVA) has been used to examine changes in individuals across time in experimental and quasi-experimental designs. Hypothesis tests can be conducted to determine whether the means of the variables measured at different time points are equal or to determine the shape of the growth trend (e.g., linear, quadratic, exponential). Researchers have identified a number of limitations with repeated measures ANOVA, however (Bryk & Raudenbush, 1992, Hox, 2002; Raykov & Marcoulides, 2000 ). Unfortunately, some of the assumptions of the method are often not tenable when used in real situations. These shortcomings include the normality of the data across between-subject factors and the equality of the covariance matrices across measurements. For example, if we are investigating changes in male and female salaries within a profession over time related to their education and experience, we may observe differences in the normality of the salary data (e.g., if women have been denied equal entry to the profession, if their participation is restricted to certain areas of practice). Initial inequities between males and females might influence subsequent measurements of their salaries (e.g., if one group's salary becomes more varied over time in ways that aren't related to education and experience).

***Growth Modeling and Other Approaches.***        In recent years, there have been increased options other than repeated measures ANOVA for examining changes over time. Having several options for statistical modeling allows greater flexibility in how the change is modeled and for determining how other variables may affect changes across time. For example, unlike in repeated measures ANOVA, where growth appears as an interaction of repeated occasions by subjects, in random coefficients growth modeling, the change in successive measurements can be directly modeled. This results in each individual having a separate growth curve or trajectory. Increased modeling options also open up possibilities for examining more complex relationships in the data where both independent and dependent variables may be changing over time, where changes in individuals and groups are examined simultaneously, and where separate growth trends can be compared before and after a treatment is introduced (called piecewise growth functions).

Similar to multilevel data analysis, growth models may be proposed and tested against the data, and their adequacy assessed through various fit indices, analyses of residuals, and comparisons between simpler or more complex models. The types of models used to examine longitudinal data vary widely, not only in the types of research and data problems they address, but also in the terminology used to describe their specific features (see Davies & Dale, 1994, for further discussion). To some extent, the various modeling approaches are also tied to particular disciplines that may favor particular ways of examining changes over time for the types of research questions that are considered important. Interested readers can examine particular approaches more closely, depending on their research concerns and the structure of their data (e.g., see Dale & Davies, 1994).

In addition to the random coefficients and SEM approaches for modeling changes over time introduced in this chapter, alternative approaches exist for analyzing various types of longitudinal data. These include event history analysis (used to examine the timing of events within an observational period), Markov latent class models (often used in hazard models to examine changes in individuals' states over time, such as how choices at previous points in time affect subsequent choices), and Box-Jenkins (ARIMA) methods (used to examine the extent to which an outcome can be explained by a predictor over and above its own past values). Further discussion of these methods can be found in Dale and Davies (1994) and in Hershberger, Molenaar, & Corneal, (1996). The common element is that each approach deals with the high correlations between successive measurements in modeling changes over time.

## RANDOM COEFFICIENTS GROWTH MODELING

As discussed in the previous chapter, hierarchical data structures are common in education. Because they can take into consideration "random" effects, random coefficients (or multilevel regression) modeling provides a convenient means of examining variation, or change, among individuals, where heterogeneity concerns individual differences in trajectories (Bryk & Raudenbush, 1992; Muthén, 2002). Unlike "fixed" effects models, where every individual in a sample is assigned the same coefficient describing, for example, the effect of gender on outcomes, random coefficients growth modeling allows the researcher to examine the variability in selected parameters across the individuals in the study. In random coefficients growth modeling, the random variability concerns individual differences in the growth trajectories.

Many individual changes may be represented through a two-level growth model (for further discussion of random coefficients growth models, see Bryk & Raudenbush, 1992; Hox, 2002). Typically, we assume that some subjects have been sampled and measured on a number of variables over time (i.e., it is also possible to include missing occasions on individuals). At level 1, each person's successive measurements across time can be represented by an individual growth trajectory (or growth curve) and by random error. Following Bryk and Raudenbush (1992), we assume that $Y_{ti}$, the observed status at time $t$ for individual $i$, is a function of a systematic growth trajectory plus random error. Polynomial curves are often used for estimating growth because they can be estimated using standard linear modeling procedures, and they are very flexible (Hox, 2002).

*Level-1 Model.* In this formulation, the systematic growth can be represented as a polynomial of degree P, with the level-1 model written as

$$Y_{ti} = \pi_{0i} + \pi_{1i}a_{ti} + \pi_{2i} a^2_{ti} + \ldots + \pi_{pi} a^P_{ti} + e_{ti}, \qquad (1)$$

where $a_{ti}$ is a time-varying variable of interest, measured at time $t$ for individual $i$, and $\pi_{pi}$ is the growth trajectory parameter $p$ for subject $i$ associated with the polynomial of degree $P$ (i.e., $p = 0, \ldots, P$). Each person is observed on $T_i$ occasions. This general equation allows the representation of several different growth trajectories including, for example, linear ($\pi_{1i} a_{ti}$) and quadratic ($\pi_{2i} a^2_{ti}$) growth. Most commonly, a simple error structure is assumed for $e_{ti}$; that is, each error is independently and normally distributed with a mean of zero and constant variance, $\sigma^2$ (Bryk & Raudenbush, 1992). However, other error structures are also possible, such as autocorrelation among errors for each person, or error that is dependent on the individual's age. More complex error structures can be useful where there are many time points per subject.

*Level-2 Model.*   The level-1 equation assumes that growth varies among individuals. At level 2, a set of predictors (e.g., gender, socioeconomic status, health status, an experimental treatment) can be added to explain the differences in individual growth trajectories. Specifically, following Bryk and Raudenbush (1992), for each of the $P + 1$ individual growth parameters,

$$\pi_{pi} = \beta_{p0} + \sum_{q=1}^{Q_p} \beta_{pq} X_{qi} + r_{pi},$$

(2)

where $X_{qi}$ might be a characteristic of the individual's background; $\beta_{pq}$ represents the effect of $X_q$ on the $p$th growth parameter; and $r_{pi}$ is a random effect with mean of zero. The set of $P + 1$ random effects for individual $i$ are assumed to be multivariate normally distributed with full covariance matrix, **T**, dimensioned $(P + 1) \times (P + 1)$.

Because multilevel modeling does not require balanced data, it is not a problem if all measurements are not available on all participants (Hox, 2002). This can be beneficial if there are subjects who drop out during a study.

### Examining Changes in Institutions' Graduation Rates

Readers are probably familiar with situations where researchers might examine a change in students' reading or math scores related to background variables such as gender and socioeconomic status. In such cases, the unit of analysis is the individual student. In the following example, we consider an application of random coefficients growth modeling to the implementation of a policy. In this simple example, data on football players' graduation rates from 12 Division 1-A public and private institutions are compiled over a 4-year period after the implementation of a policy enacted to raise student athletes' graduation rates. In this example, institutions are the unit of analysis (as opposed to individual students). The beginning of the time series is assumed to be 5 years after the policy's implementation (i.e., since players have 5 years to complete 4 years of eligibility), which corresponds to the first freshman class of players who entered after the policy took effect.

The first concern in the analysis is whether there is any growth that takes place after the policy is implemented. For example, it might be that there is no increase in graduation rates over the series of measurements after the policy is introduced. This would provide evidence that the policy did not achieve its stated goal to raise academic standards among student athletes. Second, we might want to examine possible differences in growth between public and private institutions and according to the prestige of their football programs.

In many situations where we examine change over time, it is convenient to employ a linear growth model. When the time periods are reasonably short and there are not too many observations per individual (i.e., an individual subject or, in this case, an individual institution), the linear growth model can provide a good approximation for more complex models that cannot be fully modeled because of the sparse number of observations (Bryk & Raudenbush, 1992).

*Level-1 Model.*    For a linear model at level 1, Equation 1 reduces to the following:

$$Y_{ti} = \pi_{0i} + \pi_{1i}a_{ti} + e_{ti}, \tag{3}$$

where $\pi_{0i}$ is the intercept, and $\pi_{1i}$ is the growth rate for individual (or institution) $i$ over the data-collection period and represents the expected change during a fixed unit of time. Individual growth can therefore be captured in two parameters—an intercept and a slope. It is important to note that the meaning of the intercept parameter ($\pi_{0i}$) depends on the scaling of the time variable. In this example, the time metric is yearly intervals (scaled as 0, 1, 2, 3). Varying intervals between measurement occasions can also be accommodated (e.g., 0, 1, 3, 7). Most often, researchers code the first measurement occasion as 0, so that the intercept parameter therefore can be interpreted as the true initial status of institution $i$ at time point $a_{ti} = 0$.

Defining the intercept as initial status serves as a baseline for interpreting the subsequent growth that takes place over time for each individual in the sample. In this example, therefore, each institution has its own growth trajectory (developed from the intercept and slope), with likely variability present in the random coefficients across the set of institutions. The errors ($e_{ti}$) are assumed to be independent and randomly distributed with common variance $\sigma^2$. Although the intercept is usually coded to reflect initial status, it would also be possible to code the last measurement as 0 (reflecting a final status intercept), and then code the earlier occasions with negative values (Hox, 2002). For readers familiar with HLM, the time intervals (0–3) are actually entered in the level-1 data set as a variable (time), and each time point corresponds to a specific graduation rate for each institution. This necessitates four data lines per institution, as opposed to data sets with which the reader may be more familiar that consist of only one data line per institution.

***Unconditional Growth Model.*** In random coefficients growth modeling, the first step is to examine an unconditional (i.e., no predictors) model for the random coefficients. No level-2 predictors are introduced to explain variation in the initial status or growth rate. The initial status and slope (growth) coefficients can be described as:

$$\pi_{0i} = \beta_{00} + r_{0i} \tag{4}$$

$$\pi_{1i} = \beta_{10} + r_{1i} . \tag{5}$$

Each random coefficient ($\pi_{0i}$ and $\pi_{1i}$) has only its own intercept ($\beta_{00}$ and $\beta_{10}$, respectively) that describes the average across the set of individual institutions and an error term. It is the addition of the error term that makes the coefficient randomly varying, as opposed to fixed for the sample. This simple, unconditional model provides useful evidence in determining the specification of the level-1 model and in developing baseline statistics for evaluating subsequent models (Bryk & Raudenbush, 1992).

The unconditional model for the example is presented in Table 11.1. The intercept (or initial status) was 39.50 (which is calculated as the initial graduation rate for the low-prestige and public schools in the sample), and the mean rate of growth was 3.94. This suggests that the average graduation rate initially was about 40%, and subsequently, schools gained on average

**TABLE 11.1**
**Unconditional Model of Linear Growth**

| Fixed Effect | Coefficient | Standard Error | T-ratio | df | P-value |
|---|---|---|---|---|---|
| Mean initial status, $\beta_{00}$ | 39.500 | 3.734 | 10.579 | 11 | 0.000 |
| Mean Growth rate, $\beta_{10}$ | 3.942 | 1.778 | 2.216 | 11 | 0.048 |
| Random Effect | Variance Component | | $\chi^2$ | df | P-value |
| Initial status, $r_{0i}$ | 268.922 | | 195.968 | 11 | 0.000 |
| Growth rate, $r_{1i}$ | 28.610 | | 35.598 | 11 | 0.000 |
| Level-1, $e_{ti}$ | 63.971 | | | | |

Reliability Estimates : Initial status, ($\pi_{0i}$) = 0.944; Growth rate, ($\pi_{1i}$) = 0.691.

almost 4% more football-playing graduates per year. Significant $t$ tests (i.e., the ratio of the coefficient to its standard error) indicated that both parameters are necessary for describing the growth trajectory.

Next, it is important to consider the nature of the deviations of the individual growth trajectories from the mean growth trajectory. The estimates of the initial status ($\pi_{0i}$) and slope ($\pi_{1i}$) variances were 268.9 and 28.61 respectively. The simplest test of homogeneity, that there is no true variation in individual growth parameters, involves use of a chi-square statistic. For initial status, the chi-square was 195.97 (df = 11, $N$ = 12), $p$ < .01. This leads to rejecting the null hypothesis that there is no variation among the institutions' initial status graduation percentages. For growth rates, the chi-square was 35.60 (df = 11, $N$ = 12), $p$ < .01, also suggesting the rejection of the null hypothesis of no significant variation in their growth rates.

We can also examine the reliability of the measures of the intercept and slope. If most of the growth were due to error, we would be unlikely to account for systematic variation by adding predictors at level 2 (i.e., between individual institutions). The observed measurement of a parameter consists of parameter variance and error variance. The reliability of the estimate is defined as ratio of true parameter variance to the total variance. For these data, the reliabilities were quite acceptable for the intercept (.944) and slope (.691). It should be noted that the reliability of the slope is usually lower, owing to several problems in estimation (see Bryk & Raudenbush, 1992 for further discussion).

The random coefficients model also provides an estimate of the correlation between initial status and growth. For a linear growth model, it is the correlation between $\pi_{0i}$ and $\pi_{1i}$. In this case, the correlation was –.224, suggesting that institutions that had lower graduation rates at initial status gained at a somewhat greater rate and vice versa. It is important to note that the correlation between the intercept and growth parameter depends on the specific time point selected for the intercept and the scaling of the time variable ($a_{ti}$). It is therefore important to give some attention its definition and scaling, since this affects the meaning one attaches to the coefficients (e.g., see Hox, 2002, for further discussion).

***Explaining Individual Growth Trajectories at Level 2.***        Because there was significant variation in each parameter present among individual institutions, both the intercept and growth parameters are allowed to vary at level 2. The variation in each may likely be partially explained by institutional characteristics. Following Bryk and Raudenbush (1992), the level-2 equation for intercepts is

$$\pi_{0i} = \beta_{00} + \sum_{q=1}^{Q_0} \beta_{0q} X_{0qi} + r_{0i},$$
(6)

and the equation for slopes is

$$\pi_{1i} = \beta_{10} + \sum_{q=1}^{Q_1} \beta_{1q} X_{1qi} + r_{1i}.$$

$$(7)$$

The level-2 random effects have variances $\tau_{00}$ (for the intercept) and $\tau_{11}$(for the growth slope) and covariance $\tau_{01}$.

In this example, we will consider level-2 predictors that may account for systematic variation in the intercept and slope parameters. The first variable is prestige (i.e., each school's on-field performance record consisting of wins, championships, and Top 25 finishes compiled over several years). Prestige was constructed as a factor score ($M = 0$ and $SD = 1$) and then dummy coded, with scores above .5 of a standard deviation being defined as high prestige (coded 1). The other variable is institutional type, which was dummy coded (0 = public institutions and 1 = private institutions). The level-2 model is now:

$$\pi_{0i} = \beta_{00} + \beta_{01} (\text{private})_i + \beta_{02} (\text{prestige})_i + r_{0i}$$

$$(8)$$

$$\pi_{1i} = \beta_{10} + \beta_{11} (\text{private})_i + \beta_{12} (\text{prestige})_i + r_{1i}.$$

$$(9)$$

As the table summarizes, for the initial status model, there was no relationship between either high prestige or institutional type and graduation rates. Both t-ratios were small and not significant. The unstandardized coefficients suggest that private schools started with graduation rates slightly lower than public schools (i.e., $\beta_{01} = -3.39\%$). High prestige schools graduated fewer student athletes on average than more typical schools ($\beta_{02} = -5.36\%$). In contrast, for the growth rate model, institutional type was significantly related to institutions' growth rates. More specifically, the graduation rates for private institutions increased on average at a rate of 8.36% ($\beta_{11} = 8.36$) per year faster than the graduation rates for public institutions. This can be confirmed in Table 11.3 by examining the actual observed scores for public and private institutions in this example.

We can also determine how much variance in the random coefficients was accounted for by the predictors. The proportion of variance explained is the difference between the total parameter variance (estimated from the unconditional model) and the residual parameter variance from the fitted model relative to the total parameter variance (Bryk & Raudenbush, 1992). For intercepts, this amount of variance is not substantial, as the predictors did not account for any significant amount of variance (i.e., the variance component drops from about 269 to 252). For the growth rate ($\pi_{1i}$), the addition of institutional type and prestige reduced the size of the variance component considerably. The variance in growth accounted for would be calculated as 28.61 (the unconditional variance component for $r_{1i}$ in Table 11.1) minus 17.44 (i.e., the residual variance component $r_{1i}$ in Table 11.2), which equals 11.17, divided by

### TABLE 11.2
#### Linear Model of Graduation Growth Examining the Effects of Prestige and Institutional Type

| Fixed Effect | Coefficient | Standard Error | T-ratio | df | P-value |
|---|---|---|---|---|---|
| Model for initial status, $\pi_{0i}$ | | | | | |
| Intercept $\beta_{00}$ | 39.500 | 3.662 | 10.787 | 9 | 0.000 |
| Private, $\beta_{01}$ | −3.393 | 8.292 | −0.409 | 9 | 0.692 |
| High prestige, $\beta_{02}$ | −5.357 | 7.883 | −0.680 | 9 | 0.514 |
| Model for growth rate, $\pi_{1i}$ | | | | | |
| Intercept, $\beta_{10}$ | 3.942 | 1.376 | 2.867 | 9 | 0.019 |
| Private, $\beta_{11}$ | 8.357 | 2.357 | 3.546 | 9 | 0.007 |
| High Prestige, $\beta_{12}$ | 1.057 | 3.284 | 0.322 | 9 | 0.755 |

| Random Effect | Variance Component | $\chi^2$ | df | P-value |
|---|---|---|---|---|
| Initial status, $r_{0i}$ | 251.975 | 188.505 | 9 | 0.000 |
| Growth rate, $r_{1i}$ | 17.441 | 21.269 | 9 | 0.012 |
| Level-1 error, $e_{ti}$ | 63.971 | | | |

Reliability Estimates: Initial status, $\pi_{0i}$ = 0.952: Growth rate, $\pi_{1i}$ = 0.577.

### TABLE 11.3
#### Observed Means for Sample Public and Private Institutions

| Year | Overall Mean | SD | Public Mean | SD | Private Mean | SD |
|---|---|---|---|---|---|---|
| 1 | 43.00 | 21.43 | 45.25 | 26.03 | 38.50 | 7.85 |
| 2 | 47.17 | 18.40 | 47.13 | 21.89 | 47.25 | 11.12 |
| 3 | 53.08 | 17.22 | 52.00 | 19.71 | 55.25 | 13.09 |
| 4 | 54.17 | 19.67 | 47.63 | 21.37 | 67.25 | 3.30 |

28.61. In this example, therefore, the level-2 predictors accounted for 39% of the parameter variance in graduation growth rates.

***Other Models of Random Coefficients Models.*** Other types of growth trajectories can also be formulated (e.g., quadratic) to model non-linear relationships. In principle, a polynomial of any degree could be fitted, providing the time series is sufficiently long (see Bryk & Raudenbush, 1992 for further discussion). It is also possible to add time-varying covariates to the level-1 model, for example; differing levels of resources over time might affect growth. Researchers can also develop piecewise growth models, where the growth trajectories are split into separate linear components, each with its own model. This type of modeling would be useful in comparing growth rates during two different periods, such as the time before and the time after a policy is introduced. This latter situation is examined in more detail in the next section using SEM techniques.

## EXAMINING GROWTH WITH SEM

SEM methodology offers a contrasting framework to use with various types of longitudinal data. In this part of the chapter, two different uses are illustrated: SEM for conducting latent change analysis for repeated measures data, and SEM multiple group analysis for examining trends over time collected from separate cross-sections.

### Latent Change Analysis

The SEM approach for examining repeated measures data is often referred to as latent change analysis (LCA). In SEM, growth modeling with random effects is conceptualized similar to confirmatory factor analysis (also referred to as the measurement model in a SEM analysis), where an underlying (latent) construct is said to be measured by a set of observed variables (Muthén, 2002). The individual growth is captured as latent variables that are measured by the repeated observations. Part of the individual growth may be summarized as an intercept factor (i.e., reflecting the levels of measurement over time), and part of the growth may be summarized as one or more factors describing the shape of the growth trend over time (e.g., a linear shape, a quadratic shape, a nonlinear shape). For example, linear growth can be represented by a two-factor model (also referred to as a level and shape model), which McArdle (1989) described as a useful model in conducting longitudinal research.

In order to examine individual growth over time with SEM techniques, it is necessary to change the way the data are organized for the analysis. SEM analyses depend on the analysis of covariance structures. Covariance matrices summarize information about variables (i.e., variances are contained in the diagonal elements of the matrix, and covariances between variables are

contained in the off-diagonal elements). In order to examine growth, however, variable means are needed to determine what the pattern of growth
looks like over time. To facilitate the analysis of growth using SEM, therefore, the means of the observed variables are added as the last row and col-
umn in the covariance matrix. This results in a covariance-mean matrix,
which is common in many uses of SEM (Raykov & Marcoulides, 2000). This
additional information allows for more data points to be obtained, resulting
in more effective examinations of growth, decline, growth followed by decline, and decline followed by growth (Raykov & Marcoulides, 2000).

***Measurement Model.*** Consider the example used previously where
we were interested in examining changes in the graduation rates of freshman student athletes in 12 institutions over time. Let the random variables
$\eta_{0i}$ and $\eta_{1i}$ represent an intercept growth factor and a linear trend factor, respectively. As suggested previously, in LCA the repeated measures over
time can be expressed as a type of confirmatory factor analysis (or measurement model), where the intercept and growth factors are measured by the
multiple indicators of $y_t$. Following Muthén and Muthén (2001):

$$y_{ti} = \eta_{0i} + \eta_{1i}x_t + \varepsilon_{ti}, \tag{10}$$

where $y_{ti}$ is the graduation outcome for individual $i$ (i.e., in this case an institution, since institutions are the unit of analysis), $x_t$ is a time-related variable
($t = 1,2, \ldots, T$), and $\varepsilon_{ti}$ is the error term. This model relates the variation in
$y_{ti}$ over time (i.e., which is referred to as the level-1 model in random coefficients modeling) to the growth latent factors. Other time-varying covariates
(e.g., resources) that have direct effects on the outcomes ($y_{ti}$) could also be
added to this model.

Because the repeated measures are parameters (i.e., factor loadings) in
the LCA model, the researcher can hypothesize that they follow particular
patterns. In this example, there are four occasions of measurement ($t = 1, 2,$
3, 4), and the time scores are considered to be equidistant (i.e., measured every year) and linear ($x_t = 0, 1, 2, 3$). This scaling indicates that the time-related variable consists of successive yearly intervals, starting with initial status
as time score 0. It is important to note that centering on the first time point
(with a time score of 0) defines the intercept factor as an initial status factor.
This means that it reflects institutions' graduation rates at the point when the
time-series sequence began. It is also possible to change the centering point
to other time points in the sequence (e.g., the last time point). Selecting the
last time point, for example, would result in a factor that describes the institutions' graduation rates at the end of the time-series sequence.

By fixing the factor loadings to a particular pattern (e.g., 0, 1, 2, 3), the
hypothesized growth pattern may then be tested against the actual data and
its fit determined by examining various SEM fit indices. The two-factor
LCA formulation allows the researcher to consider both the levels of the

growth or decline over time as well as the steepness of the linear trend (which summarizes the growth rate). The researcher can observe whether the change is positive or negative, whether the individual institutions are converging over time, and whether there is heterogeneity in level and rate of change across the institutions in the sample (Willett & Sayer, 1996).

**Structural Model.**  After the measurement model is used to relate the successive observed measures to the initial status and growth rate factors (similar to factor analysis), the second SEM model (i.e., the structural model) is used to relate other time-invariant variables in the model to the initial status and growth trend factors:

$$\eta_{0i} = \alpha_0 + \gamma_0 x_i + \zeta_{0i}, \tag{11}$$

$$\eta_{1i} = \alpha_1 + \gamma_1 x_i + \zeta_{1i}, \tag{12}$$

where $\alpha_0$, $\alpha_1$, $\gamma_0$, and $\gamma_1$ are structural parameters and $x_i$ refers to a time-invariant covariate (e.g., institutional type). The errors in the equations describing the measurement and structural models are denoted by $\varepsilon_{ti}$ and $\zeta$. In this case, the substantive meaning of the model formulation would be that institutional type (i.e., public or private institution) is a time-invariant (i.e., not changing over the time series) variable that affects the level of institutions' graduation rates and their graduation growth trajectory.

It is important to keep in mind that the random-coefficients approach and the LCA approach model individual growth in a slightly different manner. The SEM formulation allows the individual growth model to be conducted at a single level of analysis. This is because the outcome is considered to be multivariate, consisting of the number of repeated observations which comprise a $T$-dimensional vector $y = (y_1, y_2, \dots, y_T)'$. This formulation accounts for the correlation across time by the same random effects influencing each of the variables in the outcome vector (Muthén & Asparouhov, 2003). The SEM approach therefore contrasts with the multilevel regression approach, which typically views outcomes as univariate and accounts for correlation across time by having two levels in the model.

A second difference is the manner in which the time scores (i.e., the scaling of the observations) are considered. For random coefficients growth modeling, the time scores are data; that is, they are pieces of information entered in the data set to represent what the individual's level of outcomes were at that point in time. For latent change analysis, however, the time scores are considered as model parameters; hence their coefficients are estimated as factor loadings on the growth factors. The individual time scores are therefore not represented as data points within the data set.

Finally, LCA proceeds from an analysis of means and covariance structures. In contrast, random coefficients (multilevel) growth modeling creates a separate growth trajectory with intercept and slope for each individual. As Raudenbush (2001) notes, random-coefficients multilevel models cannot be summarized in terms of means and covariance structures.

In conducting latent growth analysis, the researcher's first concern is typically to establish the initial status and growth rates. The proposed model is summarized visually in Figure 11.1. Fitting the two-factor latent change model is accomplished by fixing the intercept factor loadings to 1.0, which ensures that it is interpreted as an initial status factor. Because the repeated measures are considered as factor loadings, there are several choices regarding how to parameterize the growth rate factor. As previously suggested, we can formulate this as a linear growth model by fixing all of the time scores in a linear pattern (i.e., with 0, 1, 2, 3). In this case, none of the time scores is freely estimated. Because the loading from the growth rate factor to Y1 is 0, it is not shown in Fig. 11.1. As a result of using a linear time score pattern, the mean of the growth rate factor describes the growth taking place between yearly intervals. In contrast, if we fixed the first measurement to 0 and the last measurement to 1 (while allowing the other two middle occasions be freely estimated), then we would have a growth rate factor describing the overall change that took place during the 4 years of data collection (as opposed to the yearly change). It would also be possible to include nonlinear growth by specifying some of the time scores as being freely estimated (e.g., 0,1,*,* or 0,1,2,*). This will allow the program to compute estimates of these time scores. For example, if the last time score were allowed to be freely estimated, the program might estimate the final time score as 4.5. This would mean that the growth between the third and fourth

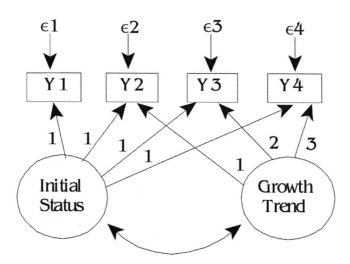

FIG. 11.1.   Two-Factor LCA Model.

intervals was not conforming to a linear trend (i.e., which would be estimated as 3 for the fourth time score).

   *Model Identification.*   As previously suggested, the SEM approach
to model fitting involves specifying a proposed set of relationships and then
testing those relationships against the data. Models that are consistent with
the data will produce stronger evidence of fit (as assessed through various fit
indices). Estimation of the proposed SEM model assumes that it has been
properly identified. If a model were not identified (called underidentified),
it would be possible to find an infinite number of values for its parameters,
and each set would be consistent with the covariance equation. It is therefore necessary to have just enough information to solve each parameter
(just identified) or more than enough information (overidentified). In general, the problem of estimation is dealt with by restricting the number of parameters actually estimated from the total number of parameters in the
model that could be estimated. This should result in a positive number of
degrees of freedom in the model (i.e., a just identified model would result in
no degrees of freedom and therefore be a perfect fit to the data). In a
covariance structure analysis, the restriction is that the number of parameters estimated must be less than or equal to $k(k+1)/2$, where k is the number
of observed variables in the model. Thus, there is one covariance equation
for each of the independent elements of the $k \times k$ covariance matrix. In the
case where there are four indicators, this would result in 10 nonredundant
elements in the covariance matrix. In a mean structure analysis of $k = 4$ repeated measures, there are altogether $q = k(k+1)/2 + k$ pieces of information that must be fit. The number of parameters in the model is estimated in
the following manner: $4(5)/2 + 4 = 14$ data points.
   The model in Fig. 11.1 has 9 parameters to be estimated (i.e., 4 error
variances, 2 latent factor variances, 1 covariance between the factors, and 2
latent factor means). In this example, all of the factor loadings are fixed to
assigned values. In order to obtain the number of degrees of freedom in the
model, it is necessary to subtract the number of model parameters from $q$.
So there are $14 - 9$, or 5 degrees of freedom in this model. This results in an
overidentified model.

   *Model Estimates.*   The estimates of the model's parameters are
presented in Table 11.4. The various fit indices all suggested that the
model fit the data well [e.g., $\chi^2 (5, N = 12) = 2.49, p = .78$]. The initial status factor mean was 43.128, and the growth rate factor mean was 4.06.
This suggests the average graduation rate grew about 4% per year over the
course of data collection. The model estimated means for the successive
measurements (corrected for error) were as follows: 43.13, 47.19, 51.25,
and 55.30. These means were very consistent with the original observed
means summarized in Table 11.3 (i.e., 43.00, 47.17, 53.08, and 54.17, respectively). The correlation between the initial status factor and the

**TABLE 11.4**
**Mplus Estimates for Two-Factor Growth Model**

|  | Estimates | SE | Est./SE |
|---|---|---|---|
| Initial Status |  |  |  |
| Grad92 | 1.000 | 0.000 | 0.000 |
| Grad93 | 1.000 | 0.000 | 0.000 |
| Grad94 | 1.000 | 0.000 | 0.000 |
| Grad95 | 1.000 | 0.000 | 0.000 |
| Growth |  |  |  |
| Grad92 | 0.000 | 0.000 | 0.000 |
| Grad93 | 1.000 | 0.000 | 0.000 |
| Grad94 | 2.000 | 0.000 | 0.000 |
| Grad95 | 3.000 | 0.000 | 0.000 |
| Factor Means |  |  |  |
| Intercept | 43.128 | 5.863 | 7.356* |
| Trend | 4.058 | 1.722 | 2.357* |

*Note.* Chi-square, 5 $df$ = 2.49, $p$ = .78
* ratio of estimate to standard error is significant, $p < .05$.

growth trend factor was moderate and negative (–.62), suggesting that schools that had lower graduation rates initially tended to grow more (and vice versa) during the data collection period.

If we chose to parameterize the time scores as ranging from 0 to 1 (with the two other time scores lying between 0 and 1), we would expect the growth rate mean to be about 12 (rising 4 points between each of the three subsequent data collection points) over the course of the time series. When the model is parameterized in this fashion, it now has only 3 degrees of freedom instead of 5, because two factor loadings are estimated). The mean growth rate turns out to be 10.75, with the initial status mean as 43.61. This yields a last measurement of about 54.36 (43.61 + 10.75), which is similar to the last observed mean of 54.17. As this suggests, setting the growth metric in different ways adjusts the coefficients correspondingly, but does not affect the overall interpretation of the data.

***Adding Covariates.*** After defining and measuring the two growth factors, we can then add prestige and institutional type as predictors, as we did in the random coefficients growth example. The results are summarized in Table 11.5. Similar to the random coefficients modeling results, prestige was not significantly related to schools' growth rates, whereas institutional type was significantly related to schools' growth rates. The coefficient indicates that, on average, private schools increased at a rate of about 8.5% per year more than public schools. Adding the two predictors to the model also reduced the correlation between the initial status and growth rate factors somewhat. It is of interest to note in passing that even though the random coefficients and LCA growth models proceed from somewhat different assumptions and therefore are parameterized slightly differently, the key coefficients were similar for describing the rate of growth (3.94 and 4.06, respectively), as well as the impact of institutional type on growth rates (8.36 and 8.49, respectively).

**_Extending the LCA Model._**    This basic two-factor LCA model can be extended in a number of ways. For example, a quadratic factor could be added to capture curvilinear types of growth. The quadratic growth factor requires three random effects; an initial status growth factor ($i$), a linear growth factor ($s$), and a quadratic growth factor ($q$). As in the previous example, if the linear time scores were 0, 1, 2, 3 (for the 4 years), the time scores for the quadratic growth factor would be the squared values of the linear time scores (0, 1, 4, 9).

**TABLE 11.5**
**Mplus Model Results for Initial Status and Growth Model**

|                     | _Estimates_ | _SE_   | _Est./SE_ |
| ------------------- | ----------- | ------ | --------- |
| Initial Status      |             |        |           |
| Private             | −8.375      | 12.375 | −0.677    |
| Prestige            | −16.263     | 12.030 | −1.352    |
| Growth              |             |        |           |
| Private             | 8.492       | 2.756  | 3.082*    |
| Prestige            | 3.388       | 2.630  | 1.288     |
| Factor Means        |             |        |           |
| Initial Status      | 46.033      | 7.145  | 6.443*    |
| Growth Trend        | 1.077       | 1.591  | 0.677     |

_Note._ Chi square = 8.562, $df$ = 9, $p$ = 0.4786. $r_{si}$ = −0.412
* ratio of estimate to standard error is significant, $p < .05$.

## MULTILEVEL LATENT CHANGE ANALYSIS

A second type of LCA model that has application to policy research is the multilevel growth model. The basic LCA model formulated as a single-level model can be expanded to include situations where we wish to include group-level variables (e.g., class or school variables) in modeling change. This model of growth within clusters can be represented as a two-level model.

In the last chapter, a two-level model was developed to examine the stability of student learning on two measurement occasions. Where three or more occasions of measurement are available, we can use the LCA modeling approach to examine change in students' learning over time. The specific analysis involves decomposing student growth (in the initial status and growth rate factors) into within- and between-class or school components and examining the effects of individual background factors and school processes (e.g., tracking, differential curricula, class size) on the growth factors. Within schools, the researcher might model how students' backgrounds affect their individual learning growth. Between schools, the researcher might model the effects of contextual variables, school inputs (e.g., class size, teacher experience), and school quality indicators on school growth rates.

### Examining Variables that Influence Student Growth in Math

Consider a policy study concerned with school accountability that focuses on the value that the quality of the school's processes adds to school growth. In many cases, comparisons are made between schools on the basis of outcome levels, without taking into consideration schools' growth over time. In cross-sectional studies of school outcomes, for example, the contribution of the school is often underestimated in the process of adjusting schools' achievement scores for the backgrounds of their students. Because the quality of school processes is believed to be cumulative and to apply to all students, however, growth in student achievement is the most appropriate criterion for judging school effectiveness. Monitoring the progress of students over time, however, has presented a number of technical problems for evaluators (e.g., the stability of the scores, how to incorporate measurement error in models, how to demonstrate the relationship between school processes and achievement).

Multilevel growth modeling can be useful in this type of research situation because it attends to many of these previously identified problems. For example, because the successive outcome measurements are used as loadings on latent growth factors, LCA provides a means of examining the stability of scores over time. If a proposed growth model does not fit the data adequately (e.g., because the observed trajectory is not consistent with the proposed one), it may provide evidence that the scores are not stable from one measurement occasion to the next. Defining growth through latent variables also provides corrections for measurement errors on the observed indicators. The correction for measurement errors results in more accurate assessments of schools' growth and the impact of other variables on school growth. This can be important in determining the extent to which schools add value to student achievement growth.

In this example, the focus is on determining the impact of measures of school quality on student learning, after controlling for student background within schools and community socioeconomic status between schools. The data consisted of 2,200 students randomly selected from within a sample of 50 middle schools. Students were measured on three yearly occasions on a standardized achievement test in math. The math outcomes were reported as scaled scores. For the within-school model, student background variables included gender and socioeconomic status. For the between-school model, school quality was a composite variable comprised of items assessing school leadership, expectations for students, classroom instructional practices, evaluation of student progress, school climate, and home/school relations. The quality variable was standardized ($M = 0$, $SD = 1$) such that higher scores indicate higher quality processes. The school level control was school socioeconomic level (CSES), which was compiled from information about student and community SES. It was coded such that higher scores indicate higher community SES.

*Model Estimates.* The model summarized in Fig. 11.2 fit the data reasonably well, $\chi^2$ (10, $N_B = 50$, $N_W = 2,200$) 60.8, $p = .000$. Although this chi-square is a bit high, it is likely due to the large sample size. In contrast, other fit indices (e.g., CFI = .99) suggested a strong fit to the data. The scaled score mean of the initial status factor was 598. In this example, the time scores were scaled so the growth rate factor would reflect the average growth over the 3-year data collection period (0, *, 1). The resulting mean was 84.0. Within schools, low SES (–.15.1) and female (5.8) were both significantly related to the initial status factor. In particular, this suggests an initial achievement gap for students of low socioeconomic background compared with their average and high socioeconomic background peers. Regarding growth rate, however, neither background variable was significant. This finding indicates that the initial gap in achievement for students of low socioeconomic background was not closed over the time they were in middle school.

Between schools, the perceived quality of school processes significantly impacted school growth over time (4.5). This can be interpreted as a standard deviation increase in perceptions about school quality yielded 4.5 scaled-score growth in achievement outcomes. As we might expect, community socioeconomic status (CSES) affected the initial level of school outcomes (3.1). Importantly, however, the figure suggests that CSES did not affect school growth.

Overall, the findings have important implications for policy and assessment. First, they suggest that it is more equitable to compare schools in terms of their growth controlled for school socioeconomic status, as op-

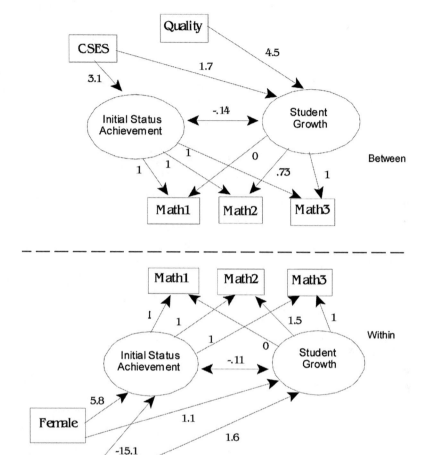

FIG. 11.2.  Multilevel model of math achievement (unstandardized coefficients).

posed to just their outcome levels. Second, the relationship between school quality and growth provides an indication of the value that schools add as measured by the quality of their school processes. This suggests it is useful to continue to develop indicator systems to monitor school processes and accommodate them into assessments of school progress, because they can provide information on the school's capacity, types of instructional strategies, and change processes implemented to improve learning outcomes.

## COMPARING TRENDS OVER TIME USING LCA

Policy studies are often concerned with determining the impact of a policy in changing behavior in an intended way. One design that is useful in examining trends before and after a policy is introduced is the time-series design. As suggested in chapter 8, the essence of a time-series design is the presence of periodic measurements and the introduction of an experimental change into this time series of measurements. The basic LCA model developed previously can be extended to compare trends within time-series designs.

Consider the case used earlier in this chapter about Division 1-A institutions and their football programs. We may wish to determine whether the introduction of Proposition 48 had any effect on changing institutions' behavior. Proposition 48 was implemented during the mid-1980s to increase institutions' graduation rates by upgrading their academic standards for admitting student athletes. In the earlier example, we examined changes in graduation rates from the point where the policy was introduced. A more thorough test of the policy's impact on changing institutions' behavior, however, would require the analyst to compare the behavioral trend before the policy was introduced with the trend afterward (see also Takahashi, 2002).

*Time-Series Design.*    In a time-series design, evidence of a treatment's effect is indicated by a discontinuity in the measurements recorded in the time series (Campbell & Stanley, 1963). In this example, the time-series design may be diagramed as follows:

$$0_1 \; 0_2 \; 0_3 \; X \; 0_4 \; 0_5 \; 0_6 \; 0_7 \; 0_8 \; 0_9$$

where the three 0's preceding the X represent a yearly trend of outcomes prior to the introduction of the policy. The design is a sound quasi-experimental design, provided certain threats to internal validity can be successfully argued away (Campbell & Stanley, 1963). Basically, the problem of internal validity reduces to the question of whether plausible competing hypotheses offer likely alternate explanations for any shift in the time series other than the introduction of the policy (Campbell & Stanley, 1963).

The major threats to the internal validity of the single-group time series design are instrumentation, testing, and history. Instrumentation and testing can be argued away more easily in this case, because the data were collected utilizing the same variables and no repeated testing on individuals was done (i.e., as might be the case if the data were collected from individuals who received a treatment of some type). The determination of change is determined solely on the fluctuations in the institutional data over the years prior to Proposition 48 and following its implementation. Threats due to history, however, could be a potential problem. Rival explanations could include changes in the institutional norms within the set of schools (that may or may not correspond to the policy's introduction) or perhaps cyclical events. The observational series can be arranged to hold these types of cycles relatively constant (e.g., data are collected at the same time and over a relatively long period of time). This lessens the possibility that some other corresponding extraneous event would produce the expected trends other than the implementation of Proposition 48. To deal with history as a rival explanation, however, it is important for the researcher to specify in advance the expected relationship between the introduction of the treatment and the manifestation of an effect (Campbell & Stanley, 1963); that is, how soon the effect would be seen. Importantly, as the time between implementation and resultant effect increases, the effects of extraneous events become more plausible.

By raising institutions' academic standards to increase graduation rates (i.e., the policy's intended effect), it is likely that the policy resulted in a reduction of freshman athletes being admitted to programs, especially in some types of institutions. If this were true, over the course of data collection, we should note a discontinuity of measurements (i.e., a decline of freshmen being admitted) after the policy was introduced. Moreover, it is likely that a shrinking pool of student athletes might affect the football recruiting practices of some schools more than others. For example, we might hypothesize that highly prestigious schools (i.e., schools with outstanding on-field performance) would be less affected in their efforts to recruit freshmen athletes than would less prestigious schools. It is likely, therefore, that the proposition also affected recruiting tactics of some institutions more than others.

We can formulate an LCA model to test these hypotheses against the data. In terms of the time-series design, the 0s preceding the X (or point where the policy was implemented) represent the outcome data on freshman entrance rates for the years 1983, 1984 and 1985. Proposition 48 was officially implemented in 1986. The 0s following the X represent the yearly freshman entrance rates for 6 years following the policy's implementation (i.e., 1986, 1987, 1988, 1989, 1990, 1991). The analysis involves comparing the initial status and growth trend factors before Proposition 48 was implemented ($0_1$–$0_3$) against the initial status and growth trend factors after Proposition 48 was implemented ($0_4$–$0_9$). A second part of the analysis involves examining how covariates such as prestige and institutional type might affect the growth factors before and after the policy was implemented.

## Growth Models to Compare Trends

Models that compare two different trends have been referred to in the past as "spline" regression models (Freund & Littell, 1991). To test the similarity of two trends, the idea is to fit one linear model segment to the data before the introduction of the policy (or, if data are not available, shortly after its introduction) and another linear model segment to the point where the plotted behavior changes abruptly. The two separate regression coefficients may then be compared against each other. Although linear spline models are one relatively easy way to examine changes over time, they have been criticized because the abrupt change in trend going from one segment to the next does not represent what would naturally occur (Freund & Littell, 1991). For example, it may be that there is a lag effect where a change does not take place immediately. Visual inspection of the overall trend, as well as the before and during trends, can aid in making some of these determinations, however.

Another way to compare the trends is through piecewise growth modeling. This approach can be used to represent different phases of development or change and to capture nonlinear growth. One way to do this is to examine whether there is a "jump" in the time series at the point where the policy is introduced (X), or at some specified point afterward. In this example, it is likely that both the initial status (intercept) factor and the growth factor would be affected by the introduction of Proposition 48. Therefore, we can develop separate growth factors associated with the key time points in the growth trend (e.g., before and after the policy is introduced). We can also have separate intercept factors to capture separate levels of outcomes at different parts of the overall data collection period. First, we might hypothesize that the effects of the policy will be seen immediately after the policy is introduced. We could then compare this model against other models with various lag (delayed) effects. In this way, it is possible to test for policy effects immediately after the policy is introduced or to test for various lag (delayed) effects.

Moreover, covariates (e.g., institutional type, institutional prestige) may also be added to the model to help refine the examination of the contrasting trends.

### Determining Whether the Trends Are the Same or Different

In the SEM framework, determining whether there are separate initial status and growth trends before and after the introduction of a policy can be approached as a type of simultaneous test of model invariance across groups (or time periods). As a prerequisite to testing models across groups, the researcher first develops a baseline model. Then the baseline model is compared across subsequent groups. To conduct tests of model invariance, the researcher imposes constraints on particular parameters of interest across the groups (or trends) involved and estimates these parameters simultaneously. The fit of the models is then examined in order to determine whether the parameters are the same or different across the time periods under consideration.

In the case of comparing trends, the parameters of interest are the initial status and growth trend latent factors for each period of time being compared. The complete model including covariates (prestige and institutional type) is conceptualized in Fig. 11.3 with separate intercept factors and growth factors before and after the policy was introduced (see Takahashi,

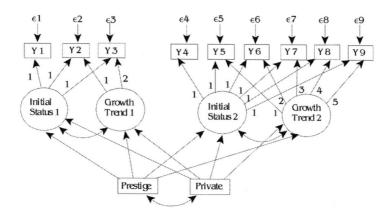

FIG. 11.3. Proposed Linear Growth Model of freshmen student athletes admitted before and after the introduction of proposition 48.

2002). Notice in the figure that there are 3 years (Y1–Y3) comprising the first trend (before the policy was introduced). If the researcher thought a one-year lag effect might exist, she or he could test the first model against a second model where Y4 (the year the policy was first implemented) was included in the first trend. The fit of the two models could then be compared to determine which one fit the data better. The model was tested with data from Division 1A football programs ($N = 105$).

*Freely Estimating the Initial Status and Growth Trends.* The necessary model tests were then conducted in a series of steps. The first step was to test a model where the initial status and growth factors for both trends were freely estimated (i.e., the hypotheses are that Initial Status 1 does not equal Initial Status 2, and Growth Trend 1 does not equal Growth Trend 2). This proposed model resulted in a relatively small, and nonsignificant chi-square coefficient, $\chi^2 = (31, N = 105) = 42.075$, $p = .09$. The factor means summarized in Table 11.6 were as follows: Initial Status 1 $M = 22.13$; Initial Status 2 $M = 20.33$; Growth Trend 1 $M = -.165$; Growth Trend 2 $M = -.479$. This result suggests the mean number of entering freshmen in the years before the policy was introduced differed from the mean number after it was introduced. Similarly, one can notice that the growth trend of entering freshmen was declining slightly (–.165 per year) before the policy was introduced. The slope declined even more sharply (–.479 per year), however, after the policy was introduced. The first step, therefore, provides preliminary evidence that the policy had an effect on numbers of freshmen student athletes admitted.

**TABLE 11.6**

**Model Testing Separate Trends Before and After**
**Proposition 48 was Introduced**

|                  | Estimates | SE    | Est./SE  |
|------------------|-----------|-------|----------|
| Latent Means     |     .     |       |          |
| Initial Status 1 | 22.128    | 0.465 | 47.576*  |
| Initial Status 2 | 20.327    | 0.396 | 51.310*  |
| Growth Trend1    | −0.165    | 0.266 | −0.618   |
| Growth Trend2    | −0.479    | 0.098 | −4.877*  |

*Note.* chi-square = 42.075, *df* = 31, *p*-value = 0.0886
* ratio of estimate to standard error is significant, *p* < .05.

***Constraining the Initial Status and Growth Trend Factors to be Equal.*** At step 2, the researcher tries to argue away the separate trends by constraining the two initial status factors to be equal and the two growth factors to be equal. If the model holding the two sets of factors equal provided the strongest fit to the data, it would suggest that the policy did not have any effect on the trends regarding the admittance of freshmen student athletes. For this constrained model, the chi-square coefficient was $\chi^2$ (33, $N$ = 105) = 69.436, $p$ = .00. The fit of successive models can be compared by using delta chi-square (i.e., the change in $\chi^2$ per degrees of freedom). In this model, the delta $\chi^2$ (2, $N$ = 105) = 17.361, $p$ = .00 was significant (i.e., a delta $\chi^2$ of 5.99 for 2 df is significant at $p$ = .05).

***Constraining Only the Initial Status Factors to be Equal.*** Next, only the two intercept factors were constrained to be equal (i.e., with Growth Trend 1 and Growth Trend 2 freely estimated). This model resulted in a smaller chi-square coefficient than the second model, $\chi^2$ (32, $N$ = 105) = 53.337, $p$ = .01, but was still considerably larger than the first model. Because the delta $\chi^2$ between the third and first models, $\chi^2$ (1, $N$ = 105) = 11.162, $p$ = .00, was larger than the required 3.84, it suggests that restricting the intercepts to be equal did not provide a plausible representation of the data. Therefore, the conclusion is that two separate growth sequences were the most appropriate to describe these data. This suggests the policy was significant in altering the trends in behavior. The comparison of observed means versus model estimated means before and after the proposition was introduced is shown in Fig. 11.4. The figure summarizes visually that the observed model fit the actual data quite well.

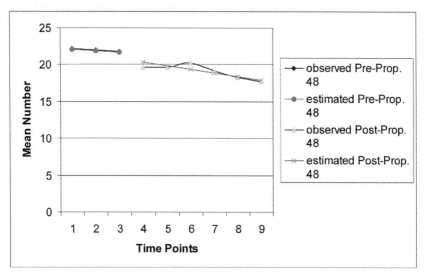

FIG. 11.4.   Comparison of trends for entering freshmen before and after the implementation of Proposition 48 ($N = 105$).

***Adding Time-Invariant Covariates.***     Finally, after establishing that there were two separate growth trends, the covariates were added to the model. This final model (as hypothesized in Fig. 11.3) also fit the data well, $\chi^2$ (41, $N = 105$) = 48.734, $p = 0.19$. The relevant effects are presented in Table 11.7. The coefficients suggest that institutional type (i.e., private) and prestige had no influence on the Initial Status 1 factor (i.e., before the policy was implemented). Prestige and institutional type also had no impact on growth rates before the policy was implemented (i.e., Growth Rate 1 factor).

After the policy was implemented, prestige was significantly related to the Initial Status 2 factor. Both prestige and institutional type were significantly related to individual schools' growth rates. Interpreting how covariates affected the growth rates is a little more complicated. In situations where the change is declining, marked positive coefficients for covariates tend to be those individuals who decline the least (Raykov & Marcoulides, 2000), whereas low covariate values represent those who decline the most. In contrast, for negative coefficients, those with high values decline the most, whereas those with low values decline the least. More specifically, then, because the overall trend in entering freshmen was declining, private school freshman numbers tended to decline less sharply (.792) than did public schools. In contrast, for schools with higher prestige (on field performance), freshman numbers declined less sharply (–.232) than did their lower prestige counterparts.

**TABLE 11. 7**

**Impact of Prestige and Institutional Type on Growth Trends**

|                    | Estimates | SE    | Estimate/SE |
|--------------------|-----------|-------|-------------|
| Initial Status 1   |           |       |             |
| High Prestige      | 0.854     | 0.504 | 1.695       |
| Private            | −0.343    | 1.551 | −0.221      |
| Initial Status 2   |           |       |             |
| High Prestige      | 1.232     | 0.426 | 2.892*      |
| Private            | −1.719    | 1.312 | −1.311      |
| Growth Trend 1     |           |       |             |
| High Prestige      | −0.118    | 0.277 | −0.426      |
| Private            | 0.716     | 0.852 | 0.840       |
| Growth Trend 2     |           |       |             |
| High Prestige      | −0.232    | 0.112 | −2.076*     |
| Private            | 0.792     | 0.344 | 2.305*      |
| Latent Means       |           |       |             |
| Initial Status 1   | 22.310    | 0.525 | 42.503*     |
| Initial Status 2   | 21.128    | 0.444 | 47.600*     |
| Growth Trend 1     | −0.410    | 0.288 | −1.420      |
| Growth Trend 2     | −0.791    | 0.116 | −6.802*     |

*Note.* chi-square = 48.734, $df$ = 41, $p$ = 0.1899
* ratio of estimate to standard error is significant, $p < .05$.

## EXAMINING REPEATED CROSS-SECTIONS WITH SEM

An analysis of repeated cross-sections can also be conducted using multiple group analysis capability in SEM. Multiple group comparisons are often conducted to determine whether a model holds over different subgroups of a population or over time. For example, data are routinely collected year to year on different students in the fourth grade, and then comparisons are made across years to determine whether the school is improving or not. Unfortunately, studies comparing achievement outcomes using repeated cross-sections of students generally report large annual fluctuations in many schools' scores. This suggests that ratings of schools as outstanding or poor might be made solely on the basis of random fluctuations, as opposed to the quality of their educational processes (Linn & Haug, 2002).

Consider a situation where a principal wants to chart the academic progress of students over a 3-year period. One way is to simply look at the scores of each year's third graders and chart the progress against a baseline year. Although this is commonly done in practice, there are a number of problems in examining progress in this manner. First, the groups of students being compared may differ in various ways including ethnicity, socioeconomic status, previous learning levels, and motivation, to name a few. Second, there may be various kinds of error involved (random error, measurement error, sampling error) that influence the scores. All of this can lead to random fluctuation in scores on a year-to-year basis.

Before making any tentative conclusions across time from data collected from different samples of individuals, therefore, it is important to have a methodological means that allows researchers to pinpoint various similarities or differences (Raykov & Marcoulides, 2000). For example, respondents' perceptions of items and constructs may change dramatically over time from how they were originally conceived (Pedhazur & Schmelkin, 1991). To compare scores across successive years assumes that there is compatibility between the scores. Examining the compatibility of scores ensures that the meaning and interpretation of scores are the same for all groups of students. For comparing test scores, three kinds of evidence regarding compatibility can be examined; reliability, factor structure, and item functioning (Pomplun & Omar, 2003; Willingham et al. 1988).

*Using Equality Constraints.*    Group comparisons necessitate the simultaneous estimation of proposed models in all samples involved. By placing equality constraints on the model across the samples (i.e., similar to how we constrained the initial status and growth factors across time in the last example), one can assess the extent to which it holds across time. Because instruments are often group specific, after each administration of an instrument to different groups, it is important to reassess the psychometric qualities of the constructs being measured to ensure that the instrument has construct validity across groups, settings, or temporal conditions.

For score compatibility, it is necessary to have invariance of the factor structure and item loadings at a minimum to ensure that instruments are not group specific. If this hypothesis holds, then it is also possible to test whether factor variances and covariances hold, as well as the error structures. To the extent that the model holds across the samples, there is a stronger basis for assessing whether change has in fact occurred. After establishing model invariance, then comparisons can be made involving differences in means across the groups being compared. It is also possible to add covariates (e.g., student background) to make a more refined assessment of progress.

Simultaneous tests of models across groups can be facilitated easily with SEM software. The analysis requires the researcher to establish that the proposed model is conceptually and metrically equivalent across the groups being studied before comparing the scores produced across groups. For example, one might have random samples of students drawn on three or four occasions. After a baseline model is developed that links items or subtests to their hypothesized constructs, it can be compared simultaneously across the successive samples of students by testing a series of increasingly restrictive hypotheses about the means and covariance structures.

*Constraining the Factor Structure.* In this case, the focus is on the three subtests (reading, math, language) comprising the latent achievement factor. At the first step, the intercepts and factor loadings for the test scores are held equal across the three time-related groups. This implies that the same factor structure exists—that is, the same number of factors, invariant factor loadings, and invariant intercepts of the observed variables. It is important to establish the conceptual and metric equivalence before examining differences in scores, although this is seldom done in the literature. One observed variable on the achievement factor is set at 1.0 to establish a common metric for interpreting the similarity of the factor structure across the groups. The proposed model is then tested against the data for the three groups simultaneously. Through this procedure, the researcher may determine the extent to which the conceptual model is similar across the groups being investigated and whether there are sources of conceptual and metric nonequivalence (see Johnsrud & Heck, 1998, for one example study).

*Constraining Factor Variances and Errors.* Second, after determining that the same factor model holds across groups, the researcher can test whether there are differences in factor variances across time and whether there are differences in errors of measurement. This step involves holding the factor variances and error terms to be equal across groups. This additional step can help answer questions about whether error variances are larger for some years. This could provide clues about the difficulty of the tests for some groups of students.

*Comparing Means.* Third, after establishing conceptual and at least partial metric equivalence (i.e., step 1), then it is possible to determine whether there are differences in the factor means across the successive samples. Required at a minimum for tests of mean structures are the same number of factors and invariant factor loadings. To compare latent means correctly, it is necessary to define them on the same scale across all of the groups. Then the model fit can be compared across the samples simultaneously. The means and intercepts of the latent variables are fixed to zero in the first group and are free to be estimated and not equal in the other groups.

The model tests are presented in Table 11.8. Several hypotheses were tested. The first examined whether there was an equal factor structure, factor loadings, and intercepts across time. This hypothesis was accepted, $\chi^2$ (20 df, $N = 313$) = 35.93, $p = .02$, CFI = .98, SRMR = .04. The second hy-

**TABLE 11.8**

**Tests of Model Invariance**

| Hypothesis Tests | $\chi^2$ | df | p | CFI | SRMR | RMSEA |
|---|---|---|---|---|---|---|
| 1. Equal factors, loadings and intercepts | 35.93 | 20 | .02 | .98 | .04 | .087 |
| 2. Equal factor variances | 36.61 | 22 | .03 | .98 | .05 | .080 |
| 3. Equal errors | 112.91 | 31 | .00 | .87 | .11 | .159 |
| 3a. Equal errors, reading | 92.64 | 25 | .00 | .89 | .11 | .161 |
| 3b. Equal errors, language | 71.89 | 25 | .00 | .93 | .10 | .134 |
| 3c. Equal errors, math | 38.25 | 25 | .04 | .98 | .05 | .071 |
| 4. Model #2 with no student covariates | 80.28 | 35 | .00 | .93 | .13 | .111 |

pothesis of equal factor variances was also accepted, $\chi^2$ (22 df, $N$ = 313) = 36.61, $p$ = .03, CFI = .98, SRMR = .05. The third hypothesis regarding equal error terms on the tests across time was not accepted, $\chi^2$ (31 df, $N$ = 313) = 112.91, $p$ = .00, CFI = .87, SRMR = .11). This suggests that the error variances for the various subtests across time were different. Further tests were conducted to determine if there was partial invariance of errors. Models 3a to 3c summarize these tests. They suggest that only the math errors were invariant across time. In contrast, the hypotheses of invariant reading errors and invariant language errors were rejected. This result could indicate that there are year-to-year differences in the ways students respond to reading and language tests (e.g., some items are more difficult for some students in particular years, other unknown factors may interfere). This could also point to possible sample selection bias regarding the students taking the tests year to year.

### Examining Growth With and Without Controls for Student Background.
After establishing partial metric equivalence (i.e., loadings, intercepts, factor variances), it is possible to examine growth. Growth was examined with and without controls for student background (i.e., in this case, gender and SES) variables known to affect achievement. The model with background controls (Model #2) fit the data better, $\chi^2$ (22 df, $N$ = 313) = 36.61, $p$ = .03, CFI = .98, SRMR = .05, than model #4 that had no controls, $\chi^2$ (35 df, $N$ = 313) = 80.28, $p$ = .00, CFI = .93, SRMR = .13. Within each year, the size and pattern of effects varied. In Year 1, the effects of low student SES (–30.6) and female (21.2) were significant and sizable. In Year 2, low SES was significant (–23.2), whereas female (7.0) was not. Finally, in Year 3, neither low SES (–1.4) nor female (7.4) was significant. These results indicate

the considerable systematic variation in test scores that can occur year-to-year due to the specific demographics of students taking the tests.

One can compare the growth in the two situations in Fig. 11.5. To the extent that covariates are related to achievement, they can provide important controls to make the charting of growth more accurate. After adjusting for student background, the actual mean progress looks considerably better in this school over time. This approach also provides a means of modeling where the school is with respect to policies such as No Child Left Behind that require assessment of progress over time for particular groups of students.

The approach used in this example provides a means of making more refined school comparisons by examining the unreliability of schools' scores over time and by examining the compatibility of scores in a very technical way. Sources of error could include sample selection error (i.e., different groups of students), measurement error, and variability in school conditions year-to-year (e.g., teacher turnover, student demographics, disruptive groups of students). Some of these problems can be addressed, or at least modeled, with greater attention to the design and technical analysis. However, the potential for sample selection error remains a potential threat to the validity of the results in studies and assessment systems using this approach.

## SUMMARY

Longitudinal analysis represents a rapidly growing application of multi-level modeling techniques. Because it provides stronger ways for dealing with causal relationships between variables than do cross-sectional analyses,

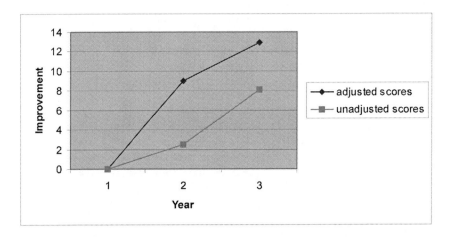

FIG. 11.5. Examining school growth with and without adjustments for student differences.

it should continue to draw increased attention from researchers. Both of the approaches presented in this chapter are very flexible for using with a number of research purposes and designs (e.g., experimental, time-series, nonexperimental). Although the actual programming of the example models was beyond the scope of this chapter, readers are encouraged to consult a number of introductory sources that provide overviews of the assumptions, uses, and programming of these methods (e.g., Hox, 2002; Muthén & Muthén, 2001; Raudenbush et al., 2000; Raykov & Marcoulides, 2000).

## EXERCISES

1. Compare and contrast several different methods of collecting longitudinal data discussed in the chapter. What are the strengths and limitations of each approach with respect to conducting policy research?

2. Think of a policy problem that could be studied with a time-series design. What type of data would you need to collect in order to test whether a policy implemented had an effect on changing behavior? Would the changes in behavior be expected to occur immediately after implementation, or is it possible that there could be a lag effect? Would there be any other issues to consider in conducting the study?

3. Compare and contrast some of the assumptions of conducting cross-sectional versus longitudinal analyses.

# IV

## *Epilogue*

Recent turmoil surrounding the purposes of public education and its reform have significantly impacted the intellectual focus of the field of educational policy. For a number of years the field has been a ship in search of a destination. The dominant intellectual underpinnings, methods of inquiry (rational models, positivism, quantitative analysis) and the utility of the research have been harshly criticized over the past two decades. Critics questioned whether the metaphor of "policy as science" really fit the investigation of educational endeavors. They argued that because political and educational institutions were socially constructed, natural science methods based on scientific laws logically derived from mathematical relationships representing causes and effects were ill-suited to understand the relationship between policymaking and schools. In the years following, a number of scholars have suggested alternative ways to conceptualize the field. These alternative discourses, norms, and routines of practice (referred to as "disciplinary practices"), which are connected to larger historical, political, economic, and cultural contexts, shape the ways in which a field of study and its related practices constitute themselves (Anderson, 1996; Robinson, 1996).

Today, this metaphor represents "contested space" in terms of its conceptual underpinnings, goals, methods, and contribution of its research in building a knowledge base that can be used to improve practice and to transform schooling. Despite criticism, however, it is clear that the scientific approach to educational policy has provided cumulative empirical knowledge about the policymaking process, as well as practices that work in certain subfields of education (e.g., school effects, school improvement processes). As the previous chapters indicate, considerable scholarly activity has taken place over the past 40 years that places theoretical propositions either at the center of the analysis (i.e., by testing particular frameworks, theories, and models) or uses theory more generally as a conceptual and methodological underpinning to guide a program of research.

315

Some newer perspectives also suggest that policy research should be used to promote advocacy (i.e., representing the field as a moral undertaking), as opposed to scientific neutrality. This discussion illuminates a concern with not only improving educational practice, but also promoting social justice and democracy, for example, by including alternative knowledge or discourses that have been subjugated, neglected, or missing (e.g., Anderson, 1996; Blackmore, 1996; Kahne, 1994). In several concrete ways, this knowledge accumulated from diverse perspectives has had an impact on changing educational practices. At the same time, most commentary on the field's progress and directions suggests that it is more diverse and fragmented today.

There are a number of factors that work against efforts to move toward more disciplined inquiry about educational policy. Changing political and social contexts may affect priorities, definitions of important problems, expectations for education and other institutions, as well as the definitions and focus of research over time. One challenge is the re-examination of the role of scholarly discourse in educational policy can (and should) play in contributing to increased understandings of educational problems. A second is to increase its utility in reducing or solving those problems.

Serious divisions within the academic community have surfaced more recently regarding the over-reliance on particular ways of looking at problems, processes, solutions, and methods. Others argue that our research has not gone far enough in changing educational practices, nor in identifying oppressive structures and working to replace them. It is clear that research based on the assumption of advancing knowledge through testing models and accumulating knowledge through separate studies (i.e., despite the various ways in which they are conducted) is built on a different set of intellectual traditions from critique and advocacy. Although new perspectives may illuminate particular aspects of problems that have been previously unnoticed, it is incumbent on researchers to establish their documented utility for producing desired changes. Each approach tends to emphasize different features and provide somewhat different explanations of events.

Chapter 12 provides a short synthesis of what has been presented previously in the book and its relevance to conducting policy research and in contributing to policy scholarship in the future. Currently, we have a tremendous number of conceptual and research tools at our disposal. In thinking about future directions, we should not lose our focus on empirical results (i.e., produced from a broader conceptualization of science) that provide knowledge that policymakers and practitioners can use, but it should be knowledge that leads to educational reforms that improve life in schools for all children. Hence, we cannot ignore the moral nature of what educators do. To make a difference in schooling will require the sustained commitment of groups of policymakers, practitioners, and scholars to identify, prioritize, and study significant policy problems and proposed solutions in a variety of settings, under varied conditions, and using diverse methods of examination.

# Chapter 12

# Further Thoughts

The intent of the book was to examine the context in which educational policymaking unfolds and how it is studied. The concern was primarily on the interplay between conceptual lenses and methodology in examining policy problems. In this final chapter, I continue to expand the discussion of policy problems and their study. I also suggest how the book might contribute to wider discussions about educational and social policy and speculate about some of the needs for the future.

Among the objectives of science are to identify regularities and form general explanations of phenomena. Frameworks, theories, and models represent ways that we create foundations for scientific knowledge. They play a central role in linking processes of scientific investigation to descriptions and explanations of findings (Everhart, 1988). They affect the research endeavor by influencing how problems are defined, what constitute data, and what data mean (Everhart, 1988). Yet, as Cibulka (1999) reminded us, they are at best imperfect representations of reality. Identifying regularities and general explanations of how phenomena work in educational and social research is made more difficult by the influence of contexts (e.g., historical settings, culture, social and political environments). For example, social context can affect what we deem is important to study, how it is studied, and also the extent to which policy changes are actually implemented (Berliner, 2002). Because of the potential of the context to impact on policy actions, it makes it difficult to replicate results of empirical studies. What works in one context may not work in another. Moreover, contextual conditions often interact with various types of other variables (e.g., school processes, resources, personnel characteristics and values) and outcomes such as student learning. Because of the complex nature of problems and interventions that interact with context, it suggests that multiple types of conceptual perspectives and scientific methods are often useful in generating valued (and successful) solutions.

317

That said, currently there is less emphasis on the support or falsification of universal theories (e.g., the theory movement in educational administration), given the added complexity of contextual influences on social problems and corresponding research endeavors. Adherence to one particular view perpetuates blind spots in our understanding of phenomena and fails to recognize the validity of alternative theoretical perspectives (Johnson, 2003). Although epistemology, conceptual frames, and methodology are at the center of how research gets done, they are often not explicitly discussed in evaluating the contribution of research to solving social problems. This is an important issue to address, especially because critics of past policy research have suggested that it often yielded inconsistent or conflicting findings, illuminated parts of problems while obscuring others, or generated controversy over policy choices in more sensitive policy areas (e.g., choice, student progress, access to resources).

In the past, researchers did not always made explicit the assumptions underlying their analyses. Boyd's (1988) chapter on policy analysis in the first *Handbook on Research in Educational Administration* (Boyan, 1988) was an exemplar in assessing the progress and maturity of the first generation of educational policy research. Boyd captured this progress in the metaphor "through a glass darkly." As he argued, policy analysis is an important, but problematic, window on the educational world because it may illuminate or obscure what it views. Boyd concluded that policy research was likely to retain both its importance and problematic qualities well into the future. On one hand, he noted that scientific analysis is strategic in making policy choices, while on the other, the limitations of social science to describe, explain, and predict human behavior make the development of an agreed-upon knowledge base of policy problems and solutions difficult. It is perhaps this tension that continues to vex those who would prefer greater integration of priorities, problems, and results in making some headway on significant social and educational problems.

Considerations about conceptual models and methods are essential to understanding changing policy scholarship in that at present, competing lenses and methods have legitimacy (Cibulka, 1999). Whereas previously there was little diversity in conceptual and methodological approaches used to examine policy problems, researchers at present hold more diverse views of scientific investigation. As Kahne (1994) concluded, traditional policy analysis was often so technically oriented toward efficiency that it lacked the ability to examine the type of research question related to emerging concerns for ideals such as democratic community and social justice:

> Indeed, policy analysts lack the vocabulary, the conceptual frameworks, and the technical procedures needed to consider systematically and articulate concern for these alternative ideals.... More generally, evaluators and policy analysts rarely devote systematic attention to the transformative power of education; they rarely assess educators' ability to graduate students with the skills,

knowledge, and social orientation needed to strengthen our democracy....
Until policy analysts work to develop and promote the language and set of
techniques needed to consider these concerns simultaneously, they will have
few ways to respond to this question. (p. 246)

Kahne's assessment of the limitations of previous policy research suggests that today, there is a moral purpose underlying our efforts to study
policy—one that sets aside to some extent rational and technical ends (e.g.,
finding the most efficient choice) and focuses on transforming institutions
and practices for the benefit of all citizens.

It is important to engage in dialogue about scope, essential problems,
and methods for the field, such that there is further understanding of what
aspects are elitist and exclusionary and what aspects are essential and productive (Johnson, 2003; Scribner et al., 2003). Challenges to dominant ways
of thinking open up the complexities of problems and help us think about a
more diverse range of solutions. They are also useful because they question
our assumptions, our ways of knowing, and our methods of investigation
(Heck & Hallinger, 1999). Newer ways of examining phenomena include
variants on traditional science (naturalist, phenomenological), advocacy
(critical theorist, feminist), and perspectives that undercut the reliance on
theory altogether (postmodern, poststructural).

In policy research, theory development along different paths has yielded
insights into politics, policy processes, and the ability of policy changes to
penetrate the educational system. Despite sustained criticism of its impact,
policy research has significantly contributed to our understanding of how political processes influence the formulation and implementation of educational and social policies. This has been influential in suggesting better ways
to design, implement, and administer policies (Boyd, 1988). Evidence has accumulated suggesting that the results of policy studies figure into policymakers' future activities, perhaps more indirectly than directly; that is, policy
results help sharpen and reformulate policy issues and sometimes provide
new strategies for approaching problems (Boyd, 1988; Weiss, 1991).

Sustained research on school effectiveness and school improvement has
resulted in a more complete understanding of how school variables (e.g.,
resources, curriculum, teacher characteristics) influence student learning
at multiple levels of the educational system. Although the research has not
attended enough to how political and social contexts influence the structuring of schooling experiences within and between schools, it has nonetheless
played a major role in shifting attention away from the impact of students'
backgrounds on learning outcomes to a focus on the school, classrooms,
and personnel (e.g., teachers, principals) as important aspects of policy reforms to improve student learning. Although improvement research has
identified the local context and the school's culture and academic processes
as central to the success or failure of efforts to change schools, it has been
less successful, however, in measuring the impact of changes in improve-

ment programs and policies on student outcomes (Teddlie & Reynolds, 2000).This research has also identified leadership as significant in contributing to school effectiveness and school improvement through identifying needs; providing moral purpose, direction and support; and empowering others to share in the stewardship of the school.

Research has also identified how cultural, gender, and class-related boundaries have not equated well with achieving success for many within the institutional structures controlled by the state. Institutional structures often reinforced dominant views and ensured a comparative advantage for some over other groups in economic, political, and social spheres. These produced corresponding organizational arrangements within schools that allowed the implementation of widely endorsed cultural values. From this perspective, policies to improve schools, for example, can be seen as less rationally derived (i.e., directed at improving outcomes) and more institutionally derived—that is, reflecting larger sociocultural routines that affect students differentially (Benham & Heck, 1998). Consequently, policies and their meanings are multidimensional and must be examined as social fabric woven together to produce a greater whole (Everhart, 1988).

## REVISITING THE CONCEPTUAL LENSES

One of the tests of the usefulness of a conceptual framework or theory is its ability to further our understanding of important policy problems. Thus, while new and promising approaches may describe certain realities of policy life, they should also result in programs of cumulative empirical work (Lee, 2003; Tillman, 2002; Willower & Forsyth, 1999). Although new perspectives applied to policy problems may illuminate particular aspects that have been previously unnoticed, it is incumbent upon researchers to establish their utility for examining policy problems through establishing empirical and methodological rigor. As Cibulka (1999) concluded, "The challenge now is to develop scholarship that draws upon these differences of ideological and theoretical perspective as a positive force" (p. 177).

The range of conceptual models presented in the previous chapters are not the only approaches that can be used to examine educational policy. There are other promising ones. They have, however, drawn the attention of previous researchers in examining policy problems from diverse perspectives and methods. Because there is an empirical body of knowledge for each, it permits some preliminary summary of the main purposes, concepts, and strengths and limitations of each approach. The lenses are compared in Table 12.1 in terms of the research designs that would typically be used, unit of analysis (i.e., what the typical level of the outcome examined is), research goals, and primary strengths and weaknesses.

One example of a rational approach (systems theory and cost-benefit analysis are others) is the policy stages typology. The goal of this type of research is primarily to identify and describe the sequential phases of policy

**TABLE 12.1**

**Conceptual Lenses**

| Conceptual Lens | Design | Unit of Analysis | Goal | Strengths | Weaknesses |
|---|---|---|---|---|---|
| Policy Stages Typology | Case Study | The policy cycle | Identify and describe the characteristics of sequential phases of policy activity (e.g., initiation, enactment, implementation, termination). | Provides a means of ordering various parts of the policy process. Adaptable to other analytic lenses. Has led to important research on various aspects of the policy process (e.g., agenda setting, implementation, evaluation). | Stages are not precisely described; difficult to connect causally. Model tends to focus on discrete parts; neglects the role of ideas (beliefs, values, goals, strategies) in policy evolution. Neglects role of institutional relationships. |
| Punctuated Equilibrium Theory | Case Study, Time Series | Individual-level policy decision (e.g., budget decision, resource allocation decision). Often uses a proxy such as a change in budgetary outcomes, resource allocation outcomes. | Identify and describe ideas, events, interactions (e.g., issue definition, agenda setting), leading to policy decisions and changes. Emphasizes decision situations and institutional arrangements (e.g., federalism) as defining the ideas (e.g., goals, strategies) and actions of policymakers. | Provides a means of explaining and predicting periods of stability (incrementalism) and periods of crisis that produce major change in policy and practice. Focuses on the movement of ideas and their interplay with institutional arrangements (e.g., federalism) as cyclical, long-term processes. | Tends to work best during periods of equilibrium. More difficult to predict timing of punctuations and their outcomes. Often relationships are nonlinear (small disturbances producing major outcomes; large disturbances easily being incorporated in to existing practices). |

*(continued on next page)*

TABLE 12.1 (continued)

| Conceptual Lens | Design | Unit of Analysis | Goal | Strengths | Weaknesses |
|---|---|---|---|---|---|
| Advocacy Coalition Framework | Case Study | The policy subsystem<br><br>Policy subsystem is flexible, so the unit of analysis can incorporate a particular policy or a broad subsystem. Subsystems can be nested, leading to multiple levels of analysis. | Identify and describe advocacy coalitions working within a policy subsystem and their shared belief systems (values, goals, causal assumptions, and problem perceptions). Explain how these shared belief systems influence collective actions over time. | Focuses on belief systems and their influence on policy actions leading to change. Also incorporates external variables that affect situations within subsystem. Emphasizes coalitions of actors existing over time comprised of various agencies and governmental levels (as opposed to separate agencies). | Does not direct attention to variables and processes that determine the timing of when policy changes will take place. Limited research on the relationship of key variables to actual policy changes. |
| Cultural Theory, Political Culture | Case, Nonexp. | Policy decisions | Identify policymakers' belief systems (assumptive worlds). Examine how particular ideologies (e.g., individualism, egalitarianism) and value positions (e.g., efficiency, choice) lead to policy decisions. Explain or predict policy regularities (patterns of policy activity) resulting from state political culture. | Focuses on belief systems and external societal variables as driving policy activity, particularly at state level. Has a set of basic concepts (value preferences, typology of state political cultures) that is able to explain regularities in state policy behavior over time and differences between states. | Culture is difficult to define and measure. Many critical concepts are relatively undeveloped. State political typology is only roughly defined. There is considerable variation in intensity and scope of state level activity regarding similar policies that is not well explained. Explanatory power of state political culture is limited in times where there are national currents. |

322

| Economic Models (e.g., production functions, cost/benefit, cost effectiveness) | Nonexp., Time series | Varied units of analysis (typically educational outcomes at the group level—districts, states) | Identify relative strength of various inputs that lead to higher outputs (e.g., productivity, student achievement). Estimate relative benefits or cost effectiveness of making particular policy choices, often in relation to resource constraints. | Has been somewhat successful in identifying sets of variables that influence outcomes in schools (e.g., contextual variables, student composition, resources). Useful in identifying and estimating potential costs of particular policy choices against their likely effectiveness in producing desired outcomes. | Narrow in scope—focuses on input and output relationships as opposed to processes. Does not unlock the "black box" of how inputs are translated into desired outputs. Assumes rational decision making (efficiency). Limited applicability for suggested future policy actions, since analyses tend to be at macro-levels and don't consider dynamics of local site implementation. |
|---|---|---|---|---|---|
| Institutional Rational Choice | Case, Nonexp., Time Series | Settings and questions determine unit of analysis (often the action arena) Takes into consideration multi-level nature of policy processes and decisions | Identify general variables (physical conditions, community attributes, rules) affecting action arenas (situations and actors). Focuses on examining interactions, explaining behavior, and predicting outcomes within policy action arenas. Evaluate outcome achieved versus those achieved under alternative arrangements. | Has a well developed set of general variables and interrelationships that account for policy actions. Accounts for interplay between changing external variables and policy arenas. Broad in scope so it can be applied to many policy situations. | Tends to focus on limited time frames; ignores historical antecedents. Often focuses on incremental behavior. Assumes that individuals act in rational ways to maximize self-interest. Most of the explanatory weight is on situational variables as opposed to internal beliefs and strategies. |

*(continued on next page)*

**TABLE 12.1 (continued)**

| Conceptual Lens | Design | Unit of Analysis | Goal | Strengths | Weaknesses |
|---|---|---|---|---|---|
| Institutional Theory | Case, Nonexp. | Organizations | Identify larger social and cultural values and ideologies that explain policy activity. Determine what factors lead organizations to adopt similar organizational structures and practices across varied settings. | Examines policy activity temporally. Focuses on influence of larger cultural scripts (i.e., institutions), as opposed to actors' internally derived goals, on actors' policy behavior. Emphasizes the impacts of policy environment on the adoption of institutional structures and practices. | Emergent, conceptually varied set of arguments. Little consensus on definitions of key concepts, variables, and methods of analysis. Lack of attention to processes leading to institutionalization of policy choices. Remaining need to develop theoretical propositions. |
| Postmodern, Feminist, Critical Theory | Case | Individuals (e.g., individual policies, individual targets of policies) | Critique existing structures (e.g., institutional arrangements) and social construction of processes that work to advantage some and marginalize others. Focus on personal dimensions of policy activities, particularly from perspectives of those marginalized by policy processes (e.g., women, ethnic minorities). After identifying oppressive structures, seeks to replace them with more preferable ones. | Identified blind spots in the conceptualization and exclusive focus of policy studies on actors in positions of power. Successful in identifying structural variables, social constructions, and institutional arrangements that limit access, participation, and outcomes of some groups. By focusing on individuals, these lenses provide close-up policy understandings that are contextualized. | Theories are primarily descriptive. They attend less to the processes of changing oppressive structures and arrangements. There is a need for more empirical work to identify key terms, concepts, and theoretical propositions. Little application of findings to actual policy aimed at replacing oppressive structures. |

activity surrounding a particular policy's life cycle. It tends to focus on the policy process as more linear in nature, with initiation proceeding to enactment, implementation, and impact. While the approach has been useful in helping to describe and organize some incremental regularities of policy activity, it has been difficult to connect the various stages to causal forces. It is not consistent with views that describe policy as dynamic, disorderly, and nonlinear. Moreover, environmental, beliefs and values, and other types of institutional relationships are not considered with respect to their potential to affect the policy process. Hence, although the typology has been useful for descriptive research purposes, it has not really enhanced the development of theory surrounding the explanation of why particular policy regularities take place or the ability to predict policy outcomes given certain contextual and institutional conditions.

Institutional theory is an example of a structural approach (e.g., loose coupling in federalism and institutional rational choice are other examples that include elements of structuralism) to examining policy processes. In general, the structural approach suggests individuals' behavior is externally conditioned by social and cultural beliefs and values, as opposed to the pursuit of their internal self-interests (Scribner et al., 2003). In particular, institutional theory focuses on how larger social and cultural values and ideologies (referred to as "institutions") influence policy actions and organizational responses to policy changes. One of the strengths of this approach is the examination of the interplay between organizations and their changing political, economic, and cultural milieu. It examines policy-related behavior and organizational responses as adaptive behavior to changing external conditions. This stands in sharp contrast to rational approaches that focus on the goal-oriented behavior of individuals. It is a bit more difficult to categorize institutional rational choice, because it incorporates both elements of structural and rational approaches; that is, it acknowledges changing external values and conditions but also incorporates individuals' intended rational actions.

Cultural approaches (political culture, advocacy coalition framework, theories that place culture and class at the center of the analysis) focus on how historical, social, and cultural conditions and processes contribute to policy patterns that develop over time. As Scribner and colleagues (2003) argued, the cultural approach suggests that intersubjectivity and identity are central to understanding political behavior and that the analysis of culture will yield insight into policy behavior (e.g., by focusing on values embedded in policies). More recently, the cultural perspective has expanded to include how structural arrangements that result from broader cultural patterns may influence policymaking in education. For example, particular types of sorting due to gender, class, or race may be mirrored within school structures.

Cultural perspectives emphasize patterns, values, rules of behavior, and understanding how power and influence contribute to the allocation of cultural values through policy decision making (Marshall et al., 1989; Scribner et al., 2003). As Marshall and colleagues noted, political institutions (e.g., courts, legislatures, unions) are the cultural stage sets built by the prior and present cultural understanding that policy actors hold. In contrast, however, cultural approaches also have limitations that researchers need to consider (i.e., difficulty in measuring culture, difficulties associated with attributing causal relationships to culture, explanatory power of culture seems subject to various types of external conditions). Cultural rules and values may become institutionalized and thus constrain individuals' actions in a manner similar to structuralist explanations (Scribner et al., 2003).

Finally, postmodern approaches represent a range of theories that focus on the consequences of relying too much on theoretical explanations, because they tend to privilege some accounts of phenomena while ignoring others. Collectively, postmodern approaches tend to favor multiple perspectives, because any particular theory is likely to be situated rather than universal because it is understood differently within different epistemologies (St. Pierre, 2002). Postmodernism has been instrumental in identifying limitations of policy analyses that focus primarily on those in positions of power. By focusing on individuals that have been marginalized historically, these lenses provide close-up understandings of policy development, implementation, and impact that are contextualized. There is a need, however, for further empirical work that identifies key concepts, theoretical propositions, and interventions that result in policy that replaces oppressive structures.

## AT A CROSSROADS

I suggested earlier that despite the voluminous literature on educational policy accumulated over the past several decades, reviews of its impact concluded that this work produced little agreement on the goals or methods of policy research, few classic studies that defined the area's central thrust and overall theoretical perspectives for studying policy activity, and no standard textbooks. Reviews were fairly consistent in concluding that policy research has been a type of "mixed bag"—that is, it has not fully lived up to its scientific promise. Policy research was critiqued as being narrowly focused on specific issues and timeframes, not relevant to the questions policymakers and practitioners want answered, poorly conceived and conducted, and seldom disseminated in ways that educators could put the results to use (Birnbaum, 2000; Feuer et al., 2002). There were also divisions within the academic community regarding the overreliance on particular ways of looking at policy problems, processes, solutions, and methods. Postmodern critiques of dominant perspectives pointed to the limited scope and assumptions of rational approaches, as well as to their tendency to exclude other epistemological and methodological perspectives. They emphasized that power, influence, and funding sources play a key role in what views become accepted as definitive. Alternative perspectives were able to identify oppressive structures, inequities, and barriers to the creation of more democratic learning communities, even if they were not as successful in formulating and pursuing policy changes.

Others commented on the fundamental disconnect among policymakers, practitioners, and researchers. Of course, there are a number of reasons for this disconnect that were explored in the book—different traditions, roles and responsibilities, and purposes, to name a few. Changing social contexts may affect priorities, definitions of important policy problems, expectations for education and other institutions, as well as the focus of scientific research over time. Policy activities reflect the cultural contexts and political crises of the times. The continued criticism of policy research from its stakeholder communities suggests that the field has reached a crossroads in terms of its goals, methods of investigation, and utility for solving policy problems. Despite the field's broader focus in recent years, it has been difficult for policy scholars to reconcile deep differences about the field's proper directions, its scientific underpinnings, and its conceptual and analytic methods.

At the present moment, federal policymakers are attempting to narrow the focus of policy research and its methods of investigation by imposing research standards for researchers seeking federal funding. This reflects an almost exclusive concern with identifying school-wide programs that result in improved student learning (which has been at the center of reform efforts over the past couple of decades) and an acknowledgment that policymakers do not believe that educational research is of a sufficient quality to determine what types of school improvement programs actually work. Regarding method, federal policymakers currently favor funding research that produces evidence of program effects based on the use of experimental trials. Their thinking is that this type of reform effort can be "mass produced" within schools, if one of several reform programs can be established to actually work consistently. By definition, however, because the success of reform efforts reflect local needs, contexts, cultures, and educational processes, there are difficulties apparent in attempting to "scale up" what works in the local context. Although there exists considerable evidence demonstrating the efficacy of local school reform programs that meet the needs of individual schools, the sum of research on school improvement has not produced any type of blueprint of actions that can be taken to improve educational outcomes with consistent results across diverse settings. It is debatable whether the introduction of experimental trials regarding whole-school reform programs will add considerably to this dilemma, even if it is thought to be so in policy circles. This is because of the complexity of the variables that go into the improvement process (e.g., resources, performance standards, leadership, commitment to change, professional development, upgraded standards and expectations, parent support, student readiness and motivation).

Although these recent policymaker actions suggest that leaders are again "manifesting their faith in science as a force for improved public policy" (Feuer et al., 2002, p. 4), they have led to considerable debates over intentions, the impact of these actions on our understanding of policy and practice, and their effects on policy scholarship. It is likely that policymakers are taking the lead from other fields (e.g., medicine), where it is believed that research evidence has produced more dramatic results than in education (Feuer et al., 2002). While this is certainly a carrot for some policy researchers interested in pursuing this more narrowly focused research program, it only represents a small subset of the broader scope of educational policy problems that are worthy of researchers' attention.

Most within the educational research community are united in their belief that legislating scientific methods is bad policy because of the complex nature of policy problems and the impact of social context in the implementation of policy solutions (Berliner, 2002; Feuer et al., 2002; Pellegrino & Goldman, 2002). As Berliner argued, attempts to legislate methods of investigation confuse methods with scientific goals. Because of the impact of social contexts in defining policy problems and policy actions, multiple types of methods are preferred. Various scientific designs can yield relevant information including case study, ethnography, survey, time series, and experiments. The choices about research purposes and questions should guide the selection of design and method. The imposing of one particular design on the field undermines researchers' free pursuit of other social problems better addressed through other designs and methods. Moreover, changes in the social environment often change the types of questions asked, what constitutes data, and how the data are interpreted. Such changes can even negate scientific work (Berliner, 2002). Berliner suggested that it is ironic that the federal government can impose the type of scientific design required to receive funding for conducting educational research, yet routinely ignore a wealth of empirical information from policy studies in diverse areas (e.g., long-term positive effects of high-quality early childhood education on student learning, the negative impact of grade retention of student performance, the narrowing of curricular focus due to high-stakes testing, the effects of class size on learning) that could make a difference in policy activities.

In a field where successful policy activity often depends on contextual conditions that interact with policy activity and implementation, efforts to increase the understanding and involvement of researchers, practitioners, and policymakers would likely pay dividends, rather than legislating how research should be conducted. Pellegrino and Goldman (2002) suggested improving the collaboration among researchers, practitioners, and policymakers in defining the nature of policy problems and in conducting the work. Conversations on a variety of educational issues would help all three communities achieve a greater understanding of problems and possible solutions. Pellegrino and Goldman also proposed raising the standards for the review of research projects being proposed for funding, as opposed to dictating how they should be conducted. It also seems that scholars, practitioners, and policymakers should help determine what findings are worthy of promoting in schools (Berliner, 2002).

The disconnect surrounding the focus, quality, and utility of policy research suggests the need to consider whether or not we as researchers, practitioners, and policymakers are moving in the right direction, and perhaps what types of corrections should be made. Examining the politics, research processes, results, and utility of research are a legitimate focus for the field's attention. Thoughtful discussion and self-correction are ways that a field progresses (Johnson, 2003; Popper, 1959). Political and social contexts have helped define the field's focus in the past—including examining equity in the 1960s and 1970s, state mechanisms for improving quality in the 1980s, site-based management, choice, and standards in the last decade or so. Recent federal efforts represent a more pragmatic focus on results. Undercurrents within the academic community have also challenged the goals and legitimacy of the research process itself. In the 1980s and 1990s, the emergence of postmodern theories (e.g., feminism, critical race, poststructuralism) have focused scholars' attention on how structures, patterns, and researchers themselves may facilitate or hinder social justice for marginally situated populations (Johnson, 2003). In part, this concern emerged as a reaction to the conservative agenda in politics and a concern with how the field of policy research has been constructed in the past.

These challenges have changed the field from one that was more singular and integrated to one that is more plural and diverse (Johnson, 2003). A thorough consideration of the nature of pressing problems, what we are trying to accomplish through policy, and how research can support this endeavor brings us back to the centrality of purpose, theory, and method. Choices about purposes, conceptual underpinnings, and research methods will impact what is illuminated—or what is obscured. Whereas an early purpose of policy research was to identify choices of action leading to optimal decisions, it is obvious that the purposes are more diverse today. Along with a meaningful reconsideration of purposes, some priorities could be set among practitioners, policymakers, and researchers for developing several research agendas leading to sustained empirical efforts. Because there are tensions between a more pragmatic approach to determining what types of reforms work (i.e., the federal policymaking position) and more theoretical and situated explanations of particular policy actions and their effects on intended targets, it is important to achieve some type of "buy in" from stakeholders regarding the problems, research purposes, and questions that are essential to address.

At the same time, it is important for university-affiliated researchers to realize that policymakers are losing interest in universities as places where useful policy information is generated. Policymakers perceive much of what academics research, teach, and discuss among themselves as outside of "reality." While policymakers may call for evidence they can use in decision making, in actuality, however, their actions result from a complex number of factors including their own value preferences; perceptions of others' value preferences; societal values (e.g., equality, liberty); their accumulation of power, resources, and knowledge; and their assessment of the evolving policy environment (Fowler, 2000). Most importantly, their decision making takes place in a political arena, as opposed to in an academic arena. Although universities, think tanks, foundations, and other agencies may contribute to idea development and discussion, it is unlikely that policymakers would act on the basis of a single study, even if one were to exist that answered a particular policy problem directly. At the same time, it has been shown that cumulative knowledge does creep into the policy environment over time. Some recent examples of this type of accumulated knowledge include lengthening of the school year, adopting educational standards, providing differential financing to students with greater need, and reducing class size.

By acknowledging some of the past differences that have separated them from practitioners and policymakers and by working to promote greater collaboration, policy researchers can weigh in on political discussions and debates and ultimately play an important role in building a more democratic and socially just society. Because policy often represents the views of those who can gain access to policy subsystems, policy researchers can contribute to an understanding of why some groups and values have been so much—or so little—represented in society and schooling at different times in our nation's history (Tyack, 2002). Schools as institutions have often suffered from economic dysfunction; that is, the primary flow of financial support has been invested in schools and students who are in the elite (Benham & Heck, 1998). There is much to learn about how power, culture, funding, and language that underlie policies have served to marginalize people primarily on the basis of race, gender, and social class (Bensimon & Marshall, 1997; Tillman, 2002). Policies may be read, interpreted, and negotiated into practice quite differently by various groups.

Greater sensitivity as to how policy is situated contextually will help policymakers and practitioners understand how and why particular structures, patterns, and practices exist over time. As a constructed activity, policy discourses and actions may both shape and be shaped by the norms, values, and daily operations of the school. Venturing outside the boundaries of academic settings and working with policymakers and practitioners to generate these understandings can aid in creating more socially just policy and in reducing or illuminating nonproductive and oppressive structures and practices within schools. In this manner, policy research can contribute to policymaking that acknowledges cultural plurality and challenges educators to apply new combinations of ideas and practices that enhance the life chances for all children.

# Appendix

For interested readers, I have included a couple of data sets that can be used to practice with multilevel modeling and growth modeling. The first data set can be used to run multilevel analyses similar to the model presented in Fig. 10.4. The data consist of a random sample of 24 schools with a random sample of 5 students within each school.

| Sch code | Read | Math | Lang | ess | cses | fm | Low ses | lge sch | age |
|---|---|---|---|---|---|---|---|---|---|
| 100 | 682 | 714 | 673 | −2.82 | −2.36 | 0 | 0 | 0 | 135 |
| 100 | 644 | 661 | 670 | −2.82 | −2.36 | 0 | 0 | 0 | 140 |
| 100 | 651 | 670 | 648 | −2.82 | −2.36 | 0 | 0 | 0 | 135 |
| 100 | 710 | 786 | 677 | −2.82 | −2.36 | 0 | 0 | 0 | 151 |
| 100 | 673 | 719 | 698 | −2.82 | −2.36 | 0 | 1 | 0 | 138 |
| 107 | 593 | 598 | 596 | 3.19 | 1.67 | 0 | 0 | 0 | 138 |
| 107 | 660 | 660 | 673 | 3.19 | 1.67 | 1 | 0 | 0 | 140 |
| 107 | 640 | 622 | 613 | 3.19 | 1.67 | 1 | 1 | 0 | 141 |
| 107 | 646 | 647 | 618 | 3.19 | 1.67 | 1 | 1 | 0 | 144 |
| 107 | 634 | 696 | 645 | 3.19 | 1.67 | 0 | 0 | 0 | 146 |
| 108 | 627 | 607 | 618 | −5.43 | −1.68 | 1 | 1 | 0 | 141 |
| 108 | 620 | 635 | 648 | −5.43 | −1.68 | 0 | 1 | 0 | 142 |
| 108 | 656 | 673 | 666 | −5.43 | −1.68 | 1 | 0 | 0 | 138 |
| 108 | 606 | 614 | 613 | −5.43 | −1.68 | 0 | 0 | 0 | 141 |
| 108 | 582 | 616 | 596 | −5.43 | −1.68 | 0 | 0 | 0 | 142 |
| 109 | 649 | 676 | 663 | 3.94 | −1.20 | 1 | 0 | 0 | 138 |
| 109 | 646 | 688 | 681 | 3.94 | −1.20 | 0 | 0 | 0 | 147 |
| 109 | 662 | 685 | 673 | 3.94 | −1.20 | 0 | 0 | 0 | 141 |
| 109 | 647 | 665 | 670 | 3.94 | −1.20 | 0 | 0 | 0 | 139 |

(continued on next page)

| Sch code | Read | Math | Lang | ess | cses | fm | Low ses | lge sch | age |
|---|---|---|---|---|---|---|---|---|---|
| 109 | 715 | 690 | 681 | 3.94 | −1.20 | 0 | 0 | 0 | 145 |
| 111 | 610 | 644 | 629 | 3.29 | −0.21 | 0 | 1 | 0 | 146 |
| 111 | 640 | 635 | 663 | 3.29 | −0.21 | 0 | 0 | 0 | 145 |
| 111 | 685 | 652 | 654 | 3.29 | −0.21 | 1 | 1 | 0 | 147 |
| 111 | 660 | 630 | 643 | 3.29 | −0.21 | 0 | 1 | 0 | 141 |
| 111 | 634 | 665 | 640 | 3.29 | −0.21 | 0 | 1 | 0 | 147 |
| 114 | 710 | 750 | 685 | 0.89 | −2.79 | 0 | 0 | 1 | 145 |
| 114 | 725 | 725 | 693 | 0.89 | −2.79 | 1 | 0 | 1 | 139 |
| 114 | 715 | 750 | 740 | 0.89 | −2.79 | 1 | 0 | 1 | 141 |
| 114 | 670 | 691 | 673 | 0.89 | −2.79 | 1 | 0 | 1 | 138 |
| 114 | 649 | 741 | 657 | 0.89 | −2.79 | 1 | 0 | 1 | 136 |
| 124 | 622 | 706 | 637 | 6.52 | 0.00 | 0 | 1 | 1 | 141 |
| 124 | 649 | 633 | 629 | 6.52 | 0.00 | 0 | 1 | 1 | 139 |
| 124 | 670 | 654 | 660 | 6.52 | 0.00 | 1 | 0 | 1 | 143 |
| 124 | 634 | 676 | 663 | 6.52 | 0.00 | 1 | 1 | 1 | 142 |
| 124 | 637 | 677 | 657 | 6.52 | 0.00 | 1 | 1 | 1 | 147 |
| 130 | 664 | 731 | 657 | 2.18 | −0.64 | 1 | 0 | 0 | 149 |
| 130 | 593 | 637 | 605 | 2.18 | −0.64 | 1 | 1 | 0 | 144 |
| 130 | 587 | 628 | 620 | 2.18 | −0.64 | 1 | 1 | 0 | 140 |
| 130 | 618 | 683 | 632 | 2.18 | −0.64 | 0 | 1 | 0 | 155 |
| 130 | 680 | 708 | 677 | 2.18 | −0.64 | 0 | 1 | 0 | 145 |
| 132 | 591 | 596 | 579 | −2.03 | −0.82 | 1 | 1 | 0 | 138 |
| 132 | 615 | 636 | 618 | −2.03 | −0.82 | 0 | 0 | 0 | 138 |
| 132 | 618 | 686 | 645 | −2.03 | −0.82 | 1 | 1 | 0 | 140 |
| 132 | 655 | 643 | 632 | −2.03 | −0.82 | 0 | 0 | 0 | 143 |
| 132 | 632 | 625 | 635 | −2.03 | −0.82 | 0 | 0 | 0 | 142 |
| 134 | 603 | 594 | 600 | −1.25 | −0.71 | 0 | 1 | 0 | 140 |
| 134 | 617 | 605 | 616 | −1.25 | −0.71 | 0 | 0 | 0 | 138 |
| 134 | 627 | 614 | 599 | −1.25 | −0.71 | 0 | 0 | 0 | 139 |
| 134 | 670 | 682 | 630 | −1.25 | −0.71 | 1 | 1 | 0 | 140 |
| 134 | 673 | 675 | 632 | −1.25 | −0.71 | 0 | 0 | 0 | 137 |
| 136 | 668 | 776 | 700 | 4.23 | −1.37 | 1 | 0 | 1 | 137 |
| 136 | 651 | 696 | 648 | 4.23 | −1.37 | 1 | 0 | 1 | 138 |
| 136 | 624 | 652 | 666 | 4.23 | −1.37 | 0 | 0 | 1 | 143 |
| 136 | 719 | 737 | 680 | 4.23 | −1.37 | 1 | 1 | 1 | 143 |
| 136 | 656 | 728 | 632 | 4.23 | −1.37 | 0 | 0 | 1 | 144 |
| 140 | 668 | 676 | 650 | 5.92 | −1.58 | 0 | 0 | 0 | 139 |
| 140 | 696 | 712 | 681 | 5.92 | −1.58 | 0 | 1 | 0 | 149 |
| 140 | 670 | 688 | 673 | 5.92 | −1.58 | 1 | 0 | 0 | 146 |
| 140 | 670 | 722 | 689 | 5.92 | −1.58 | 1 | 1 | 0 | 140 |

| 140 | 687 | 704 | 681 | 5.92 | −1.58 | 0 | 0 | 0 | 140 |
|---|---|---|---|---|---|---|---|---|---|
| 141 | 696 | 734 | 680 | 2.55 | −1.85 | 1 | 0 | 0 | 145 |
| 141 | 599 | 594 | 580 | 2.55 | −1.85 | 0 | 0 | 0 | 139 |
| 141 | 687 | 706 | 685 | 2.55 | −1.85 | 0 | 0 | 0 | 144 |
| 141 | 649 | 696 | 670 | 2.55 | −1.85 | 0 | 0 | 0 | 143 |
| 141 | 642 | 626 | 635 | 2.55 | −1.85 | 1 | 0 | 0 | 141 |
| 143 | 608 | 626 | 607 | 6.00 | −0.54 | 0 | 1 | 0 | 147 |
| 143 | 630 | 656 | 629 | 6.00 | −0.54 | 1 | 1 | 0 | 139 |
| 143 | 608 | 605 | 610 | 6.00 | −0.54 | 0 | 1 | 0 | 137 |
| 143 | 719 | 731 | 716 | 6.00 | −0.54 | 1 | 0 | 0 | 146 |
| 143 | 640 | 611 | 635 | 6.00 | −0.54 | 0 | 0 | 0 | 141 |
| 145 | 660 | 669 | 630 | −3.24 | 0.96 | 1 | 1 | 0 | 143 |
| 145 | 651 | 640 | 648 | -3.24 | 0.96 | 1 | 1 | 0 | 137 |
| 145 | 635 | 643 | 645 | -3.24 | 0.96 | 1 | 0 | 0 | 140 |
| 145 | 595 | 591 | 586 | -3.24 | 0.96 | 0 | 1 | 0 | 144 |
| 145 | 642 | 652 | 637 | -3.24 | 0.96 | 1 | 1 | 0 | 137 |
| 150 | 649 | 636 | 657 | 8.17 | -0.87 | 1 | 1 | 0 | 138 |
| 150 | 653 | 679 | 651 | 8.17 | -0.87 | 1 | 1 | 0 | 143 |
| 150 | 644 | 673 | 640 | 8.17 | -0.87 | 1 | 0 | 0 | 136 |
| 150 | 613 | 607 | 620 | 8.17 | -0.87 | 1 | 1 | 0 | 143 |
| 150 | 690 | 734 | 685 | 8.17 | -0.87 | 0 | 1 | 0 | 136 |
| 151 | 615 | 644 | 618 | 8.02 | −1.26 | 0 | 1 | 0 | 138 |
| 151 | 658 | 666 | 650 | 8.02 | −1.26 | 0 | 0 | 0 | 143 |
| 151 | 664 | 672 | 685 | 8.02 | −1.26 | 0 | 0 | 0 | 142 |
| 151 | 613 | 633 | 637 | 8.02 | −1.26 | 0 | 0 | 0 | 147 |
| 151 | 680 | 669 | 663 | 8.02 | −1.26 | 0 | 0 | 0 | 147 |
| 153 | 664 | 741 | 690 | −2.70 | −1.72 | 1 | 0 | 0 | 140 |
| 153 | 625 | 704 | 651 | −2.70 | −1.72 | 1 | 0 | 0 | 142 |
| 153 | 675 | 768 | 657 | −2.70 | −1.72 | 1 | 0 | 0 | 142 |
| 153 | 680 | 728 | 657 | −2.70 | −1.72 | 0 | 0 | 0 | 145 |
| 153 | 656 | 719 | 651 | −2.70 | −1.72 | 0 | 0 | 0 | 140 |
| 155 | 719 | 698 | 685 | −1.55 | −1.70 | 0 | 0 | 0 | 144 |
| 155 | 630 | 649 | 620 | −1.55 | −1.70 | 1 | 0 | 0 | 143 |
| 155 | 640 | 653 | 632 | −1.55 | −1.70 | 0 | 0 | 0 | 145 |
| 155 | 699 | 696 | 660 | −1.55 | −1.70 | 1 | 0 | 0 | 147 |
| 155 | 670 | 706 | 648 | −1.55 | −1.70 | 0 | 0 | 0 | 139 |
| 250 | 593 | 605 | 613 | −3.56 | 0.26 | 0 | 1 | 1 | 138 |
| 250 | 567 | 604 | 610 | −3.56 | 0.26 | 0 | 0 | 1 | 143 |
| 250 | 666 | 700 | 698 | −3.56 | 0.26 | 1 | 1 | 1 | 144 |
| 250 | 604 | 620 | 621 | −3.56 | 0.26 | 1 | 0 | 1 | 144 |
| 250 | 670 | 680 | 677 | −3.56 | 0.26 | 0 | 0 | 1 | 139 |
| 251 | 660 | 676 | 640 | 2.27 | 0.26 | 0 | 1 | 0 | 136 |

*(continued on next page)*

| Sch code | Read | Math | Lang | ess | cses | fm | Low ses | lge sch | age |
|---|---|---|---|---|---|---|---|---|---|
| 251 | 687 | 676 | 681 | 2.27 | 0.26 | 0 | 0 | 0 | 140 |
| 251 | 660 | 675 | 666 | 2.27 | 0.26 | 1 | 0 | 0 | 136 |
| 251 | 603 | 633 | 616 | 2.27 | 0.26 | 1 | 0 | 0 | 143 |
| 251 | 637 | 636 | 616 | 2.27 | 0.26 | 0 | 1 | 0 | 146 |
| 274 | 610 | 619 | 606 | 2.03 | 1.96 | 0 | 1 | 1 | 135 |
| 274 | 622 | 683 | 630 | 2.03 | 1.96 | 0 | 0 | 1 | 145 |
| 274 | 690 | 695 | 670 | 2.03 | 1.96 | 1 | 1 | 1 | 139 |
| 274 | 646 | 675 | 640 | 2.03 | 1.96 | 0 | 1 | 1 | 139 |
| 274 | 578 | 619 | 580 | 2.03 | 1.96 | 0 | 1 | 1 | 146 |
| 375 | 670 | 686 | 645 | -0.30 | 0.26 | 1 | 1 | 1 | 138 |
| 375 | 627 | 653 | 637 | -0.30 | 0.26 | 1 | 0 | 1 | 147 |
| 375 | 639 | 712 | 648 | -0.30 | 0.26 | 0 | 1 | 1 | 137 |
| 375 | 651 | 666 | 620 | -0.30 | 0.26 | 1 | 0 | 1 | 146 |
| 375 | 582 | 598 | 586 | -0.30 | 0.26 | 0 | 0 | 1 | 141 |
| 377 | 637 | 622 | 620 | -20.44 | 0.48 | 1 | 1 | 0 | 140 |
| 377 | 630 | 620 | 599 | -20.44 | 0.48 | 1 | 1 | 0 | 140 |
| 377 | 662 | 637 | 620 | -20.44 | 0.48 | 0 | 1 | 0 | 136 |
| 377 | 647 | 626 | 623 | -20.44 | 0.48 | 1 | 1 | 0 | 145 |
| 377 | 630 | 607 | 610 | -20.44 | 0.48 | 1 | 0 | 0 | 142 |

**Exercise 1**

Construct a multilevel SEM model to examine the influence of within- and between-group predictors on achievement outcomes. The model is summarized in the following figure. The variables are as follows. Schcode is the clustering variable. Between-school variables are ESS, a standardized scale of school quality (constructed from the indicators in Fig. 10.4); CSES, a standardized measure of school socioeconomic status (reverse coded in this data set); and Lrgsch, a dichotomous school size variable (coded 1 = 1,500+ students).Within-school variables are lowSES, a measure of student socioeconomic status (coded low SES =1); the child's age in months; fm (coded female = 1); and Read, Math, and Lang are standardized test scores.

Modeling statements are provided for Mplus and LISREL. They produce slightly different results owing to different methods of estimation (and standardization) used. For the proposed model, you may wish to note the intraclass correlations, differences in the between-group unadjusted and adjusted achievement means (i.e., adjusted for gender and student SES), which variables are significant predictors of the latent outcome variable (i.e., the ratio of the estimate to its standard error provides a $t$-ratio with values above 2.064 significant at $p = .05$ between groups, and values above 1.98 significant at $p = .05$ within groups), and differences in the variance accounted for within and between groups. Interested readers might also want to conduct the analysis as a single-level SEM and compare the differences in chi-squares, effects of the predictors, and variance in achievement accounted for between the single level and multilevel analyses.

It is possible to investigate various multilevel models with these data by using different combinations of predictors. When low SES and female are used together in LISREL, however, the resulting covariance matrix is not positive definite (likely due to small sample size), so there is no resulting solution.

The Mplus input statements used to run a model similar to Fig. 10.4 are as follows:

| | |
|---|---|
| TITLE: | Two-level Elementary School Effects Model; |
| DATA: | FILE IS C:\Mplus\Ch10ex.dat; format is 4f4.0,2f6.2,3f2.0,f8.2; |
| VARIABLE: | Names are schcode read math lang ess cses female lowSES lgesch age; |
| | Usevariables are schcode read math lang ess cses age lowSES; |
| | CLUSTER IS schcode; between is cses ess; |
| ANALYSIS: | TYPE = General Twolevel; |
| | Estimator is MUMLM; |
| Model: | %BETWEEN% |
| | bachiev by read@1 math lang; |
| | bachiev on cses ess lowSES@0 age@0; |
| | %WITHIN% |
| | achiev by read math lang; |
| | achiev on lowSES age; |
| OUTPUT: | Stampstat Standardized; |

*Note.* $\chi^2$ (14, $N_W = 120$, $N_B = 24$) = 12.69, $p = .55$, CFI = 1.00, RMSEA = .000

LISREL input statements used to run the model in the figure are as follows:

---

```
!Example Multilevel Study
Group1: Between Schools Group
DA NI=10 NG=2 MA=CM
LA
Schcode read math lang ess cses female lowses largesch age
RA FI='C:\Mplus\ch10example2.psf'
$CLUSTER SCHCODE
$PREDICT
SE
2 3 4 5 6 8 10/
MO NX=4 NY=3 NE=1 LY=FU,FI GA=FU,FI PH=SY,FR PS=DI,FR
TE=DI,FR
LE
Achieve
FR LY(2,1) LY(1,1) GA(1,1) GA(1,2)
VA 1.0 LY(3,1)
FI PH(3, 3) PH(4, 4)
PD
OU SS
Group2: Within Schools Group
DA NI=10 NG=2 MA=CM
LA
Schcode read math lang ess cses female lowses largesch age
RA FI='C:\Mplus\ch10example2.psf'
$CLUSTER SCHCODE
$PREDICT
SE
2 3 4 5 6 8 10/
MO NX=4 NY=3 NE=1 LY=FU,FI GA=FU,FI PH=SY,FR PS=DI,FR
TE=DI,FR
LE
Achieve
FR LY(2,1) LY(1,1) GA(1,3) GA(1,4)
VA 1.0 LY(3,1)
FI PH(1,1) PH(2, 2) PH(3,3) PH(4,4)
FI PH(2,1)
OU
```

---

*Note.* $\chi^2$ (14, $N_W$ = 120, $N_B$ = 24) = 10.53, $p$ = .72, RMSEA = 0.000, $p$ = .33

## Exercise 2

The data can also be used to set up and run a two-level or a three-level multivariate (i.e., similar to the previous multilevel SEM) model in HLM. Interested readers can consult Raudenbush et al. (2000) or Heck and Thomas (2000) for details on how to set up HLM files. For this example, we will set up and conduct a two-level analysis of reading scores. In this model there are two school-level predictors (CSES and ESS) and two individual-level predictors (female, low SES) in the analysis. To conduct two-level analyses, one needs to create a level-1 data set (consisting of schcode, read, math, lang, female, and low SES) and a level-2 data set (consisting of schcode, CSES, ESS, and lgesch). The two files are then merged (using schcode) into a SSM file in HLM. After the SSM files is successfully created, the descriptive statistics should be as follows:

| Variables | N | MEAN | SD | MINIMUM | MAXIMUM |
|-----------|-----|---------|-------|---------|---------|
| Level 1 | | | | | |
| Read | 120 | 647.26 | 34.07 | 567.00 | 725.00 |
| Math | 120 | 667.19 | 44.47 | 591.00 | 786.00 |
| Lang | 120 | 645.52 | 31.64 | 579.00 | 760.00 |
| Female | 120 | 0.45 | 0.50 | 0.00 | 1.00 |
| LowSES | 120 | 0.42 | 0.50 | 0.00 | 1.00 |
| Level 2 | | | | | |
| ESS | 24 | 0.66 | 5.91 | −20.44 | 8.10 |
| SCSES | 24 | −0.64 | 1.21 | −2.79 | 1.96 |
| Lgesch | 24 | 0.25 | 0.44 | 0.00 | 1.00 |

A series of models can then be tested. Often, the first is a null model (with no predictors) to obtain the intraclass correlation for reading. Following is selected output for the null model.

Model 1: Null Model

| | Coefficient | SE | t-ratio | df | p |
|---|---|---|---|---|---|
| School Reading Means | | | | | |
| Intercept, $\gamma_{00}$ | 647.26 | 3.96 | 163.63 | 23 | .000 |

*Note.* Variance components are 177.67 (between) and 989.29 (within). These can be used to calculate the intraclass correlation (177.67/177.67 + 989.29 = .152).

Next, a level-1 only model might be examined. Finally, a full multilevel model can be estimated. For the model summarized below, the predictors at each level were grand-mean centered. Readers might compare the grand-centered solution to one where the level-1 predictors are group-mean centered.

Model 2: Full Model

|  | Coefficient | SE | t-ratio | df | p |
|---|---|---|---|---|---|
| School Reading Means |  |  |  |  |  |
| Intercept, $\gamma_{00}$ | 647.26 | 3.02 | 214.37 | 21 | .000 |
| ESS, $\gamma_{01}$ | 0.55 | 0.53 | 1.05 | 21 | .307 |
| CSES, $\gamma_{02}$ | −9.38 | 2.78 | 3.38 | 21 | .003 |
| Individual Variables |  |  |  |  |  |
| Female, $\gamma_{10}$ | 11.48 | 5.89 | 1.95 | 115 | .051 |
| LowSES, $\gamma_{20}$ | −5.75 | 6.42 | −0.90 | 115 | .371 |

Variance components for the model are 22.52 (between) and 981.42 (within). The change in between-group variance components from the null to the full model suggests that ESS and CSES account for considerable between-school variance in reading outcomes ([177.67–22.52]/177.67 = .873, or 87%). The amount of variance accounted for at the individual level is much smaller.

## LONGITUDINAL ANALYSIS

The following data set can be used to run several different single-level and multilevel growth models. The data consist of a number of individual students ($N = 120$) randomly sampled within a random sample of schools. Students were assessed in math over three consecutive years.

| Sch code | math1 | math2 | math3 | fm | lwses | slep | cses | ess |
|---|---|---|---|---|---|---|---|---|
| 104 | 548 | 609 | 642 | 0 | 1 | 1 | .97 | −1.14 |
| 104 | 597 | 626 | 639 | 1 | 1 | 0 | .97 | −1.14 |
| 104 | 579 | 673 | 656 | 1 | 1 | 1 | .97 | −1.14 |
| 104 | 559 | 632 | 647 | 1 | 1 | 0 | .97 | −1.14 |
| 105 | 566 | 631 | 685 | 0 | 1 | 1 | 1.54 | −.36 |
| 105 | 602 | 640 | 640 | 1 | 0 | 0 | 1.54 | −.36 |
| 116 | 610 | 658 | 665 | 1 | 1 | 1 | −1.28 | −.54 |
| 116 | 667 | 700 | 771 | 0 | 0 | 0 | −1.28 | −.54 |

| 116 | 631 | 669 | 656 | 0 | 0 | 0 | −1.28 | −.54 |
|-----|-----|-----|-----|---|---|---|-------|------|
| 116 | 627 | 688 | 726 | 1 | 0 | 0 | −1.28 | −.54 |
| 116 | 627 | 673 | 728 | 0 | 0 | 0 | −1.28 | −.54 |
| 116 | 542 | 622 | 650 | 1 | 0 | 0 | −1.28 | −.54 |
| 148 | 562 | 650 | 650 | 1 | 1 | 0 | −.64 | .19 |
| 148 | 644 | 704 | 731 | 1 | 0 | 0 | −.64 | .19 |
| 148 | 690 | 734 | 798 | 0 | 1 | 1 | −.64 | .19 |
| 148 | 633 | 725 | 723 | 1 | 1 | 1 | −.64 | .19 |
| 152 | 648 | 712 | 749 | 1 | 0 | 1 | −.11 | −1.28 |
| 152 | 550 | 636 | 647 | 0 | 1 | 0 | −.11 | −1.28 |
| 152 | 660 | 696 | 721 | 1 | 0 | 1 | −.11 | −1.28 |
| 152 | 554 | 628 | 662 | 0 | 1 | 0 | −.11 | −1.28 |
| 152 | 637 | 722 | 771 | 1 | 0 | 0 | −.11 | −1.28 |
| 201 | 607 | 686 | 704 | 0 | 0 | 0 | −.88 | −2.06 |
| 201 | 618 | 704 | 690 | 0 | 0 | 0 | −.88 | −2.06 |
| 201 | 610 | 682 | 705 | 1 | 1 | 0 | −.88 | −2.06 |
| 201 | 623 | 715 | 726 | 1 | 0 | 0 | −.88 | −2.06 |
| 219 | 631 | 677 | 693 | 0 | 0 | 1 | −.98 | −.84 |
| 219 | 651 | 731 | 775 | 1 | 0 | 1 | −.98 | −.84 |
| 219 | 590 | 648 | 697 | 0 | 0 | 0 | −.98 | −.84 |
| 219 | 671 | 750 | 764 | 0 | 0 | 1 | −.98 | −.84 |
| 232 | 574 | 640 | 640 | 0 | 1 | 0 | .17 | −1.45 |
| 232 | 671 | 683 | 679 | 1 | 0 | 0 | .17 | −1.45 |
| 232 | 612 | 638 | 669 | 0 | 1 | 0 | .17 | −1.45 |
| 237 | 559 | 616 | 655 | 0 | 1 | 0 | −1.18 | −1.36 |
| 237 | 601 | 717 | 760 | 1 | 0 | 0 | −1.18 | −1.36 |
| 237 | 553 | 584 | 648 | 1 | 1 | 0 | −1.18 | −1.36 |
| 255 | 600 | 666 | 689 | 0 | 1 | 0 | −.93 | −1.11 |
| 255 | 548 | 619 | 631 | 0 | 0 | 0 | −.93 | −1.11 |
| 255 | 572 | 640 | 687 | 0 | 0 | 0 | −.93 | −1.11 |
| 255 | 667 | 722 | 744 | 0 | 1 | 0 | −.93 | −1.11 |
| 273 | 585 | 650 | 652 | 0 | 1 | 0 | 1.87 | −.76 |
| 273 | 543 | 635 | 669 | 0 | 1 | 0 | 1.87 | −.76 |
| 273 | 597 | 671 | 667 | 1 | 0 | 0 | 1.87 | −.76 |
| 273 | 637 | 667 | 721 | 1 | 0 | 0 | 1.87 | −.76 |
| 273 | 535 | 607 | 633 | 1 | 1 | 0 | 1.87 | −.76 |
| 273 | 605 | 652 | 656 | 1 | 1 | 0 | 1.87 | −.76 |
| 273 | 610 | 731 | 711 | 1 | 1 | 0 | 1.87 | −.76 |
| 273 | 590 | 673 | 689 | 0 | 1 | 0 | 1.87 | −.76 |
| 278 | 521 | 584 | 639 | 1 | 1 | 1 | .48 | −.75 |
| 278 | 618 | 658 | 705 | 1 | 1 | 1 | .48 | −.75 |
| 278 | 560 | 625 | 642 | 1 | 0 | 1 | .48 | −.75 |

*(continued on next page)*

| *Sch code* | *math1* | *math2* | *math3* | *fm* | *lwses* | *slep* | *cses* | *ess* |
|---|---|---|---|---|---|---|---|---|
| 278 | 527 | 584 | 631 | 0 | 1 | 0 | .48 | −.75 |
| 278 | 648 | 708 | 757 | 1 | 0 | 0 | .48 | −.75 |
| 278 | 685 | 777 | 791 | 0 | 0 | 0 | .48 | −.75 |
| 278 | 627 | 655 | 697 | . 0 | 0 | 0 | .48 | −.75 |
| 278 | 598 | 652 | 673 | 0 | 0 | 0 | .48 | −.75 |
| 278 | 590 | 651 | 653 | 0 | 1 | 0 | .48 | −.75 |
| 279 | 576 | 626 | 678 | 1 | 0 | 1 | −.22 | −1.55 |
| 279 | 637 | 685 | 693 | 1 | 1 | 1 | −.22 | −1.55 |
| 279 | 654 | 702 | 744 | 1 | 0 | 0 | −.22 | −1.55 |
| 279 | 574 | 643 | 677 | 0 | 1 | 0 | −.22 | −1.55 |
| 279 | 525 | 638 | 660 | 1 | 1 | 0 | −.22 | −1.55 |
| 279 | 579 | 639 | 647 | 1 | 0 | 0 | −.22 | −1.55 |
| 279 | 568 | 651 | 644 | 0 | 1 | 0 | −.22 | −1.55 |
| 279 | 607 | 642 | 657 | 0 | 1 | 0 | −.22 | −1.55 |
| 310 | 600 | 644 | 665 | 1 | 1 | 0 | −.91 | −1.30 |
| 310 | 554 | 644 | 665 | 1 | 0 | 0 | −.91 | −1.30 |
| 310 | 521 | 629 | 612 | 0 | 1 | 0 | −.91 | −1.30 |
| 310 | 663 | 706 | 735 | 1 | 0 | 0 | −.91 | −1.30 |
| 310 | 637 | 688 | 724 | 1 | 0 | 0 | −.91 | −1.30 |
| 310 | 583 | 646 | 663 | 1 | 0 | 0 | −.91 | −1.30 |
| 318 | 601 | 659 | 697 | 1 | 0 | 0 | −.50 | −1.00 |
| 318 | 572 | 625 | 665 | 0 | 0 | 0 | −.50 | −1.00 |
| 318 | 671 | 700 | 757 | 0 | 0 | 0 | −.50 | −1.00 |
| 327 | 577 | 666 | 691 | 1 | 1 | 1 | 1.03 | −.18 |
| 327 | 563 | 611 | 655 | 1 | 0 | 0 | 1.03 | −.18 |
| 327 | 538 | 607 | 635 | 0 | 1 | 0 | 1.03 | −.18 |
| 327 | 573 | 659 | 679 | 1 | 1 | 0 | 1.03 | −.18 |
| 365 | 559 | 646 | 653 | 1 | 1 | 0 | 1.23 | −.21 |
| 365 | 573 | 639 | 655 | 1 | 1 | 0 | 1.23 | −.21 |
| 365 | 560 | 632 | 677 | 0 | 1 | 1 | 1.23 | −.21 |
| 373 | 559 | 612 | 647 | 0 | 1 | 1 | .18 | −1.65 |
| 373 | 591 | 623 | 660 | 1 | 0 | 0 | .18 | −1.65 |
| 383 | 612 | 696 | 689 | 0 | 0 | 0 | 1.97 | −1.84 |
| 383 | 566 | 633 | 665 | 0 | 1 | 0 | 1.97 | −1.84 |
| 383 | 605 | 650 | 656 | 1 | 0 | 0 | 1.97 | −1.84 |
| 385 | 637 | 685 | 721 | 1 | 0 | 0 | −.21 | −1.16 |
| 385 | 562 | 612 | 631 | 0 | 1 | 0 | −.21 | −1.16 |
| 387 | 595 | 671 | 710 | 1 | 1 | 0 | .23 | −.74 |
| 387 | 604 | 662 | 647 | 1 | 1 | 1 | .23 | −.74 |
| 387 | 641 | 632 | 678 | 0 | 1 | 0 | .23 | −.74 |

| | | | | | | | | |
|---|---|---|---|---|---|---|---|---|
| 387 | 690 | 698 | 690 | 1 | 0 | 0 | .23 | −.74 |
| 420 | 607 | 695 | 708 | 1 | 0 | 1 | 1.03 | −1.01 |
| 420 | 594 | 673 | 681 | 0 | 1 | 0 | 1.03 | −1.01 |
| 420 | 671 | 756 | 775 | 0 | 0 | 0 | 1.03 | −1.01 |
| 420 | 601 | 654 | 675 | 1 | 0 | 0 | 1.03 | −1.01 |
| 420 | 573 | 662 | 659 | 0 | 1 | 0 | 1.03 | −1.01 |
| 420 | 616 | 680 | 716 | 1 | 0 | 0 | 1.03 | −1.01 |
| 428 | 635 | 685 | 711 | 1 | 0 | 0 | .14 | −1.10 |
| 428 | 625 | 667 | 690 | 1 | 0 | 0 | .14 | −1.10 |
| 428 | 569 | 673 | 701 | 1 | 0 | 0 | .14 | −1.10 |
| 428 | 594 | 640 | 656 | 1 | 0 | 0 | .14 | −1.10 |
| 428 | 568 | 614 | 637 | 1 | 1 | 0 | .14 | −1.10 |
| 455 | 621 | 654 | 685 | 1 | 0 | 0 | .02 | −1.80 |
| 455 | 570 | 638 | 655 | 1 | 0 | 0 | .02 | −1.80 |
| 455 | 604 | 629 | 671 | 1 | 0 | 0 | .02 | −1.80 |
| 455 | 531 | 598 | 629 | 0 | 1 | 0 | .02 | −1.80 |
| 455 | 590 | 660 | 689 | 1 | 0 | 1 | .02 | −1.80 |
| 455 | 621 | 658 | 660 | 1 | 1 | 0 | .02 | −1.80 |
| 455 | 568 | 644 | 681 | 1 | 0 | 0 | .02 | −1.80 |
| 455 | 547 | 636 | 667 | 1 | 0 | 0 | .02 | −1.80 |
| 455 | 542 | 648 | 657 | 1 | 1 | 0 | .02 | −1.80 |
| 456 | 570 | 651 | 671 | 0 | 1 | 0 | −.43 | −2.50 |
| 456 | 583 | 659 | 673 | 0 | 1 | 1 | −.43 | −2.50 |
| 456 | 590 | 647 | 686 | 0 | 0 | 0 | −.43 | −2.50 |
| 456 | 610 | 654 | 655 | 0 | 0 | 0 | −.43 | −2.50 |
| 456 | 646 | 712 | 708 | 0 | 0 | 0 | -.43 | -2.50 |
| 456 | 557 | 616 | 702 | 0 | 0 | 0 | −.43 | −2.50 |
| 456 | 610 | 680 | 721 | 1 | 0 | 0 | −.43 | −2.50 |
| 456 | 587 | 685 | 686 | 1 | 0 | 0 | −.43 | −2.50 |
| 456 | 583 | 652 | 689 | 1 | 0 | 0 | −.43 | −2.50 |

## Exercise 3

First, the data can be examined as an individual growth model with SEM. We will examine growth in math as a function of several student demographics including female (coded 1), lowSES (coded 1), and English as a Second Language (SLEP) background (coded 1). The proposed model to be tested is summarized in the following Mplus model statements. In this example, the growth model can be defined as nonlinear (by using an asterisk for Math3). Interested readers may also define the model as a linear growth model (by replacing the asterisk with @2). Readers will note that the fit of the linear model is quite poor in comparison.

The Mplus input statements used to define this model are as follows.

| | |
|---|---|
| TITLE: | Growth model for math; |
| DATA: | File is C:\Mplus\mathgrowth.dat; |
| VARIABLE: | Names are schcode math1 math2 math3 female lowSES slep cses ess; |
| | Usevariables are math1 math2 math3 lowSES female slep; |
| ANALYSIS: | Type = meanstructure; Estimator is mlm; |
| Model: | |
| | I by math1@1 math2@1 math3@1; |
| | S by math1@0 math2@1 math3*; |
| | I on female lowSES slep; |
| | S on female lowSES slep; |
| | [Math1-math3@0 I s]; |
| OUTPUT: | Sampstat Standardized; |

$\chi^2$ (3, $N$ = 120) = 6.403, $p$ = .09, CFI = .99
Note. *This parameter is estimated to be 1.379 (suggesting students' growth in math between occasion 2 and 3 is considerably less than between occasion 1 and 2).

## Exercise 4

In this final exercise, we will construct a multilevel growth model using HLM (i.e., in this particular data set, the sample size appeared to be too small between groups to fit the model with multilevel SEM techniques). To examine multilevel growth with HLM it is necessary to construct a three-level data set before making the SSM file. This requires a different way of entering the data at level 1. For the first two individuals in the data set, the new data set looks like this:

| Schcode | id | Time | Achieve |
|---|---|---|---|
| 104 | 1 | 0 | 548 |
| 104 | 1 | 1 | 609 |
| 104 | 1 | 2 | 642 |
| 104 | 2 | 0 | 597 |
| 104 | 2 | 1 | 626 |
| 104 | 2 | 2 | 639 |

Readers will notice that for each individual, the three consecutive math scores comprise separate data records (which makes the total number of observations at level 1 equal to 360). Each individual also needs to have an identification number. This ID number (along with schcode) will be used to link the level-1 data to students' background data (i.e., female, lowses, slep) at level 2. At level 3, the relevant school information (i.e., ESS, CSES) is included. Finally, notice that a time variable is also constructed to reflect the different measurement occasions. In this case, the intervals represent yearly testing in math. Readers may remember that in the previous SEM example the third interval was estimated to be almost 1.4. This reflects a basic difference in treatment of the time variable between the SEM and HLM approaches (i.e., time scores are data points for HLM and are parameters that can be estimated in SEM analyses).

After the SSM file is assembled, the descriptive data should look like the following:

| Variables | N | MEAN | SD | MINIMUM | MAXIMUM |
|---|---|---|---|---|---|
| Level 1 | | | | | |
| Time | 360 | 1.00 | 0.82 | 0.00 | 2.00 |
| Math | 360 | 647.33 | 53.33 | 521.00 | 798.00 |
| Level 2 | | | | | |
| Female | 120 | 0.57 | 0.50 | 0.00 | 1.00 |
| Low SES | 120 | 0.46 | 0.50 | 0.00 | 1.00 |
| Slep | 120 | 0.19 | 0.40 | 0.00 | 1.00 |
| Level 3 | | | | | |
| CSES | 25 | 0.10 | 0.95 | −1.28 | 1.97 |
| ESS | 25 | −1.10 | 0.62 | −2.50 | 0.19 |

The level 1 model contains the intercept for math achievement (defined as initial status) and the time variable represents the data collection period. At level 2, both the initial status intercept and the growth-rate parameter (i.e., the expected change during a fixed unit of time, depending on how the time variable is scaled) are allowed to vary randomly as a function of the background variables; therefore, there are two random effects at level 2. The level-3 model represents the variability among schools in the two parameters of interest. In general, models with no predictors at level 2 and 3 should be fit prior to considering explanatory variables at either level (Bryk & Raudenbush, 1992). This can provide important statistics for examining growth (e.g., the variability in growth that lies at each level, the correlations among growth parameters, the reliability of effects at each level).

For the unconditional model (i.e., no level 2 or 3 predictors), the following estimates were obtained. This suggested that only about 3% of the variation in initial status was between schools (48.6/[48.6 + 397.17 + 1130.35]). In contrast, about 41% of the variance in growth rates was between schools (.457/[.457 + .656]).

The final estimation of variance components is as follows:

| Random Effect | Variance Component | df | $\chi^2$ | p-value |
|---|---|---|---|---|
| Level 1 | | | | |
| Temporal variation, e | 397.16752 | | | |
| Level 2 | | | | |
| Individual initial status, $r_0$ | 1130.35401 | 95 | 868.71 | 0.000 |
| Individual learning rate, $r_1$ | 0.65556 | 95 | 102.28 | 0.286 |
| Level 3 | | | | |
| School mean status, $u_{00}$ | 48.59954 | 24 | 30.77 | 0.161 |
| School mean learning, $u_{10}$ | 0.45707 | 24 | 24.76 | 0.419 |

Finally, we can consider an explanatory model that examines the effects of individual background and school variables on initial status and growth rates. The level-1 model remains the same.

The final estimation of fixed effects (with robust standard errors) is as follows:

| Fixed Effect | Coefficient | Standard Error | t-ratio | Approx. df | p-value |
|---|---|---|---|---|---|
| Model For Initial Status | | | | | |
| Intercept, $\gamma_{000}$ | 647.947737 | 2.764316 | 234.397 | 22 | 0.000 |
| Cses, $\gamma_{001}$ | −5.153805 | 3.203139 | −1.609 | 22 | 0.122 |
| Ess, $\gamma_{002}$ | 10.128761 | 4.932553 | 2.053 | 22 | 0.052 |
| Female, $\gamma_{010}$ | −3.451797 | 4.597777 | −0.751 | 116 | 0.453 |
| Low SES, $\gamma_{020}$ | −33.331201 | 6.432808 | −5.181 | 116 | 0.000 |
| Slep, $\gamma_{030}$ | 13.066952 | 8.361861 | 1.563 | 116 | 0.118 |
| Model For Learning Rates | | | | | |
| Intercept, $\gamma_{100}$ | 43.469334 | 1.148525 | 37.848 | 22 | 0.000 |
| Cses, $\gamma_{101}$ | −1.131889 | 0.959698 | −1.179 | 22 | 0.251 |
| Ess, $\gamma_{102}$ | −0.013081 | 1.422280 | −0.009 | 22 | 0.993 |
| Female, $\gamma_{110}$ | −0.701524 | 1.584549 | −0.443 | 116 | 0.658 |
| Low SES, $\gamma_{120}$ | −0.015037 | 1.322632 | −0.011 | 116 | 0.991 |
| Slep, $\gamma_{130}$ | 2.240100 | 1.944876 | 1.152 | 116 | 0.250 |

Readers will notice the consistency between the level-2 model in HLM (focusing on individual background variables) and the LCA model conducted with SEM (i.e., only low SES is significant in explaining initial status, and none of the background variables is significant in explaining growth), even though the two models are parameterized somewhat differently.

# References

Adams, D. W. (1988). Fundamental considerations: The deep meaning of Native American schooling, 1800–1900. *Harvard Education Review, 58*(1), 1–27.

Adelman, C., Jenkins, D., & Kemmis, S. (1977). Re-thinking case study: Notes from the second Cambridge conference. *Cambridge Journal of Education, 6,* 139–50.

Alexander, K., & Alexander, M. D. (2001). *American public school law* (5th ed.). Belmont, CA: Wadsworth/Thomson Learning.

Anderson, G. (1989). Critical ethnography in education: Origins, current status, and new directions. *Review of Educational Research, 59*(3), 249–270.

Anderson, G. (1990). Toward a critical constructivist approach to educational administration. *Educational Administration Quarterly, 26*(1), 38–59.

Anderson, G. (1996). The cultural politics of schools: Implications for leadership. In K. Leithwood, J. Chapman, D. Corson, P. Hallinger, & A. Hart (Eds.), *International handbook of educational leadership and administration* (pp. 947–966). Boston: Kluwer Academic Publishers.

Anfara, V. A., Brown, K. M., & Mangione, T. L. (2002). Qualitative analysis on stage: Making the research process more public. *Educational Researcher, 31*(7), 28–38.

Angus, L. (1996). Cultural dynamics and organizational analysis: Leadership, administration and the management of meaning in schools. In K. Leithwood, J. Chapman, D. Corson, P. Hallinger, & A. Hart (Eds.), *International handbook of educational leadership and administration* (pp. 967–996). Boston: Kluwer Academic Publishers.

Atkin, J. M., & House, E. R. (1981). The federal role in curriculum development: 1950: 1980. *Educational Evaluation and Policy Analysis, 3*(5), 5–36.

Ball, S. J. (1987). *The micro-politics of the school: Towards a theory of school organization.* New York: Methuen.

Ball, S. J. (1990). *Politics and policymaking in education: Explorations in policy sociology.* London: Routledge.

Banfield, E. (1965). *Big city politics.* New York: Random House.

Banks, J. (1988). *Multiethnic education: Theory and practice.* Boston: Allyn & Bacon.

Banks, J. (1993). The canon debate, knowledge construction, and multicultural education. *Educational Researcher, 22*(5), 4–14.

Bassiri, D. (1988). *Large and small sample properties of maximum likelihood estimates for the hierarchical model*. Unpublished doctoral dissertation, Michigan State University, East Lansing.

Baumgartner, F., & Jones, B. (1993). *Agendas and instability in American politics*. Chicago: University of Chicago Press.

Beekhoven, S., De Jong, U., & Van Hout, H. (2002). Explaining academic progress via combining concepts of integration theory and rational choice theory. *Research in Higher Education, 43*(5), 577–600.

Bell, D. A. (1992). *Faces at the bottom of the well: The permanence of racism*. New York: Basic Books.

Bellah, R. (1983). Social science as practical reason. In D. Callahan & B. Jennings (Eds.), *Ethics, the social sciences, and policy analysis* (pp. 37–64). New York: Plenum.

Benham, M. K. (1993). *Political and cultural determinants of educational policymaking: Their effects on Native Hawaiians*. Unpublished doctoral dissertation, University of Hawai'i at Mānoa, Honolulu.

Benham, M. K., & Heck, R. H. (1994). Political culture and policy in a state-controlled educational system: The case of educational politics in Hawai'i. *Educational Administration Quarterly, 30*(4), 419–450.

Benham, M. K., & Heck, R. H. (1998). *Culture and educational policy in Hawai'i: The silencing of native voices*. Mahwah, NJ: Lawrence Erlbaum Associates.

Bensimon, E. M., & Marshall, C. (1997). Policy analysis for postsecondary education: Feminist and critical perspectives. In C. Marshall (Ed.), *Feminist critical policy analysis* (pp. 1–21). London: Falmer Press.

Benson, C. S. (1988). Economics of education: The U.S. perspective. In N. Boyan (Ed.) *Handbook of Research on Educational Administration* (pp. 355–372). New York: Longman.

Berliner, D. C. (2002). Educational research: The hardest science of all. *Educational Researcher, 31(8)*, 18–20.

Berman, C., & McLaughlin, M. W. (1975). *Federal programs supporting educational change, Vol. IV: The findings in review*. Santa Monica, CA: Rand.

Berman, C., & McLaughlin, M. W. (1977). *Federal programs supporting educational change, Vol. VII: Factors affecting implementation and continuation*. Santa Monica, CA: Rand.

Berman, C., & McLaughlin, M. W. (1978). *Federal programs supporting educational change, Vol. VIII: Implementing and sustaining innovations*. Santa Monica, CA: Rand.

Bernard, H. R. (1994). *Research methods in anthropology: Qualitative and quantitative approaches*. Newbury Park, CA: Sage.

Bidwell, C. E., & Kasarda, J. D. (1980). Conceptualizing and measuring the effects of school and schooling. *American Journal of Education, 88*(4), 401–430.

Birnbaum, R. (2000). Policy scholars are from Venus: Policy makers are from Mars. *The Review of Higher Education, 23*(2), 119–132.

Blackmore, J. (1996). "Breaking the silence": Feminist contributions to educational administration and policy. In K. Leithwood, J. Chapman, D. Corson, P. Hallinger, & A. Hart (Eds.), *International handbook of educational leadership and administration* (pp. 997–1042). Boston: Kluwer Academic Publishers.

Blackmore, J., Kenway, J., Willis, S., & Rennie, L. (1993). What's working for girls? The reception of gender equity policy in two Australian schools. In C. Marshall (Ed.), *The new politics of race and gender* (pp. 183–202). London: The Falmer Press.

Blount, J. (1994). One postmodernist perspective on educational leadership: Ain't I a leader? In S. Maxcy (Ed.), *Postmodern school leadership: Meeting the crisis in educational administration* (pp. 47–59). London: Praegar.

Bogdan, R. C., & Bilken, S. K. (1982). *Qualitative research for education: An introduction to theory and methods.* Boston: Allyn & Bacon.

Bogdan, R. C., & Biklen, S. K. (1998). *Qualitative research for education* (3rd ed.). Boston: Allyn & Bacon.

Boje, D. M., Gephart, R., Jr., & Thatchenkery, T. J. (1996). *Postmodern management and organization theory.* Newbury Park, CA: Sage.

Boyan, N. (1988). *Handbook of research on educational administration.* New York: Longman.

Boyd, W. (1988). Policy analysis, educational policy, and management: Through a glass darkly? In N. Boyan (Ed.) *Handbook of research on educational administration* (pp. 501–522). White Plains, NY: Longman.

Boyd, W. (1992). The power of paradigms: Reconceptualizing educational policy and management. *Educational Administration Quarterly, 28*(4), 504–528.

Boyd, W., & Kerchner, C. (1988). *The politics of excellence and choice of education.* New York: The Falmer Press.

Brewer, D., Gates, S. M., & Goldman, C. A. (2002). *In pursuit of prestige: Strategy and competition in US higher education.* New Brunswick, NJ: Transaction Press.

Brewer, D., Krop, C., Gill, B., & Reichardt, R. (1999). Estimating the cost of national class size reductions under different policy alternatives. *Educational Evaluation and Policy Analysis, 21*(2), 179–192.

Brewer, G. D. (1974). The policy sciences emerge: To nurture and structure a discipline. *Policy Sciences 5*(3), 239–244.

*Brown v. Board of Education,* 347, U.S. 483, 74 S.Ct. 686 (1954).

Bryk, A. S., & Raudenbush, S. W. (1992). *Hierarchical linear models: Applications and data analysis methods.* Newbury Park: CA: Sage.

Bryman, A., & Burgess, R. G. (1994). Developments in qualitative data analysis: An introduction. In A. Bryman & R. G. Burgess (Eds.), *Analyzing qualitative data* (pp. 1–17). New York: Routledge.

Bulmer, M. (1982). *The uses of social research.* London: Allen & Unwin.

Burgess, R. G., Pole, C. J., Evans, K., & Priestley, C. (1994). Four studies from one or one study from four? In A. Bryman & R. G. Burgess (Eds.), *Analyzing qualitative data* (pp. 129–145). London: Routledge.

Callahan, D., & Jennings, B. (Eds.). (1983). *Ethics, the social sciences, and policy analysis.* New York: Plenum.

Callahan, R. (1960). *An introduction to education in American society.* New York: Knopf.

Callahan, R. (1962). *Education and the cult of efficiency.* Chicago: University of Chicago Press.

Campbell, D. T., & Stanley, J. C. (1963). *Experimental and quasi-experimental designs for research.* Chicago: Rand McNally.

Campbell, R., Cunningham, L. Nystrand, R., & Usdan, M. (1990). *The organization and control of American schools* (6th ed.). Columbus, OH: Merrill Publishing.

Catterall, J. (1997). Reflections on economic analysis and education policy: Introduction. *Educational Evaluation and Policy Analysis, 19*(4), 297–299.

Cibulka, J. G. (1995). Policy analysis and the study of the politics of education. In J. D. Scribner & D. H. Layton (Eds.), *The study of education politics* (pp. 105–126). Washington, DC: Falmer.

Cibulka, J. G. (1999). Ideological lenses for interpreting political and economic changes affecting schooling. In J. Murphy & K. Seashore Louis (Eds.), *Handbook of research on educational administration* (2nd ed., pp. 163–182). San Francisco: Jossey-Bass.

Cobb, R. W., & Elder, C. D. (1972). *Participation in American politics: The dynamics of agenda building.* Boston: Allyn & Bacon.

Cohen, D. (1982). Policy and organization: The impact of state and federal educational policy on school governance. *Harvard Educational Review, 52,* 474–499.

Cohen, M., March, J., & Olsen, J. (1972). A garbage can model of organizational choice. *Administrative Science Quarterly, 17*(1), 1–25.

Cohen, M. R. (1988). *Statistical power for the social sciences* (2nd ed.). Mahwah, NJ: Lawrence Erlbaum Associates.

Coleman, J. S. (1972). *Policy research in the social sciences.* Morristown, NJ: General Learning Press.

Coleman, J. S., Campbell, E. Q., Hobson, C. J., McPartland, J., Mood, A., Weinfeld, F., & York, R. L. (1966). *Equality of educational opportunity.* Washington, DC: Government Printing Office.

Connelly, F. M., & Clandnin, D. J. (1990). Stories of experience and narrative inquiry. *Educational Researcher, 19*(5), 2–14.

Cook, T. D. (2002). Randomized experiments in education: Why are they so rare? *Educational Evaluation and Policy Analysis, 24*(3), 175–200.

Cook, T. D., & Campbell, D. T. (1979). *Quasi-experimentation: Design and analysis issues for field settings.* Boston: Houghton Mifflin Co.

Coplin, W. D., & O' Leary, M. K. (1981). *Basic policy studies skills.* Croton-on-Hudson, NY: Policy Studies Associates.

Corson, D. (1996). Emancipatory discursive practices. In K. Leithwood, J. Chapman, D. Corson, P. Hallinger, & A. Hart (Eds.), *International handbook of educational leadership and administration* (pp. 1043–1067). Boston: Kluwer Academic Publishers.

Cox, R. W. (1981). Social forces, states and world orders: Millennium. *Journal of International Studies, 10*(2), 126–155.

Cremin, L. (1970). *American education: The colonial experience, 1607–1783.* New York: Harper & Row.

Cuban, L. (1990). Reforming again, again, and again. *Educational Researcher, 19*(1), 3–13.

Cubberley, E. P. (1916). *Public school administration: A statement of the fundamental principles underlying the organization and administration of public education.* Boston: Houghton Mifflin.

Cubberley, E. P. (1929). *Public school administration.* Boston: Houghton Mifflin.

Culbertson, J. A. (1988). A century's quest for a knowledge base. In N. Boyan (Ed.), *Handbook of research on educational administration* (pp. 3–26). New York: Longman.

Darling-Hammond, L. (1994). Performance-based assessment and educational equity. *Harvard Educational Review, 64*(1), 5–29.

Darling-Hammond, L. (2002, September 6). Research and rhetoric on teacher certification: A response to "teacher certification revisited." *Education Policy Analysis Archives, 10*(36), 1–57.

Davies, R. B. (1994). From cross-sectional to longitudinal analysis. In R. B. Davies & A. Dale (Eds.) *Analyzing social & political change: A casebook of methods* (pp. 20–40). Newbury Park, CA: Sage.

Davies, R. B., & Dale, A. (1994). Introduction. In R. B. Davies & A. Dale (Eds.), *Analyzing social and political change* (pp. 1–19). Newbury Park, CA: Sage.

De Leeuw, J. & Kreft, I. (1995). Questioning multilevel models. *Journal of Educational Statistics, 20*(2), 171–189.

deLeon, P. (1999). The stages approach to the policy process. In P. Sabatier (Ed.) *Theories of the policy process* (pp. 19–32). Boulder, CO: Westview Press.

Derrida, J. (1976). *Of grammatology.* Baltimore, MD: Johns Hopkins University.

Derrida, J. (1977). *Writing and difference.* London: Routledge & Kegan Paul.

Desimone, L., Porter, A. C., Garet, M. S., Yoon, K. S., & Birman, B. F. (2002). Effects of professional development on teachers' instruction: Results from a three-year longitudinal study. *Educational Evaluation and Policy Analysis, 24*(2), 81–112.

DesJardins, S. L. (2002). Understanding and using efficiency and equity criteria in the study of higher education policy. In J. Smart (Ed.), *Higher education: Handbook of theory and research* (Vol. XVII, pp. 173–219). New York: Agathon Press.

Dewey, J. (1972). The influence of the high school upon educational methods. In *The early works of John Dewey, 1882–1898* (pp. 270–271). Carbondale, IL: University of Illinois Press.

Dillard, C. (2000). The substance of things hoped for, the evidence of things not seen: Examining an endarkened feminist epistemology in educational research and leadership. *International Journal of Qualitative Studies in Education, 13*(6), 661–681.

Dimaggio, P., & Powell, W. (1983). The iron cage revisited: Institutional isomorphism and collective rationality in organizational fields. *American Sociological Review, 48,* 147–160.

Donmoyer, R. (1996). This issue: Talking "truth" to power. *Educational Researcher, 25*(8), 2, 9.

Downs, A. (1957). *An economic theory of democracy.* New York: Harper.

Downs, A. (1972). Up and down with ecology: The issue-attention cycle. *Public Interest, 28,* 38–50.

Duemer, L. S., & Mendez-Morse, S. (2002, September 23). Recovering policy implementation: Understanding implementation through informal communication. *Education Policy Analysis Archives, 10*(39), 11 pages. Retrieved from http://epaa.asu.edu/epaa/v10n39.html.

Dunbar, C. (2001). *Does anyone know we're here: Alternative schooling for African American youth.* New York: Peter Lang.

Dye, T. (1966). *Politics, economics, and the public.* Chicago: Rand McNally.

Dye, T. R. (1972). *Understanding public policy.* Englewood Cliffs, NJ: Prentice-Hall.

Dye, T. R. (1990). *American federalism: Competition among governments.* Lexington, MA: Lexington Books.

Easton, D. (1953). *The political system.* New York: Knopf.

Easton, D. (1965). *A systems analysis of political life.* New York: Wiley.

Elazar, D. (1970). *Cities on the prairie.* New York: Basic Books.

Elazar, D. (1984). *American federalism* (3rd ed.). New York: Harper & Row.

Eliot, T. H. (1959). Toward an understanding of public school politics. *American Political Science Review, 53*(4), 1032–1051.

Elmore, R., & McLaughlin, M. (1982). *Reform and retrenchment: The politics of school finance reform.* Cambridge, MA: Ballinger.

Elster, J. (Ed.). (1986). *Rational choice.* Oxford, England: Blackwell.

Everhart, R. (1982). The nature of "goofing off" among junior high school adolescents. *Adolescence, 17*, 177–188.

Everhart, R. (1988). Fieldwork methodology in educational administration. In N. Boyan (Ed.), *Handbook of research on educational administration* (pp. 703–726). New York: Longman.

Evers, J., & Lakomski, G. (1996). Science in educational administration: A postpositivist conception. *Educational Administration Quarterly, 32*(3), 379–402.

Fairbanks, D. (1977). Religious forces and "morality" politics in the American states. *Western Political Quarterly, 30*, 411–417.

Fay, B. (1987). *Critical social science.* Ithaca, NY: Cornell University Press.

Ferman, B. (1991). Chicago: Power, race, and reform. In H. Savitch & J. Thomas (Eds.) *Big city politics in transition: Urban Affairs Annual Reviews* (Vol. 38, pp. 47–63). Newbury Park, CA: Sage.

Feuer, M. J., Towne, L., & Shavelson, R. J. (2002). Scientific culture and educational research. *Educational Researcher, 31*(8), 4–14.

Fine, M., & Weiss, L. (1993). Introduction. In L. Weiss & M. Fine (Eds.) *Beyond silenced voices: Class, race, and gender in United States schools* (pp. 1–6). Albany, NY: SUNY Press.

Finkelstein, B. (1978). Pedagogy as intrusion: Teaching values in popular primary schools in nineteenth century America. In D. R. Warren (Ed.), *History, education, and public policy* (pp. 239–270). Berkeley: CA: McCutchen.

Finn, J. D. (2002). Small classes in American schools: Research, practice, and politics. *Phi Delta Kappan, 83*(7), 551–560.

Firestone, W. (1989). Educational policy as an ecology of games. *Educational Researcher, 18*(7), 18–24.

Firestone, W., & Corbett, H. (1988). Planned organizational change. In N. Boyan (Ed.), *Handbook of research on educational administration* (pp. 321–340). White Plains, NY: Longman.

Firestone, W. A. (1990). Continuity and incrementalism after all: State responses to the excellence movement. In J. Murphy (Ed.), *The education reform movement of the 1980s: perspectives and cases* (pp. 143–166). Berkeley, CA: McCutchan.

Flyvbjerg, B. (2001). *Making social science matter.* Cambridge, UK: Cambridge University Press.

Fotiu, R. (1989). *A comparison of the EM and data augmentation algorithms on simulates small sample hierarchical data from research on education.* Unpublished doctoral dissertation, Michigan State University, East Lansing.

Foucault, M. (1970). *The order of things.* London: Tavistock.

Foucault, M. (1973). *The archeology of knowledge.* New York: Vintage.

Fowler, F. C. (2000). *Policy studies for educational leaders.* Upper Saddle River, NJ: Prentice-Hall.

Fraenkel, J. R., & Wallen, N. (2000). *How to design and evaluate research in education.* (4th ed.). Boston: McGraw-Hill.

Freund, R. J., & Littell, R. C. (1991). *SAS System for Regression* (2nd ed.). Cary, NC: SAS Institute.

Garms, W., Guthrie, J. W., & Pierce, L. C. (1978). *School finance: The economics and politics of education.* Englewood Cliffs, NJ: Prentice-Hall.

Gee, J., Michaels, S., & O'Conner, M. (1992). Discourse analysis. In M. LeCompre, W. Millroy, & J. Preissle (Eds.), *The handbook of qualitative research in education* (pp. 227–292). San Diego: Academic Press.

Gergen, K. J. (1968). Assessing the leverage points in the process of policy formation. In R. A. Bauer & K. J. Gergen (Eds.), *The study of policy formation* (pp. 182–203). New York: Free Press.

Glaser, B. J., & Strauss, A. L. (1967). *The discovery of grounded theory.* Chicago: Aldine.

Glenn, C. (1988). *The myth of the common school.* Amherst: University of Massachusetts Press.

Godwin, R. K., & Kemerer, F. R. (2002, May 15). School choice trade-offs. *Education Week, 21*(36) 52, 39.

González, F. E. (2001). *Haciendo que hacer*—cultivating a Mestiza worldview and academic achievement: Braiding cultural knowledge into educational research, policy, and practice. *International Journal of Qualitative Studies in Education, 14*(5), 641–656.

Goodwyn, L. (1978). *The populist movement.* New York: Oxford University Press.

Gordon, E. (1997). Task force on the role and future of minorities, American Educational Research Association. *Educational Researcher, 26*(3), 44–53.

Gormley, K. (1988). Ten adventures in state constitutional law. *Emerging issues in state constitutional law.* Washington, DC: National Association of Attorneys General.

Grant, L., & Fine, G. (1992). Sociology unleashed: Creative directions in classical ethnography. In M. LeCompre, W. Millroy, & J. Preissle (Eds.) *The handbook of qualitative research in education* (pp. 405–446). San Diego: Academic Press.

Grodzins, M. (1960). The federal system. In *Goals for Americans: The report of the President's Commission on National Goals.* New York: Columbia University Press.

Grodzins, M. (1966). *The American system.* Chicago: Rand McNally & Co.

Guthrie, J., & Reed, R. (1991). *Educational administration and policy: Effective leadership in American education* (2nd ed.). Boston: Allyn and Bacon.

Guthrie, J. W. (1988). Educational finance: The lower schools. In N. Boyan (Ed.), *Handbook of research on educational administration* (pp. 373–389). New York: Longman.

Hallinger, P., & Heck, R. H. (1996). The principal's role in school effectiveness: An assessment of the methodological progress, 1980–1995. In K. Leithwood, J. Chapman, D. Corson, P. Hallinger, & A. Hart, (Eds.), *International handbook of educational leadership and administration* (pp. 723–783). London: Kluwer Academic Publishers.

Hanson, R. (1980). Political culture, interparty competition and political efficacy in the American States. *Publius: The Journal of Federalism, 10*(2), 17–36.

Hanushek, E. A. (1997). Outcomes, incentives, and beliefs: Reflections on analysis of the economics of schools. *Educational Evaluation and Policy Analysis, 19*(4), 301–308.

Harding, S. (1986). *The science question in feminism.* Ithaca, NY: Cornell University Press.

Hays, S. (1963). The politics of reform in municipal government in the progressive era. *Pacific Northwest Quarterly, 55*, 163.

Heck, R. (1991). Public school restructuring in Chicago: Indicator of another revolution in the politics of education? *Equity and Excellence, 25*, 216–221.

Heck, R. H. (1991–1992). Systems dynamics and Chicago school reform: A model for redefining who governs. *Administrator's Notebook, 35*(4), 1–6.

Heck, R. H.(2003). Examining the stability of school effects and school effectiveness criteria. *Journal of Effective Schools, 2*(1), 49–61.

Heck, R. H., Brandon, P., & Wang, J. (2001). Implementing site-managed educational changes: Examining levels of implementation and impact. *Educational Policy, 15*(2), 302–322.

Heck, R. H., & Crislip, M. (2001). Direct and indirect writing assessments: Examining issues of equity and utility. *Educational Evaluation and Policy Analysis, 23*(3), 275–292.

Heck, R. H., & Hallinger, P. (1999). Next generation methods for the study of leadership and school improvement. In J. Murphy & K. Seashore Louis (Eds.), *Handbook of research on educational administration* (2nd ed., pp. 141–162), San Francisco, CA: Jossey-Bass.

Heck, R. H., & Thomas, S. L. (2000). *An introduction to multilevel modeling techniques.* Mahwah, NJ: Lawrence Erlbaum Associates.

Heclo, H. (1974). *Social policy in Britain and Sweden.* New Haven: Yale University Press.

Heller, D. E. (2002). The policy shift in state financial aide programs. In J. C. Smart (Ed.) *Higher education: Handbook of theory and research* (Vol. XVII, pp. 221–261). New York: Agathon Press.

Henry, A. (1998). Complacent and womanish: Girls negotiating their lives in an African centered school in the U. S. *Race, Ethnicity, and Education, 1*(2), 151–170.

Herman, R. (1999). *An educator's guide to schoolwide reform.* Arlington, VA: Educational Research Service.

Hershberger, S. L., Molenaar, P. C. M., & Corneal, S. E. (1996). A hierarchy of univariate and multivariate time series models. In G. A. Marcoulides & R. E. Schumacker (Eds.), *Advanced structural equation modeling: Issues and techniques* (pp. 159–194). Mahwah, NJ: Lawrence Erlbaum Associates.

Hess, G. A., Jr. (1991). *School restructuring, Chicago style.* Newbury Park, CA: Sage.

Hill, P., & Rowe, K. (1996). Multilevel modelling in school effectiveness research. *School Effectiveness and School Improvement, 7*(1), 1–34.

Hox, J. J. (1995). *Applied multilevel analysis.* Amsterdam: T.T. Publikaties.

Hox, J. J. (1998). Multilevel modeling: When and why? In I. Balderjahn, R. Mathar, & M. Schader (Eds.), *Classification, data analysis, and data highways* (pp. 147–154). New York: Springer Verlag.

Hox, J. J. (2002). *Multilevel analysis: Techniques and applications.* Mahwah, NJ: Lawrence Erlbaum Associates.

Hox, J. J., & Maas, C. M. (2001). The accuracy of multilevel structural equation modeling with pseudobalanced groups and small sample sizes. *Structural Equation Modeling, 8*(2), 157–174.

Iannaccone, L. (1975). *Education policy systems: a study guide for educational administrators.* Fort Lauderdale, FL: Nova University Press.

Iannaccone, L. (1977). Three views of change in educational politics. In the seventy-sixth yearbook of the National Society for the Study of Education, *Politics of Education* (pp. 255–286). Chicago: University of Chicago Press.

Iannaccone, L. (1988). From equity to excellence: Political context and dynamics. In W. Boyd & C. Kerchner (Eds.), *The politics of excellence and choice in education* (pp. 49–65). London: Falmer.

Iannaccone, L., & Cistone, P. (1974). *The politics of education.* Eugene, OR: ERIC Clearinghouse on Educational Management, University of Oregon.

Isaak, A. (1987). *Politics.* Glenview, IL: Scott, Foresman.

Jacobson, L. (2002). Report relates better schools and diversity. *Education Week, 22*(3), 1, 14.

Jenkins-Smith, H. (1990). *Democratic politics and policy analysis.* Pacific Grove, CA: Brooks/Cole Publishing Company.

Jenkins-Smith, H., & St. Clair, G. (1993). The politics of offshore energy. In P. Sabatier & H. Jenkins-Smith (Eds.), *Policy change and learning: An advocacy coalition approach* (pp. 149–175). Boulder, CO: Westview.

Johnson, B. (2001). Toward a classification of nonexperimental quantitative research. *Educational Researcher, 30*(2), 3–13.

Johnson, B. L. (2003). Those nagging headaches: Perennial issues and tensions in the politics of education field. *Educational Administration Quarterly, 39*(1), 41–67.

Johnsrud, L. K., & Heck, R. H. (1998). Faculty worklife: Establishing benchmarks across groups. *Research in Higher Education, 39*(5), 539–555.

Jöreskog, K., & Sörbom, D. (2003). *LISREL 8.54.* Lincolnwood, IL: Scientific Software International.

Jung, R. K. (1988). The federal role in elementary and secondary education: Mapping a shifting terrain. In N. Boyan (Ed.) *Handbook of research on educational administration* (pp. 487–499). New York: Longman.

Kaestle, C. F. (1988). Recent methodological developments in the history of American education. In R. M. Jaeger (Ed.), *Complementary methods for research in education* (pp. 61–71). Washington, DC: American Educational Research Association.

Kahne, J. (1994). Democratic communities, equity, and excellence: A Deweyan reframing of educational policy analysis. *Educational Evaluation and Policy Analysis, 16*(3), 233–248.

Kahumoku, W. (2000). *The dynamics of cultural politics and language policy in public education: The case of Native Hawaiians.* Unpublished doctoral dissertation, University of Hawai'i at Mānoa, Honolulu.

Kaplan, A. (1964). *The conduct of inquiry: Methodology for behavioral science.* San Francisco: Chandler.

Kaplan, D., & Elliott, P. (1997). A didactic example of multilevel structural equation modeling applicable to the study of organizations. *Structural Equation Modeling, 4*(1), 1–23.

Katznelson, I. (1976). The crisis of the capitalist city: Urban politics and social control. In W. Hawley & M. Lipsky (Eds.), *Theoretical perspectives on urban politics* (pp. 214–229). New York: Prentice-Hall.

Kaufman, H. (1956). Emerging conflicts in the doctrines of public administration. *American Political Science Review, 50*(4), 1057–1073.

Kearney, C. P. (1967). *The 1964 Presidential Task Force on Education and the Elementary and Secondary Education Act of 1965.* Unpublished doctoral dissertation, University of Chicago, Chicago, IL.

Keith, N. (1996). A critical perspective on teacher participation in urban schools. *Educational Administration Quarterly, 32*(1), 45–79.

Kemmis, D. (1990). *Community and the politics of place.* Norman, OK: University of Oklahoma Press.

Kenway, J. (1992, October). *Making hope practical rather than despair convincing: Some thoughts on the value of post-structuralism as a theory of and for feminist change in schools.* Paper presented at the Women's Studies Conference, Sydney, Australia.

Kenway, J., Willis, S., Blackmore, J., & Rennie, L. (1994). Making hope practical rather than despair convincing: Feminist post-structuralism and change. *British Journal of Sociology, 15*(2), 187–210.

Key, V. C. (1949). *Southern politics in state and nation.* New York: Knopf.

Kramnick, I. (1987). Editor's introduction. In I. Kramnick (Ed.), *The federalist papers* (pp. 11–82). Harmondsworth, UK: Penguin.

Kreft, I., & De Leeuw, J. (1998). *Introducing multilevel modeling*. Newbury Park, CA: Sage.

Ladson-Billings, G. (2000). Racialized discourses and ethnic epistemologies. In N. Denzin & Y. Lincoln (Eds.), *Handbook of qualitative research* (2nd ed., pp. 257–277). Newbury Park, CA: Sage.

Lagemann, E. C. (1997). Contested terrain: A history of education research in the United States, 1890–1990. *Educational Researcher, 26*(9), 5–17.

Lankford, H., Loeb, S., & Wyckoff, J. (2002). Teacher sorting and the plight of urban schools: A descriptive analysis. *Educational Evaluation and Policy Analysis, 24*(1), 37–62.

Lasswell, H. D. (1951). The policy orientation. In D. Lerner & H. Lasswell (Eds.), *The policy sciences* (pp. 3–15). Palo Alto, CA: Stanford University Press.

Lasswell, H. D., & Kaplan, A. (1950). *Power and society*. New Haven: Yale University Press.

Lather, P. (1986). Issues of validity in openly ideological research: Between a rock and a soft place. *Interchange, 17*(4), 63–84.

Lather, P. (1990). *Feminist research in education: Within/Against*. Geelong, Australia: Deakin University Press.

Lather, P. (1991). *Getting smart. Feminist research and pedagogy with/in the postmodern*. New York: Routledge.

Lather, P. (1992). Critical frames in educational research: Feminist and post-structural perspectives. *Theory Into Practice, 31*(2), 87–99.

Lecercle, J. J. (1990). *The violence of language*. London: Routledge.

Lee, C. D. (2003). Why we need to re-think race and ethnicity in educational research. *Educational Researcher, 32*(5), 3–5.

Lee, J. (1997). State activism in education reform: Applying the Rasch Model to measure trends and examine policy coherence. *Educational Evaluation and Policy Analysis, 19*(1), 29–43.

Levin, H. M. (1983). *Cost-effectiveness: A primer*. Newbury Park, CA: Sage.

Levin, H. M. (1984). About time for educational reform. *Educational Evaluation and Policy Analysis, 6*(2), 151–163.

Levin, H. M. (1988). Cost-effectiveness and educational policy. *Educational Evaluation and Policy Analysis, 10*(1), 51–69.

Levin, H. M. (1991). Cost-effectiveness at quarter century. In M. McLaughlin & D. Philips (Eds.), *Evaluation and education at quarter century* (pp. 189–209). Chicago: University of Chicago Press.

Levin, H., Glass, G., & Meister, G. (1987). A cost-effectiveness analysis of computer-assisted instruction. *Evaluation Review, 11*(1), 50–72.

Levinson, B. A. U., & Sutton, M. (2001). *Policy as practice: Toward a comparative sociocultural analysis of educational policy*. London: Ablex Publishing.

Lewellen, T. C. (1992). *Political anthropology: An introduction* (2nd ed.). London: Bergin & Garvey.

Lichbach, M. I. (1997). Social theory and comparative politics. In M. I. Lichbach & A. S. Zucherman (Eds.), *Comparative politics: Rationality, culture, and structure* (pp. 239–276). New York: Cambridge University Press.

Lindblom, C. E. (1968). *The policy-making process*. Englewood Cliffs, NJ: Prentice-Hall.

Lindblom, C. E., & Cohen, D. (1979). *Usable knowledge: Social science and social problem solving*. New Haven, CN: Yale University Press.

Linn, R. L., Baker, E. L., & Betebenner, D. W. (2002). Accountability systems: Implications of requirements of the No Child Left Behind Act of 2001. *Educational Researcher, 31*(6), 3–16.

Linn, R. L., & Haug, C. (2002). Stability of school building scores and gains. *Educational Evaluation and Policy Analysis, 24*(1), 27–36.

Lipsitz, D. (1986). *American democracy.* New York: St. Martin's Press.

Lomawaima, K. (2000). Tribal sovereigns: Reframing research in American Indian education. *Harvard Educational Review, 70*(1), 1–21.

López, G. R. (2003). The (racially neutral) politics of education: A critical race theory perspective. *Educational Administration Quarterly, 39*(1), 68–94.

Louis, K. S., & Miles, M. (1990). *Improving the urban high school: What works and why.* New York: Teachers College Press.

Louis, K. S., & Miles, M. (1991). Managing reform: Lessons from urban high schools. *School Effectiveness and School Improvement, 2*(2), 75–96.

Louis, K. S., Toole, J., & Hargreaves, A. (1999). Rethinking school improvement. In J. Murphy & K. S. Louis (Eds.), *Handbook of research on educational administration* (2nd ed., pp. 251–276). San Francisco: Jossey-Bass.

Lutz, F. W., & Iannaccone, L. (1978). *Public participation in local school districts.* Lexington, MA: D. C. Heath.

Lutz, F. W., & Merz, C. (1992). *The politics of school/community relations.* New York: Teachers College Press.

Majchrzak, A. (1984). *Methods for policy research.* Newbury Park, CA: Sage.

Malen, B., Croninger, R., Muncey, D., & Redmond-Jones, D. (2002). Reconstituting schools: "Testing" the "Theory of Action." *Educational Evaluation and Policy Analysis, 24*(2), 113–132.

Mann, D. (1975). *Policy decision-making in education.* New York: Columbia University, Teachers College Press.

March, J. G., & Olsen, J. P. (1989). *Rediscovering institutions: The organizational basis of politics.* New York: Free Press.

Marcoulides, G. A., & Heck, R. H. (1990). Educational policy issues for the 1990s: Balancing equity and excellence in implementing the reform agenda. *Urban Education, 25*(1), 55–67.

Marshall, C. (1993). The new politics of race and gender. In C. Marshall (Ed.), *The new politics of race and gender* (pp. 1–6). London: Falmer.

Marshall, C. (1997). Preface. *Feminist critical policy analysis* (pp. ix–x). Washington, DC: Falmer.

Marshall, C., & Anderson, G. (1995). Rethinking the public and private spheres: Feminist and cultural studies perspectives on the politics of education. In J. Scribner & D. Layton (Eds.), *The study of educational politics* (pp. 201–212). London: Falmer Press.

Marshall, C., Fuhrman, S., & O'Day, J. (1994). National curriculum standards: Are they desirable and feasible? In R. Elmore & S. Fuhrman (Eds.), *The governance of curriculum: 1994 yearbook of the Association for Supervision and Curriculum Development* (pp. 12–30). Alexandria, VA: ASCD.

Marshall, C., Mitchell, D., & Wirt, F. (1986). The context of state level policy formulation. *Educational Evaluation and Policy Analysis, 8*(4), 347–378.

Marshall, C., Mitchell, D., & Wirt, F. (1989). *Culture and education policy in the American states.* New York: Falmer.

Martin, J., & Sugarman, J. (1993). Beyond methodolatry: Two conceptions of relations between theory and research in research on teaching. *Educational Researcher*, *22*(8), 17–24.

Mawhinney, H. (1993). An advocacy coalition approach to change in Canadian education. In P. Sabatier & H. Jenkins-Smith (Eds.), *Policy change and learning* (pp. 59–82). Boulder, CO: Westview Press.

Maxcy, S. (1995). Responses to commentary: Beyond leadership frameworks. *Educational Administration Quarterly*, *31*(3), 473–483.

Mayer, D. (1999). Measuring instructional practice: Can policymakers trust survey data? *Educational Evaluation and Policy Analysis*, *21*(1), 29–45.

Mazzoni, T. L. (1993). The changing politics of state education policy making: A 20-year Minnesota perspective. *Educational Evaluation and Policy Analysis*, *13*(4), 357–379.

Mazzoni, T. L., & Clugston, R. M., Jr. (1987). Big business as a policy innovator in state school reform: A Minnesota case study. *Educational Evaluation and Policy Analysis*, *9*(4), 312–324.

McArdle, J. (1989). A structural modeling experiment with multiple growth functions. In P. Ackerman, R. Kanfer, & R. Cudek (Eds.), *Learning and individual differences: Abilities, motivation, and methodology* (pp. 71–117). Hillsdale, NJ: Lawrence Erlbaum Associates.

McArdle, J. (1998). Modeling longitudinal data by latent growth curve methods. In G. Marcoulides (Ed.), *Modern methods for business research* (pp. 359–406). Mahwah, NJ: Lawrence Erlbaum Associates.

McArdle, J., & Hamagami, F. (1996). Multilevel models from a multiple group structural equation perspective. In G. A. Marcoulides & R. Schumacker (Eds.), *Advanced structural equation modeling: Issues and techniques* (pp. 89–124). Mahwah, NJ: Lawrence Erlbaum Associates.

McDonald, R. P. (1994). The bilevel reticular action model for path analysis with latent variables. *Sociological Methods and Research*, *22*, 299–413.

McDonald, R. P., & Goldstein, H. (1989). Balanced versus unbalanced designs for linear structural relations in two-level data. *British Journal of Mathematical and Statistical Modeling*, *42*, 215–232.

McDonnell, L. M., & Elmore, R. F. (1987). Getting the job done: Alternative policy instruments. *Educational Evaluation and Policy Analysis*, *9*(2), 133–156.

McFarland, A. (1983). Public interest lobbies versus minority faction. In A. Cigler & B. Loomis (Eds.), *Interest group politics* (pp. 326–335). Washington, DC: CQ Press.

McLaughlin, M. (1990). The RAND change agent study revisited: Macro perspectives, microrealities. *Educational Researcher*, *19*(9), 11–16.

Meek, V. L. (1988). Organizational culture: Origins and weaknesses. *Organization Studies*, *9*(4), 453–473.

Merelman, R. M. (1984). *Making something of ourselves: On culture and politics in the United States*. Berkeley: University of California Press.

Merelman, R. M. (2002, February 6). Dis-integrating American public schools. *Education Week*, *21*(21), 52, 36–37.

Merriam, S. B. (1988). *Case study research in education: A qualitative approach*. San Francisco: Jossey-Bass.

Meyer, J. W., Boli, J., & Thomas, G. (1987). Ontology and rationalization in Western cultural account. In G. Thomas, J. Meyer, F. Ramirez, & J. Boli (Eds.), *Institutional structure: Constituting state, society, and the individual* (pp. 12–37). Newbury Park, CA: Sage.

Meyers, M. (1973). *Sources of the political thought of James Madison*. London: Brandeis University Press.

Miles, K. H., & Darling-Hammond, L. (1998). Rethinking the allocation of teaching resources: Some lessons from high-performing schools. *Educational Evaluation and Policy Analysis, 20*(1), 9–29.

Miles, M. B., & Huberman, A. M. (1984). *Analyzing qualitative data: A source book for new methods*. Newbury Park, CA: Sage.

*Milliken v. Bradley*, 418 U.S. 717, 94 S.Ct. 3112 (1974).

Miron, G., & Nelson, C. (2002, May 15). What's public about charter schools? *Education Week, 21*(36), 38–39.

Mitchell, D. (1984). Educational policy analysis: The state of the art. *Educational Administration Quarterly, 20*(3), 129–160.

Moe, T. (1990). Political institutions: The neglected side of the story. *Journal of Law, Economics, and Organization, 6*, 213–253.

Mok, M. (1995). Sample size requirements for 2-level designs in educational research. *Multilevel Modeling Newsletter, 7*(2), 11–15.

Monk, D. H., & Hussain, S. (2000). Structural influences on the internal allocation of school district resources: Evidence from New York State. *Educational Evaluation and Policy Analysis, 22*(1), 1–26.

Monk, D. H., & Plecki, M. L. (1999). Generating and managing resources for school improvement. In J. Murphy &. K. S. Louis (Eds.), *Handbook of research on educational administration* (2nd ed., pp. 491–510). San Francisco: Jossey-Bass.

Montesquieu. (1748). *The spirit of laws*. D. W. Carrithers (Ed.). Berkeley, CA: University of California Press, 1977.

Moore, K. M., & Sagaria, M. D. (1993). The situation of women in research universities in the United States: Within the circles of power. In J. S. Glazer, E. M. Bensimon, & B. K. Townsend (Eds.), *Women in higher education: A feminist perspective* (pp. 227–249). Needham, MA: Ginn Press.

Morgan, G. (1986). *Images of organization*. Beverly Hills, CA: Sage Publications.

Mort, P., & Cornell, F. (1941). *American schools in transition: How our schools adapt their practices to changing needs*. New York: Teachers College Press.

Mosteller, F., & Boruch, R. (Eds.). (2002). *Evidence matters: Randomized trials in education research*. Washington, DC: Brookings.

Murphy, J. T. (1971). Title I of ESEA: The politics of implementing federal education reform. *Harvard Educational Review, 41*, 35–63.

Muthén, B. O. (1989). Latent variable modeling in heterogeneous populations. *Psychometrika, 54*, 557–585.

Muthén, B. O. (1990). *Mean and covariance structure analysis of hierarchical data*. Los Angeles: UCLA Statistical Series #62.

Muthén, B. O. (1991). Multilevel factor analysis of class and student achievement components. *Journal of Educational Measurement, 28*, 338–354.

Muthén, B. O. (1994). Multilevel covariance structure analysis. *Sociological Methods and Research, 22*(3), 376–398.

Muthén, B. (2002). Beyond SEM: General latent variable modeling. *Behaviormetrika, 29*, 81–117.

Muthén, B. O., & Asparouhov, T. (2003). *Advances in latent variable modeling, Part I: Integrating multilevel and structural equation modeling using Mplus*. Unpublished manuscript.

Muthén, B. O., & Satorra, A. (1995). Complex sample data in structural equation modeling. In P. Marsden (Ed.), *Sociological methodology* (pp. 267–316). Washington, DC: American Sociological Association.

Muthén, B. O., & Satorra, A. (1989). Multilevel aspects of varying parameters in structural models. In R. D. Bock (Ed.), *Multilevel analysis of educational data* (pp. 87–99). San Diego, CA: Academic Press.

Muthén, L., & Muthén, B. O. (1998–2001). *Mplus user's guide*. Los Angeles: Author.

Muthén, L., & Muthén, B. O. (2001 March 28–31). *Growth modeling with latent variables using Mplus*. Paper presented at the *Mplus* Short Courses meeting, Boston,.

Nagel, S. (1980). The policy studies perspective. *Public Administration Review, 40*, 391–396.

Nagel, S. S. (1984). *Contemporary public policy analysis*. University, AL: University of Alabama Press.

National Academy of Sciences. (1996). *Research and education reform: Roles for the Office of Educational Research and Improvement*. Washington, DC: National Academy Press.

National Center for Educational Statistics. (1993). *120 years of American education: A statistical portrait*. Washington, DC: Government Printing Office.

National Center for Educational Statistics, (2003). *Overview of public elementary and secondary schools and districts: School Year 2001–02*. NCES-2003-411. Washington, DC: US Department of Education.

National Commission on Excellence in Education. (1983). *A nation at risk: The imperative for educational reform*. Washington, DC: US Department of Education Government Printing Office.

National Research Council. (2002). Accumulation of scientific knowledge. In R. J. Shavelson, & L. Towne (Eds.), *Scientific research in education. National Research Council, Committee on Scientific Principles for Educational Research* (pp. 28–49). Washington, DC: National Academy Press.

Nelson, R. H. (1991). Economists as policy analysts: Historical overview. In C. E. Van Horn (Ed.), *The state of the states* (2nd ed., pp. 15–32). Washington, DC: Congressional Quarterly Press.

Nye, B., Hedges, L. V., & Konstantopoulos, S. (2002). Do low-achieving students benefit more from small classes? Evidence from the Tennessee class size experiment. *Educational Evaluation and Policy Analysis, 24*(3), 201–217.

Odden, A. R., & Clune, W. H. (1998). School finance systems: Aging structures in need of renovation. *Educational Evaluation and Policy Analysis, 20*(3), 157–178.

Odden, A. R., & Picus, L. O. (1992). *School finance: A policy perspective*. New York: McGraw-Hill.

Ogawa, R. T. (1992). Institutional theory and examining leadership in schools. *International Journal of Educational Management, 6*(3), 14–21.

Ogawa, R. T., & Bossert, S. T. (1995). Leadership as an organizational quality. *Educational Administration Quarterly, 31*(2), 224–243.

Ogawa, R. T., Sandholtz, J. H., Martinez-Flores, M., & Scribner, S. P. (2003). The substantive and symbolic consequences of a district's standards-based curriculum. *American Educational Research Journal, 40*(1), 147–176.

Oleszek, W. J. (1996). *Congressional procedures and the policy process* (4th ed.). Washington, DC: Congressional Quarterly Press.

Ostrom, E. (1999). Institutional rational choice: An assessment of the institutional analysis and development framework. In P. A. Sabatier (Ed.), *Theories of the policy process* (pp. 35–71). Boulder, CO: Westview Press.

Ouston, J. (1999). School effectiveness and school improvement: Critique of a movement. In T. Bush, L. Bell, R. Bolam, R. Glatter, & P. Ribbins (Eds.), *Educational management: Redefining theory, policy, and practice* (pp. 166–177). London: Paul Chapman.

Park, S. M. (1996). Research, teaching, and service: Why shouldn't women's work count? *Journal of Higher Education, 67*(1), 46–84.

Parker, L., & Lynn, M. (2002). What's race got to do with it? Critical Race Theory's conflicts with and connections to qualitative research methodology and epistemology. *Qualitative Inquiry, 8*(1), 7–22.

Patterson, S. (1968). The political cultures of the American states. *Journal of Politics, 30,* 187–209.

Patton, M. Q. (1990). *Qualitative evaluation and research methods.* Newbury Park, CA: Sage.

Pearce, R. H. (1965). *The savages of America: A study of the Indian and the idea of civilization.* Baltimore, MD: Johns Hopkins Press.

Pedhazur, E. J., & Schmelkin, L. P. (1991). *Measurement, design, and analysis: An integrated approach.* Mahwah, NJ: Lawrence Erlbaum Associates.

Pellegrino, J. W., & Goldman, S. R. (2002). Be careful what you wish for—you may get it: Educational research in the spotlight. *Educational Researcher, 31*(8), 15–17.

Peterson, P. E. (1985). *The politics of school reform, 1870–1940.* Chicago: University of Chicago Press.

Peterson, P. E., & Wong, K. K. (1985). Toward a differentiated theory of federalism: Education and housing policy in the 1980s. *Research in Urban Policy, 1,* 301–324.

Pierce, P. R. (1934). *The origin and development of the public school principalship.* Chicago: University of Chicago Press.

*Pierce v. Society of Sisters,* 268 U.S. 510, 45 S.Ct. 571 (1925).

Plank, D. N., Scotch, R. K., Gamble, J. E. (1996). Rethinking progressive school reform: Organizational dynamics and educational change. *American Journal of Education, 104,* 79–102.

*Plessy v. Ferguson,* 163 U.S. 537, 16 S.Ct. 1138 (1896).

Pomplun, M., & Omar, M. H. (2003). Do minority representative reading passages provide factorially invariant scores for all students? *Structural Equation Modeling, 10*(2), 276–288.

Popkewitz, T. (1981). Qualitative research: Some thoughts about the relation of methodology and social history. In T. Popkewitz, & B. Tabachnick (Eds.), *The study of schooling: Field-based methodologies in educational research and evaluation* (pp. 155–178). New York: Praeger.

Popper, K. R. (1959). *The logic of scientific discovery.* New York: Basic Books.

Pressman, J., & Wildavsky, A. (1984). *Implementation* (3rd ed.). Berkeley, CA: University of California Press.

Pulliam, J. (1987). *History of education in America* (4th ed.). Columbus, OH: Merrill.

Rains, F. W., Archibald, J., & Deyhle, D. (Eds.). (2000). Through our own eyes and our own words—The voices of indigenous scholars. *International Journal of Qualitative Studies in Education, 13*(4), 377–428.

Raudenbush, S. W., Bryk, A., Cheong, Y. K., & Congdon, R. (2000). *HLM5: Hierachical linear and nonlinear modeling.* Chicago: Scientific Software.

Raudenbush, S. W., Fotiu, R. P., & Cheong, Y. F. (1998). Inequality of access to educational resources: A national report card for eighth-grade math. *Educational Evaluation and Policy Analysis, 20*(4), 253–267.

Rawls, J. (1971). *A theory of justice.* Cambridge, MA: Harvard University Press.

Raykov, T., & Marcoulides, G. A. (2000). *A first course in structural equation modeling.* Mahwah, NJ: Lawrence Erlbaum Associates.

Reagan, M. D., & Sanzone, J. G. (1981). *The new federalism.* (2nd ed.). New York: Oxford University Press.

Redford, E. S. (1969). *Democracy in the administrative state.* New York: Oxford University Press.

Reynolds, D., & Teddlie, C., with Creemers, B., Scheerens, J., & Townsend, T. (2000). An introduction to school effectiveness research. In C. Teddlie & D. Reynolds (Eds.), *The international handbook of school effectiveness research* (pp. 3–25). New York: Falmer Press.

Rice, J. K. (1994). Meeting the educational needs of at-risk students: A cost analysis of three models. *Educational Evaluation and Policy Analysis, 16*(1), 1–19.

Rice, J. K. (1997). Cost analysis in education: Paradox and possibility. *Educational Evaluation and Policy Analysis, 19*(4), 309–317.

Rich, A. (1993). Toward a woman-centered university. In J. S. Glazer, E. M. Bensimon, & B. K. Townsend (Eds.), *Women in higher education: A feminist perspective* (pp. 121–134). Needham, MA: Ginn Press.

Richards, L., & Richards, T. (1994). From filing cabinet to computer. In A. Bryman & R. G. Burgess, (Eds.), *Analyzing qualitative data* (pp. 146–172). London: Routledge.

Ripley, R. B. (1988). *Congress: Process and policy* (4th ed.). New York: W. W. Norton.

Rist, R. (1977). On the relations among educational research paradigms: From disdain to détente. *Anthropology & Education Quarterly, 8*(2), 42–49.

Ritchie, J., & Spencer, L. (1994). Qualitative data analysis for applied policy research. In A. Bryman & R. G. Burgess (Eds.), *Analyzing qualitative data* (pp. 173–194). New York: Routledge.

Robinson, V. M. J. (1996). Critical theory and the social psychology of change. In K. Leithwood, J. Chapman, D. Corson, P. Hallinger, & A. Hart (Eds.), *International handbook of educational leadership and administration* (pp. 1069–1096). Boston: Kluwer Academic Publishers.

Rollow, S., & Bryk, A. (1993). Democratic politics and school improvement: The potential of Chicago school reform. In C. Marshall (Ed.), *The new politics of race and gender* (pp. 97–106). London: The Falmer Press.

Rousseau, J. (1758). *A discourse on political economy.* G. D. H. Cole (Ed.). London: J. M. Dent and Sons, 1973.

Rubin, I. S. (1990). *The politics of public budgeting.* Chatham, NJ: Chatham House.

Rudolph, F. (1990). *The American college and university: A history.* Athens, GA: University of Georgia Press.

Sabatier, P. A. (1993). Policy change over a decade or more. In P. Sabatier, & H. Jenkins-Smith (Eds.), *Policy change and learning: An Advocacy coalition approach* (pp. 13–39). Boulder, CO: Westview Press.

Sabatier, P. A. (1999). *Theories of the policy process.* Boulder, CO: Westview Press.

Sabatier, P. A., & Jenkins-Smith, H. C. (1993). *Policy change and learning: An advocacy coalition approach.* Boulder, Colorado: Westview Press, 13–39.

Sabatier, P. A., & Jenkins-Smith, H. C. (1999). The advocacy coalition framework: An assessment. In P. A. Sabatier (Ed.), *Theories of the policy process* (pp. 117–166). Boulder, CO: Westview Press.

Sachen, D. M., & Medina, M., Jr. (1990). Investigating the context of state-level policy formation: A case study of Arizona's bilingual education legislation. *Education Evaluation and Policy Analysis, 12*(4), 378–399.

Sackney, L., & Mitchell, C. (2002). Postmodern expressions of educational leadership. In K. Leithwood, & P. Hallinger (Eds.), *Second international handbook of educational leadership and administration* (pp. 881–913). Boston: Kluwer Academic Publishers.

Sarason, S. B. (1971). *The culture of the school and the problem of change.* Boston, MA: Allyn & Bacon.

Sarason, S. B. (1990). *The predictable failure of educational reform.* San Francisco, CA: Jossey-Bass.

Savitch, H., & Thomas, C. (1991). *Big city politics in transition.* Newbury Park, CA: Sage.

Schattschneider, E. E. (1957). Intensity, visibility, direction and scope. *The American Political Science Review, 51*(4), 933–942.

Schattschneider, E. E. (1960). *The semisovereign people.* New York: Holt, Reinholt, & Winston.

Schlager, E. (1999). A comparison of frameworks, theories, and models of policy processes. In P. A. Sabatier (Ed.), *Theories of the policy process* (pp. 233–260). Boulder, CO: Westview Press.

Schon, D. A., & Rein, M. (1994). *Frame reflection.* New York: Basic Books.

Schultze, C. L. (1977). *The public use of private interest.* Washington, DC: The Brookings Institution.

Schumacher, E. F. (1975). *Small is beautiful: Economics as if people mattered.* New York: Perennial Library, Harper & Row.

Scott, W. R. (1995). *Institutions and organizations.* Thousand Oaks, CA: Sage.

Scribner, J. D., Aleman, E., & Maxcy, B. (2003). Emergence of the politics of education field: Making sense of a messy center. *Educational Administration Quarterly, 39*(1), 10–40.

Scribner, J. D., & Englert, R. M. (1977). The politics of education: An introduction. In J. D. Scribner (Ed.), *The politics of education: The 76th yearbook of the National Society for the Study of Education, Part II* (pp. 1–29). Chicago: University of Chicago Press.

Shakeshaft, C., & Hanson, M. (1986). Androcentric bias in the *Educational Administration Quarterly. Educational Administration Quarterly, 22*(1), 68–92.

Shapiro, J. Z., & McPherson, R. B. (1987). State board desegregation policy: An application of the problem-finding model of policy analysis. *Educational Administration Quarterly, 23*(2), 60–77.

Shaw, K. E. (1978). Understanding the curriculum: The approach through case studies. *Journal of Curriculum Studies, 10*(1), 1–17.

Shipman, G. A. (1969). Role of the administrator—policy making as part of the administrative process. In F. J. Lyden, G. A. Shipman, & M. Kroll (Eds.), *Policies, decisions, and organization* (pp. 118–129). New York: Appleton-Century-Crofts.

Simon, H. A. (1945). *Administrative behavior.* New York: Free Press.

Slavin, R. E. (2002). Evidence-based education policies: Transforming educational practice and research. *Educational Researcher, 31*(7), 15–21.

Sleeter, C. (2000). Epistemological diversity in research on preservice teacher education for historically underserved children. *Review of Research in Education, 25,* 209–250.

Smart, J. C. (2002, November). *Attributes of exemplary research manuscripts employing quantitative analyses.* Paper presented at the annual Meeting of the Association of the Study of Higher Education, Sacramento, CA.

Smith, A. (1776). *An inquiry into the nature and causes of the wealth of nations*. Reprinted in 1981. Indianapolis: Liberty Classics.

Smith, J. K. (1983). Quantitative versus qualitative research: An attempt to clarify the issue. *Educational Researcher, 12*(3), 6–13.

Smith, J. K., & Heshusius, L. (1986). Closing down the conversation: The end of the quantitative-qualitative debate among educational researchers. *Educational Researcher, 15*(1), 4–12.

Southwest Educational Research Laboratory. (2002). *CSRD database of schools*. Retrieved from http://www.sedl.org/csrd/awards.html

Spring, J. (1986). *The American school 1642–1985*. New York: Longman.

St. Pierre, E. A. (2002). "Science" rejects postmodernism. *Educational Researcher, 31*(8), 25–27.

Stanfield, J. (1994). Ethnic modeling in qualitative research. In N. Denzin, & Y. Lincoln (Eds.), *Handbook of qualitative research* (pp. 175–188). Newbury Park, CA: Sage.

Stewart, J. (1991, June). Policy models and equal educational opportunity. *Political Science and Politics, 24*, 167–173.

Stout, R., Tallerico, M., & Scribner, K. P. (1995). Values: The "what" of the politics of education. In J. D. Scribner, & D. H. Layton (Eds.), *The study of educational politics: The 1994 commemorative yearbook of the Politics of Education Association, 1969–1994* (pp. 5–20). Washington, DC: Falmer.

Supovitz, J. A., & Brennan, R. T. (1997). Mirror, mirror on the wall, which is the fairest test of all? An examination of the equitability of portfolio assessment relative to standardized tests. *Harvard Educational Review, 67*(3), 472–506.

Sullivan, W. M. (1982). *Reconstructing public philosophy*. Berkeley, CA: University of California Press.

Swanson, C. B., & Stevenson, D. E. (2002). Standards-based reform in practice: Evidence on state policy and classroom instruction from the NAEP state assessments. *Educational Evaluation and Policy Analysis, 24*(1), 1–27.

Swartz, M. J., Turner, V., & Tuden, A. (1966). *Political anthropology*. Chicago: Aldine.

Takahashi, R. (2002). *The effects of policy on intercollegiate football programs: The intended and unintended effects of Proposition 48*. Unpublished doctoral dissertation, University of Hawai'i at Mānoa, Honolulu.

Tamura, E. (1994). *Americanization, acculturation, and ethnic identity: The Nisei generation in Hawai'i*. Chicago: University of Illinois Press.

Teddlie, C., & Reynolds, D. (2000). *The international handbook of school effectiveness research*. London: Falmer.

Teddlie, C., Reynolds, D., & Sammons, P. (2000). The methodology and scientific properties of school effectiveness research. In C. Teddlie & D. Reynolds (Eds.), *The international handbook of school effectiveness research* (pp. 55–133). London: Falmer Press.

Teddlie, C., Stringfield, S., & Reynolds, D. (2000). Contextual issues within school effectiveness research. In C. Teddlie, & D. Reynolds (Eds.), *The international handbook of school effectiveness research* (pp. 160–185). London: Falmer Press.

Thurston, L. M., & Roe, W. H. (1957). *State school administration*. New York: Harper & Row.

Tierney, W., & Bensimon, E. M. (1996). *Promotion and tenure community and socialization in academe*. New York: SUNY Press.

Tillman, L. C. (2002). Culturally sensitive research approaches: An African-American perspective. *Educational Researcher, 31*(9), 3–12.

Tolbert, P. S., & Zucker, L. G. (1996). The institutionalization of institutional theory. In S. R. Clegg, C. Hardy, & W. R. Nord (Eds.), *Handbook of organizational studies* (pp. 175–190). London: Sage.

Tong, R. (1989). *Feminist thought: A comprehensive introduction*. Boulder, CO: Westview.

Townsend, B. K. (1993). Feminist scholarship in core higher education journals. *The Review of Higher Education, 17*(1), 21–41.

Tribe, L. H. (1972). Policy science: Analysis or ideology? *Philosophy & Public Affairs, 2*(1), 55–110.

True, J. L., Jones, B. D., & Baumgartner, F. R. (1999). Punctuated-equilibrium theory: Explaining stability and change in American policymaking. In P. A. Sabitier (Ed.) *Theories of the policy process* (pp. 97–115). Boulder, CO: Westview Press.

Turner, F. J. (1894). *The frontier in American history*. Washington, DC: Government Printing Office.

Tyack, D. B. (1974). *The one best system: A history of American urban education*. Cambridge, MA: Harvard University Press.

Tyack, D. B. (1976). Ways of seeing: An essay on the history of compulsory schooling. *Harvard Education Review, 46*(3), 355–389.

Tyack, D. B. (1991). Public school reform: Policy talk and institutional practice. *American Journal of Education, 99*(1), 1–19.

Tyack, D. B. (2002). Introduction. In S. Mondale & S. B. Patton (Eds.), *School: The story of American public education* (pp. 1–8). Boston: Beacon Press.

Tyack, D. B., & Cuban, L. (1995). *Tinkering toward utopia: A century of public school reform*. Cambridge, MA: Harvard University Press.

Tyack, D. B., & Hansot, E. (1981). Conflict and consensus in American public education. *Daedalus, 110*(3), 1–26.

Tyack, D. B., & Hansot, E. (1990). *Learning together: A history of coeducation in American schools*. New Haven: CT: Yale University Press.

U.S. Congress (1990). Individuals with Disabilities Education Act. Pub. L. No. 105–476.

U.S. Congress (2001). *No Child Left Behind Act of 2001*. Pub. L. No. 107–110.

U.S. Department of Education. (1999). *Guidance on the comprehensive school reform program*. Washington, DC: Author.

U.S. Department of Education. (2002). *Strategic plan, 2002–2007*. Washington, DC: Author.

Van Geel, T. (1987). *The courts and American education law*. Buffalo, NY: Prometheus Books.

Van Geel, T. (1988). The law and the courts. In N. Boyan (Ed.), *Handbook of research on educational administration* (pp. 623–653). New York: Longman.

Van Horn, C, Baumer, D., & Gormley, W. (1992). *Politics and public policy* (2nd ed.). Washington, DC: Congressional Quarterly Inc.

Viadero, D. (2001). The dropout dilemma. *Education Week, 20*(21) 26–29.

Wagner, J. (1993). Ignorance in educational research: Or, how can you not know that? *Educational Researcher, 22*(5), 15–23.

Walsh, K. (2001). *Teacher certification reconsidered: Stumbling for quality*. Baltimore, MD: Abell Foundation. Available: http://www.abellfoundation.org.

Ward, J. G. (1993). Demographic politics and American schools: Struggles for power and justice. In C. Marshall (Ed.), *The new politics of race and gender* (pp. 7–18). Washington, DC: Falmer Press.

Warfield, M. E. (1994). A cost-effectiveness analysis of early intervention services in Massachusetts: Implications for policy. *Educational Evaluation and Policy Analysis, 16*(1), 87–99.

Warwick, D. P., & Pettigrew, T. F. (1983). Towards ethical guidelines for policy research. *Hastings Center Report, 13*, 9–16.

Weick, K. (1976). Educational organizations as loosely coupled systems. *Administrative Science Quarterly, 21*, 1–19.

Weick, K. (1984). Small wins: Redefining the scale of social issues. *American Psychologist, 39*, 40–50.

Weiss, C. (1982). Policy research in the context of diffuse decision making. *Journal of Higher Education, 53*(6), 619–639.

Weiss, C. (1991). Knowledge creep and decision accretion. In D. Anderson & B. Biddle (Eds.), *Knowledge for policy: Improving education through research* (pp. 183–192). London: Falmer Press.

Weiss, J., & Gruber, J. (1987). The managed irrelevance of federal education statistics. In W. Alonso & P. Starr (Eds.), *The politics of numbers* (pp. 363–391). New York: Russell Sage Foundation.

Welch, S., & Peters, J. (1980). State political culture and the attitude of state senators toward social, economic welfare, and corruption issues. *Publius: The Journal of Federalism, 10*(2), 59–68.

White, L. (1959). *The evolution of culture*. NY: McGraw-Hill.

White, M. (1983). Policy analysis and management science. In S. Nagel (Ed.), *Encyclopedia of policy studies* (pp. 3–15). New York: Marcel Dekker.

Wildavsky, A. (1987). *Frames of reference come from cultures: A predictive theory*. Working Paper Series, Survey Research Center, University of California, Berkeley.

Willet, J., & Sayer, A. (1996). Cross-domain analysis of change over time: Combining growth modeling and covariance structure analysis. In G. Marcoulides & R. Schumacker (Eds.), *Advanced structural equation modeling: Issues and techniques* (pp. 125–158). Mahwah, NJ: Lawrence Erlbaum Associates.

Willingham, W. W., Rogosta, M., Bennett, R. E., Braun, H., Rock, D. A., & Powers, D. E. (1988). *Testing handicapped people*. Boston: Allyn & Bacon.

Willms, D. (1992). *Monitoring school performance: A guide for educators*. London: Falmer Press.

Willower, D. J., & Forsyth, P. B. (1999). A brief history of scholarship in educational administration. In J. Murphy & K. Seashore Louis (Eds.), *Handbook of research on educational administration* (2nd ed., pp. 1–23). San Francisco: Jossey-Bass.

Wilson, S., Floden, R., & Ferrini-Mundy, J. (2001). *Teacher preparation research: Current knowledge, gaps, and recommendations*. Seattle, WA: Center for the Study of Teaching and Policy.

Windshuttle, K. (1996). *The killing of history*. San Francisco: Encounter Books.

Wirt, F. (1980). Does control follow the dollar? School policy, state-local linkages and political culture. *Publius: The Journal of Federalism, 10*(2), 69–88.

Wirt, F., & Harman, G. (1986). *Educational recession and the world village*. Lewes: Falmer Press.

Wirt, F. M., & Kirst, M. (1982). *Schools in conflict*. Berkeley, CA: McCutchan Publishing.

Wirt, F. M., & Kirst, M. (1989). *Schools in conflict* (2nd ed.). Berkeley, CA: McCutchan Publishing.

Witte, J. F. (1998). The Milwaukee voucher experiment. *Educational Evaluation and Policy Analysis, 20*(4), 229–251.

Wolcott, H. (1994). *Transforming qualitative data: Description, analysis, and interpretation.* Newbury Park, CA: Sage.

Wong, K., & Rollow, S. (1990). A case study of the recent Chicago school reform. *Administrator's Notebook, 34*(5–6), 1–6.

Yin, R. K. (1989). *Case study research: Design and methods* (Rev. ed.). Newbury Park, CA: Sage.

# Author Index

# Subject Index

**378**

SUBJECT INDEX

33–34, 99, 157, 159–160,
172–173, 181–182, 185–186,
190–191, 195, 282, 315, 318,
320, 326–329
*Methods for Policy Research*, 191
*Milliken v. Bradley*, 51
Model, xxi–xxii, 58, 25–26, 80, 185, 208,
315
Modernist, 138–139
Morrill Act, 48
Multilevel modeling
defined, 183, 242–243
in policy research, 153, 248–250,
269–275
Multilevel regression, *see* Quantitative re-
search methods
Multilevel structural equation modeling, *see*
Quantitative research methods
Multiple regression, *see* Quantitative re-
search methods
Multiple streams theory, *see* Garbage can
model
Municipal Reform, 60, 93, 98, 103, 106,
109–110, 114–115, 154

**N**

National Collegiate Athletic Association
(NCAA), 145
National Defense Education Act, 41
Neo-Marxism, 161
No Child Left Behind Act of 2001, viii,
xiii, xv, 5, 19, 52, 182, 198, 312

**O**

Old Deluder Satan Act, 45
Ordinance of 1785, 44
Ordinance of 1787, 44

**P**

Participant observation, *see* Qualitative
research methods
Phenomenology, 28, 31, 165, 195,
215–216, 226, 319
*Pierce v. Society of Sisters*, 48–49, 52
P.L. 94–142, 42
*Plessy v. Ferguson*, 50–51
Policy

actor influence, xiii, 4, 36, 68–70, 79,
95–96, 110–114, 330
analysis, 9–10, 31, 318
cycle, *see* Issue-attention cycle
defined, 6–8
development, *see* Policy formulation
evaluation, *see* Policy outcomes
formulation, ix, xvi, xix, 1–2, 6, 17,
23, 43, 55, 57, 59–60, 63,
65–66, 69–71, 74–75, 79,
175, 319, 326
images, 106–107, 110–112, 115, 315
implementation, ix, xix, 1–3, 6, 17,
22–23, 27, 29, 43, 52,
56–57, 59, 61, 65–66,
72–77, 79–80, 175–179,
319, 325–326
outcomes, xix, 2, 4, 11–12, 16–17,
22–23, 27, 28, 50, 55–57,
61–62, 65–66, 72–73, 80,
179, 194, 199, 319, 325–326
research
compared with technical research,
186
conceptualization of, xx–xxiii, 30,
34, 186–196, 329
goals, 9–13, 30, 186–188,
318–319, 326
influence, 17–22, 28–30, 315–316,
318–319, 329–330
temporal issues, xvi, xix, 30–31,
188, 326
utility, xix, 18–19, 22, 27,
187–188, 315–316, 319,
326, 329–330
scholarship, vii,xvi–xviii, 12–18, 28,
30, 32, 34, 188–189,
315–316, 318, 328–329
stages heuristic, x, 14, 55–56, 60,
64–76, 79, 117, 158, 320,
321, 325
subsystem, xviii–xix, 1, 7, 26–27,
29–30, 35–36, 40, 60–64,
67–68, 93, 108–109,
117–122, 125–126, 141
talk, 4–5, 115–116
values, *see* Value positions
Policymaking, *see* Policy
Politics of education, 15–17, 31
Positivist research, 158, 160, 181, 198,
218, 315